Coffee and Power

COFFEE
AND
POWER

*Revolution and the Rise of
Democracy in Central America*

~

Jeffery M. Paige

HARVARD UNIVERSITY PRESS
Cambridge, Massachusetts
London, England

First Harvard University Press paperback edition, 1998

Library of Congress Cataloging-in-Publication Data

Paige, Jeffery M.
    Coffee and power : revolution and the rise of democracy in Central America /
Jeffery M. Paige.
        p.   cm.
    Includes bibliographical references and index.
    ISBN 0-674-13648-9 (cloth)
    ISBN 0-674-13649-7 (pbk.)
    1. Coffee trade—Costa Rica—History—20th century.   2. Coffee trade—El
Salvador—History—20th century.   3. Coffee trade—Nicaragua—History—20th
century.   4. Costa Rica—Politics and government—20th century.   5. El
Salvador—Politics and government—20th century.   6. Nicaragua—Politics and
government—To 1960.   7. Nicaragua—Politics and government—1960–
8. Elite (Social sciences)—Costa Rica—History—20th century.   9. Elite (Social
sciences)—El Salvador—History—20th century.   10. Elite (Social sciences)—
Nicaragua—History—20th century.   I. Title.
HD9199.C82P35   1997
338.1'7373'09728—dc20   96-34693

To the people of Central America,
in sorrow and in hope

Contents

~

Tables and Figures

Preface

The research on which this book is based began and ended, like so much else in Central America during the decade of catastrophe, with news of violent death. The project began on a busman's holiday to Guatemala in August of 1980. I had never visited Central America before, but Guatemala had been a puzzling case in my earlier book, *Agrarian Revolution.* Despite having the largest migratory wage labor force in agriculture of any country in the world, it had not had the revolutionary movement in the countryside that my theory predicted. The revolution began almost at the moment I arrived and would consume much of the Guatemalan highlands in the next two years. Perhaps 100,000 people, most of them members of the Mayan peoples of Guatemala, were brutally murdered in a counter-revolutionary campaign of military terrorism unprecedented in the contemporary Western Hemisphere. Some of them almost certainly were people I met on that first trip in the village of Santiago Atitlán, on the shores of what is surely one of the most beautiful highland lakes in the world, Atitlán, from which the village takes it name. The day I first saw it was particularly beautiful. A brilliant sun brought out the intense natural colors of the lake and the bold hues of Mayan textiles with a vibrancy that I remember still.

The contrast between the beauty of that day, the grace and dignity of the people I met in the village, and the holocaust that followed has haunted me ever since and provoked this book. I remember in particular the courtesy and gentleness of the women in the local market, who tolerated gringo ignorance of the ways of a highland market with patience and good humor. Like many other North Americans, including the not inconsiderable number of countercultural Californians living around Lake Atitlán, I was touched by some quality of this culture, however brief and superficial my contact. A week after my visit, however, the Organization of the People in Arms, the principal guerrilla group in the area, visited the village, called the villagers and the North American tourists together, lectured them on the need for revolution, and departed with some weapons purloined from the local police outpost. A week after that the Guatemalan army arrived and began a rampage of murder, rape, and pillage that would become their principal tactic in a war in which Mayan civilians were assumed to be the enemy. I could only wonder what had happened to those gentle women I had met in the village.

I never returned to Atitlán or the highlands, but over the next decade I visited Central America with increasing frequency and began the research that eventually led to this book. As the project evolved, my focus shifted further south to the three countries that are the subject of this book, El Salvador, Costa Rica, and Nicaragua. I never forgot Guatemala, however, and my work there finds it way into this book as a contrasting case in Chapter 2 and an implicit example of authoritarianism throughout. Indeed, the contrast between militarized Guatemala and demilitarized Costa Rica started me thinking about how these two small countries only a brief plane ride apart could have such dramatically different politics. As I learned more about Central America, I discovered that many others had had the same experience and had been puzzled by the same question. Edelberto Torres-Rivas, whose brilliant analyses of Central American social structure are the intellectual starting point for this work, told me that he too had begun thinking about the puzzle of Central American comparative politics after a trip from Guatemala to Costa Rica. Edelberto was not, however, going on a research trip or a vacation. His high school friend and then-Vice President of Guatemala, Villagrán Kramer, had warned him that he could not guarantee his and his family's safety in their native Guatemala for more than twenty-four hours. Edelberto left for Costa Rica, where he remains in safety but in exile from his native land.

As my own research progressed, I decided to substitute El Salvador for Guatemala as a case of authoritarianism and political repression to contrast with peaceful, social democratic Costa Rica and—at that time—revolutionary Sandinista Nicaragua. It seemed that these three cases encompassed an extraordinary range of political variation while resembling one another in many ways, including their dependence on coffee as their principal export commodity from the late nineteenth century to the present. Guatemala too depended on coffee, but its semi-feudal labor relations and repressed indigenous population made it a special case in many respects. I had, by then, decided that the way to understand the differences in the political structures in the region was to interview members of the coffee dynasties that had created them. I did not think it would have been psychologically possible for me to conduct interviews with representatives of the ruling elites of two societies as repressive as Guatemala and El Salvador. One was difficult enough.

As I pursued my research in El Salvador, I found that the interviews I had planned with members of the Salvadoran coffee elite had turned into a murder mystery—the mystery of who had killed Segundo Montes, the distinguished Jesuit sociologist with whom I had hoped to work in El Salvador. He and his Jesuit colleagues at the University of Central America, their housekeeper, and her daughter had been murdered by the Salvadoran army a little more than a month before I was scheduled to arrive in El Salvador. Zoila Innocente, who courageously assumed the position of chair of the Sociology Department vacated by Montes's death, graciously extended to me an invitation to affiliate with the department. My office at the University looked out on the Jesuits' residence, where the physical scars of the attack were still plainly visible. Among the principal suspects in the murders (at least in my mind) were the people I was interviewing. That most of them professed to be as horrified by the murders as I was was not entirely reassuring. In the end, of course, as we now know, it was the high command of the Salvadoran armed forces which gave the order for the murders, without necessarily consulting their allies in the upper class or the government. Still, the murders of Segundo Montes and his colleagues haunted the final phase of my research in Central America just as the pillage of Santiago Atitlán haunted its beginnings

Many times since I started this research I have been asked how I could or would want to work in such a violent and troubled region. The truth of the matter is that, despite the violence or perhaps because of it, never have I seen such courage and personal conviction at work in the ways I witnessed in Central America. I will long remember the social scientists and other brave people I met there (and, of course, one that I did not meet), and the courage of peoples inspired by revolutionary hope. The hundreds of ways great and small in which the people of the region bore the burdens of a revolutionary war and foreign intervention will remain with me for a long time. That this intervention and much of the resulting carnage was the responsibility of my own government gave this courage a special poignance. At the end of the revolutionary decade, if all this hope and valor did not create the utopia that some, perhaps unrealistically, dreamed of, neither did it leave the world unchanged. Central America has been transformed in fundamental ways by the tumult of the 1980s, which opened up the possibility of a future long denied to the majority of its peoples. To realize this future will require even greater courage and hope than did the armed struggles themselves. Hope is in increasingly short supply even in Central America, where it accomplished so much, yet at such a terrible cost.

The debts of this author are many. To the people in the region who welcomed a stranger with remarkable courtesy and patience I owe a general debt. I am particularly grateful to the many people who helped me both with this research and my general education on Central America. In El Salvador Zoila Innocente and other members of Segundo Montes's former department helped me both personally and professionally more than I think they realize. I also am deeply indebted to Joaquín Salaverría, Director of the National Archive of El Salvador, whose friendship and commitment to scholarship were indispensable in carrying out my research there. Rubén Piñeda of the Salvadoran Coffee Council helped in many ways with the project and provided many valuable insights into the workings of the coffee sector. I hope that neither Rubén nor Joaquín will find the present work objectionable. I am also indebted to the United States Information Agency and the Fulbright Program in El Salvador; without their support it would have been impossible to do the kind of work I wished to do.

In Nicaragua I owe a tremendous debt to Dennis Gilbert, who generously shared with me his extensive knowledge of Latin American and Nicaraguan elites and showed me the ropes of field research.

Rose Spaulding too has been immensely helpful, not only in Nicaragua, where we met in the field, but also during a term at the Kellogg Center at Notre Dame and on other occasions. She has been a perceptive critic and a wonderful source of ideas about the Nicaraguan elite. David Kaimowitz graciously extended his hospitality and shared his extensive first-hand experience in Nicaragua with me on numerous occasions. Eduardo Baumeister has also been a valued colleague and a continuing source of intellectual stimulation. David Dye kindly shared some of his own data on the Nicaraguan coffee sector, making the problem of selecting subjects to interview much easier than it might otherwise have been. Rosario Sanabria made valuable contributions to the project when she was at Michigan as a Fellow of the Latin American Scholarship Program of American Universities. I am also grateful to the Sandinista Government of Nicaragua for inviting me as an International Observer on a Conference on the Atlantic Coast, which provided me with the opportunity to begin the interviews in Nicaragua.

I owe a special debt to the social science community of Costa Rica, surely a country with one of the highest concentrations of such talent in the hemisphere. Víctor Hugo Acuña has been an unfailing source of inspiration, hospitality, ideas, and sources since my first visits to Costa Rica in the early 1980s. My understanding of the conflicts of the 1930s in Costa Rica owes much to him as well as to Héctor Pérez Brignoli, whose broad grasp of Central American reality has deepened this work at numerous points. I wish to extend special thanks to Gertrude Peters and Samuel Stone, both of whom generously shared their own researches on the Costa Rican coffee elite with me. Ciska Raventos's scholarly work has also been an invaluable source for this book. Carolyn Hall provided many helpful suggestions in the early stage of this project. I am indebted to Mario Samper for much useful information on the history of Costa Rican coffee and for inviting me to conferences that gave me the opportunity to compare my ideas with those of others working on this subject. I also would like to thank Mitch Seligson and Rick Tardanico for their helpfulness and counsel both in Costa Rica and at home. Lowell Gudmundson's subtle insights into Costa Rican history have been an inspiration to me.

Many institutions have lent their support to this project over the years. I am particularly grateful for the financial support of the National Science Foundation (award SES 8920899) and the Fulbright Program. The Fulbright people were as helpful in San José as they were in Washington and San Salvador. The Office of the Vice President for Research and the LSA Faculty Assistance Fund provided crucial seed money for this project at its early stages and OVPR once again provided difficult-to-find support for data analysis and writing. I also benefited from a term of residence at the Kellogg Center at Notre Dame and from a term as a visiting lecturer at the Latin American Caribbean Center of Florida International University. The stimulating environments these centers provided did much to advance the project. I am also grateful to students and colleagues at the Center for Research on Social Organization of the University of Michigan, who over the years have probably heard more than they ever thought they wanted to know about the troubled politics of these small countries. I am particularly grateful for the support of Howard Kimeldorf, Rick Lempert, and Mark Mizruchi, who have been dogged readers and critics in the final stages of this manuscript. The Center's Administrative Assistant, Pat Preston, has been a great help in the final preparation of the manuscript. I am also grateful to Susan Eckstein, Peter Evans and Maurice Zeitlin for the support and encouragement they have provided at various stages of the project.

The staffs and administrations of the many research collections in which I worked also deserve thanks. These include, in Costa Rica, the National Archive, National Library, Bureau of the Census, and the libraries of the University of Costa Rica and the Superior Council of Central American Universities, all in San José; in Nicaragua, the libraries of the National Bank, Institute for Economic and Social Studies, Central American Institute for Business Administration, Central American Historical Institute of the University of Central America, the Nicaraguan Coffee and Cotton boards, and the Center for Investigations and Studies for the Agrarian Reform, all in Managua; in Guatemala, the Bureau of the Census and Statistics, Guatemala City; in El Salvador, the National Library, the National Museum Library, the National Archive, the Library of the University of Central America, the Library of the University's Human Rights Institute, the Library of the Central Bank in San Salvador, and the private library of Dr. Manuel Gallardo in Santa Tecla; in the United

States, the Library of Congress, the National Agricultural Library, the Central American collections of Tulane University and Michigan State University, and the Bancroft collection of the University of California at Berkeley. I am particularly grateful to the archivists and librarians at the Institute of Coffee in Costa Rica and the Salvadoran Coffee Council in El Salvador for granting me access to their periodical clippings and other collections.

Finally I would like to thank the Central Americans I interviewed for this study—the coffee growers, millers, and exporters themselves. I could scarcely have asked for more courteous, helpful, and friendly treatment than I received in the offices, farms, and homes of these men and women. Despite the cultural, national, and, in many cases, political differences that separated us, I came to like and admire the energy, passion, and enthusiasm with which they talked of their industry and themselves. I learned a lot about their societies and my own by talking with them. I hope I have done justice to their views in the summaries reported here. These reports and the conclusions drawn from them are, of course, my own and neither the persons I interviewed nor the many individuals or institutions that helped me bear any responsibility for them. Nevertheless my debts, in particular to the people of Central America, are many. People on both sides of the Central American conflicts who shared their hopes and fears with me made this work possible. It is to them that this book is dedicated.

Introduction

~

On January 16, 1992, Alfredo Cristiani Burkard, President of El Salvador, and representatives of the Frente Farabundo Martí para la Liberación Nacional (FMLN) signed peace accords at Chapultepec Castle in Mexico City, ending more than eleven years of civil war in El Salvador. The accords represented the culmination of a regional peace process begun by President Oscar Arias Sánchez of Costa Rica in February 1987. In October 1987, even before the fruits of his peace plan had been realized, Arias received the Nobel Prize for Peace. In February 1990, elections prescribed in the Arias plan brought to power Violeta Barrios de Chamorro, widow of martyred editor Pedro Joaquín Chamorro; ended a decade of rule by the Sandinistas; and brought the civil war in Nicaragua to an uncertain conclusion. The Chapultepec Castle ceremony brought to a close an epoch of Central American revolution and civil war that had begun with the Sandinista Revolution in 1979.[1] It also marked the end of the last revolutionary conflict of the Cold War era and may have marked the end of a cycle of Marxist-Leninist revolution that began with the October Revolution of 1917.

The wars of the 1980s in Central America had left close to 200,000 people dead and created 2,000,000 refugees.[2] They had been wars of extraordinary brutality and viciousness, particularly to civilians. If the most enduring international image of the beginning of the decade of revolution was that of the casual, cold-blooded murder of ABC journalist Bill Stewart as he lay prone beneath the guns of the Nicaraguan National Guard in June 1979, the most enduring image of its end was certainly the blasted bodies of six Jesuit priests, their housekeeper, and her daughter— murdered, as we now know,

1

at the direct orders of the High Command of the Salvadoran Armed Forces during the FMLN's last great offensive in November 1989. In the 1980s El Salvador, in particular, earned an unenviable international reputation for "death squads" and mass murder equalled in Latin America only by the "scorched Communist" campaigns of General Ríos Montt in neighboring Guatemala.

In the United States the Central American wars of the 1980s became a peculiar obsession of the Reagan administration, which saw them as an opportunity to reverse declining United States international prestige and hold the line against the putative "evil empire" of the then extant Soviet Union. The Reaganites' obsession with Central America, far beyond anything justified by the region's marginal strategic and inconsequential economic importance, led the United States into association with some of the most unsavory figures in the South American military and police establishment, to violations of international law and human rights, and ultimately to the betrayal of its own Constitution in the Iran-Contra scandal of 1986–87. The ultimate casualty in the Central American wars of the 1980s was an American government that saw its high officials indicted and some convicted for lying to Congress or worse. The discomfiture of the Reagan administration in Central America deepened a public mood of cynicism and distrust of government that was already well advanced from the earlier American failure in Vietnam.

The Central American civil wars were, in the end, settled by the Central Americans themselves, although not before the demise of both the Reagan administration and its nemesis, the Soviet Union, ended the Cold War. President Cristiani's signature on the Chapultepec accords, like the election of Violeta Chamorro in Nicaragua, represented a major evolution in the region's political institutions as well as a substantial change in the thinking of much of its elite. In other ways, however, the pacification of Central America represents a continuation of traditional social and political institutions. Alfredo Cristiani Burkard, Oscar Arias Sánchez, and Violeta Barrios de Chamorro are all representatives of the leading dynastic families that have controlled Central American politics from the early colonial period to the present. The role of these elites in the civil wars of the 1980s has received relatively less attention than have the ideologies and ambitions of the rebels or the international diplomatic and human rights aspects of the struggle. Yet they are no less central to understanding both the origins and the resolution of the crisis.

Although North American policy makers saw the Central American conflicts as episodes in the cold war, they were in fact deeply rooted in the social and economic structures of the region. These structures in turn were shaped by a single commodity that has dominated these small export economies from the nineteenth century to the present—coffee. The Central American dynastic elite is overwhelmingly an elite of coffee producers, processors, and exporters that rose to power everywhere on the Isthmus (except in Honduras) between 1850 and 1893. This coffee elite shaped the political institutions that emerged in the early twentieth century and survived the collapse of these institutions in the economic and political crises of the 1930s. When the world economy again entered a prolonged downturn after 1970, the elites faced a political crisis that was even more profound than the one they had faced in the 1930s. Once again, however, they appear to have survived a determined revolutionary challenge from below. Coffee and power have been closely linked in Central America since the nineteenth century. Coffee created the dynastic elites and shaped the political institutions that faced revolutionary crisis in the 1980s.

Both Alfredo Cristiani and Oscar Arias are members of leading coffee dynasties of their respective countries. Cristiani is the descendent of Italian immigrants who came to El Salvador at the height of the nineteenth-century coffee boom and intermarried with local elite families. The Cristianis and other Italian immigrant families such as the Borgonovos, Prietos, and Meardis now constitute an important nucleus of coffee growers, processors, and exporters. Alfredo Cristiani's family firm was in 1980–81 the tenth largest coffee processing firm in El Salvador.[3] Oscar Arias Sánchez is the grandson on his mother's side of legendary Costa Rican coffee grower and processor Julio Sánchez Lépiz, and on his father's side of the prominent coffee growing Arias family through which Oscar can trace his ancestry to the conquistador of Costa Rica, Juan Vázquez de Coronado.[4] During his presidency he was a business partner of the German-Costa Rican Peters family, the largest coffee processors in Costa Rica.[5] Violeta Chamorro, like Arias, can trace both her and her late husband's families to the colonial aristocracy but although the Chamorros produced and exported coffee, the family origins are in the pre-coffee cattle ranching and merchant nobility of Granada.[6]

Unlike the family fortunes of Cristiani or Arias, the wealth and prominence of the Chamorros (five Nicaraguan presidents since independence) in the twentieth century is based on sugar, not coffee. No coffee producer has played a prominent role in Nicaraguan politics since the abortive presidency of Carlos Solórzano in 1925, and coffee growers have largely been excluded from ultimate power since the overthrow of Managua coffee planter José Santos Zelaya in 1909. Both presidencies were ended by coups organized by Emiliano Chamorro, a collateral relative of Pedro Joaquín Chamorro. (Anastasio Somoza García made himself the largest coffee grower in Nicaragua only after he had been assisted to the presidency by the United States Marines.) Coffee producers were notably absent both from the ruling Sandinista elite and from the close circle of elite families surrounding President Chamorro.[7] The role of the coffee elite in Nicaragua was largely defined by its exclusion from power after 1909. This exclusion would profoundly influence Nicaraguan politics and, ultimately, the Nicaraguan revolution.

Cristiani, Arias, and Chamorro are representative of the dynastic elites of their respective nations. During the 1980s the coffee elite of El Salvador backed a violently anti-Communist party founded by death-squad organizer Roberto D'Aubuisson and remained unified in opposition to social change in general and the FMLN rebels in particular. Cristiani was the presidential candidate of D'Aubuisson's party, but he led the party and the coffee elite to a democratic and peaceful accommodation with the rebels. In Costa Rica during the 1980s important sectors of the coffee elite, led by Oscar Arias, remained committed to the traditional Costa Rican values of peace, democracy, and progressive social change despite increasing tensions and determined pressure by the Reagan administration to join its anti-Communist crusade in Central America. In Nicaragua a substantial (although minority) sector of the coffee elite, along with other members of the agro-export elite and old aristocratic families like the Chamorros, joined the Sandinista revolution even though they knew it was led by Marxist-Leninists. Mrs. Chamorro was a member of the first revolutionary junta in 1979. These differences in elite behavior profoundly influenced the outcome of the 80s crisis in each country. Unified opposition to the FMLN by the coffee elite contributed significantly to the rebels' failure to take power in El Salvador, just as elite support for the Sandinistas was crucial to their victory in Nicaragua. The commitment of Oscar Arias and other members of the coffee elite to social democracy and peace kept Costa Rica out of the revolutionary crisis altogether.

What accounts for these profound differences in elite ideology and behavior? This book attempts to answer this question in two ways: through conversations with members of the coffee elite themselves in the midst of the revolutionary crisis of the 1980s, and by tracing the historical origins of elite ideology in the rise of the nineteenth-century coffee economy and its crisis in the Great Depression. It is a study of both ideological and political transformation. It is of course impossible to separate the ideology and actions of the elite from the greater political and social systems of which they are a part, but these systems were in part a creation of the coffee elite. The revolutionary crises of the 1980s were crises of the coffee elites and the societies they made at the end of the nineteenth and the beginning of the twentieth centuries. Understanding their views and the historical origins of the 1980s conflicts, it is hoped, will provide insight not only into the common outcome—neo-liberalism and democracy— but also into the profound differences among the political systems of these three countries as the 1980s began.

At the beginning of that decade it would have been difficult to find anywhere in the world three political systems as different as those of El Salvador, Costa Rica, and Nicaragua. El Salvador was still under the control of a military junta and associated death squads that, with the backing of the coffee elite, were trying to hang on to the power they had held almost without interruption since 1932. El Salvador, before the beginnings of democracy in the mid-eighties, had the longest-lived series of military dictatorships in Latin America. Costa Rica, on the other hand, had the longest-lived stable democracy in Latin America, with contested elections and a universal franchise since 1948. Its welfare state had provided a general level of well-being for its population far beyond what would be expected from its modest levels of economic development. After the Sandinista revolution in 1979, Nicaragua was for more than a decade the only revolutionary socialist state on the Latin American mainland

and one of two in the Western Hemisphere. After a period of revolutionary turmoil, the three societies seem to be converging on a common model of electoral democracy and neo-liberal economic policy, but they took very different routes to arrive there.

The divergence in the political systems of these three countries was even more striking given their underlying similarities. El Salvador, Costa Rica, and Nicaragua are all small, peripheral, agricultural export economies that were once part of the same province of the Spanish colonial empire and share a common culture, common Isthmian location, and common history of foreign domination. A single agricultural export commodity, coffee, has dominated all three societies, as well as neighboring Guatemala, from the mid-nineteenth century to the present. El Salvador, Costa Rica, and Nicaragua were selected for this study precisely because of these similarities. Honduras did not enter the coffee export economy until well into the twentieth century. It was, and to some extent still is, the exemplar "banana republic." The large indigenous population of Guatemala, like El Salvador a nation with a ferocious authoritarian tradition, makes it in many respects a special case, despite the fact that it too is a coffee export economy. The choice of El Salvador, Costa Rica, and Nicaragua for this study maximizes the divergence in political outcomes while minimizing the underlying variability among the cases. At the beginning of the 1980s, and for much of the postwar period, these political differences were profound. The social origins of dictatorship, democracy, and revolutionary socialism were all represented in Central America.

Readers familiar with Barrington Moore's monumental *Social Origins of Dictatorship and Democracy* (1966) will note that the three routes taken by El Salvador, Costa Rica, and Nicaragua to the 1980s crisis parallel his three political routes into the modern world: through revolution from above and conservative authoritarianism (what he calls "fascism"), through revolutionary socialism, and through democracy.[8] The coffee elites are not the only factor influencing the diverse political routes Central American political systems followed in the twentieth century, but the political systems of El Salvador, Costa Rica, and Nicaragua were largely constructed by them, and the crisis of the 1980s was in large part a crisis of the coffee elites. Both the political divergence of the three societies at the beginning of the revolutionary decade and their eventual political convergence at its end provide important tests of Moore's theory and other theories of the origins of dictatorship, democracy, and socialist revolution.

Furthermore, as Lowell Gudmundson has pointed out, Moore's ideas on the relationship between agrarian structures and political development have had such impact on the study of Central America that they form the framework for both the classic works of Ciro F. S. Cardoso, Edelberto Torres-Rivas, and Héctor Pérez-Brignoli and the more recent analyses by Enrique Baloyra, Robert Williams, Anthony Winson, and myself.[9] The contrast between the authoritarian North (El Salvador and especially Guatemala) and the democratic South (Costa Rica) has been viewed, after Moore, as a consequence of the greater importance of labor-repressive forms of export agriculture in the North and the greater importance of small holders and merchant capitalists in the South. The Moore framework as it has been applied to Central America has considerable validity, especially in regard to labor repression and authoritarianism in the North, but this book will attempt to demonstrate that in important respects both Moore's model and its applications in Central America fall short in accounting for differences in the twentieth-century politics of El Salvador, Costa Rica, and Nicaragua.

A revised model is necessary not only to account for the historical differences among Central American political systems, but also to explain the current convergence of all three, whatever their past agrarian structures, on some version of representative democracy. The Central American transitions to democracy in the 1980s share important parallels with democratic transitions in the Southern Cone, the former Soviet Union, and elsewhere as well as with the historic experience of Western democracies. It will be argued here, however, that the characteristics of the Central American cases are sufficiently distinct, both in historical and contemporary terms, to suggest that a new model of democratic transition may be necessary—through socialist revolution from below.

The transformation of Central America in the 1980s was one of politics and economics, but it was also a transformation in the realm of ideas. Twice in this century, in the 1930s and again in the 1980s, the liberal ideology of the nineteenth-century Central American coffee elites has been challenged by revolutionary alternative visions of society. In both cases elite thinking was profoundly changed by the experience, in part through the ideological work required in the repression and denial of the revolutionary vision. It is elite ideology as revealed by interviews with members of Central American dynastic elites that is the central empirical focus of this study. When members of the dynastic elites were interviewed at the height of the revolutionary tumult of the 1980s, they were in the midst of a profound ideological transformation. This transformation was in part a consequence of the revolutionary decade and in part reflected a deeper transformation in the class relations of the agro-export sector itself. In class relations, politics, and ideology the three societies started at very different points and converged on a common model. These transformations are the central focus of this book.

Part I of the book describes the origins of the coffee elite in the class relations of the late nineteenth- and early twentieth-century coffee export economy and the remarkable continuity of its influence down to the present. Chapter 1 introduces the cast of characters in this particular historical drama—the families of the coffee elite itself—and describes their divergent behavior in the revolutionary decade of the 1980s. Chapter 2 describes the elite's class position in the social organization of agro-export production and how this position changed over the course of the twentieth century. The distinction between the *agrarian* and *agro-industrial* class fractions of the elite, rooted in the social organization of coffee production itself, is critical for understanding the politics and ideologies of the elites. It profoundly affects the elites' relationships to subordinate classes and the state. As subsequent chapters will attempt to demonstrate, these patterns of class relations and their transformation account for both the divergence of the elite politics and ideology at the beginning of the revolutionary decade and their convergence at its end.

Differences in class relations set the framework in which the crises of both the 1930s and the 1980s unfolded, but the elite ideologies are also influenced by the complex personal and political histories of the elite itself. Part II explains how these histories unfolded in the crisis of the 1930s. In this decade the liberal ideology of the nineteenth-century coffee elite was modified substantially by interaction with insurrectionary movements associated with counter-ideologies—sometimes, as in Costa Rica, for the better, and sometimes, as in El Salvador, for the worse. The crisis of the 1930s is therefore the key to understanding the ideologies of the elites in the 1980s. It is the ultimate source of the stories they tell in the interviews. Most of their families, or the older interviewees themselves, were intimately involved in these events. Their consciousness as a class is shaped as much by these complex series of events and, particularly in Costa Rica, by improbable historical conjunctures, as it is by the organization of production. At the end of the thirties, the traditional liberalism of the elite had evolved into a consciousness that led to dramatically different politics at the beginning of the eighties.

In Part III the book turns to the crisis of the 1980s and examines both how elite narratives influenced the genesis of the crisis and how these narratives changed in response to the crisis. This is the story of the 1980s as told by members of the coffee elite. The ideological structure in which elite narratives were constructed was provided by Central American liberalism as elaborated by the nineteenth-century Liberal parties. Each of the elites emphasizes one particular part of this Liberal heritage—*Progress* in El Salvador, *Liberty* in Nicaragua, and *Democracy* in Costa Rica. At the end of the decade these different stories had converged on a common ideology of neo-liberalism and democracy. Each of the elite stories has peculiar silences and areas of tension—forbidden zones that the interviewer had to approach with care. Hidden beneath these silences, it will be argued, are the forbidden counter-narratives of the long dead insurrectionaries of the 1930s and the new stories of the revolutionaries of the 1980s. Maintaining these silences proved extremely costly for the elite both personally and politically. Things unsaid in the interviews proved as interesting as things said.

Finally, in the concluding chapter, the book returns to the questions with which we began. How did the coffee elite come to support conservative authoritarianism in El Salvador, revolutionary socialism in Nicaragua, and social democracy in Costa Rica? And how did the eighties crisis lead all three elites to converge on parliamentary democracy and neo-liberalism? The answers to these questions involve transformations in both the political economy and the ideology of Central America and its coffee elites. In the 1980s Central America took a journey, which much of the world has followed in the twentieth century, through democracy, dictatorship, and revolutionary socialism to a still uncertain political future in neo-liberal democracy. It is hoped that the stories of the coffee elite will help us to understand not only the revolutionary crisis of the 1980s in Central America, but also the political ideologies and political structures of the cold-war era now ended, and the emerging new political order in which all of us, including particularly the United States, have been and continue to be so deeply embedded.

I

Social Origins of the Central American Crisis

1

Revolution and the Coffee Elite

The origins of the revolutionary crisis of the 1980s in Central America are to be found in the origins of the coffee elite itself, in the export economy of nineteenth-century Central America. It was this coffee export economy that created the deep divisions between a privileged elite and impoverished rural masses that exploded in revolution twice in this century. The expansion of the export economy was associated with the rise of a new elite ideology, liberalism, that served as both a justification and program for the political and economic transformations that consolidated the new agro-export order. The coffee elite survived the revolutionary challenges of both the 1930s and 1980s but with both its ideology and its political program deeply transformed. At the end of the second revolutionary decade, however, the coffee elite emerged with its power, if anything, enhanced. Power in Central America in the late twentieth century is still held by the coffee elite that arose with the export economy of the late nineteenth century.

Social Origins of the Coffee Elite

The coffee dynasties of nineteenth-century Central America were built at the expense of much of the rest of the population, just as the colonial aristocracies from which many of them descended had

13

been built on the destruction of indigenous civilizations. The rise of coffee, first in Costa Rica, then in El Salvador, and finally in Nicaragua, brought with it revolutions by Liberals opposed to colonial restrictions on labor, land, and markets. The victorious Liberals then set about remaking their societies to fit the needs of the new export economy. As Ciro F. S. Cardoso notes, the date of the beginning of the Liberal reforms in El Salvador and neighboring Guatemala corresponds exactly to the moment at which coffee exports exceeded traditional exports of dye stuffs.[1] Liberal revolutions in El Salvador (1885) and Nicaragua (1893) (as well as Guatemala, 1871) deepened the social transformations that accompanied the rise of coffee. Similar changes had begun more gradually in Costa Rica in the 1840s. The Liberal revolutionaries dispossessed traditional Indian communities, disestablished Church control over property, raffled off public lands, encouraged European immigration and foreign investment, developed ports and railroads, and forcibly recruited a largely unwilling rural population to work on their coffee estates. They built new wealth and created vast poverty, setting in motion social forces that would explode under them twice in this century.

The period from 1880 to the Great Depression was the golden age of the coffee elite. In El Salvador in 1895 a majority of national legislators were coffee growers. After the 1898 coup d'etat by General Tomás Regalado, founder of one of El Salvador's legendary coffee dynasties, coffee growers held the Salvadoran presidency without interruption until 1931. In Costa Rica the coup d'etat of General Tomás Guardia in 1870 initiated an uninterrupted rule by the coffee elite that did not end until 1948. The "organic intellectuals" of the coffee elite, the "Generation of 1888" or "the Olympians," ruled for much of this period in the formidable personages of thrice-president (1910–1914, 1924–1928, 1932–1936) Ricardo Jiménez Oreamuno and twice-president (1906–1910, 1928–1932) Cleto González Víquez. In Nicaragua, Managua coffee planter José Santos Zelaya seized power in 1893 and held it until 1909, initiating a whirlwind series of reforms that doubled coffee exports and consolidated elite control over a newly expanded state apparatus. At the turn of the century coffee was the primary export, the foundation of wealth, the determinant of social status, and the arbiter of political power in all three countries as well as in neighboring Guatemala.

Immigrants and Aristocrats: The Coffee Dynasties of El Salvador, Costa Rica, and Nicaragua

The new elite was composed of traditional aristocratic families, usually of pure Spanish descent, from the colonial and republican periods, and of newer European immigrants who arrived in Central America to take advantage of the economic opportunities provided by the coffee boom. The colonial and republican aristocracies had the advantage of political influence, social standing, and often control over land. The European immigrants lacked these advantages but brought with them technical, commercial, and financial skills notably lacking in the overwhelmingly agrarian societies of nineteenth-century Central America, with their minuscule professional and merchant classes. For the most part the immigrants were not part of mass migrations but were single men attracted by expanding opportunities. They married into the local gentry and were assimilated into the Hispanic elite, although German and other Axis nationals found during World War II that their nationality could be a distinct handicap. For the most part, though, the new immigrants became part of a new and powerful elite.

The new immigrants generally used their skills to move into the more technical and financially demanding but also much more profitable processing and exporting activities, and sometimes into production. The traditional colonial and republican elites were more likely to begin by growing coffee and sometimes expanded into the other activities. For example, in Costa Rica in 1850, at the start of the coffee age, *three-quarters* of all major coffee growers were descended from just two Spanish colonial families, one of them that of the conquistador Juan Vázquez de Coronado himself.[2] Foreigners were almost without representation. By 1935, however, 44 percent of coffee processing and a greater percentage of exports were in the hands of foreigners.[3] In El Salvador in the 1930s, of the 24 largest coffee processors 17 were immigrants. By 1980–81, 12 of the 15 largest coffee processing firms were controlled by immigrants and their descendents.[4] In the north central Nicaraguan coffee zone by 1910 two-thirds of the largest estates were in the hands of foreigners, many of them Americans.[5] The Germans were the single most important group in Nicaragua and Costa Rica, while the Italians and English were more important in El Salvador.

These coffee dynasties are cognatic descent groups that trace their lineage through both males and females to a founding male ancestor, usually the nineteenth-century immigrant or colonial aristocrat who founded the family coffee enterprise. The family is invariably referred to by the surname of the male founder and can extend through both blood and marriage to large groups of descendents. The effective kin group, however, is members of the family with a stake in the family economic enterprise, frequently a group of coffee estates organized around a family-owned processing plant, but in the more successful lineages, particularly in El Salvador, organized family holding companies or financial groups. The enterprise is usually managed by an elder son of the lineage. Even if these economic organizations are incorporated as Sociedades Anónimas (S.A.), ownership and management are closely or exclusively held by family members. Although vague feelings of allegiance may unite relatives outside the charmed circle of economic power, the economic enterprise reinforces the loyalty and sentiments of kinship with the sinews of property. These lineage groups have proved to be surprisingly resilient, providing political and social power as well as material sustenance to their members. The nature of dynastic economic activities varies considerably in the three countries, but the general dynastic form is the same.

Costa Rica: Montealegres, Peterses, and Julio Sánchez Lépiz. The Montealegres were by far the most successful of the Spanish colonial aristocrats who moved into the expanding coffee export economy in Costa Rica, but nevertheless illustrate the process by which political and social power translated into control of coffee. The Montealegres are direct descendents of both the conquistador Juan Vázquez de Coronado and the seventeenth-century Spanish nobleman, Antonio Acosta de Arévalo. The family's dominance of the coffee trade began with the activities of the brothers José María Montealegre and Mariano in the 1850s. By this time both were prominent growers, processors, and exporters. José María became president of Costa Rica in 1860 by overthrowing the nation's leading coffee processor and exporter, President Juan Rafael Mora, himself also a descendent of conquistador Vázquez de Coronado, after Mora's plans to found a bank threatened other exporters' hold over the coffee trade. New

President José María's brother, Mariano, then founded his own bank in 1863, the Banco Anglo Costarricense, which remained until its bankruptcy in 1995 one of the most important financial institutions in the country. In 1990 the Montealegre family still controlled the third largest processing and exporting business in a highly concentrated industry.[6]

Wilhelm Peters Schuster, on the other hand, did not arrive in Costa Rica until the last decade of the nineteenth century. He first worked in a pharmacy with German chemist Carlos Beutel and then as an estate administrator, before beginning to assemble an economic empire that would make him one of the most important producers, processors, and exporters before World War II. His properties were expropriated after Pearl Harbor because he was a German national, and he was forced to return to his homeland. He came back to Costa Rica penniless after the war and rebuilt his coffee empire. The enterprise, now run by his son, Werner Peters Scheider, was in the 1980s the leading coffee processing and exporting firm in the country. Werner Peters is the business partner of President Oscar Arias Sánchez. Another German immigrant, Julio Francisco Rohrmoser Harder, who arrived in Costa Rica in 1853 and founded a second coffee dynasty, became so assimilated into Costa Rican society that his descendents were considered Costa Rican, not German, in World War II and were not expropriated. Julio Francisco's granddaughter Amelia married Juan José Montealegre to create another branch of one of Costa Rica's most powerful coffee families.[7]

Julio Sánchez Lépiz, Oscar Arias's maternal grandfather, is the exception that proves the rule on the social origins of the coffee elite. His father was a mule skinner and oxcart driver, and was not descended from Vázquez de Coronado, Acosta de Arévalo, or any aristocrat whatsoever. He was one of the poor who made up the overwhelming majorities of Costa Rica, El Salvador, and Nicaragua but played almost no role in the origins of the coffee elite. Julio began buying as well as transporting coffee and eventually came to own 25 coffee estates and several processing plants. By 1935 he was the largest single coffee exporter in Costa Rica. Oscar Arias's mother, Lilliam, is mentioned prominently in Julio Sánchez Lépiz's will, and the family coffee empire was run by his great uncle before being managed in partnership with the Peterses.[8] The Arias-Sánchez family empire is unusual in one other respect, at least among Costa Rican families. The family also controls extensive sugar and cattle properties, in a pattern of agro-export diversification rare among Costa Rican (but not Salvadoran) coffee families.[9] Coffee elite families of non-aristocratic and non-immigrant origins are even rarer, however. *None* of the leading Salvadoran coffee families and no more than one or two of the leading Nicaraguan producers was from such a family.[10]

El Salvador: Regalados, de Solas, and Hills. The "fourteen families" of El Salvador are a journalistic invention, but the families themselves are not. Dynasties like the Peterses or Montealegres of Costa Rica are, if anything, even more important in El Salvador. The Regalado dynasty, for example, founded by General and President Tomás Regalado, who wielded immense political as well as economic power in the nineteenth century, became, in alliance with the Republican Mathies and Dueñas families, the largest single producer of coffee in El Salvador in the 1970s, as well as the single largest sugar producer, although only the 21st largest coffee exporter. The base of the family fortune lay in its vast estates of more than 6,000 hectares in six different Salvadoran provinces, and it suffered heavy losses in the Salvadoran land reform of 1981.[11] The Regalados, in alliance with the Dueñas and Alvarez clans, were founders of one of Salvador's principal banks, the Banco de Comercio, and the family also came to control electrical utilities, sugar refineries, an automobile agency, and an investment company.[12] The Regalados had the reputation of being one of the most intransigent of the Salvadoran oligarchic clans during the crisis of the 1980s. The FMLN's attacks on the Salvadoran coffee oligarchy began with the kidnapping and subsequent murder of Ernesto Regalado Dueñas.[13]

If the economic base of the Regalados was political power and control over land, the base of Salvador's leading coffee exporter before 1979, the de Sola family, was in commerce. The de Solas were Sephardic Jews from the Dutch possession of Curaçao, an important entrepot in the insular and littoral Caribbean trade. The founder of the Salvadoran dynasty, Orlando de Sola, learned the intricacies of international commerce from his father, a prominent Curaçao merchant. At the age of twenty he had already become a partner in a French commercial firm in Panama. He arrived in San Salvador in

1896 with business introductions from his French partners and a consular appointment from the Dutch Government. De Sola established himself in merchandising, expanded into manufacturing and transportation, and then, making use of his extensive international and commercial knowledge and connections, moved into the export of sugar and coffee. He did not purchase his first coffee processing plant until 1923 and his first coffee estate until 1935, but by 1970–71 the firm of H. de Sola and Sons was the largest coffee exporter in El Salvador and the center of a diversified business empire employing thousands. Except for the family black sheep Orlando (the founder's grandson), the de Solas had the reputation of being one of the most liberal of the Salvadoran dynasties in the 1970s and 1980s.[14]

Although Orlando de Sola did not marry into a Salvadoran family, his descendents and most other immigrant dynastic founders did. Appendix I shows the pattern of intermarriage with Salvadoran families of another prominent immigrant family, the Hills. The family founder, the redoubtable James Hill, arrived in El Salvador from England in 1889 and, like de Sola, was the representative of a European firm who began in retail merchandising. In 1899 he married a Salvadoran woman, Dolores Bernal Nájera, and became interested in coffee through her mother, who owned an estate. A friend of plant wizard Luther Burbank, Hill became one of El Salvador's most technically sophisticated producers, introducing many innovations that were widely adopted by other Salvadorans. As the genealogy in Appendix I indicates, his descendents intermarried widely with leading colonial and republican families including the Escalóns, Orellanas, Guriolas, and Regalados. James Hill's granddaughter, Ellen O'Sullivan Hill, was married to Ernesto Regalado Dueñas when he was kidnapped and murdered by the FMLN. In 1980–81 J. Hill y Cía. was the fifteenth largest coffee processor in El Salvador, and Llach y Cía., controlled by the Llach Hills, was the fifth largest. The Hill family has interests in cotton, banking, cement, textiles, finance, and an industrial park.[15] The family coffee enterprise is managed by Harold Hill, second son of James Hill's first son, Jaime Hill.

Nicaragua: The Bolts and the Cuadras. With the exception of the Somoza dynasty, which is a special case, the Nicaraguan coffee elite were less likely to form great economic empires like those of their counterparts elsewhere in the region. Although powerful coffee processing and exporting families such as the Baltodanos and Rappaciolis did emerge in Nicaragua, more typical are the Matagalpa coffee dynasties founded by John Bolt and Salvador Cuadra. Bolt was an English miner who migrated to Nicaragua at the turn of the century to work in the goldfields of the north central region, married a Nicaraguan woman, and purchased the coffee estates La Grecia and Las Canas, which had 50,000 trees under production in 1930. His estate was divided among his three sons. The son who received the least land, Guillermo Bolt Martínez, became the most successful, acquiring his own estate of about 50,000 trees and establishing a substantial coffee processing business (later expropriated by the Sandinistas). Three of Bolt's grandchildren (two of them children of Guillermo) owned substantial estates in Matagalpa before the revolution. The Bolt family is typical of the turn-of-the-century immigrant pioneers who established the Matagalpa coffee industry in the first two or three decades of this century. The relatively small scale of the Bolt enterprise, when contrasted with the diversified business empire of the de Solas or the coffee processing empire of the Montealegres, is typical of the Nicaraguan coffee elite, as is the small scale of his processing plant and the importance of coffee land, as opposed to processing or export, in the family's activities.[16]

Salvador Cuadra, a descendent of one of the leading families of the Granada colonial nobility, also acquired a Matagalpa estate a few years before John Bolt. In 1910 he had 60,000 coffee trees in production and by 1930, 100,000 trees.[17] His grandson Jaime Cuadra is now proprietor of Salvador Cuadra's estate El Gorrión, and one of Jaime's sisters owns La China, another of the original Cuadra Matagalpa properties. The Cuadras were in the prerevolutionary period the doyens of Matagalpa provincial society, and Jaime Cuadra became president of the Coffee Association of Matagalpa, the most powerful private producers' organization in the post revolutionary era. Unlike Bolt and all the Costa Rican and Salvadoran coffee families discussed thus far, he did not own a plant that processed coffee from other growers.[18] Like Bolt and most other Nicaraguan coffee families, Cuadra's wealth depends almost exclusively on production, not on processing and export, and despite his social and political eminence, he has few holdings outside his coffee farm.

The Bolts and Cuadras are typical of most Nicaraguan coffee families in the relatively small scale of their enterprise, its limited economic scope, and dependence on production rather than processing and export. They are also typical of an important political minority among Nicaraguan coffee growers. Both were early and active supporters of the Sandinistas. In the prerevolutionary era Cuadra was close to many Sandinista activists, including later Sandinista *comandante* Victor Tirado, and was arrested and imprisoned by Somoza for pro-Sandinista activities. Cuadra gained his freedom only as part of an exchange, after the Sandinistas raided a 1974 Christmas party for the American ambassador and took the gusts hostage. The hostages included many close associates of Somoza (but not the Ambassador, who had left early). Cuadra joined such prominent Sandinistas as Daniel Ortega in the mass release and later flight to Cuba. He then spent five years in exile in Canada before returning to Nicaragua after the revolution. He was offered a high position in the Ministry of Agriculture by the Sandinistas, but declined. By the mid eighties, however, his Matagalpa Association was one of the strongest voices in opposition to Sandinista rule. When Violeta Chamorro was elected President, he was offered the Agricultural Ministry but again declined because of Chamorro's close ties to the Sandinistas.[19]

Guillermo Bolt's daughter Gladys, married to Matagalpa planter Noel Rivera, became one of the most important leaders of the Sandinista Farmers and Ranchers Union (UNAG), where she was an influential defender of those private coffee farmers who, like her husband and herself, had remained in Nicaragua after the revolution. Her role and her support for a Sandinista organization, even if in the interests of private farmers, gained her national publicity and the hatred of many in the counter-revolution who regarded her as a traitor to her class. In 1984 contra raiders took her husband prisoner at the family's isolated farm and beat and bayoneted him to death. After her husband's death, Gladys Bolt sold the family's farm but remained active in UNAG, which became increasingly responsive to her and other private farmers over the years. She never joined the Sandinista Party but remained a firm supporter of the revolution before and after her husband's death.[20]

In one way or another, the events of the 1980s in El Salvador and Nicaragua touched most of these families, some as deeply as they touched the family Bolt. Most members of the Salvadoran elite lived and worked in heavily armed compounds and were escorted by armed guards when they traveled to their estates. Many were threatened with kidnapping by army death squads as well as the FMLN.[21] In Nicaragua contra raids threatened almost any coffee planter in the north central region who was sympathetic to the Sandinistas; conversely, suspected contra sympathizers risked confiscation of their estates and arrest (but not torture or death) from the Sandinistas.[22] The coffee elite had been among the principal targets of both the Salvadoran and Nicaraguan revolutions, and by the time they were interviewed by the author in 1986, 1987, and 1990, at the height of the civil wars, they were under tremendous physical, political, and psychological pressure, apparent in both their conversation and demeanor.

Crisis and Change: The Persistence of Coffee Elite Power

Although the coffee elites of El Salvador, Costa Rica, and Nicaragua retained immense economic and social power well into the 1980s, after the 1920s their direct control over Central American politics was much reduced. The Great Depression put an end to direct rule by the coffee oligarchies and generated powerful oppositional movements that nearly brought down the social and economic structures created by the Regalados, the Montealegres, and other coffee barons of the nineteenth century. The elite survived the Great Depression (except in Nicaragua) with its economic and social power intact, by ceding direct power to military dictatorships in El Salvador and Nicaragua and, paradoxically, to a democratic regime imposed by a military junta in Costa Rica. In El Salvador after 1932 and Nicaragua after 1934 the political systems were organized around an implicit alliance between the oligarchy and a military dictatorship, with the latter holding ultimate power. After 1930 the Central American coffee elites traded the right to rule for the right to make money, although in Nicaragua even this right would eventually be threatened by the greed of the Somozas. In Costa Rica in 1948 the victorious revolution of José Figueres excluded the coffee elite from the direct political power they had held since 1870.

At the outset of the revolutionary decade of the 1980s, however, the coffee elites remained a power to be reckoned with in Central

American society. This was particularly true in El Salvador, whose coffee elite emerged as the most economically powerful on the Isthmus despite its loss of formal political power in 1932. Leading coffee families, including the Regalados and the Hills, continued to control the major domestic banks before their nationalization in 1980. When new export crops began to be produced after World War II, the coffee elite controlled these as well. Twelve of the fourteen largest cotton producers before 1979, including the Hill-Llach-Hills and the Cristianis, were among the 26 largest coffee growers, as were nine of the ten largest sugar growers including the Regalados (the largest), the Cristianis, and the de Solas.[23] This wealth in export agriculture enabled the coffee elite to move into finance, real estate, commerce, tourism, and, in the heyday of the Central American common market in the 1960s, manufacturing for domestic and regional markets. The coffee elite came to control not only coffee but most of the rest of the economy.[24] The diversified Regalado, de Sola, and Hill enterprises are representative of Salvadoran coffee elite economic power.

Furthermore, the coffee elite seems to have staged something of a political comeback in El Salvador, after fifty years in the political wilderness. The election of Alfredo Cristiani in 1989 marked the first time since 1931 that a coffee grower had held the Salvadoran presidency. Cristiani and his administration were closely tied to the core of coffee elite power. Cristiani's family is the proprietor of the tenth largest coffee processing firm. The administration's eminence grise, Cristiani's brother-in-law and grandson of James Hill, Roberto Llach-Hill, is the proprietor of Llach y Cía., the fifth largest processor. His friend and choice for the critical diplomatic mission in Washington during his administration was Miguel Angel Salaverría, himself a member of a leading coffee family and general manager of Prieto S.A., the eighth largest processor, founded by another Italian immigrant. These three men and two of their first cousins together control five of the fifteen largest coffee processing firms in El Salvador. Although Cristiani was followed in office in 1994 by former San Salvador mayor Armando Calderón Sol, the dominance of the coffee elite continues. In 1970–71 the Sol Millet branch of the family was the eighth largest coffee exporter in El Salvador.[25] The paradoxical outcome of the Salvadoran civil war has been a coffee elite restoration and a displacement, perhaps temporary, of the military from direct rule. The coffee elite that took power at the end of the revolutionary decade was, however, very different from the one that existed at its beginning, and far different from the elite when it last ruled in 1931.

In Costa Rica the traditional families of the coffee elite, including the Montealegres and the Peterses, continue to dominate coffee processing or export although they are increasingly hard pressed by a growing cooperative movement on the one hand and foreign transnationals on the other. Unlike the Salvadoran elite, they have not (with some notable exceptions, including the Arias-Sánchez family) moved into other forms of export agriculture nor into industry. Their control over banking was terminated by the nationalization of the banking system in 1948. Only one family of the Costa Rican coffee elite, the formidable Jiménez de la Guardia clan, approaches the wealth and economic diversification of the Salvadoran families. The Jiménez de la Guardias, in addition to owning coffee estates, control rice, cattle, and sugar production, the nation's largest newspaper, La Nación, the largest brewery, and a host of other enterprises including the first McDonald's franchise to be established outside of North America.[26] The almost complete absence of coffee families in industry, overwhelmingly controlled by North American corporations, or (in textiles) by Jewish Eastern European immigrants, is particularly notable.[27] The Costa Rican elite, having lost its political hegemony in 1948, has not compensated by developing the diversified economic power of its Salvadoran counterpart. Its interests are still largely limited to coffee.

The "dynasty of the conquerors," in Samuel Stone's notable phrase, does continue to dominate Costa Rican politics.[28] Although not all descendents of the early colonial nobility are themselves coffee growers, the dynasty of the conquerors has retained a striking hold over the Costa Rican presidency. Every presidential election in Costa Rica since 1948 has had least one contender who was a descendent of the conquistador Cristóbal de Alfaro, and in all but three elections both contenders were descendents of Alfaro. Oscar Arias Sánchez, a scion of one of Costa Rica's most notable coffee families and business partner of another, as well as a descendent of Alfaro, was succeeded by Rafael Angel Calderón Fournier, himself the son of the last pre-1948 coffee elite president and another descendent of Alfaro.[29] Calderón Fournier's first Vice President was Arnulfo López, a lawyer for the Peters firm and past president of the Coffee Association. One of his chief advisers was Rodolfo Jiménez Borbón, scion of the Jiménez de La Guardia family.[30] The current (1996) Costa Rican President, José María Figueres, is the son of the only postwar Costa Rican president not descended from the conquerors, the founder of modern Costa Rica, José Figueres *père.*[31]

Only in Nicaragua does the coffee elite remain outside the charmed circle of power. Jaime Cuadra's opposition to the policies of the successive ruling regimes of the Somozas, the Sandinistas, and the Chamorros may be taken as representative of the political exclusion of the coffee elite since the overthrow of their great hero José Santos Zelaya in 1909. Violeta Barrios de Chamorro is at the center of a kinship network of families descended, not from the coffee elite, but from the colonial merchant aristocracy of the city of Granada and associated with the Nicaraguan Conservative Party (Zelaya and the rest of the coffee elite were Liberals). This network of families not only held supreme political power in the Chamorro administration but commanded the economic heights of the Somoza regime. Surprisingly, as Carlos Vilas has demonstrated, these same families were also integrated into the power structure of the revolutionary Sandinista regime, leading one cynical Sandinista (not from an aristocratic family) to observe that the change from the Sandinistas to Chamorro simply meant that the "government had crossed Calle Atravesada [the street where Granada's aristocratic families traditionally have their homes] from one sidewalk to the other."[32] While this is, to be sure, an exaggeration (neither Sandinista President Daniel Ortega, his brother, Sandinista Defense Minister Humberto Ortega, nor Interior Minister and Sandinista Party founder Tomás Borge, for example, are from the Granada or any other aristocracy), it underscores the Conservative family ties that linked the Chamorro administration to its predecessors and facilitated the Chamorro-Sandinista coalition when it controlled Nicaragua.

At the core of this network was Doña Violeta's martyred husband, Pedro Joaquín Chamorro Cardenal, editor of Nicaragua's leading newspaper *La Prensa,* leader of the Conservative anti-Somoza opposition, and board member of one of prerevolutionary Nicaragua's two

leading bank-based financial groups, BANIC (after the Banco Nicaragüense). The other financial group, BANAMERICA (after the
Banco de America), was led by his first cousin, Alfredo Pellas Chamorro, who also controlled Central America's largest sugar mill, San
Antonio, in partnership with several other Conservative Granada
families, including that of Pedro Joaquín Chamorro. In the Sandinista period both *La Prensa* and the official party newspaper, *Barri-
cada*, were controlled by Pedro Joaquín's and Doña Violeta's sons,
Pedro Chamorro Barrios and Carlos Fernando Chamorro Barrios, respectively, and the independent but pro-Sandinista newspaper, *El
Nuevo Diario*, was controlled by Pedro Joaquín's brother and partner
in BANIC, Xavier Chamorro Cardenal. The Chairman of the National Bank of Nicaragua was a descendent of another noble Granada
family and another cousin of Pedro Joaquín, Joaquín Cuadra Chamorro. Joaquín Cuadra's son was General Joaquín Cuadra Lacayo,
Chief of Staff of the Sandinista Army (Ejército Popular Sandinista,
EPS); his mother was a member of another colonial Granada merchant family, the Lacayos. Antonio Lacayo, married to Doña Violeta's
daughter, was her principal adviser, effective prime minister, and
principal architect of the de facto alliance with the Sandinistas.[33]

The Heritage of Underdevelopment:
Revolution and Dynastic Rule

What accounts for the astonishing persistence of dynastic power in
Central America? The institutional, political, and economic backwardness of the region that made it so prone to revolution also created the conditions that promoted the dominance of family dynasties. The absence of effective markets for securities, capital, and
credit, and the lack of a stable legal environment for business have
made family ties the best guarantee of contractual compliance and
therefore the sine qua non of business success.[34] Similarly, the dominance of lawless military regimes has made family ties the only
effective guarantee of personal safety and the only institutional route
to political power. The general political disorder in the region has
had the same effect. The absence of any effective parliamentary institutions, mass parties, or even associational interest groups has left
families as the only institutions through which political power can

be acquired.[35] The extreme shortage of capital and dominance of a single export commodity have sucked capital into the coffee economy controlled by the dynasties and also insured that capital for new enterprises will come from the traditional elite.[36] Finally, the limited development of higher education (until very recently) has insured that professional educations must be purchased abroad, giving wealthy families a stranglehold over the professions and hence entry to the political class.[37]

Although these conditions have persisted longer in Central America than elsewhere in Latin America, family dynastic power is likely to persist wherever politically unstable, dependent export economies dominated by reactionary military or personalistic dictatorships impede the development of the political and economic institutions of modern capitalism. Because such conditions were common in Latin America, it is not surprising to find family dynasties in countries outside Central America. In Peru, as Dennis Gilbert has demonstrated, dynastic power lasted until the modernizing military coup of 1968; the period from World War II to the 1960s was the heyday of the Peruvian agro-export dynasties.[38] Maurice Zeitlin has demonstrated that leading Chilean families whose wealth derived from land ownership and mineral exports in the nineteenth century continued to dominate the much more advanced and corporate-controlled Chilean economy as late as the 1960s. In 1973 one of these families, the Edwardses, was instrumental in organizing the coup that overthrew Salvador Allende.[39] Although in semi-peripheral areas of Latin America such as Mexico, Brazil, and Argentina family dominance seems to have ended earlier,[40] it is likely to be an important part of politics wherever underdevelopment and personalistic rule persist.

Despite the immense power of the coffee elite and other dynastic families in Central America, the narrowly based political regimes they constructed at the turn of the century proved to be extraordinarily prone to revolutionary crises. The elite barely survived the crisis of the thirties by ceding direct rule to military dictatorships (even in Costa Rica, where Figueres's revolutionary regime ruled by decree for seventeen months). In Nicaragua and El Salvador an oligarchic-dictatorial alliance emerged as the ruling political structure after the thirties. It proved to be no more stable in the long run than the direct oligarchic rule it had replaced. The long economic boom in Central America and the world economy after 1945 created new social and economic forces that could not be contained in the rickety oligarchic-dictatorial structures of the twentieth-century political order. The end of this boom after 1973 detonated the social explosion that had been gathering force throughout the long period of postwar economic expansion. Only Costa Rica, whose institutional structure had evolved in a social democratic, if elite-dominated, direction survived the crisis. The archaic oligarchy-dictator alliances collapsed into a revolutionary conflagration.

The Revolutionary Decade of the 1980s: The Coffee Elite Under Fire

For most of their long tenure, the oligarchic-dictatorial regimes did not rely on the ferocious and promiscuous violence that characterized their twilight years in the late 1970s and early 1980s. Anastasio Somoza García assembled a formidable political coalition which included a tamed coffee elite, a subordinate labor movement, a loyal following of public employees, and, at the core of his power, the Nicaraguan National Guard.[41] Elite opponents of his rule were co-opted by formal power-sharing arrangements and a cut of the economic pie. Somoza García's huge personal economic empire became merged with the assets of the state in a pattern that Edelberto Torres Rivas, after Max Weber, has characterized as Sultanic rule.[42] The elder Somoza was astute enough to provide a favorable business climate for agro-exporters, including coffee growers, and he avoided large scale interference in their affairs despite his own growing empire. His policies were continued by his equally astute older son, Luis.[43] Only when his younger son, Anastasio, took power after the death of his brother did the situation begin to deteriorate. For almost fifty years, however, the Somozas managed to cling to power with an astute combination of cooptation and repression.

In El Salvador the military continued its implicit partnership with the oligarchy until 1979. Occasional reformist openings in 1944, 1960, and 1972 were followed directly by a return to authoritarian rule, although the wide-scale massacres that had brought the army to power in 1932 were not repeated until after 1979. The Salvadoran coffee elite was left completely free to pursue its economic fortunes, unhindered by state strictures or economic competition from the military or the state. Soldiers loyal to the oligarchy could expect to be rewarded by lucrative positions in the private business world after retirement, but the military itself, dominated by the cohesive graduating classes of the Salvadoran military academy (called "tandas") was a society apart, with its own traditions and institutions and virtually complete legal impunity. Salvadoran elite families did not participate in the military, and its officers were typically recruited from the lower middle classes. Conflict between the military and the coffee elite, joined in an implicit alliance for more than sixty years, was rare, but when it did occur, the military called the shots. The state was no mere instrument of the bourgeoisie but the more powerful member of an alliance.[44]

The New Agro-Export Economy and the Revolutionary Challenge

The implicit exchange of the right to make money for the right to rule worked reasonably well for both parties and no serious challengers to the oligarchic-dictatorial alliance emerged until the 1970s. But in both Nicaragua and El Salvador new social forces had been gaining momentum in the intervening years, and by the 1970s they could no longer be contained. Once again the agro-export economy created the new social forces that challenged the old order. The rapid expansion of sugar, beef, and, above all, cotton production in Central America after World War II began to challenge the coffee monoculture that was the basis of the old order. The coffee industry itself experienced a substantial expansion and technical transformation. The fifties and sixties were boom years for the Central American agro-export economies, and new fortunes grew up to challenge the old. The expansion of the Central American common market in the 1960s, particularly in El Salvador, created a nascent industrial bourgeoisie. These industrialists, together with the new agro-industrial cotton kings, made up a new social and political force within the elite. For the upper classes, the postwar agro-export bonanza was a new Golden Age.[45]

The consequences for the rest of the population, still heavily rural, were disastrous. While meat exports climbed, Central American meat consumption declined; both agro-exports and food imports increased as export crops expanded at the expense of food production. Real wages stagnated and declined while prices, particularly after the oil shock of 1973, increased.[46] The dramatic expansion of both cotton and cattle created massive displacements of the rural population of a magnitude unseen since the days of the Liberal land tenure revolutions of the nineteenth century. All of the new export crops, including the new coffee system, were more capital- and less labor-intensive than the systems they replaced. Unemployment increased dramatically as owners cleared unproductive serfs and squatters from their lands and replaced payment in subsistence rights and kind with cash wages and rents.[47] The massive displacement of the rural population from the land created two new classes unseen before in Central America—a semi-proletariat of part-time wage laborers, renters, and subsistence farmers, and an urban informal sector of petty merchants, artisans, and day laborers.[48] In many cases the two classes converged into a great mass of desperate people with no firm ties to the labor market, the institutions of property, or the societies of which they were a huge majority.

An increasing body of research indicates that it was these growing classes of unemployed and underemployed rural semi-proletarians and urban informal sector workers, joined, in the case of El Salvador, by a small but well organized formal proletariat in the Common Market manufacturing sector, that made the mass base of the revolutions.[49] Where the two classes converged—in Nicaragua, for example, it was where the cotton fields met the city in the urban Indian *barrios* of Subtiava (in León) and Monimbó (in Masaya)—a critical point of social combustion was reached. Both *barrios* were in the vanguard of the popular insurrections that brought down the Somozas.[50] The rural semi-proletariat that combined the ownership or rental of tiny parcels of land with migratory wage labor in the cotton, sugar, and coffee harvests formed the unshakeable rural base of Salvador's FMLN in Chalatenango and Morazán during more than a decade of civil war.[51] The urban informal sector in Managua, Masaya, León, Matagalpa, and other major Nicaraguan cities were the shock troops of this predominantly urban insurrection and suffered disproportionate casualties in the fighting that followed.[52] The rural base of the FSLN (Frente Sandinista de Liberación Nacional, or Sandinistas) was among angry farmers in north central Nicaragua displaced by the expanding ranch economy.[53] The coffee export economy created the oligarchic political structures of Central America; cotton and cattle destroyed them.

Only in El Salvador did a formal industrial proletariat play an important role in the struggle. Here Communist-led unions became an important part of the FMLN's popular coalition in the early stages of the war.[54] Elsewhere, conventional Marxist class analysis proved a poor guide to sources of popular discontent despite the prominence of Marxist-Leninists in the revolutionary leadership in both El Salvador and Nicaragua. These new revolutionary levies were, as one of them told Jenny Pearce in Chalatenango in 1984, a "pobretariado" ("pooretariat"), not a *proletariado* (proletariat).[55] The oligarchic-dictatorial government's retrograde social and economic policies provided neither housing nor public or social services for the "pobretariado." Without stable employment or ties to the land, concentrated in miserable urban slums, deprived of public services, schools, clinics, even potable water, and met with fierce repression when they mobilized to protest any of these things, the "pobretariado" had only their families, their communities, and themselves to rely on in resisting the new agro-export order. New faiths and new political doctrines were necessary to speak to the concerns of people who were as far from the industrial working class of orthodox Marxists as they were from the dynastic privilege of the coffee elite.

This new faith came first from an old one. Catholic priests influenced by the doctrines of Liberation theology began working in the Salvadoran countryside around the town of Aguilares, and the Catholic labor union FECCAS (Federación Cristiana de Campesinos Salvadoreños) spread like wildfire through Morazán and Chalatenango, inculcating its doctrines of God's love for the poor and salvation through direct action.[56] Similar groups sprang up in Nicaragua, initiated by Jesuit priest and poet Ernesto Cardenal, and became influential in the development of the decidedly unorthodox Sandinista ideology.[57] It was the sermons of Archbishop Arturo Romero and his defense of the human and spiritual rights of the poor as much as Marxist-Leninist ideology that brought the rural population of El Salvador to the revolution. The "pobretariado" found its way to Marx though Jesus Christ. In the Manichean world of Salvadoran politics the Church became the enemy. The slogan of one right-wing death squad was "Be a Patriot, Kill a Priest." In 1977–78 alone 15 priests and lay religious leaders were murdered in El Salvador.[58] Many more would die thereafter. Christianity itself had become a threat to the agro-export order.

After long debate, the leaders of the new revolutionary party in Nicaragua decided to call themselves Sandinistas after Augusto César Sandino, the nationalist but decidedly non-Marxist hero of the struggle to throw the U.S. Marines out of Nicaragua in the 1920s and 1930s.[59] His was a powerful image of national pride counterposed to the national humiliation of a dynasty imposed on the country by those same Marines. The FSLN made his slouched, hatted figure an almost universal sight in revolutionary Nicaragua. The Sandinistas' eclectic revolutionary doctrine was broad enough to include progressive Catholics and anti-Somoza nationalists, as well as exploited workers and peasants. Although at its theoretical core and in its top leadership the party was based in Marxism and, for the most part, Leninism, its dominant faction preached a mixed economy, political pluralism, non-alignment, and coalition with progressive sectors of the bourgeoisie.[60] In the end this decidedly unorthodox strategy worked. The popular insurrection began in Monimbó, not with evocations of the heroes of Marxism but with outrage at the murder of indomitable Somoza foe and Granada aristocrat, Pedro Joaquín Chamorro. In the end the urban informal sector, students, businessmen, and even some cotton and coffee barons combined with FSLN guerrillas to throw out Somoza in the mass urban insurrections of 1978–79.

The Salvadoran rebels, particularly those factions derived historically from the Communist Party, were considerably more orthodox in their theory and practice than the Sandinistas. They waged a classic guerrilla war in the countryside and twice, in 1981 and 1989, unsuccessfully attempted revolutionary uprisings in the cities and countryside. At the top levels the movement was committed to Marxism-Leninism, although how deep that commitment was, particularly among rebel factions that had split from the Christian Democratic Party, is now open to some question. The leader of one of these factions, Joaquín Villalobos, has now declared himself a social democrat and announced that "Marxism is a theory just like any other." During the war, however, the rebels followed orthodox Marxist principles, attacking their class enemies in the bourgeoisie and the military and rejecting the broad coalitions sought by the Sandinistas. Significantly, they chose to name the unified revolutionary movement after Farabundo Martí, the founder of the Communist Party of El Salvador and leader of the failed insurrection of 1932: Frente Farabundo Martí para la Liberación Nacional (FMLN). Although their rural base of support remained loyal, they were never able to put together the broad coalition that brought the Sandinistas to power.

Elite Responses to Revolution: Fight Back, Join, or Stay Out

The revolutionary upsurge of the "pobretariado" and the rise of the FMLN and FSLN represented the greatest challenge the coffee elite had ever faced. The responses of the three nations' elites could not have been more different. The Salvadorans began as unified, intransigent opponents of the FMLN and revolution but ended up negotiating a peace settlement that gave the rebels a place in the national legislature. A majority of the Nicaraguan coffee elite stayed with Somoza to the end and went down with him, losing their estates in the wave of confiscations that followed the revolution. A substantial minority, however, among them the Cuadras and the Bolts, backed the Sandinistas and stayed in Nicaragua after the revolution. These events also reverberated in Costa Rica, where hard-line segments of the elite pushed for deeper involvement in the anti-Communist struggle of the Reagan administration. More moderate forces in the elite won out in the end, keeping Costa Rica out of the war of the eighties. Each of these responses reflects not only the tactics of the revolutionaries but also the economic structure, historical experience, and social views of the respective elites.

El Salvador: From Death Squads to Limited Democracy. On October 15, 1979, the coalition between the Salvadoran oligarchy and the military collapsed when young officers, faced with armed guerrilla groups and an upsurge of urban and rural protest, and terrified by the Nicaraguan revolution of the previous July, staged a military coup and initiated a series of reforms directed squarely at the institutional power of the coffee elite. On March 6 and 8, 1980, the military officers initiated a land reform which, if carried out fully, would have eliminated the land holdings of most of the coffee elite, and nationalized the banking system, controlled by coffee capital since the beginning of the century. Even more important from the point of view of the coffee elite was the nationalization of coffee export in December of the previous year, which broke the power of the processing-export elite and reduced them to mere agents of the government. In less than six months the junta had struck against the control over land, processing, exports, and finance that was the heart of coffee elite power. As Enrique Baylora observes, the beginning of the Salvadoran civil war can reasonably be dated to the state of siege imposed the day after the land reform decrees.[61]

The outraged coffee elite found itself without even a political party to defend it against the assaults of what they came to see as an obscene conspiracy of the Carter administration in league with the radical officers and Christian Democrats of the revolutionary junta.[62] They turned, as they had in the past, to their allies in the military in an effort to reverse the policies of the junta and crush the upsurge of the left with a wave of violence. As William Stanley has demonstrated, the resulting catastrophic violence of 1980–81, in which perhaps 30,000 died, was closely related to competition between military factions intent on gaining support from different sectors of the traditional oligarchy by demonstrating their ferocity in the face of the left.[63] As military terror intensified, whole categories of people suspected because of their dress or demeanor of being "subversives" were murdered in numbers that reached thousands a month. Many of the victims were poor rural people slaughtered in the increasingly violent struggle over land reform.

During this period of massive violence, retired army major Robert D'Aubuisson, whose former position as head of military intelligence proved advantageous for waging war against the left, rapidly emerged as the dominant figure. D'Aubuisson, described with some accuracy by former Ambassador Robert White as a "pathological killer," personally organized the assassination of Archbishop Romero and worked closely with his former colleagues in military intelligence in organizing the mass slaughter. D'Aubuisson would appear on television and read off lists of "subversives" from purloined intelligence files (or perhaps simply from his own imagination). In the next few days the corpses of many of those he had named would end up in one of a number of favored dumping places of the death squads in the suburbs of San Salvador. On February 24, 1980, D'Aubuisson read off the name of Attorney General Roberto Zamora. The next night a death squad tracked Zamora down and killed him at a party in his own home. After several failed efforts at organizing counter-coups, however, D'Aubuisson went underground to avoid arrest. When he emerged in September 1981, it was to announce that he had renounced military adventurism and would henceforth pursue electoral politics through a new political party, the Alianza Republicana Nacionalista (ARENA).[64]

At its official founding on September 30, 1981, ARENA was a coalition of D'Aubuisson and his backers on the hard right and the Alianza Productiva (Productive Alliance), itself a coalition of conservative industrialists and businessmen that included much of the traditional oligarchy. D'Aubuisson had been backed by Guatemalan Mario Sandoval Alarcón and his right wing National Liberation Movement, by Conservative members of the U.S. Republican Party, including members of Jesse Helms's staff, by veterans of the French Algerian OAS, and by a group of right-wing oligarchs in Miami led by the outspoken right-wing grandson and namesake of Orlando de Sola. The businessmen were led by hard-line but shrewd industrialist and former Foreign Minister Rodríguez Porth, who declared that ARENA had two enemies to fight: the communism of the FMLN and the "communitarianism" of the Christian Democrats.[65] A charismatic crowd pleaser on the stump, D'Aubuisson would delight crowds by slicing a watermelon in two with a machete to illustrate the Christian Democrats were green (the party's color) on the outside, but red on the inside. ARENA emerged as the principal opposition to the Christian Democrats, the party supported by the United States and the army. Real power, however, was still held by traditional military officers who soon displaced the young Turks on the junta.

Reversing the reforms of the junta and opposing the Christian Democrats and the United States became ARENA's rallying cry. ARENA's economic policies followed the laissez-faire liberalism of the traditional peak business associations in El Salvador—free enterprise and an end to all government interference in the economy. Although ARENA contested elections, the Productive Alliance was ambivalent about democracy, and the more conservative elements in ARENA favored a complete annihilation of the left along the lines of the 1932 massacre that had ended the previous communist insurrection in El Salvador. Private-sector leaders talked openly of killing up to 100,000 people to restore the pre-1979 status quo.[66] A large part of ARENA's appeal was a muscular, violent anti-Communist nationalism that D'Aubuisson, who struck a defiantly macho pose in campaigns, could embody better than anyone else. ARENA's early success owed much to its association with violent and antidemocratic solutions to complicated problems. But these associations also limited its appeal as a mass party, even in El Salvador.

D'Aubuisson, however, proved to be a much shrewder politician than his many detractors had anticipated. After electoral defeats in 1984 and 1985, which brought to power Christian Democrat Napoleón Duarte, a man still committed to the reforms of the junta, the ARENA leader began a conscious effort to transform his party's image and constituency. Industrialist Rodríguez Porth was the key figure in D'Aubuisson's efforts to reach out to more moderate sectors of the coffee elite and the business community. ARENA decided that the land reform, only partially implemented, had become a political sacred cow and dropped its effort to reverse this key reform, causing the ever militant Orlando de Sola to quit the party in disgust. But ARENA continued to oppose the other reforms, particularly the nationalization of the banks and coffee export economy, and remained true to its laissez-faire principles. The party retained, too, its fiery nationalism and militant anti-communism, but increasingly D'Aubuisson spoke of electoral democracy, not mass murder, as the future for El Salvador.[67]

A critical element in D'Aubuisson's new ARENA was the recruitment of Cristiani to the party in 1984, followed by his anointment by D'Aubuisson as the party's presidential candidate in 1989. Cristiani, as we have seen, was a key figure among the immigrant coffee processors, who represented the less regressive wing of the elite. He was also a leading figure in a new business sector organization founded in 1983, FUSADES (Fundación Salvadoreña para el Desarrollo Económico y Social or Salvadoran Foundation for Economic and Social Development). Salvador Simán was president of the Foundation at the time of Cristiani's election, and Simán is the most frequently occurring name on the list of founders. The Simán dynasty was based in commerce and retail sales, not coffee. They were Palestinian immigrants, part of a wealthy but socially distinct sector of the elite (disparagingly called "los Turcos" by old line families) that also includes the Zablahs, another family prominent in FUSADES. The Hill-Llach-Hills, the Alvarezes (Colombian immigrant coffee processors), and the processing branch of the huge Salaverría coffee dynasty are also well represented. Notably absent or underrepresented are traditional agrarian families of the old Republican elite—Regalados, Dueñas, Escalóns, Quiñónez, Meléndez. Although many other prominent coffee families are represented, most of the members listed, except for the processors, are in industry, finance, real estate, and construction, not in agro-export.[68]

Many of President Cristiani's closest advisers, including Roberto Llach-Hill and Miguel Angel Salaverría, are members of FUSADES, and the Foundation's position papers became the basis for ARENA administration policy. FUSADES clearly represents the manufacturing rather than the agrarian sector of the coffee elite. Support for land reform was much more palatable to manufacturers than it was to traditional landowners, including coffee growers. ARENA became even more fully committed to limited democracy. In a stunning move D'Aubuisson nominated Rubén Zamora, the brother of the Attorney General whose death the ARENA leader had successfully demanded a decade before, for the position of Vice President of the National Assembly. Even more heretical, the party of violent anti-communism began to talk of a negotiated settlement of the war, particularly after the great FMLN offensive of 1989 made it clear to the elite that the war could not be won. War was bad, indeed catastrophic, for business. If ending it required the sacrifice of a few landowners or exceptionally homicidal commanders, so be it. It was Cristiani and the new ARENA that negotiated the Chapultepec accords. In a decade the coffee elite had moved from violent opposition to revolution to tentative accommodation with it.

Nicaragua: From Revolution to Counter-Revolution. The mass base of the Nicaraguan revolution was among the urban informal sector and students who made up the majority of the participants in the insurrections of 1978–79. FSLN guerrillas led the final military offensive in 1979. The elite, however, played a decisive role in the revolution, which could not have succeeded without them. The bourgeois opposition to Somoza crystalized around two men, Pedro Joaquín Chamorro of the Granada aristocracy, and Alfonso Robelo Callejas, who was from an old León family but had become a millionaire in the cotton boom. Chamorro had been a leader of an abortive armed rebellion by Conservatives in 1959 and kept up a steady rain of criticism of Somoza from his position as editor of *La Prensa*. In 1974, disgusted by still another Somoza deal to coopt the Conservative opposition, he founded his Unión Democrática de Liberación (UDEL) with support from dissident Conservatives, businessmen, and other opponents of Somoza. His assassination in January 1978 sparked a wave of protests and demonstrations organized in part by his widow Violeta. UDEL declared a general strike of both business and labor, the first of many in the next ten months that destabilized the regime. The popular insurrection began in Monimbó in February, when the National Guard attacked a memorial service for Chamorro.[69]

Chamorro's assassination was a critical turning point for the Nicaraguan bourgeoisie. He had been at the center of a dense network of Conservative Granada families and was a national symbol of opposition to Somoza. His death indicated to many members of the bourgeoisie that no one was safe.[70] One astute member of the coffee elite told me that in a meeting with prominent businessmen in 1978 in which he attempted to caution them about the consequences of supporting a revolution led by "communists," another elite member stood up and declared, in what appeared to be an expression of a general sentiment, that he would rather live under communism than under Somoza.[71] Chamorro led an important sector of the elite into the revolution, although most of the elite members wanted it to go no further than the departure of Somoza himself and hoped to preserve the National Guard and other institutions of Somoza rule. Even before Chamorro's assassination, however, other prominent businessmen—including his cousin Joaquín Cuadra Chamorro; the banker and another Granada aristocrat, Arturo Cruz Porras; coffee exporter Emilio Baltodano Pallais; and León aristocrat and supermarket-chain owner, Felipe Mántica—had joined "los Doce," a group of twelve professional and business men who announced their support for "patriotic alliance" with the FSLN.[72] Alfredo César, general manager of the Pellas-Chamorro San Antonio Sugar Mill (and later contra leader), fought in the revolution with his close friend, Joaquín Cuadra Chamorro's son and later Sandinista Chief of Staff, Joaquín Cuadra Lacayo.[73]

Despite Chamorro's leadership, many of the elite associated with the main financial groups BANIC and BANAMERICA held back from joining the struggle. The most militant sector was a group of smaller businessmen and agro-exporters, including coffee growers, organized into the Consejo Superior de Iniciativa Privada (Superior Council of Private Initiative or COSIP, later COSEP).[74] The driving force in the group was Alfonso Robelo, who served as president in 1977. During the Sandinista period it was the Bolaños-Geyers, a nineteenth-century Spanish and twentieth-century German immigrant family, who ran the organization. COSIP was the organizational expression of the new business groups created by the postwar agro-export boom,which in Nicaragua was centered on cotton. Robelo's fortune was based on a cotton seed oil processing plant, GRACSA (Grasas y Aceites, S.A.), of which Antonio Lacayo, Violeta Chamorro's son-in-law and minister, was then general manager.[75] The Bolaños-Geyers, one of very few Nicaraguan coffee families to diversify into other crops, owned SAIMSA (Servicio Agrícola Industrial Masaya), one of Nicaragua's largest agro-industrial cotton producers.[76] In the literature on the revolution, the Bolaños-Geyers and other agro-industrialists outside the main financial groups have come to be called the "middle bourgeoisie."

Robelo organized the first modern political party of the "middle bourgeoisie," the Movimiento Democrático Nacional (National Democratic Movement or MDN). In May 1978 the MDN, "los doce," the UDEL, and anti-Somoza Conservatives joined the FAO (Frente Amplio Opositor, or Broad Opposition Front) in opposition to Somoza and in implicit alliance with the FSLN. During the revolution many members of the elite and a significant fraction of the agro-export bourgeoisie supported the FAO or even the FSLN. Although many large coffee and cotton growers remained loyal to Somoza, a significant number, perhaps as many as half, at least tacitly supported the revolution and remained in Nicaragua in the Sandinista period.[77] Some coffee and cotton growers gave money to the Sandinistas, others allowed their farms to be used by Sandinista combatants, and some, like Jaime Cuadra, did much more, including sheltering Sandinista leaders in their homes or even taking up arms themselves. Many had sons, daughters, or other close relatives with the FSLN.[78] The revolution was based on an implicit coalition between the FSLN, the aristocratic elite, and the agro-industrial middle bourgeoisie including many coffee and cotton growers.

The victorious revolutionary coalition was based on principles enunciated by the dominant Ortega faction of the FSLN—a mixed economy, political pluralism, and non-alignment. The first revolutionary junta included Violeta Chamorro and Alfonso Robelo in coalition with Sergio Ramírez of "los Doce," Moisés Hassán of the FSLN's popular coalition, and Daniel Ortega, FSLN *comandante* and later President of Nicaragua. The junta therefore included both the Conservative Granada aristocrats, the new cotton barons, and FSLN representatives. Since Ramírez and Hassán were both FSLN, the party actually had a working majority. Growing FSLN power eventually led to a breakdown of the revolutionary alliance. The resignation of Robelo and Chamorro in April 1980 over Sandinista plans to create a FSLN majority in the Council of State began the alienation of the dynastic elite and the agro-export bourgeoisie from the revolution. The post-Sandinista working alliance between the Ortega brothers and Violeta Chamorro actually represented a return to the alliance that carried the revolution in the first place. The initial alliance, however, scarcely survived the first anniversary of the revolution.[79]

In August 1980 Humberto Ortega, concurrently Defense Minister, FSLN National Directorate member, and brother of Daniel Ortega, announced that elections would be postponed until 1985 and that no campaigning would be permitted until 1984. He reaffirmed the dominance of the Sandinista National Directorate. The election of an outspoken anti-Communist as president of the United States hardened attitudes on both sides. Less than a week after the U.S. election COSEP attacked the Sandinistas for attempting to impose a "Communist system" in Nicaragua. The next day COSEP representatives and three opposition political parties resigned from the Council of State to protest the government's refusal to allow

Robelo's MDN to hold a rally and the sacking of MDN headquarters by a Sandinista mob. The successful revolutionary alliance had collapsed. The Granada aristocrats formally represented by Mrs. Chamorro, and both the coffee and cotton growers of the middle bourgeoisie represented by COSEP and Robelo, were in the political wilderness.[80] For the coffee growers in particular it was a familiar role. Displaced from power by the United States in 1909–1912, submerged by the Somoza dynasty in 1937, they had once more been excluded from power, this time by the victorious revolution many of them had backed.

Despite the breakdown of the alliance, many coffee and cotton growers and other members of the middle bourgeoisie stayed in Nicaragua and continued trying to function in the mixed economy. They became increasingly alienated by the regime and by 1986, when they were interviewed by me, most had became private, if not public, supporters of the armed rebellion of the counter-revolutionary "contras." A few, like Gladys Bolt, remained loyal to the revolution, and most paid a price as the civil war intensified. With tension rising on both sides, the position of the agro-export bourgeoisie became increasingly precarious. Although the Sandinistas attempted a reconciliation after 1986, for most of the middle bourgeoisie it was too little too late. The election of Violeta Chamorro seemed to promise them relief from Sandinista rule, and in fact many regained control of estates they had lost in the Sandinista period.[81] At the height of the contra war, however, the coffee growers among them were again frustrated by their exclusion from power, a seeming constant in Nicaragua since 1909. They had made a journey which was the reverse of the Salvadorans—from coalition with revolution to support for armed counter-revolution. After the Sandinistas' electoral defeat some of the elite, led by the Chamorro-Lacayo faction, made the journey back to coalition, but others, notably those associated with COSEP, did not.[82]

Costa Rica: The Price of Peace. Although Costa Rica has the reputation of a country with a deeply ingrained culture of peace and democracy, in the 1980s that culture was put under considerable strain as the divisions that were tearing apart El Salvador and Nicaragua emerged there too. The economic crisis of the 1980s triggered unrest in both the city and the countryside, and pressures from the Reagan administration to join the contra war threatened traditional Costa Rican neutrality. Land seizures by peasants and strikes by urban workers multiplied. The banana-plantation zones experienced what many union leaders hoped would be an insurrectionary strike wave. Extremist right-wing groups appeared demanding firm action against unrest and Nicaragua. Deeply in debt, Costa Rica was forced to accept military aid and training missions that threatened to turn its small rural guard into the army that it had abolished in 1948. U.S. Green Berets appeared on the streets of San José and CIA missions were flown from secret bases in Guanacaste. Clashes with Sandinista troops occurred, and relations with Nicaragua soured. President Luis Alberto Monge celebrated his ties to the Reagan administration, denounced communism, and while publicly proclaiming Costa Rican neutrality, seemed to be leading the country deeper into the Central American abyss.[83]

The 1986 election, which began as a conventional struggle between the two parties that had amiably alternated in power since 1948, rapidly turned into a referendum on the Central American conflict. Oscar Arias Sánchez, scion of the great coffee family but candidate of the vaguely social democratic PLN (Partido de Liberación Nacional or National Liberation Party), was opposed by Rafael Calderón Fournier, a much more conservative politician than was his father, the great social reformer of the coffee elite, President Rafael Angel Calderón Guardia. Although President Monge and presidential candidate Arias were of the same party, it was the opposition's Calderón who seemed more sympathetic to Monge's and Reagan's policies in the Central American conflict. Since Arias was from the conservative wing of Liberación, differences in economic policy between the candidates were not great. Arias won a very close race by making himself the candidate of peace, opposing militarization and defending Costa Rica's traditional neutrality.[84] In February 1987 he put his campaign promises into action by proposing the Arias Peace Plan. His plan put him on a collision course with the Reagan administration. As one of Arias's close associates and another prominent coffee processor told me, "It was scary, little Oscar and his plan against the big United States."[85]

The essence of the Arias plan was democratization. Unlike the earlier peace plans, the Arias plan recognized the legitimacy of all Central American governments, including the Sandinistas, but called for an ending of aid and sanctuary for irregular forces, including the contras. After Sandinista gunners downed a CIA supply plane piloted by Eugene Hasenfus, Arias moved to close contra bases in Costa Rica. His defection from the contra war brought immediate American pressure. Oliver North appeared in Costa Rica and threatened a total cutoff of American aid, which had reached an incredible $634 million in the first three years of the Monge administration. AID funds were frozen and U.S. aid was reduced substantially.[86] The Reagan administration was in no position, however, to resist peace plans for Central America. Revelations that the inept Mr. Hasenfus had ties to the U.S. government led to the beginnings of the Iran-Contra scandal in November 1986. The weakened position of the Reagan administration provided an opening for the Costa Rican peace initiative. On August 7, 1987, the five Central American presidents signed the accords that would eventually end the Central American conflict on terms first outlined by Oscar Arias. The grandson of Julio Sánchez Lépiz had led not only his own country but the region from revolutionary war to a shaky democratic peace.[87]

At the beginning of the decade, the Costa Rican coffee elite was still committed to the social democracy and peace that it had supported since 1948. After a rough passage, it ended the decade at the same point. The Salvadorans began the decade committed to mass murder in defense of an oligarchic-dictatorial alliance they had supported for almost fifty years. They began the 1990s formally committed to peace, accommodation, democracy, and a purge of their most ferocious allies in the military. The Nicaraguan coffee elite began the decade once again trying to continue the revolution they had begun a century earlier, this time in a bizarre alliance with Marxist-Leninist revolutionaries. They ended the decade supporting armed opposition to this revolution. The coffee elites, more than any other single group, had created the regimes and the societies that began the eighties crisis. Both they and the societies would undergo significant transformations in the course of a wild and violent decade. These transformations were political and military. There were also, however, transformations in the realm of ideas.

From Liberalism to Neo-Liberalism: The Transformation of Elite Ideology

The Liberal revolutions that ushered in the age of coffee in the nineteenth century were, to be sure, a response to opportunities for agro-exports in the expanding economy of imperial capitalism. They were also profound revolutions in the realm of ideas. The ideology of the Central American Liberals, their vision of the political, economic, and social order (or "project," as it is called in Latin America), transformed the material as well as the legal, political, and social bases of the society, creating the agro-export order that collapsed in the 1980s. Liberalism also created the hegemonic construction of Central American reality that ruled in the realm of ideas as well as in the political economy of power. Twice in this century, in the 1930s and the 1980s, alternative visions of this reality arose to challenge the Liberal ideological order. In both cases these challenges changed important elements of hegemonic liberalism, but also left much of its core untouched. At the beginning of the 1990s, hegemonic neo-liberalism was both very similar to, yet very different from, the liberalism of the nineteenth-century coffee elites.

Liberalism in the Golden Age of the Coffee Elite

Nineteenth-century liberalism in Central America, like twentieth-century socialism, or, for that matter, sixteenth-century Catholicism, was an imported doctrine. All three doctrines underwent significant changes in response to Central American realities. Central American Liberals, like their nineteenth-century European capitalist counterparts, believed that material progress depended on economic freedom. In Central America economic freedom meant an end to the special guilds, communal rights, monopolies, tithes, taxes, duties, estates, and noble and clerical privileges that had hamstrung the colonial economy and hindered the rise of the new export order. The Central American Liberals also believed in the intellectual freedom to pursue the new insights of science and technology unconstrained by religious or other traditional orthodoxies. The Liberals' great hero was the French Positivist (and inventor of the term "sociology") Auguste Comte. The Central Americans were true heirs of the

French Enlightenment and prided themselves on their commitment to rationality, science, and progress.[88]

In one respect, however, the Central American Liberals differed significantly from their European and North American contemporaries. Unlike classic nineteenth-century liberals in the United States and Britain, the Central Americans believed in a powerful central state that could intervene to promote economic and technological development.[89] The laissez-faire state beloved of North American and British nineteenth-century liberals and their twentieth-century ideological heirs (now called "conservatives" in both countries) was not part of the Central American plan. It was the Central American Liberals who were ever promoting an ever bigger state through Central American union. It was they who wanted the state to undertake expensive infrastructure development projects, especially roads, ports, and railroads, to facilitate agro-exports; to intervene in labor markets to coerce labor; to break the power of religious orders and the Church; to maintain domestic tranquility through a vastly expanded constabulary and modern armies; and to guarantee new industries through concessions and subsidies to foreign and domestic businessmen alike. They did not, like later socialists, envision a state-controlled economy, but they did believe the state should do everything possible to facilitate private enterprise. Their slogans were "Order and Progress" or, more euphemistically, "Peace, Progress, and Liberty."

Despite their French Enlightenment origins and dedication to liberty and equality before the law, the institutions of parliamentary democracy were not part of the Liberals' nineteenth-century project. To be sure, all the Central American Republics modeled their constitutions after that of the United States and promised elections and representative government. In practice, however, the Liberals ruled by decree, imposing oligarchic control through the vastly strengthened state apparatus and modern military institutions they created. Even in nominally democratic Costa Rica, oligarchic control of elections was nearly total until the 1940s, and real parliamentary democracy did not emerge until 1948. Liberals saw themselves as the vanguard of modern civilization, leading backward societies into a new age of progress and enlightenment by replacing backward Iberian institutions with modern ones modeled after the United States and Great Britain. Although they promoted popular education, they ruled in the name of an enlightened elite which, in practice, corresponded to the families described in this chapter. The backwardness, as they saw it, of the Indian societies and rural mestizo communities of the Isthmus was a particular source of concern. These peoples would have to be led into the modern age.

The revolution from above instituted by the nineteenth-century Liberals was a disaster for most the population. The most direct assaults on the people were the land and labor laws that abolished communal control over the land by indigenous communities, sold off the commons and public lands to large holders, and instituted systems of state control over labor with varying degrees of stringency. The subsidies, infrastructure improvements, and special concessions went entirely to benefit the elite. The pattern of concentrated land ownership in the agro-export sector and mass poverty and landlessness among much of the population in the 1980s was a heritage of the Liberal revolutions of the 1880s. As Ralph Lee Woodward has observed, "The Indian and rural peasant gained little from the new liberals . . . who used the impoverished masses as the manpower to provide the material advances for the regime. One landed oligarchy . . . simply gave way to another which, in concert with foreign investors, used the advances of modern civilization for itself. The social costs of this were very high."[90] These costs are still being paid.

This nineteenth-century liberalism became the hegemonic force in both nineteenth- and twentieth-century Central American social and political thought and runs like a thread through the conversation of the contemporary descendents of the nineteenth-century Liberal revolutionaries. The concepts of progress and liberty continued to guide the organizing principles of coffee elite thinking in this century just as they did in the last. Except in Costa Rica, democracy was not part of the heritage of Enlightenment liberalism in Central America, and recent democratization efforts have neither institutional nor ideological roots. Together, progress, liberty, and democracy have more recently become the organizing principle of the new neo-liberal order in Central America, just as they are the core values in the capitalist industrial democracies of the developed world. The close relationship between capitalism and democracy, often assumed in both Marxist and non-Marxist social science, has proved in practice to be problematic. Capitalism can coexist with a wide variety of political systems, and it appears that the bourgeoisie has seldom been the principal force pushing for full parliamentary democracy.[91] Democracy seems even less compatible with the agro-export order of Central America. Nevertheless, all three concepts—progress, liberty, and democracy—are important organizing principles in the thought of the contemporary coffee elite.

Liberalism Transformed: Narratives of a Class in Crisis

The hegemonic construction of Central American reality by liberalism was challenged in both the 1930s and 1980s by other ideologies that tried to include those left out of the Liberals' vision of progress and order—the poor, the Indian, the mestizo, the disenfranchised, and the dispossessed. These ideologies too were European imports. In Central America in the 1930s they were represented by the Communism of the Third International in El Salvador and Costa Rica, and the idiosyncratic pan-Latin American version of European nationalism of Augusto César Sandino in Nicaragua. In the 1980s, revolutionary socialism and nationalism would again be the dominant oppositional currents, even if both took a very different form than they did in the 1930s. The dominant liberal ideology of the coffee elite was substantially affected by these counter-ideologies in the 1930s, largely through the work of ideological and political reconstruction necessary for their repression and denial. The beliefs with which the coffee elite faced the 1980s are those that were forged in the ideological and political combat of the 1930s. Liberalism emerged triumphant, but transformed by the counter-ideologies of the 1930s.

It is these ideologies of the coffee elite in the 1980s that are the principal empirical focus of this book. Although I have referred to them as ideologies, in conversations with members of elite families these beliefs had as much the structure of stories or narratives as of formal ideologies. The coffee elite does have well-developed formal ideologies and political programs, and the questions in the interviews were designed to elicit them. In the midst of the tumult of the 1980s, however, members of the elite had to make sense of their own personal and familial histories as well as the histories of their nation and their class. These families, more than most, illustrate what C. Wright Mills called the intersection of history and personal biography.[92] They made sense of the 1980s crisis by telling themselves and me stories about themselves, their families, their enemies, their countries, and their histories—their pasts, their presents, and their futures. At the height of the civil wars these stories were told with great urgency and feeling, verging at times almost on desperation. The stories were influenced by formal ideologies, including most notably liberalism, but they were not limited to ideology only. The term "narrative" as it is increasingly used in the historical and sociological literature seems to best capture the actual structure of the interviews.[93]

The stories of the Central American coffee elite during the revolutionary crisis of the 1980s were collected through interviews with 57 members of 53 different coffee dynasties in the three countries. In Nicaragua, five members of five cotton dynasties were also interviewed. These elite interviews were supplemented by interviews with officials in government and private coffee organizations. Statements made or issued to the press by individuals (some of whom were members of elite families) and organizations in the coffee industry were reviewed for the period 1979–1989 in the collections of clippings maintained by the national coffee offices of El Salvador and Nicaragua.[94] At the height of the civil wars confidentiality was deemed essential by most respondents, and specific families and individuals, except for public figures such as President Cristiani in El Salvador or Nicolás Bolaños in Nicaragua, both of whom were interviewed, cannot be identified here. In each country the goal was to interview economically active members of each of the twenty leading families in coffee processing (El Salvador and Costa Rica) or production (Nicaragua), although only in Costa Rica did it prove feasible to follow a formal population frame. In El Salvador and Nicaragua interviews almost invariably required personal introductions. In most cases the head of the family coffee enterprise was the person interviewed, but if the enterprise head declined or was unavailable, other members of the same dynasty were substituted. Details of the selection procedures are presented in Appendix II.

Representatives of 58 different dynastic families constitute a substantial proportion, and in Costa Rica virtually the entire population, of the Central American agro-export elite. Those interviewed included members of most of the influential coffee families in the region. Most of the Salvadorans interviewed belonged to the immigrant processing fraction of the elite. They included the then-president and four past presidents of the major processors' association (among them President Cristiani and his Ambassador Miguel Angel Salaverría), as well as presidents or representatives of seven of the fifteen leading firms in the coffee processing industry. A substantial minority of those interviewed were not large processors but producers associated with a separate producers' association. These included two presidents of that organization, the widow of a third, a close associate of a deceased past president, and representatives of leading cooperative and governmental coffee organizations. Almost all of those interviewed were members of leading coffee dynasties, particularly among the processors. They were interviewed in 1987 and 1990, during the civil war. It proved impossible to gain access to members of the hard-line old Republican families like the Regalados and their representatives. Orlando de Sola, in particular, declined several requests for an interview. It was possible to talk to close associates of de Sola, however, and the views of this faction can also be reconstructed from their many public statements.

In Costa Rica those interviewed included 22 executives of 18 of the 20 largest (and four of the top five) firms in coffee processing in the period 1950–1980. Together these firms control 80 percent of the privately processed coffee in Costa Rica. All but one were members of the traditional coffee aristocracy descended either from the conquistadors, the seventeenth-century colonial nobility, or from nineteenth-century German immigrants. All were interviewed in 1990. In Nicaragua, 17 large-scale coffee growers and—given the importance of cotton in the Nicaraguan revolution—five cotton growers were interviewed. Together, these coffee growers contributed almost ten percent of total Nicaraguan production. The cotton growers included two of the five largest producers. Eight of these growers were officers or past officers of major regional or national producers associations. Most were from distinguished Nicaraguan families, although most were not related to the great families of the Granada colonial aristocracy. Most of the Nicaraguans were affiliated with COSEP through their crop organizations and are therefore representatives of the "middle bourgeois" fraction of the Nicaraguan agro-export bourgeois that remained in the country after the revolution. All were interviewed in Nicaragua in 1986 during the contra war.

The interviews averaged one hour and fifty minutes and were conducted in Spanish or English according to the preference of those interviewed. Most were conducted in Spanish. Not infrequently, the formal interviews led to more extended tours of the enterprise or to social occasions in which less formal but sometimes more informative conversations could take place. Although my intention was to conduct an open-ended but structured interview, it soon became evident that most of those interviewed had a message they wanted me to hear and managed to tell it no matter what the specific questions. For the most part, these stories were told with considerable feeling and urgency. Sometimes they became almost confessional. In both Nicaragua and El Salvador the elite was under tremendous psychological pressure and seemed to view the presence of a North American interviewer as an opportunity to get out their side of the story, which most felt had been neglected by the American press and public. Almost all of these men and women have a sufficiently sophisticated knowledge of United States politics and society to know that the views of a North American social science professor are not likely to be the same as their own. In the end this seemed to matter less than a willingness to take seriously what they had to say. This I endeavored to do.

Neo-Liberalism, Democracy, and the "New World Order"

When the members of the coffee elites were interviewed, they were in the midst of an ideological sea change from the reconstructed liberalism that emerged from the crisis of the Great Depression to a neo-liberalism that included democratic principles unheard of (except in Costa Rica) in either classic Central American liberalism or its post-Depression variant. Neo-liberalism's minimalist notion of the state and dogmatic commitment to the market were also doctrines that broke sharply with the Central American Liberal tradition. As one skeptical member of the Salvadoran coffee elite observed, "It's back to basics—pure Adam Smith." The economic principles of neo-liberalism in Central America, as elsewhere, emphasized privatization, deregulation, trade liberalization, and a dramatically reduced state.[95] In a kind of market utopianism, neo-liberalism placed its faith in the magical powers of completely unrestricted markets to rescue the region from underdevelopment. Although neo-liberal economic doctrine represented a distinct change from the statism and nationalism of the traditional Central American Liberals, in other respects, particularly in its belief in progress through export-led economic growth, the new liberalism shared much with the old.

The neo-liberal economic agenda was enthusiastically implemented by the new, democratically elected governments in both El Salvador and Nicaragua. In a pre-election interview, Alfredo Cristiani told the author that he intended to privatize land, banking, and agro-exports, and once elected, that is exactly what he did. Both Cristiani and Violeta Chamorro in Nicaragua returned the agro-export economy to its former private owners and began the privatization of their countries' nationalized banking systems. Although neither one attempted to entirely reverse land reform (Cristiani in particular was committed by the peace agreement to extending it), both moved to privatize reform lands, either by returning them to former owners or titling them to small holders. Cristiani was so devoted to neo-liberal doctrines that he attempted to privatize the outpatient facilities of San Salvador's main public hospital in the midst of a cholera outbreak. Chamorro not only set about returning urban and rural properties confiscated in the Sandinista era to their private owners, but introduced user fees in such formerly free public services as hospitals and schools. Resistance to the neo-liberal agenda was strongest in Costa Rica, and despite the enthusiastic embrace of neo-liberalism by Oscar Arias's successor (and former defeated presidential rival) Calderón Fournier, little was accomplished beyond the privatization of the money-losing state development corporation and the re-legalization of private banking.[96]

Although neo-liberal policies were promoted by the United States and internal lending agencies, often as part of orthodox "structural adjustment programs" demanded as conditions for debt relief or renewed international lending, it would be a mistake to regard these changes in Central America simply as a result of external pressure.[97]

The policies were vigorously pursued by emerging agro-industrial sectors in both El Salvador and Nicaragua, and both Alfredo Cristiani and Violeta Chamorro had made them the centerpieces of their electoral campaigns. Even in Costa Rica, where external pressure was most important and resistance to the neo-liberal agenda most pronounced, changes in the structure of the agro-export economy had created internal pressures for change (see Chapter 8). The rise of neo-liberalism was a product of deep-seated changes in Central American society and class relations. In a strange twist of fate, neo-liberalism was the principal economic heritage of the failed socialist revolutions of Central America in the 1980s.

In the revolutionary decade Central America underwent a dual transformation in politics and ideology. Authoritarian regimes in El Salvador and Nicaragua gave way to tentative but recognizable democracies. Costa Rica survived the decade with its democracy intact, creating a political convergence that few would have predicted at the beginning of the decade. In the realm of ideology, nineteenth-century liberalism laced with the anti-communism that was the heritage of the Depression crisis gave way to neo-liberalism; the Liberals' faith in the economic efficacy of the nation-state was abandoned, but their devotion to progress through exports was retained. Democracy too was incompatible with the authoritarianism of traditional liberalism, and ideology as well as institutions shifted accordingly. The "order and progress" of the nineteenth-century Liberals became the democracy and progress of the neo-liberal "new world order."

The shift from liberalism to neo-liberalism and from authoritarianism to democracy was in part a response to the revolutionary decade and the breakdown of the old order that these events represented. The transformations also reflected deep-seated changes in the class relations of the agro-export economy itself. Underlying the rapid and violent earthquake that is a revolution are the more gradual tectonic shifts of the underlying class relations. The class relations of the agro-export sector had changed considerably from the coffee export economy of the early nineteenth century. These changes underlay the revolutionary upsurge of the 1980s and the convergence of elite ideology and national politics on neo-liberalism and democracy.

2

Class and Class Relations

Were the families of the Central American coffee elite a class? They have been referred to as an "elite" because this term best captures their strategic position in a number of different institutional hierarchies including, but not limited to, the organization of production. The coffee dynasties controlled not only the coffee industry but elite political, professional, and social positions, as well as many sectors of the economy outside coffee. They were also a hereditary elite in a society in which position in aristocratic lineage was an important determinant of class position. The coffee elite, as its origins in Spanish and other European immigration would suggest, is also a racial elite, much "whiter" than the rest of the population. Its positions in these different institutional hierarchies reinforced dynastic power and guaranteed class position. Often political position and lineage were more important in maintaining social standing, particularly in times of political or economic instability, than class position in the limited sense of ownership of the means of production. This dominance in many different institutional sectors suggests that the members of the coffee dynasties might more accurately be described as an elite than a class.

Nevertheless, the wealth and power of this elite are rooted in the social relations of coffee production, processing, and export, that is, in a class position. But what class? A coffee grower in Central America is a member of a landed class, and labor relations in some of the more benighted regions like Guatemala approach feudal serfdom. Coffee processors, on the other hand, who often purchase coffee from other growers and subject it to chemical and physical operations to separate the seed or "bean" from the surrounding skin and pulp, a critical step in the preparation of the final product, are manufacturers using an agricultural raw material. Although processing technology can be primitive, it can also involve substantial industrial installations. The coffee processors are mill owners employing wage laborers—that is, they are manufacturing capitalists. The export trade, and usually the financing of the crop, are forms of financial or mercantile activity closely tied to the banking system. So the coffee elite is a financial and commercial class as well. The coffee elite ties together different positions in the organization of production ordinarily associated with different classes. The economic interdependence of these different positions, however, and the capitalist organization of the industry as a whole suggest that these positions might be thought of as defining divisions within a class rather than distinct classes. In the terminology of class analysis such divisions are usually called class "fractions."

At the heart of the class dynamics of the coffee elite is a fundamental dualism—between its landed or *agrarian* and manufacturing or *agro-industrial* fractions. This dualism is inherent in the division within the coffee production process between coffee growing and harvesting on the one hand, and coffee processing and export on the other. Although one family may do both, different families may also specialize in one of the two forms of activity. The division between Spanish noble and immigrant families in the elites tends to parallel, although far from perfectly, the split between land ownership and processing. Spanish colonial or republican families like the Regalados are more likely to be owners of vast tracts of land and coffee trees, while immigrant families like the de Solas tend to be coffee processors or exporters. The Regalados export coffee, however, and the de Solas owned extensive farms, so the distinction is one of degree. Nevertheless, it is an important one and influences the politics and ideology as well as the economic behavior of the elite. The two class fractions are bound together by ties of kinship, economics, and function into a single elite. Frequently, a mill owned by a key member of the family will process coffee from the landed estates of other family members.

The fundamental division of the elite into agrarian and agro-industrial fractions is reinforced by the fact, already noted, that the elite, particularly in El Salvador, controls other sectors of the economy, including, but not limited to, other agro-export sectors. Coffee producers in El Salvador, for example, are also cotton and sugar producers. The latter two enterprises under contemporary Central American conditions are highly industrialized forms of agri-business. Urban manufacturing is also controlled by leading coffee families in El Salvador, as is much of banking, commerce, real estate, tourism, and finance. Although much less common in the other two countries, the same patterns of economic diversification also exist there. As Edelberto Torres Rivas has pointed out, the elite in Central America, like agro-export elites throughout Latin America, derives its power from both the feudal social relations of the landed estate, and the manufacturing sectors of agri-business and urban industry.[1] Political models based on class divisions between agrarian landlords and an industrial bourgeoisie can be applied only with difficulty to Central America. The two classes are part of one elite.

Nevertheless, the agrarian and agro-industrial fractions of the elite differ in their political orientations. The agrarian fraction has been a bulwark of authoritarian politics throughout the region. The agro-industrial fraction is less closely tied to the authoritarian order and, under some circumstances, more open to democratic initiatives. The close ties between the two fractions have often suppressed these differences, and, particularly in times of crisis, the two converge on the authoritarianism of the retrograde agrarians. This is what happened in the 1930s, when the elite presented a united front against a revolutionary upsurge from below. In the 1980s, a new wave of revolutionary mobilizations markedly increased tensions along this fundamental fault line within the elite, causing it to begin to break apart. The break is critical for assessing the prospects for a successful democratic transition in the region. Without a break with the power and the authoritarian politics of the agrarian fraction, no such transition would be possible. Such a division within the elite, however, has been inhibited by the immense power of the agrarians in an agro-export order and by the close ties between the two fractions that are characteristic of Central American, and Latin American, elite politics. Breaking the two fractions apart is thus a key issue in twentieth-century elite politics.

The distinction between the agrarian and agro-industrial parts of the coffee elite is also essential to understanding the national differences in the political behavior of these elites and the pattern of class conflict and type of political system in each country. While all three countries export the same commodity, the social and material base of coffee production—the "relations" and "forces" of production—are actually very different. These differences in the organization of production led to profound differences in class relations, both between the agro-industrial and agrarian fractions within the upper classes, and between the upper and lower classes in the agro-export sector as a whole. Fundamental changes in class relations occurred after World War II; hence class conflicts took very different forms in the 1930s and 1980s, and the political outcomes in the two crises were also very different. Although the historical development of political structures and political ideology in Central America cannot be reduced to class relations alone, it is not possible to understand these developments without understanding the substantial differences in relations within and between classes in the coffee agro-export sectors of El Salvador, Costa Rica, and Nicaragua, and examining how these relations changed over the twentieth century. Both stability and change in these class relations are rooted in the social and material organization of agro-export production.

Agrarian and Agro-Industrial Origins of Coffee Elite Power in the Early Twentieth Century

The dead hand of the Spanish colonial and even the Indian imperial past exerted a profound effect on the way in which coffee production developed in Central America. This was particularly true in Guatemala, which has been included in this chapter as a comparative case even though it is not one of the countries included in the project research design. It is, however, an extreme case of a country dominated both by a landed elite and by its pre-Colombian past. Whatever their colonial or pre-Colombian heritage, however, the coffee elites had to solve the same four fundamental problems common to coffee production everywhere: (1) acquisition and control over land, (2) organization and rationalization of production, (3) mechanization of processing, (4) finance and control over exports.[2] Solutions to the first two problems are associated with the development of a landed class. The more land the elite controlled or the more productive its system of growing coffee, the more powerful the agrarian fraction of the coffee elite. Solutions to the third and fourth problems are associated with the industrial fraction of the elite. The greater the technological and commercial development of processing and exports under elite control, the stronger the agro-industrial fraction of the elite.

Control over land and control over production strengthen the agrarian base of the coffee elite, but for different reasons. Control over land also provides political control over vast numbers of rural people. Control over an efficient and profitable coffee production system provides increased economic power. Power based on production is still closely tied to the investment in land and standing crops, and to the huge amount of hand labor associated with coffee production everywhere. Processing and export, on the other hand, are agro-industrial and commercial activities, respectively. Neither activity is dependent on land ownership or the control of a large dependent wage labor force. Both are capital-intensive and both are the more profitable phases of the coffee production sequence and the source of vast financial power. As the base of power of the elite moves from land and production into processing and exports, the elite becomes less like landlords and more like capitalists, that is, there is a shift from an agrarian toward an agro-industrial elite. The four Central American coffee producers differ substantially regarding the strength and weakness of the agrarian and agro-industrial fractions of their elites and the importance of land versus production in the base of the agrarian elite.

The Agrarian Elite: Control Over Land and Production

Although—all other things being equal—the more land controlled the more coffee produced, control over land and production are frequently alternative bases of power for the agrarian elite. Control over land in an inefficient production system usually means that there is a large class of legally or paternalistically bound laborers living on the estate. This confers great political power over the rural population, but not necessarily great economic power. Investment in an efficient production system through technical innovations in varieties, fertilizers, pruning, and spacing can substantially increase yields and profits, although it cannot much reduce the demand for hand labor. An efficient production system therefore can create considerably greater economic power than an inefficient system. Technological innovation, however, is also associated with the capitalist rationalization of production and the substitution of wage and often migratory labor for resident labor as coffee land becomes too valuable to be set aside for subsistence plots. Control over the rural population may actually decline as a cash nexus replaces direct paternalistic or coercive controls (or both) over a resident labor force. These different bases of coffee elite agrarian power are thus associated with different patterns of class relations. Nevertheless, the more the income of the elite depends on either land or productive efficiency (or both), the stronger the agrarian fraction of the elite. The four countries differ substantially along these dimensions.

Land, Production and People. There is little disagreement among authors writing about Guatemala or in official statistical sources about the absolute domination of Guatemalan coffee land and total production by large estates.[3] Similarly, there is little disagreement about the domination of a planter oligarchy over both land and production in El Salvador, although there are substantial differences between these two systems.[4] There is, however, considerable debate about the true distribution of land and production and the relative size and importance of the large estate in the cases of both Costa Rica and Nicaragua, and consequently a debate about the pattern of class relations in each country. For Costa Rica, the opposing positions are most forcefully stated by Carolyn Hall and Mitchell Seligson; Hall's position has also been argued by Cardoso and Torres-Rivas, and Seligson's work has been echoed by Anthony Winson.[5] Hall argues that Costa Rican coffee landownership and production have been dominated by small holders, and that estate production is of less relative importance and the estates themselves smaller than elsewhere in Central America. Seligson contends that the rise of coffee production transformed the traditional small-holding pattern of Costa Rican agriculture and led to dominance by large estates, unequal land distribution, and the growth of a landless proletariat.

For Nicaragua, Jaime Wheelock (later Sandinista Minister of Agriculture and Agrarian Reform) argued in his influential work, *Imperialismo y dictadura,* that the coffee estate was simply an extension of patterns of colonial agriculture, and that large manorial units dominated coffee production. In Wheelock's view, Nicaragua differed from El Salvador in the technical development of coffee production and processing, but not in the importance of the large estate. Eduardo Baumeister, on the other hand, proposed a model of the Nicaraguan agrarian economy suggesting that Nicaragua, like Costa Rica, is an exception to the Latin American pattern of large estate dominance and that small holders and what he calls a bourgeoisie *chapiolla,* or small-employer stratum, were the most important factors in pre-revolutionary Nicaraguan coffee production.[6] As is often the case in such debates, there is more than a little truth in both positions, and in part the continued discussion reflects the more varied internal structures of coffee production in Nicaragua and Costa Rica, in contrast to Guatemala and El Salvador. In all four countries, however, an accurate assessment of the true distribution of land and production and its relationship to class position requires a consistent and sociologically meaningful definition of estate and small-holder production. For purposes of statistical comparison, this definition needs to be expressed in area of production units employed in Central American censuses, but it also needs to approximate real differences in class relations in the different size categories.

Table 1 shows coffee area and production in Guatemala, El Salvador, Costa Rica, and Nicaragua organized into five size categories based on the likely class position of producers in that category. *Subfamily* or mini-farms control too little coffee to support a family and require outside wage labor. *Family farms* have enough coffee to support a family and can be worked with family labor and a minimum of hired labor at harvest. *Small employers* control sufficient coffee to require hiring additional labor, but are usually directly involved in managing and working their farms themselves. *Estate producers* have a hired manager as well as hired labor and control enough land to permit an aristocratic life style. Finally, *integrated producers* have

Table 1. Coffee Area and Production for Costa Rica (1955), Nicaragua (1957–58), El Salvador (1940, 1957–58), and Guatemala (1966–67) by Class Position of Producers

Class position	Farm area in coffee	Costa Rica (1955) Number of farms	Percentage of total area	Nicaragua (1957–58) Number of farms	Percentage of total area	El Salvador (1940) Number of farms	Percentage of total area	Guatemala (1966–67) Number of farms	Percentage of total area
				Coffee area in *manzanas*					
Sub-family	0–4.9	19,049	33.6 } 47.8	5,762	11.4 } 24.5	9,768	— } 18.9	25 to 30,000	— } 11.6
Family	5–9.9	1,775	14.2	2,059	13.1				
Small employer	10–49.9	979	22.1	1,256	22.6	1,322	27.4	606	4.6
Estate	50–99.9	101	8.6 } 30.6	314	19.2 } 52.8	263	16.4 } 53.7	1,148	17.2 } 83.7
Integrated producer	100+	83	21.6	212	33.6	192	37.3	636	66.5
Totals		21,987	100.1	9,603	99.9	11,545	100.0	—	99.9
Total area		80,574		123,253		117,216 (1940) 178,070 (1957–58)		330,900 (1964)	

Coffee production in *quintales* of green coffee

		Costa Rica (1955)		Nicaragua (1957–58)		El Salvador (1940)		Guatemala (1966–67)	
		Yield	Percentage of national production	Yield	Percentage of national production	Yield	Percentage of national production	Yield	Percentage of national production
Sub-family	0–4.9	5.6	29.5 } 42.2	1.2	3.5 } 12.8	7.4 }	— } 13.5	— }	— } 13.1
Family	5–9.9	5.7	12.7	2.7	9.3		—	—	—
Small employer	10–49.9	5.9	20.3	3.9	22.9	10.7	28.4	12.8	7.3
Estate	50–99.9	7.3	9.8 } 37.5	4.3	21.3 } 64.2	12.5	19.7 } 58.1	8.6	17.1 } 79.5
Integrated producer	100+	8.2	27.7	4.9	42.9	11.9	38.4	7.6	62.4
Totals		$\bar{X}$ = 6.5	100.0	$\bar{X}$ = 3.9	99.9	$\bar{X}$ = 10.6	100.0	$\bar{X}$ = 6.6	99.9
Total produced		522,998		474,683		1,891,201		2,188,517 (1964)	

Sources: Costa Rica: Dirección General de Estadística y Censos, *Censo agropecuario 1955* (San José, 1957), pp. 101, 230; Nicaragua: Dirección General de Estadística y Censos, *El café en Nicaragua* (Managua, 1961), p. 7; El Salvador: Asociación Cafetalera de El Salvador, *Primer censo nacional del café* (San Salvador, 1940), p. 26; Dirección General de Estadística y Censos, *Compendio del segundo censo nacional del café* (San Salvador, 1961), p. 51; Guatemala: Dirección General de Estadística, *Censo cafetalero 1950* (Guatemala City, 1953), p. 5; and *Censo agropecuario* (Guatemala City, 1964), pp. 245, 248; M. J. Biechler, "The Coffee Industry of Guatemala: A Geographic Analysis" (Ph.D. diss., Michigan State University, 1970), p. 109.

enough land so that they are likely also to control more than one farm and own a mill processing their own and other growers' coffee. The categories are approximate and may vary over time depending on the degree of technical rationalization of production. The size categories are intended to capture class relations as they existed approximately at mid-century, providing a view of class relations as they existed before the post-World War II rationalization of production in all four countries. These class relations can be assumed to have changed little from the beginning of the century.[7]

The data in Table 1 make it possible not only to clarify some of the issues raised in the debates over coffee and class in Costa Rica and Nicaragua, but also to compare the class systems of each of the Central American coffee producers. Three major conclusions can immediately be drawn by inspection of Table 1. First, concentration of both land and production is notably greater in Guatemala than anywhere else in Central America. Not only are coffee area and production in Guatemala more concentrated than in Costa Rica or Nicaragua, but they are also much more concentrated than in oligarchic El Salvador. Approximately two-thirds of both Guatemalan coffee area and production are controlled by integrated producers, and an additional 17% is controlled by estate producers. Family and sub-family producers are so inconsequential that little systematic data is collected on them, and the small-employer stratum is of little greater importance. In Guatemala, the dominance of the large estate in the control of coffee land is almost complete.

The second conclusion is that Salvadoran and Nicaraguan coffee land and production are dominated by large estates, although not as completely as in Guatemala. The data in Table 1 show almost identical levels of concentration in both coffee area and production. Approximately 500 estate and integrated producers (of the approximately 10,000 growers in both countries) controlled 53% of the total coffee area in both countries, and these two classes of large growers actually controlled a greater proportion of production in Nicaragua (64.2%) than in El Salvador (58.1%). Nicaragua is not an exception to the pattern of estate dominance in Latin American agriculture. The data in Table 1 indicate that Nicaragua more closely resembles El Salvador, a country with a well-deserved reputation for oligarchic dominance, than it does Costa Rica. Neither in Nicaragua nor in El Salvador do the numerous small holdings of family and sub-family farmers make any substantial contribution to production; they control less than a quarter of the coffee area in Nicaragua and less than 20% in El Salvador.[8] On the basis of the coffee-class structure in Nicaragua and El Salvador revealed in the data in Table 1, similar patterns of landed elite dominance would be expected in both countries.

Despite these similarities in the relative distribution of land ownership and production, Salvadoran yields are *three times* as great as those in Nicaragua, so that the absolute wealth and potential for oligarchic dominance by coffee growers are much greater in El Salvador than in Nicaragua. Furthermore, there are substantial internal divisions within Nicaragua. As Table 2 indicates, the original area of Nicaraguan production in Managua and Carazo revealed levels of concentration of land ownership similar to those of Guatemala, not El Salvador, with 92% and 81% of the area, respectively, controlled by estate or integrated producers in the 1950s. In the newer coffee region of Matagalpa and Jinotega the small-employer stratum was expanding rapidly in the post-World War II period. Even though patterns of land ownership for the nation and the Managua-Carazo region support Wheelock's contention, Baumeister's argument is supported by the low yields and relative poverty of even large Nicaraguan growers and the emergence of the small-employer stratum in the most dynamic coffee region. Class relations are clearer and class polarization more advanced in El Salvador, despite the similarities in land ownership.

The third conclusion suggested by the data in Table 1 is that both small holders and large estates are important in Costa Rica. It is clear that compared to El Salvador and Nicaragua, to say nothing of Guatemala, the small-holding farmers control a much more substantial share of coffee area and production, and that the estate sector is correspondingly smaller. Small holders are approximately twice as important in area and three times as important in production as they are in either Nicaragua or El Salvador, and the estate sector is proportionately a third less important in both area and production. Differences of this magnitude reflect substantial differences in the political and economic power of the coffee elites of Nicaragua and El Salvador relative to Costa Rica, and tend to support Hall's con-

Table 2. Distribution of Production by Class Position of Producers for Nicaragua, 1910 and 1957

Class position	Production (qq)	Managua 1910		Managua 1957		Carazo 1910		Carazo 1957	
						Regions III–IV			
Sub-family	10<	.0		.3		.2		.6	
Family	10 < 40	.4	.4	.9	1.2	3.5	3.7	3.7	4.3
Small employer	40 < 200	11.3		7.1		21.4		15.0	
Estate	200 < 500	33.9		21.1		22.7		22.5	
Integrated producer	≥500	54.3	88.2	70.5	91.6	52.1	74.8	58.3	80.8
Total percentage		99.9		99.9		99.9		100.1	
Total produced		67,440		81,004		47,187		119,087	
Percentage of nation		38.8		17.1		27.1		25.1	

Class position	Production (qq)	Matagalpa 1910		Matagalpa 1957		Jinotega 1910		Jinotega 1957	
						Region VI			
Sub-family	10<	1.1		1.8		.3		5.3	
Family	10 < 40	3.1	4.2	9.9	11.7	3.5	3.8	14.1	19.4
Small employer	40 < 200	19.2		30.9		19.4		23.5	
Estate	200 < 500	33.1		24.7		28.9		21.3	
Integrated producer	≥500	43.5	76.6	32.7	57.4	47.9	76.8	35.8	57.1
Total percentage		100.0		100.0		100.0		100.0	
Total produced		18,444		116,734		16,484		65,894	
Percentage of nation		10.6		24.6		9.4		13.9	

Sources: República de Nicaragua, *Censo cafetalero* (Managua, 1910), calculated from census listing. Nicaragua: Dirección General de Estadística y Censos, *El café en Nicaragua* (Managua, 1961), p. 7.

tentions regarding the strength of small holders and the weakness of the large estates in Costa Rican coffee production.

This conclusion must, however, be immediately qualified by noting that the most important small-holding class is *not* the family farmers but rather the sub-family farmers, who are not only much more numerous but control more production and area. Since 19,000 of the 22,000 coffee growers in Costa Rica in 1955 fell into the sub-family category, Seligson might well contend that Costa Rican coffee farmers were a semi-proletariat of land-starved mini-farmers rather than an autonomous yeoman farmer class. The family farm is actually relatively insignificant in numbers, area, and production. Furthermore, a small number of large estates (184 of 22,000) controlled 30.6% of total coffee area and 37.5% of production. As Seligson contends, there is in fact a high degree of concentration in Costa Rican coffee production, although not so much as elsewhere in Central America. Although naive views of Costa Rica as a nation of Jeffersonian family farmers will find no support from the data in Table 1, Hall's position does receive some support from the cross-national comparison. The small-holder sector is much more important in Costa Rica than elsewhere. On the other hand, Seligson's image of a Costa Rica divided between a few large estates and a mass of semi-proletarians is also supported by the data. But the situation is even worse elsewhere.

The data in Table 1 do not, therefore, provide support for the idea that the dominance of an independent yeoman farmer class provides the economic base for Costa Rican democracy and Costa Rican exceptionalism in Central America. Although comparison between Costa Rica and either Nicaragua or El Salvador gives the impression of relative small-holder dominance in Costa Rica, the data suggest that estate and, especially, integrated producers are in a position to exert considerable economic and political power over a dispersed and impoverished class of sub-family farmers. As the integrated producers also control the processing of the small farmers' crop, the dominance is even greater than the area and production data alone would suggest. The substantial difference in the political behavior of the Salvadoran and Costa Rica elites, as well as the much greater success of democracy in the latter country than in the former, cannot be explained simply by the greater importance of family farmers in the latter. Both countries were dominated economically by estate owners even though the degree of dominance was greater in El Salvador.

The data in Table 1 not only provide a comparative portrait of the entire class structure of Central American coffee production, but also include information that makes possible an assessment of the absolute economic and political strength of Central American coffee producers, both individually and as a class. Table 3 presents the information in Table 1 in a slightly different form to emphasize these differences. The data on mean area and mean production of estates with 100 *manzanas* (1 *mz.* = .69 hectares) or more in coffee by country provide indirect information about landed power—best measured by mean area—and wealth—best measured by mean production—of the average individual large estate in each country. Once again, Guatemala is unique. The extremely large mean coffee land area controlled by individual estate owners (342 *manzanas*) is almost one-and-one-half times the mean size of large estates elsewhere in Central America. It is also notable that the optimum size of an estate seems to be approximately the same in Costa Rica, Nicaragua, and El Salvador—200 *manzanas*. Costa Rican estates are not markedly smaller than those of El Salvador and are in fact larger on average than those of Nicaragua. Comparison with Guatemala is, of course, misleading, as in both overall distribution and average size of large estates it is an exceptional case.

Table 3. Mean Area and Mean Production of Estates with 100 *manzanas* or More Planted in Coffee, and Total Area and Total Production of Estates with 50 *manzanas* or More Planted in Coffee by Country

| | Estate Area in Coffee | | | |
| | ≥100 mz. | | ≥50 mz. | |
Country	Mean area (mz.)	Mean production (qq)	Total area (1000 mz.)	Total production (1000 qq)
Costa Rica	210	1,722	24.7	196.1
Nicaragua	195	955	65.1	304.8
El Salvador	228	2,713	95.6	1,098.8
Guatemala	342	2,479	202.1	1,278.3

Source: Table 1. Guatemala area and production data based on average of 1950 and 1964 census figures.

The data on mean production indicate a distinctly different pattern of economic power by country. Salvadoran growers manage to produce more coffee per estate than Guatemalan growers, despite the much smaller average area in coffee on their estates. Inasmuch as the Salvadorans are producing more coffee on less land, their efficiency and hence profitability and financial power should be greater than the approximately equal average production per estate in the two countries would suggest. The average production of large Costa Rican estates lags somewhat behind the average production of Salvadoran or Guatemalan estates, and the Nicaraguan integrated producers are the weakest in Central America by a considerable margin (half the production per estate of Costa Rica, approximately a third of that of Guatemala or El Salvador). This pattern of efficiency, productivity, and economic strength of Salvadoran growers and inefficiency, backwardness, and economic weakness of Nicaraguan producers also appears in data on technology and processing still to be presented. Although the distribution of coffee land and production does not differ appreciably in the two countries, differences in productivity make the Salvadoran and Nicaraguan growers, respectively, the economic strong and weak classes of Central America.

The data on total area and production for all estates with more than 50 *manzanas* in coffee in the third and fourth columns of Table 3 provide an index of the absolute political and economic power of the coffee-growing classes as a whole. Measured once again by control over land, the Guatemalan agrarian elite is in a class by itself. The total coffee area controlled by all large growers in Guatemala is twice that of El Salvador, three times that of Nicaragua, and eight times that of Costa Rica. Total production, however, is almost as high in El Salvador as it is in Guatemala, even though Guatemalan growers as a class control twice as much land. Once again, the Salvadoran elite is distinguished by its greater productivity and efficiency. Nicaraguan and Costa Rican agrarian elites lag far behind the region's two leaders in both total area and total production. Although individually and as a class Costa Rican estate owners produce more coffee per unit area than do Nicaraguan growers, the total power of the Costa Rican agrarian elite as a whole—assessed in terms of either coffee land or production—is actually less than that of the Nicaraguan elite. The reasons for the relative weakness of the Nicaraguan and Costa Rican agrarian elites are, however, different. The Nicaraguan elite was weak because it was inefficient; the Costa Rican elite was weak because it lost control over a substantial share of production to a class of small holders.

It has been assumed throughout that control over land implies control over people, although it is clear that some forms of productive organization lead to more control over people than others, even if the same amount of land is involved. Table 4 assesses this idea directly by presenting the number of workers under administrative control by estate owners (resident or permanent workers) and the number under temporary control (harvest migrants) for the three Central American producers for which data are available. Data are from coffee censuses conducted from 1935 to 1942. No data on labor force organization are presented in later censuses. It is clear from the data in Table 4 that the Guatemalan coffee elite controlled approximately three times as many resident laborers as did the Salvadoran elite, even though Salvadoran production was only slightly less than Guatemalan. The absolute difference in the size of populations controlled is actually greater than these figures suggest, because the families of resident laborers usually lived with them on the estate. As families of permanent workers could be mobilized to help in the

Table 4. Number of Small Holders and Number of Resident and Non-Resident Workers Employed on Estates with More Than 50 *manzanas* in Coffee in El Salvador (1940), Guatemala (1942–43), and Costa Rica (1935)

Category	Costa Rica	El Salvador	Guatemala
Small holders	23,641	9,768	9,340
Resident adult males	—	27,396	76,767
Permanent workers	23,636	—	—
Harvest migrant (all workers)	—	231,710	142,941
Total harvest labor	75,000	310,000	350,000
Estate area (1000 mz.)	21.0	62.9	164.5
Estate production (1000 qq)	194.7	784.4	895.2

Sources: El Salvador: Asociación Cafetalera, *Primer censo*, pp. 26, 34, 35, 39; Guatemala: Oficina Central del Café, *Informe cafetalero de Guatemala* (Guatemala City, 1946); Costa Rica: Instituto de Defensa del Café de Costa Rica, "El instituto levanta el censo cafetalero del país: resumen general de la república," *Revista del Instituto de Defensa del Café de Costa Rica* 3, 14 (1935):58–74.

harvest, the number of outside harvest migrants is greater in El Salvador than in Guatemala. Nevertheless, the total harvest labor force including hired outsiders, permanent workers, and the working members of their families is greater in Guatemala (350,000) than in El Salvador (310,000).

The data in Table 4 support the assessment of the relative positions of the Salvadoran and Guatemalan coffee elites suggested by the land and production distribution data of Tables 1 and 3. Control over more land does translate into control over more people, all other things being equal. The comparative labor force data in Table 4 also indicate that the Salvadoran growers used their permanent labor force much more efficiently, because output per permanent worker is almost three times higher in El Salvador than in Guatemala. The limitations of hand picking restrict any such dramatic productivity differences in harvesting, however. Once again the Salvadoran elite is distinguished by its vastly more efficient production system; the Guatemalan elite by its greater control over land and people in a relatively inefficient system.

The difference between El Salvador and Guatemala in control over people is actually much greater than the data in Table 4 suggest, because control is qualitatively as well as quantitatively distinct in the two countries. Since its origins in the late nineteenth century, the Guatemalan coffee production system has been dominated by various forms of forced labor that have varied only in whether effective control was exercised by the state or by individual planters.[9] Either the state required a certain number of days of forced labor from every Indian inhabitant, or it backed debt servitude and labor contractors under the control of estate owners. In the latter system, which continues to function today, laborers were advanced money by estate owners but never managed to work off their debts and became permanently indebted.[10] Because debts could be inherited, by the beginning of this century a distinct class of hereditary serfs (*colonos*) had developed on coffee estates, and institutionalized serfdom (*colonaje*) had come to be formalized in Guatemalan law and custom. The resident *colono* labor force was supplemented by gangs of harvest migrants, recruited into fixed-term debt servitude by a system of advances controlled by unscrupulous labor contractors. These gang laborers were seldom able to work off all their debts and differed from the resident *colonos* principally in the fixed-term nature of their contracts and the absence of even the limited legal protection afforded the *colonos.*

This elaborate legal system of forced labor is not duplicated elsewhere in Central America, although varying degrees of extra-economic coercion were universal: the use of company stores in Nicaragua, rural patrols in El Salvador, and estate housing or subsistence plots in Costa Rica.[11] Guatemala is unique not only in the numbers of people and vast amounts of land controlled by its coffee elite, but also in the elaboration of an institutionalized system of forced labor backed by both the informal armed power of the coffee planters and the formal armed power of the state. A North American visitor observed in 1908 that Guatemala had so many soldiers that it looked like a penal colony; this is as true today as it was then.[12] Owning Guatemala's most productive land, producing its most important source of wealth, and controlling a vast dependent population through state-sanctioned forced labor, the Guatemalan coffee elite became a political force that has no exact parallel in the other coffee-producing countries. Not even in El Salvador was such extensive control over land and people possible.

The Costa Rican data in Table 4 are not directly comparable with those of El Salvador and Guatemala, because the 1935 Costa Rican coffee census reports the number of persons *working* on coffee estates, not the number of workers *resident* on the estates as in El Salvador or Guatemala. Because many Costa Rican coffee workers were day rather than resident laborers, the data may reflect a difference in reporting conventions rather than real differences between the systems. The principal value of the data in Table 4 for Costa Rica is to indicate that the ratio of small holders to hired laborers was much higher in Costa Rica than in either El Salvador or Guatemala, although the small holders and hired laborers could, of course, be the same people. Nevertheless, it is clear that a large portion of the Costa Rican lower class were small property owners. Class polarization was considerably more acute in El Salvador and Guatemala than it was in Costa Rica. This difference would have profound consequences when the Depression of the 1930s heightened class tensions in both El Salvador and Costa Rica.

Production Technology and Productive Efficiency. The differences in production per unit area evident in Tables 1, 3, and 4 are the result of substantial differences in the technology of production. As might be expected, El Salvador has been the traditional leader in production technology, followed by Costa Rica, with Guatemala and Nicaragua lagging far behind. Table 5 presents three readily accessible indices of technical sophistication in production: coffee variety; fertilizer use; and density of plantings. Each innovation substantially increases yields and profits. By the 1950s Salvador had already made the tran-

Table 5. Distribution of Coffee Varieties, Fertilizer Use, and Planting Density by Country, 1950–1957

Technical Index	Costa Rica 1955		Nicaragua 1957		El Salvador 1957		Guatemala 1950	
Variety	*Percentage of total coffee area*							
Típica	67.9		80.1		29.3		48.5	
Maragogipe	—	} 67.9	4.3	} 84.4	—	} 29.3	5.0	} 53.5
Típica-Bourbon	—		—		—		32.1	
Bourbon	16.4		15.4		58.8		14.3	
Others	15.7	} 32.1	0.1	} 15.5	11.9	} 70.7	—	} 14.3
Total	100.0		99.9		100.0		99.9	
Fertilizer use	*Percentage of total coffee area*							
Organic	10.4		2.0		—		6.6	
Chemical	25.3	} 35.7	3.0	} 5.0	—		5.3	} 11.9
None	64.4		95.0		—		88.2	
Total	100.1		100.0		—		100.1	
	Number of trees per manzana							
Density	—		1,000		1,258		635	

Sources: Costa Rica: Estadística y Censos, *Censo agropecuario 1955*, pp. 40, 42, 44, 233; Nicaragua: Estadística y Censos, *El café*, pp. 11, 13, 18; El Salvador: Estadística y Censos, *Segundo censo*, pp. 3–5; Guatemala: Estadística, *Censo cafetalero de 1950*, pp. 7, 37, 71.

sition from the traditional Central American coffee varieties, Típica and Maragogipe, to the hardier and higher-yielding Bourbon strain. In 1957 more than two-thirds of Salvadoran coffee area was in the more advanced varieties, whereas the transition had hardly begun in either Nicaragua or Guatemala and extended to only approximately a third of the coffee area in Costa Rica. Although fertilizer-use statistics by area are not available for El Salvador, the relative position of Costa Rica compared to Nicaragua and Guatemala is the same as in the variety sub-table. In the 1950s organic or chemical fertilizers were used on 35.7% of the total Costa Rican coffee area. The corresponding figures for Nicaragua and Guatemala are 5% and 11.9%, respectively. Density of plantings was almost twice as great in Salvador as it was in Guatemala.[13]

The technical superiority of El Salvador is indicated most clearly in yields expressed in *quintales* (1 *quintal* = 100 lbs.) per *manzana,* for selected periods from World War II to the present (Table 6). For most of the period, Salvadoran yields are more than twice those of Guatemala or Nicaragua and substantially greater than those of Costa Rica. By 1978 government-sponsored technical development programs in Costa Rica had reversed the relative positions of El Salvador and Costa Rica and by 1980 Costa Rica was clearly in the

Table 6. Yields in *Quintales* of Green Coffee per *Manzana* for Selected Periods by Country

Period	Costa Rica	Nicaragua	El Salvador	Guatemala
1942 or before	7.6 (1935)	6.1 (1910)	11.1 (1940)	6.3 (1942–43)
1948–1952	6.9	5.3	10.1	5.4
1961–1965	9.1	5.2	12.4	8.0
1969–1971	13.2	6.9	17.1	8.3
1978	17.8	9.2	16.7	9.7
1980	21.2	9.0	14.7	9.5

Sources: United Nations Food and Agriculture Organization, *Production Yearbook,* vols. 14 and 34 (New York, 1960), p. 129 (1981), p. 184; Costa Rica: Instituto de Defensa, "Censo cafetalero," p. 59; Estadística y Censos, *Censo agropecuario, 1963,* p. 151; Nicaragua: República de Nicaragua, *Censo cafetalero,* p. 644; A Gariazo, E. Incer, D. Dye, and R. Soley, "El subsistema del café en Nicaragua," presented at the Second Seminar on Central America and the Caribbean, Managua, Feb. 9–12, 1983, app. table 7; El Salvador, Asociación Cafetalera, *Primer censo,* p. 26; Guatemala: Oficina Central, *Informe cafetalero,* pp., 152, 194; Estadística, *Censo agropecuario,* 1964, pp. 245, 248.

lead. This increase was particularly pronounced for small producers. Still, for most of the period El Salvador had the highest yields not only in Central America but in all of Latin America and, with the exception of some relatively minor producers, the highest yields in the world. By 1980 Costa Rica had assumed the lead in both Central and South America and, excepting minor producers, had the third highest yield in the world.[14] During most of the twentieth century the Salvadoran elite were the world leaders in the technological revolution of coffee production.

The differences in production technology between El Salvador and Costa Rica, on the one hand, and Guatemala and Nicaragua, on the other, are pronounced and have been so for some time. In June 1937 the Colombian agronomist Juan Pablo Duque made a survey of Central American production for the Colombian coffee board, which was worried about increased competition.[15] His description of the relative technical sophistication of the four Central American coffee systems, summarized in Table 7, is echoed in other cross-national surveys, as well as in studies of the technical organization of individual systems.[16] Duque found that harvesting techniques were similar in Costa Rica, El Salvador, and Guatemala. In Nicaragua, however, then as now, pickers strip or "milk" the branches of a mixture of ripe and unripe berries, leaves, twigs, buds, and other detritus, damaging the trees, reducing yields, and producing a low grade of coffee.[17] It is not entirely clear why this practice has persisted in the face of determined government and private efforts to suppress it, but it may be related to the relative backwardness of the Nicaraguan processing technology, which cannot produce higher grades of coffee no matter what quality of harvested fruit is used as input.[18]

Duque found that Costa Rica and El Salvador had a distinct advantage in pruning technique; in most areas of Nicaragua and Guatemala the coffee bush was allowed to grow freely with only maintenance cutting. In Nicaragua, an elaborate pruning system developed by the progressive grower Arturo Vaughan ("poda Vaughan") is used on some of the larger estates on the Carazo plateau but not elsewhere.[19] The distinct Costa Rican style of pruning, which encouraged candelabra-like branching, had some success among progressive planters in Guatemala but was not generally adopted.[20] In 1937 Duque found a "great preoccupation" with the use of chemical

Table 7. Estimates of the Technological Organization of Central American Coffee Production by Juan Pablo Duque for the Colombian Coffee Board, June 1937

	Costa Rica	Nicaragua	El Salvador	Guatemala
Harvesting	Mature beans only	Stripping ripe and unripe beans, leaves	Mature beans only	Mature beans only
Pruning	Intense	Free growth	Intense but variable	Free growth
Fertilizer	"Great preoccupation with spreading the use of chemical fertilizers"	None	Izote (*Yucca* sp.) and mineral fertilizers	General use[a]
Transport	Ox carts, trucks	Trucks (Carazo); pack animals (Matagalpa-Jinotega)	Carts, trucks	Carts, trucks, pack animals, human bearers
Processing machinery	Imported, sophisticated; "constant preoccupation with improving processing plant"	Local, primitive	Imported, sophisticated; similar to Costa Rica	Imported, sophisticated (but lags behind Costa Rica and El Salvador)
Quality control	High	Nonexistent	High	High
Machine drying	Yes	No	Yes	Yes

[a]M. Domínguez, "The Development of the Technological and Scientific Coffee Industry in Guatemala 1830–1930" (Ph.D. diss., Tulane University, 1970), p. 167, reports that fertilizer use was confined to German planters and that "inorganic fertilizers were, broadly speaking out of reach of all but the most prosperous planters." See also Table 4 above.

Source: Juan Pablo Duque, *Informe del jefe de departamento técnico sobre su viaje de estudio a algunos países cafeteros de la América Central* (Managua: Asociación Agrícola de Nicaragua, 1938).

fertilizers in Costa Rica, and the 1935 coffee census recorded that 30% of Costa Rican coffee lands was fertilized.[21] Duque found an active interest in fertilizers in El Salvador as well as the extensive use of the *izote* plant (*yucca* sp.) as a fertilizer supplement or substitute. He also found substantial interest in fertilizer among Guatemalan planters, but Domínguez reports that only German planters used it.[22] Costa Rican and El Salvadoran planters used the most advanced techniques of harvesting, pruning, and fertilization. Nicaraguan growers used the most primitive methods in all three areas, and Guatemalans used advanced techniques in harvesting only. The relative technical lead of Costa Rica and, especially, El Salvador over Guatemala and, especially, Nicaragua in production technology persisted for most of the century.

The analysis of land, production, and production technology demonstrates that the agrarian fractions of both the Guatemalan and Salvadoran elites were powerful but for different reasons. The Guatemalan coffee elite controlled more land and people and had a tighter hold on the people than did any other coffee elite in Central America. Its power rested on the captive allegiance of its serfs and the armed force at its command. The Salvadoran agrarian elite became the most productive, efficient, and profitable in Central America. But it controlled fewer people less securely. As early as the 1920s the labor force of El Salvador had relatively few resident laborers and consisted almost entirely of wage laborers. The Guatemalan elite was a backward, semi-feudal landed class that faced little opposition from its captive labor force bound to the land. The landed fraction of the Salvadoran elite was wealthy and therefore powerful, but it nonetheless depended on land concentration and massive amounts of harvest labor. This labor was not the politically demobilized serfs of Guatemala, but a proletarianized and potentially explosive mass of wage laborers. In the 1930s this potential became reality.

The agrarian fractions of the coffee elites of Nicaragua and Costa Rica gained neither the military and political power of the Guatemalans nor the economic power of the Salvadorans. Although control of Nicaraguan coffee land was as concentrated as it was in El Salvador, the Nicaraguan coffee elite never approached the productive efficiency of the Salvadorans and remained the least productive planter class in Central America. Although many Costa Rican growers controlled estates as large as any in Central America outside Guatemala, and were almost as efficient as the Salvadorans, as a class they never gained the absolute control over land and production achieved in El Salvador or Guatemala. Instead, they shared this control with a persistent class of sub-family farmers. These differences are further accentuated by substantial differences in control over processing and export.

The Agro-Industrial Elite: Control Over Processing and Export

Under Central American conditions processing, unlike production, can be extensively mechanized, and consequently the capital requirements are considerably greater in processing than in production. Harvested coffee beans begin to ferment almost immediately, and if the crop is not to be lost, it must be processed within 8 to 36 hours after picking.[23] Processing must remove the seeds of the coffee berry—the source of coffee as a beverage—from the surrounding organic material. Each coffee berry has an outer skin surrounding a thick pulp that constitutes the greater part of the mass of the berry. Surrounding the seeds is a thick, sticky substance known as mucilage, a paper-like membrane called the parchment, and a thin coating called the silver skin. Processing must dispose of the skin and pulp, separate the mucilage from the parchment, and strip off the parchment and silver skin without contaminating or damaging the beans themselves.[24] In the Central American system of "wet" processing the skin and pulp are mechanically removed and the mucilage is allowed to ferment until it can be washed away. The beans are then dried in the open or in mechanical dryers and then mechanically threshed to remove the parchment. Central American wet processing plants (called *beneficios*) have ranged from rudimentary hand-driven wooden devices of local manufacture to elaborate power-driven industrial installations.[25]

Although many small estate-based processing systems require little investment, the capital requirements of a large, technologically sophisticated industrial processing plant are substantial and have been so since the technology was developed at the end of the nineteenth century. The owners of such plants are industrial capitalists using an agricultural raw material rather than agriculturalists. It is, of course, entirely possible for a coffee producer to integrate downstream into processing, and in fact many large producers in Central America have owned their own industrial processing plants.[26] The greater the importance of industrial processing in a coffee elite's activities, however, the greater the strength of the agro-industrial as opposed to the agrarian fraction of the elite. Many of the most successful coffee processors purchase additional coffee from other growers to realize economies of scale; this in turn may lead them to make advances to other growers and hence assume the role of banker.[27] Many coffee processors also become involved in exporting the coffee they buy, giving them a position in the lucrative export phase of the business. Similarly, a processor possesses a fund of capital that may allow diversification into other agricultural activities or into industry, tourism, or real estate.[28] To the degree that the coffee elite is involved in industrial processing, it becomes more an agro-industrial, financial, or commercial class and less a purely agrarian class.

In processing, Costa Rica and El Salvador are the clear leaders, with Guatemala and Nicaragua again trailing at remarkably low levels of efficiency. In both Nicaragua and Guatemala primitive transportation restricted the development of centralized processing plants by preventing coffee berries from being transported to processing plants rapidly enough to prevent spoilage. Transportation technology was most highly developed in El Salvador and Costa Rica, where good roads made it possible to use ox carts and later trucks to quickly bring harvested berries from farm to mill.[29] The primitive roads of north central Nicaragua made even the use of ox carts difficult, and much coffee was moved on the backs of mules. Roads were better in the Managua-Carazo area, but much of the crop was still moved by mule or ox cart rather than by truck.[30] In Guatemala there were also regional variations, but in general carts, pack animals, and—unique in Central America—human bearers were used to transport coffee. In the remote Alta Verapaz region, human bearers carried 100-pound bags of coffee as far as 40 miles.[31] In Guatemala much coffee was still sold in the partially processed parchment stage.[32]

Processing technology itself was most advanced in Costa Rica and El Salvador, where imported European and North American power-driven equipment was used extensively in large industrial installations frequently located off the farm in cities or other central locations.[33] European, especially German, growers in Guatemala were responsible for many of the technical innovations in the coffee processing industry worldwide, but technological innovation ceased after World War I, and the processing industry stagnated.[34] In the 1930s Duque found that the processing industry in Guatemala trailed those of Costa Rica and El Salvador, and the gap is even wider today.[35] In the Managua-Carazo region of Nicaragua the development of processing was handicapped not only by poor transportation but also by a shortage of water, and before World War II as much as half of the crop was processed using the simpler "dry" method. Even though, by the 1950s, 90% of the crop was wet-processed, the shortage of water led to the improper washing of much of it. In north central Nicaragua there was plenty of water but so few roads that partial wet processing was done with homemade equipment, and much coffee was stored for weeks or months before being sent to final milling.[36] As a result, it was impossible to maintain quality standards in Nicaraguan coffee, whereas quality control was high in Costa Rica, El Salvador, and even in Guatemala.

Duque's observations on the superiority of Costa Rican and El Salvadoran processing technologies are also supported by the data in Table 8 showing the number of processing plants in each of the four countries for the period from the late nineteenth century to the present. As a general rule, the smaller the number of plants, the greater their technological sophistication, the greater the number of farms served by a given processor, the better the supporting transportation system, and the more likely that both wet processing and final polishing of parchment coffee are done in the same installation. Costa Rica and El Salvador have always had a relatively small number of processing plants—approximately 200 before World War II—and by 1972 the number declined to 114 in El Salvador and 83 in Costa Rica. Nicaragua and Guatemala had more than 1,000, almost all of them on-farm installations processing only to the parchment stage. Since in the 1950s El Salvador and Guatemala processed approximately equal amounts of coffee, the average Salvadoran plant processed more than *ten times* as much coffee as the typical Guatemalan plant. In fact, El Salvador possesses what is said to be the

Table 8. Number of Coffee Processing Plants (*beneficios*) for Selected Periods by Country

Period	Costa Rica	Nicaragua	El Salvador	Guatemala
1888–1910	256	423	—	—
1940–1942	221	—	207	4,243
1950–1957	—	1,263[a]	—	1,334[a]
1972	114	—	83	—

[a]Data for farms producing 220 qq. or more of coffee berries in Guatemala only. For comparative purposes the Nicaraguan total includes only farms producing 400 qq. of green coffee or more (5 qq. of berries yield approximately 1 q. of green coffee).

Sources: Costa Rica: Samuel Stone, *La dinastía de los conquistadores* (Editorial Universitaria Centroamericana, 1982), p. 256; Instituto de Defensa, "Censo cafetalero," p. 59; Mitchell Seligson, *Agrarian Capitalism and the Transformation of Peasant Society: Coffee in Costa Rica.* Special Studies Series, no. 69 (Buffalo: Council on International Studies, State University of New York at Buffalo, 1975), p. 24; Nicaragua: República de Nicaragua, *Censo cafetalero*, calculated from census listings; Estadística, *El café*, p. 25; El Salvador: Asociación Cafetalera, *Primer censo*, pp. 183–189, calculated from listings of *beneficios*; H. Castenada, "El café en El Salvador," unpublished manuscript (Managua: Instituto Centroamericano de Administración de Empresas, 1977); Guatemala: Oficina Central, *Informe cafetalero*, p. 146; Estadística, *Censo cafetalero 1950*, p. 80.

largest processing plant in Central America, El Molino.[37] The relative numbers of Salvadoran and Costa Rican plants suggest that the scale of Costa Rican technology is similar. Although El Salvador has traditionally been the leader in production technology, both Costa Rica and El Salvador have highly developed processing systems.

Given the substantial economic gains to be realized through scientific cultivation and industrial processing, it might be asked why all the Central American countries did not follow the path of El Salvador and later Costa Rica towards the full rationalization of both production and processing. For Nicaragua, Wheelock argues, the answer is to be found in the politics of intervention. The reversal of the Liberal revolution of the coffee elite after 1909 and the United States protectorate that ensued prevented the Liberals from realizing their full coffee development program. In 1910 Nicaragua, under the influence of the Liberals, took its first coffee census—a remarkably detailed document.[38] In 1912 the United States Marines arrived, not to leave for good until 1933. Their war against Augusto César Sandino was fought in the heart of the Matagalpa-Jinotega coffee belt, and there is little doubt that the intervention stopped the rationalization and expansion of production in what later would become Nicaragua's most dynamic coffee zone. It was not until the 1950s that expansion resumed in this region. Nicaragua did not take another coffee census until 1957. The intervention also deprived the coffee elite of control over exports and finance, which passed into the hands of American banks. The backwardness of the Nicaraguan coffee elite in both production and processing is a direct result of the American intervention.

In Guatemala, United States intervention involved bananas rather than coffee, and estate sizes were certainly large enough to generate capital for modernization. The failure to rationalize the industry is clearly related to the temptations of forced labor and a racist social structure. With labor virtually free for the taking, thanks to state-enforced debt servitude, and the Indian population having almost no protection from planter land grabs, there was little incentive to rationalize production. Land costs remained vastly lower in Guatemala than in Costa Rica, and wage levels were the lowest in Central America.[39] Indeed, what is surprising about Guatemala is not how little rationalization of production took place, but how much. But it took place almost entirely among German planters, who were more closely tied to world capitalism than to the extractive society of colonial Guatemala. Once the Germans were expropriated during World War II, the Guatemalan coffee elite reverted to doing what it had always done best — living in luxury on the tribute of a captive Indian population. Technological innovation stopped, and planters and their allies in the military devoted themselves to the rationalization not of coffee production but of state terror.

Costa Rica lagged behind El Salvador in production technology but not in the industrialization of processing. Although the elite of integrated producers rapidly modernized, and large estates such as Aquiares, studied by Morrison and Norris, or Concavas, studied by Hall, were models of productive efficiency, the yield figures for smaller growers (see Table 1) indicate that they were slow to rationalize production.[40] The small growers remained captives of the owners of processing plants until the economic crisis of the Depression, when the establishment of the Instituto de Defensa del Café (Institute for the Defense of Coffee) shifted some measure of control to the state. After the 1948 revolution, the Oficina del Café (Office of

Coffee) pushed through a technical development program that substantially benefited the small growers and caused Costa Rican yields to exceed those of El Salvador by the 1970s.[41] As long as the impoverished sub-family coffee farmers of Costa Rica were under the unrestricted control of the coffee-processing elite, they lacked both the capital and the technical knowledge necessary to rationalize production. The failure of the small producers to modernize without state intervention is another indication of the unequal distribution of wealth and power in the Costa Rican coffee system.

Deprived of complete control over production, land, and production technology by the persistence of small holders, the Costa Rican elite emerged as an elite of processors and exporters rather than growers. The agrarian fraction of the elite was therefore weaker in Costa Rica than anywhere else in Central America, with the possible exception of Nicaragua. Contrary to the myth of rural egalitarianism, Costa Rica did have a substantial class of wealthy, landed coffee estate owners. This group was less important in coffee, both relatively and absolutely, than its counterparts were elsewhere in the region. Class relations in the Costa Rican coffee system were based on a fundamental division between the processing elite, many of whom owned large estates themselves, and a large class of small holders from whom they purchased their coffee. This division between large property owners and small, rather than the division between coffee pickers and coffee growers, was to influence Costa Rican politics throughout the twentieth century.

In El Salvador the complete rationalization of production and processing early in the century enabled the coffee elite to move downstream into export and thereby gain control of what Sebastián calls the "power pyramid" of coffee land, processing, and export.[42] The data in Table 9 show this pattern as it existed in 1940 according to the first Salvadoran coffee census.[43] The left half lists (by family) the number of processing plants *(beneficios)* and export brands controlled by the leading processors; the right half of the table shows the same information for leading exporters. It is clear from these data that almost all large processors were also active exporters and vice-versa. The names on both lists represent a *Who's Who* of the Salvadoran oligarchy.[44] The power pyramid of coffee production, processing, and export conferred control over other export crops, especially cotton

Table 9. Number of Coffee Processing Plants (*beneficios*) and Number of Legal
Export Trademarks Held by Largest Holders in El Salvador in 1940

Holders of largest number of *beneficios*			Holders of largest number of export brands		
Family or company	*Beneficios*	Export	Family or company	Export	*Beneficios*
Meardi	12	60	Meardi	60	12
Daglio	8	17	Alvarez	22	4
Sol Millet	7	5	Curaçao Trading	19	1
Guirola	7	6	de Sola	18	6
de Sola	6	18	Daglio	17	8
Salaverría	5	6	J. Hill	16	1
Alfaro	5	5	Goldtree-Liebes	9	2
Cáceres	5	—	Delpech	8	1
Bonilla	5	—	Meza Ayau	7	1
Regalado	4	6	Nottebohm Trading	7	2
Alvarez	4	22	Dueñas	6	4
Magaña	4	—	Guirola	6	7
Dueñas	4	6	Morán	6	1
Lima	4	4	Matamoros	6	1
			Regalado	6	4
			Salaverría	6	5
			Vides	6	1

Source: Asociación Cafetalera, *Primer censo*, pp. 183-199.

and sugar, and frequently over finance and industry as well. Edelberto Torres-Rivas has called the Central American elite a "three-footed beast" with one foot in export agriculture, one in finance, and one in industry.[45] No coffee elite in Central America fits this description better than the Salvadoran. An elite of fully integrated producers controlled the coffee system and much else as well.

The most dramatic contrast to the fully integrated production system and powerful coffee elite of El Salvador is the case of Nicaragua. The Nicaraguan coffee elite achieved neither the rationalization of coffee production nor hegemonic power in Nicaraguan economy and society. Table 10 presents a list of individuals who might have been the founders of the Nicaraguan coffee oligarchy if U.S. intervention, civil war, and the rise of the Somoza dynasty had not undermined their economic and technical progress. The Table shows the 11 largest growers in the Department of Carazo recorded in the

Table 10. Principal Producers in the Department of Carazo, 1910

Producer	Estates	Area (mz.)	Produc- tion (qq)	Total area	Total produc- tion	Number of *beneficios*
Arturo Vaugham	San Francisco	222	5,000	222	5,000	1
José E. González	La Providencia	240	1,200	590	3,000	2
	Monte Cristo	175	1,500			
	La Palmera	175	1,300			
Adolfo Benard	San Dionisio	123	1,300	238	2,200	1
	Santa Rosa	50	500			
	San Francisco	65	400			
Rappaccioli	El Paraíso	145	1,000	330	2,000	2
(Vincente y Hnos.)	El Pochotón	100	400			
	La Moca	85	600			
Fernando Chamorro	La Amistad	90	800	210	1,700	2
	El Brasil	120	900			
Teodoro Tefel	Chilamatal	305	1,500	305	1,500	1
Vincente Rodríguez	Santa Cecilia	100	1,100	175	1,450	1
	San Ramiro	75	350			
José Ig. González	San Jorge	60	600	160	1,400	1
	Las Delicias	100	800			
Ignacio Baltodano	El Brasilito	180	1,100	180	1,100	1
José M. Siero	Santa Gertrudis	56	600	146	900	0
	Andalucía	90	300			
Anastasio Somoza	Santa Julia	5	50	94	730	2
	El Convoy	14	80			
	El Porvenir	75	600			

Source: República de Nicaragua, *Censo cafetalero,* pp. 666–671.

1910 coffee census on the eve of the 1912 United States intervention.[46] The largest producer was Arturo Vaughan (misspelled
Vaugham in the census), the developer of the system of pruning that
bears his name. This technologically advanced producer's yields of
22.5 *quintales/manzana* in 1910 actually exceeded the 1982 national
average of Costa Rica, Latin America's technological leader. Vaughan
was a rare Nicaraguan example of the Salvadoran-type rationalized
integrated producer—the kind of grower who might have formed,
along with other technologically progressive planters, the nucleus of
a Nicaraguan coffee oligarchy. Vaughan's estate, San Francisco, is
still owned by his family and is in production today; the current

owner, also named Arturo, has diversified to become one of Nicaragua's largest egg producers.

But it was not the descendents of Arturo Vaughan and other technologically sophisticated producers, such as Carlos Wheelock in nearby Managua, who became the masters of Nicaragua. Instead, it was the son of the eleventh largest producer in Carazo, whose yields were only a third (7.8 *quintales/manzana*) of those of Arturo Vaughan, and who did not control sufficient land to be included in the "integrated producer" category. The rise of Anastasio Somoza as ruler of Nicaragua and its largest coffee producer was, of course, a consequence of international power politics, not coffee wealth. Anastasio Somoza García had been poor enough to have worked as a used car dealer, and he gained his political prominence in part through his command of English.[47] It would take a revolution to bring to power the coffee-growing Wheelock family in the person of Jaime Wheelock, a member of the FSLN since 1969 and Minister of Agriculture and Agrarian Reform in the Sandinista period. By that time, however, Wheelock had become committed not only to the industrialization of Nicaraguan agriculture, but to revolution against the coffee elite itself.

Some members of the 1910 Carazo planter elite owned their own processing plants (Table 10), but none owned as many as members of the Salvadoran elite; in fact, Carazo coffee-processing technology was in a prolonged state of arrested development because of the shortage of water. Exports were controlled by American banks in partnership with the Nicaraguan national bank. Two families of Carazo planters listed in Table 10, the Rappacciolis and the Baltodanos, did become major exporters in the 1950s, but by then they had fallen behind their counterparts in El Salvador and Costa Rica in accumulating export-based economic power. Furthermore, their ability to diversify into other areas of the economy or even expand their coffee holdings was limited severely by the dominance of the Somoza family. Technologically backward in both production and processing, deprived of control over exports, and hemmed in by the Somozas, the Nicaraguan coffee elite never completed the transition to agro-industrial production. If the Salvadoran coffee oligarchy rested on a power pyramid of coffee, processing, and export, the Nicaraguan coffee economy was a pyramid without a base.

Class, Politics, and Ideology in the Agro-Export Economy in 1920–1950, 1950–1979, and 1992

The data presented thus far summarize the coffee systems of El Salvador, Guatemala, Costa Rica, and Nicaragua as they existed in the first half of the twentieth century, between 1920 and 1950. With the exception of Nicaragua, these systems were essentially those established by the Liberal revolutions of the coffee elite in the second half of the nineteenth century. They were also the systems that defined class relations in the first of the two great crises of the coffee elite in this century, that of the 1930s. By the time of the second great crisis, that of the 1980s, however, class relations had been fundamentally transformed. The unprecedented post-World War II expansion of world capitalism stimulated a new boom in the Central American agro-export economies. Although coffee itself underwent a significant expansion, the most dynamic sectors were the new agro-exports of cattle, sugar, and above all cotton. Class relations in these sectors were very different from those in the coffee economy of the first half of the century. Nevertheless, the political systems with which Central America entered the crisis of the 1980s were shaped by the resolution of the class conflict of the 1930s, and this conflict and its resolution were shaped by the organization of coffee production from 1920 to 1950. Class relations in both the 1920–1950 period and the 1950–1980 period are therefore fundamental to understanding the politics and class relations of the 1979–1992 period.

Class Relations, 1920–1950

The pattern of class relations in El Salvador, Costa Rica, Guatemala, and Nicaragua in this period and its relationship to the organization of coffee production in each country is summarized in Figure 1. The horizontal dimension shows the relative power of the agrarian fraction in each country based on either land or productive efficiency; the vertical dimension shows the relative power of the agro-industrial fraction based on processing. The two diagonals show the relative importance of land and productive efficiency respectively as bases of economic and political power of the *agrarian* fraction of the

Figure 1. Strength and Power Bases of the Agrarian and Agro-Industrial Fractions of Coffee Elites and Relations between Upper and Lower Classes in the Coffee Sector, 1920–1950

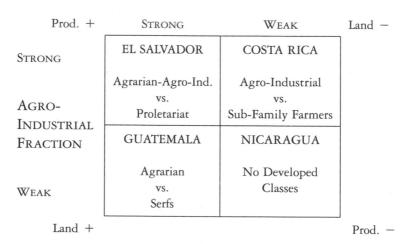

AGRARIAN FRACTION

	STRONG	WEAK	
Prod. +			Land −
STRONG	EL SALVADOR	COSTA RICA	
AGRO-INDUSTRIAL FRACTION	Agrarian-Agro-Ind. vs. Proletariat	Agro-Industrial vs. Sub-Family Farmers	
	GUATEMALA	NICARAGUA	
WEAK	Agrarian vs. Serfs	No Developed Classes	
Land +			Prod. −

elite. The position of each country in the four cells of the Figure shows the particular combination of the strength or weakness of the agrarian and agro-industrial fractions of the elite in that country. Each cell also shows the pattern of relations between the elite and the lower classes in the coffee production system in that country. The position of Guatemala in the Figure, for example, indicates that its coffee elite has a strong agrarian and weak agro-industrial fraction and that the base of power of the agrarian elite is land (+). The coffee class system is divided between the large estate owners of the agrarian fraction and the *colonos,* or "serfs." The Figure summarizes the empirically observed (as opposed to logically possible) combinations of land, production, and export types in Central American coffee, and also the within- and between-class relations that would be expected from the social organization of production based on these combinations.

As the Figure indicates, the Guatemalan elite, particularly in its national sector, was characterized by large estates, large amounts of land under estate control, and large numbers of people under tight seigniorial restrictions. Estates owned by Guatemalan nationals never adopted rationalized production technology, and before World War II, processing and exports were largely controlled by Germans. The Guatemalan elite was overwhelmingly landed and agrarian, with a relatively weak agro-industrial fraction. Debt servitude, serfdom, and other forms of legal bondage created class relations similar to those of the European feudal manor: the Spanish and European immigrant landlord class ruled over an unfree Indian labor force. Although these relations began to change with the post-World War II rationalization of coffee, before the 1970s institutions of coerced labor inhibited rural popular mobilization and created a strong interest in authoritarian political structures to control the unfree population. Guatemala had so many soldiers that it resembled a penal colony because it *was* a penal colony based on forced labor. The European and Spanish coffee elites ruled over its captive indigenous population like the occupying army they in fact were. As long as the agrarians of the coffee elite ruled in Guatemala, neither popular mobilization nor democracy was on the political agenda.[48]

The most striking contrast with the Guatemalan elite was that of Costa Rica, in which the agrarian fraction was relatively weakly developed because it lost control over substantial amounts of land to a persistent class of family farmers. The agro-industrial fraction, however, was relatively strong. Because it was able to buy cherry coffee from the small farmers, as well as process coffee from its own estates, it developed a highly industrialized form of processing that gave it control over banking, exports, and the small-holder population. The Costa Rican elite was overwhelmingly an elite of processors. Class relations revolved around the relationship between these processors and the small holders, not between the landowners and their laborers. Agricultural laborers on the large estates in Costa Rica were controlled by ties of paternalism that delivered them as a reliable political base for the coffee elite until well after World War II. No substantial popular challenge ever developed from the laborers in coffee. Politics revolved around the gentlemanly disagreements between large and small property owners, and the elite soon found that such conflicts could be easily managed by the gradual extension of the franchise to rural property owners and the establishment of democratic institutions.

El Salvador had both a strong agrarian and a strong agro-industrial fraction in its coffee elite. The power of the agrarian fraction was not, however, based on control of land and captive serfs as in Guatemala, but on the most technically advanced coffee production system in the world. The unintended consequence of this capitalist rationalization of coffee production was the creation of the huge rural proletariat and semi-proletariat that have characterized Salvadoran rural life down to the present. Driven by the profitability of its highly efficient production, the Salvadoran coffee system expanded dramatically, driving a very dense population of small farmers off the land and *colonos* and other captive laborers from their subsistence plots. The agro-industrial fraction of the elite also developed rapidly in response to the need to process the immense volumes of coffee generated in the production system, but never achieved independence from the equally powerful and wealthy agrarian fraction. Salvadoran elite politics tended to oscillate between the policies of the slightly more progressive agro-industrial fraction and the agrarians, who proved at least as reactionary as their Guatemalan equivalents. A well-justified fear of popular mobilization from the rural proletariat kept the two fractions united in support of the reactionary policies of the agrarians throughout much of this century.

As the cases of Guatemala, Costa Rica, and El Salvador clearly indicate, the relative success of democratic or authoritarian political institutions in Central America is closely related to the agrarian or agro-industrial bases of their coffee elites. The greater the weight of the agrarian fraction in the elite, the greater the likelihood of authoritarian institutions to discipline and control the mass of hand labor that is the inescapable condition of estate-based coffee production. Whether that system was institutionalized in formal debt servitude as in Guatemala, or in the form of a militarized rural constabulary as in El Salvador, it functioned to inhibit democratic institutions wherever a strong agrarian fraction arose. As Barrington Moore so persuasively and accurately argued in *Social Origins*, the presence of a landed elite dependent on labor-repressive agriculture is an insurmountable obstacle to democratic institutions. Only in Costa Rica was the coffee elite dominated by the agro-industrial rather than the agrarian fraction, and only in Costa Rica did democratic institutions develop before the 1990s. Similarly, the inability of the agro-industrial fraction of the Salvadoran elite to separate itself from the retrograde agrarians has inhibited the development of democracy in that country.

The failure of democracy to develop in Nicaragua was only indirectly related to the pattern of class relations in the coffee industry. United States intervention in 1912 reversed the coffee elite's Liberal revolution of 1893 and inhibited the development of the coffee industry. Nicaragua remained backward in both production and processing and therefore developed neither a strong agrarian nor agro-industrial elite in coffee. Similarly, neither a large rural proletariat nor a substantial class of commercial small holders developed in the Nicaraguan coffee production. Capitalist class relations remained weak or non-existent in the Nicaraguan coffee economy throughout most of the twentieth century. The relative absence of well-defined classes and the United States military occupation insured that popular mobilization, when it came, would be based not on the class-centered doctrines of socialism but on anti-imperialist nationalism. The coffee elite itself, on the other hand, continued trying to resume the Liberal revolution of 1893, interrupted by the U.S. intervention. In 1979 some members of the elite viewed the Sandinista revolution as such an opportunity. Their support for the revolution was critical to its initial success. Elite support for dictatorship, democracy, and revolution was closely related to the pattern of class relations in the early twentieth-century coffee industry.

Class relations in the coffee industry also influenced the mass movements that arose in response to the political and social crisis of the Great Depression. In El Salvador the rural proletariat rose up in the only mass-based Communist insurrection in Latin American history, and was savagely repressed by a unified elite following the hard line of the agrarian fraction. In Costa Rica a moderate reformist movement of small coffee farmers arose to successfully challenge the monopoly of the processors, although here, as in El Salvador, popular mobilization outside the coffee sector was led by the Communists. In Nicaragua an anti-Yankee nationalist movement arose in the north central coffee zone to challenge both foreign control of the Nicaraguan economy and foreign occupation by the United States. Advanced proletarianization in Salvadoran coffee cultivation favored the Communists; small-holder dominance in Costa Rica favored populist reformism; the absence of developed class relations in Nicaragua and the presence of the United States favored nationalism. The elite response to the protest movements of the 1930s led directly to the political regimes that confronted in such different ways the crisis of the 1980s.

In El Salvador the repression of the desperate insurrection launched by the coffee proletariat in 1932 led directly to the imposition of a ferocious military authoritarianism that would dominate that country until 1979. In Nicaragua the repression of the anti-imperialist nationalism of Sandino in the 1930s by the Marines created the Nicaraguan National Guard and the Somoza regime that dominated Nicaragua too until 1979. In Costa Rica the processor elite easily handled the modest challenge from small growers in the 1930s, but vehemently and finally violently opposed the challenge from the Communists and reformers in their own ranks. Yet the absence of a powerful agrarian fraction in Costa Rica made expansion of democracy possible after 1948, even if the coffee elite had initially opposed it. The social origins of dictatorship, democracy, and socialist revolution in Central America at the start of the 1980s are to be found in the political response to the crisis of the 1930s. The social origins of the crisis of the 1980s are also to be found in the class relations of the agro-export sector, but by then both the class relations and the agro-export sector itself had changed fundamentally from what they had been in the first half of the century.

Class Relations, 1950–1980

Table 11 summarizes the macro-economic pattern of change in the Central American agro-export economy in the period 1950–1980. As is immediately evident, the most obvious change is the spectacular expansion of the new exports—cattle, sugar, and cotton. Cotton production scarcely existed in Central America in 1950. By the 1970s the narrow coastal strip of Central America had become, after the United States South and Egypt, the third greatest cotton-producing region in the world.[49] In Nicaragua in particular the expansion was spectacular, and cotton made up almost half of total exports by the 1970s. There was also exponential growth in cotton exports in El Salvador and Guatemala (but not in Costa Rica), although they

Table 11. Cotton, Cattle, Sugar, and Coffee Area and Production 1950–1979 in Costa Rica, El Salvador, Guatemala, and Nicaragua

| | Cotton | | | | | Cattle | |
| | 1948–52 | | 1967 | | 1979 | (1,000 head) | |
	Area[a]	Prod.[b]	Area	Prod.	Prod.	1947–52	1974
Costa Rica	—	—	12	.10	.10	601	1,767
El Salvador	30	.18	76	.80	1.58	795	1,009
Guatemala	3	.04	130	1.72	3.21	977	1,916
Nicaragua	68	.40	211	2.24	2.40	1,068	2,600

| | Sugar | | | | Coffee | | | |
| | 1961–65 | | 1977 | | 1950 | | 1977 | |
	Area	Prod.[c]	Area	Prod.	Area	Prod.[b]	Area	Prod.
Costa Rica	35	1,082	54	2,160	74	.51	115	1.74
El Salvador	36	1,060	55	3,300	162	1.64	213	3.96
Guatemala	46	1,960	123	6,800	235	1.27	391	3.23
Nicaragua	30	971	51	2,578	39	.43	61	1.36

[a]Area = thousands of *manzanas*
[b]Production = millions of *quintales*
[c]Production = thousands of metric tons
Source: Adapted from James Dunkerly, *Power in the Isthmus* (London: Verso, 1990), Tables 11a and 11b, pp. 187–189. Dunkerly's tables are adapted from an unpublished paper by Edelberto Torres-Rivas, "The Beginning of Industrialization in Central America" (Washington, D.C.: Latin American Program, Wilson Center, 1984).

constituted a much smaller proportion of total exports.[50] Traditional Central American cattle production was reoriented toward export and technologically transformed by meat packing plants, refrigeration, and container ships. Meat exports, which scarcely existed in 1950, exploded throughout the region. The redistribution of the Cuban sugar franchise to loyal anti-Communist regimes created a bonanza for the Central American sugar industry. Between 1950 and the late 1970s Central American cotton production expanded by a factor of ten, cattle herds doubled, and sugar production almost tripled.

Even coffee expanded substantially, in both area and production (Table 11). Particularly in Costa Rica and to a lesser extent El Salvador, this was accompanied by a technological transformation of the industry. Chemical pesticides, fertilizers, and sun-tolerant high-density varieties dramatically increased yields, lowered resident and even harvest labor requirements, and increased the ratio of migratory to resident labor, dramatically increasing the size of the semi-proletariat. Nicaragua and Guatemala lagged far behind in these changes, but even here yields almost doubled between 1950 and 1980 (see Table 6 above), although they still barely reached the level of El Salvador in 1950. Except for Costa Rica and Honduras, where bananas had been an important factor, before the war the region had been virtually a monoculture in coffee. Despite the more than doubling of coffee exports in the period 1950–1980, the real story of the postwar expansion is the bonanza of new agro-export crops. Production of these new crops gave rise to class relations that were very different from those under even the most technologically advanced forms of coffee production. All of the new crops were produced by agro-industrial enterprises that required vastly more capital and considerably less labor than even efficient coffee production.[51] The result of the rise of these new industries, and of the technological transformation of coffee itself, was a dramatic expansion of the agro-industrial fraction of the Central American elite and an equally dramatic expansion of marginally employed and unemployed former rural workers who made up the new semi-proletariat and informal sector.

The cotton boom was made possible by the massive use of pesticides, and ever-increasing amounts of chemical fertilizers were necessary to maintain soil fertility. Production was extensively mechanized. Crop-dusting aircraft, tractors, and cultivating equipment were widely used, and, toward the end of the boom, harvesting machinery was introduced in Nicaragua. Cotton also stimulated associated manufacturing activities, not only in cotton gins but in textiles and cottonseed oil production, both for domestic markets. Similarly, meat-packing plants, refrigeration, and containerized shipping were the key to meat exports; ranching itself, practiced with little concern for animal husbandry since colonial times, was transformed by improved breeds, imported feed grains, and fertilized pastures. Sugar had always been an agro-industrial crop, so that its expansion reproduced the factory-in-the-field organization typical of this crop. The largest cotton and sugar mills in Central America were located in Nicaragua, even though coffee milling remained backward. The agro-industrial fraction of the elite was enormously strengthened by these developments.

The agro-industrial elite in these industries was critical in the crisis of the 1980s. Owners of the large Nicaraguan sugar and cotton mills backed the revolution, as did the owner of the largest cotton-seed oil plant, owners of the most mechanized cotton production operation, many of the cotton growers themselves, and even a substantial minority of the coffee growers, particularly the more efficient producers. The Chamorro family was one of the principal partners in the largest sugar mill, San Antonio. In El Salvador the agro-industrial coffee elite controlled sugar and cotton as well. Alfredo Cristiani, as noted, was the sixth largest cotton producer as well as the tenth largest coffee processor in El Salvador. He also owned a firm selling agro-chemicals to cotton growers. Oscar Arias's family controlled one of Costa Rica's largest sugar mills and had extensive interests in cattle and meat exports. One of Arias's partners in the sugar mill was Alfonso Robelo, owner of Nicaragua's largest cotton-seed oil plant, leader of the cotton agro-industrialists of León, and member of the first Sandinista revolutionary junta. The Borgonovos of El Salvador, leading coffee and cotton producers, were also partners in the Arias family sugar mill. As these examples make clear, the agro-industrial elite emerged as the decisive class in Central America in the 1980s both nationally and internationally.

The expansion of cotton, sugar, and coffee ate up three-quarters of a million *manzanas* of some of the best agricultural land in Central America. The expansion of cattle consumed four million *manzanas* of grazing, forest, and agricultural land. Since the new crops were capital- rather than labor-intensive, the result was a failure to absorb the growing Central American population and the displacement of large numbers of *colonos* and small holders, legal and illegal, from the land. The prewar system of Central American agriculture had been based on labor exploitation; the new system was based on labor expulsion. The postwar transformation created the massive semi-proletariat and informal sector that were characteristic of the region. Perhaps a half million part-time migratory laborers were involved in the cotton harvest, a quarter million in Nicaragua alone. Many of them were desperate subsistence farmers without enough land to support themselves. Many other displaced farmers collected in the cities, where the languid pace of industrial expansion failed to absorb them and left them to live as best they could. As was noted in Chapter 1, the consensus of current research indicates that these new classes were the decisive popular force in the Central American revolutions.

The new agro-export economy dramatically changed Central American class relations. The new pattern of class relations as it existed at the start of the revolutionary decade of the eighties is outlined in Figure 2. In comparison to the pattern of class relations in the 1920–1950 period outlined in Figure 1, the most notable change is the rise of the agro-industrial elite to preeminence everywhere except Guatemala, and the creation of a semi-proletariat particularly in El Salvador and Nicaragua. In El Salvador, as the Figure indicates, the agro-industrial fraction of the elite became economically (although not as yet politically) dominant over the agrarian fraction, whereas the opposite was the case in the 1920–1950 period. In Nicaragua, which had no developed classes in the earlier period, the new agro-industrial fraction now dominated, but the agrarian fraction had also been strengthened. In both countries the semi-proletariat became the overwhelming majority of the lower class. In Costa Rica the agrarians lost out to a powerful agro-industrial fraction after 1948, but semi-proletarianization has been re-

Figure 2. Class Relations in Agro-Export Sectors, 1950–1979

EL SALVADOR	COSTA RICA
Agro-Ind.-Agrarian vs. Semi-Proletariat	Agro-Ind.-Farmer vs. (Semi-Proletariat)
GUATEMALA	NICARAGUA
Agrarian-Agro-Ind. vs. Semi-Prol./Serfs	Agro-Ind.-Agrarian vs. Semi-Proletariat

sisted because of the government's development and social welfare policies. A newly strengthened farmer class has become a de facto ally of the agro-industrial elite against an emerging semi-proletariat much smaller than elsewhere in the region. In Guatemala the agrarian order of landlords and serfs is still present, but so are agro-industrialists and a growing semi-proletariat in a mixed system.

The political implications of these developments are described in much greater detail in the chapters that follow. It is sufficient to note here that the rise of the agro-industrialists and the semi-proletariat created a revolutionary crisis not only between the popular classes and the elite but between the two fractions of the elite itself. During the 1980s, immense revolutionary pressure from below began to cause the two fractions of the elite, united in all previous crises, to split apart. By 1992 the agro-industrial elite had managed to separate itself from the agrarians everywhere except in Guatemala, and the agrarian order and the authoritarian regimes that had supported it were in ruins. The ultimate beneficiaries of the revolutionary crisis of the 1980s were the agro-industrialists. By 1992 they had emerged triumphant everywhere, again except for Guatemala. In the three cases that are the focus of this study, class relations in 1992 converged on a single pattern—a dominant agro-industrial elite divested from a now largely defunct agrarian fraction, and a large and ever increasing semi-proletariat. The three societies had also converged on the common political form of representative democracy, and the common economic program and ideology of neo-liberalism. How this came about is a matter not only of class relations but of ideology, politics, and the flux of human action and experience that defined the history of the coffee elite. In this history the crisis of the 1930s was a decisive event.

II

History and Memory:
The Crisis of the 1930s

3

Farabundo Martí and the Failure of Revolutionary Socialism

As the twentieth century began, the coffee elite was in economic, political, and ideological control of Central American society. Its positivist vision of European civilization, agro-exports, infrastructure development, laissez-faire capitalism, and authoritarian rule defined the limits of the possible. The worldwide economic crisis that began with the crash of 1929 initiated a protracted political and social crisis that challenged the agro-export order built on that vision. The resolution of the crises, in turn, created regimes that for better or for worse were to confront the revolutionary crisis of the 1980s. In El Salvador the outline of this new order was already evident in 1931, with the rise to power of General Maximiliano Hernández Martínez, whose sixteen-year authoritarian rule initiated a series of military juntas that would endure until the Salvadoran civil war of the 1980s. In Nicaragua the rise to power of Anastasio Somoza García in 1937 began the dynasty that would endure until 1979. In Costa Rica the crisis was not finally resolved until the civil war of 1948, by which time the economic shocks of the Depression had been confounded by the political and economic dislocations of World War II. In all three cases the coffee elite lost direct power over the political system. In all three cases, however, the new political arrangements preserved the economic and social position of the elite despite determined challenges from other quarters.

The crisis of 1929 also produced alternative ideological visions to challenge the elite's positivist vision of order and progress. In Nicaragua the idiosyncratic Indo-Hispanic nationalism of Augusto César Sandino defined the alternative vision; in both Costa Rica and El Salvador the ideas of the international Communist movement, particularly the position of the Third Communist International, profoundly influenced the alternative visions of society. In all three countries these visions asserted the positions of those left out of the Liberal narrative of order and progress—the poor, the indigenous, the landless, the disenfranchised—and demanded a fundamental redistribution of wealth and power, both nationally and internationally, as a prerequisite for any sustained economic or social development. The challengers expressed their messages in their own national discourses, but all definitively rejected the idea that agro-export development based on a narrow Europeanized social and economic elite would ever lead to improvement for the poor majority in each country. At their most radical, these demands not only struck at the Liberal vision of the coffee elite but at the social and political order derived from the Spanish conquest on which that vision was based.

The alternative visions of the Central American future that emerged from the Depression can be identified with the movements led by three men: Agustín Farabundo Martí (1893–1932), leader of the Salvadoran Communist Party in the insurrection of 1932; Manuel Mora Valverde (1909–), secretary general of the Communist Party of Costa Rica from its founding in 1929 until his resignation in a party split in 1983; and Augusto César Sandino (1895–1934), dissident Liberal general, founder of the guerrilla Army of National Sovereignty, and leader of the successful campaign to expel the United States Marines from Nicaragua. Martí and Sandino were the names chosen by the revolutionary guerrilla fronts of the 1980s in El Salvador (Frente Farabundo Martí para la Liberación Nacional, FMLN) and Nicaragua (Frente Sandinista de Liberación Nacional, FSLN), but it may have been Mora who had the most enduring impact on Central American government and society. The execution of Martí in 1932 and the murder of Sandino in 1934 not only silenced these leaders but effectively suppressed their movements and ideologies for a half-century. Mora survived the Depression and lived to see many of his ideas enacted in law by a Costa Rican governing coalition (1943–1948) his party backed.

Until the renewal of hostilities in the 1980s, the ideas and movements of Martí and Sandino existed as a suppressed undercurrent in Central American society, without a place in the official histories, popular ideologies, and reigning myths of the authoritarian governments that were built on their corpses. In El Salvador public documents and even newspapers from the period of the 1932 insurrection disappeared from libraries and archives, and an official story of Communist savagery was substituted for the actual history of the massacre carried out by the troops under the command of General Maximiliano Hernández Martínez.[1] In Nicaragua Anastasio Somoza García went to the extraordinary length of writing a book to discredit Sandino, justify his murder, and defend the legitimacy of Somoza's own illegal seizure of power.[2] Even though not the slightest trace of the ideas of Martí and Sandino was to be found in the policies and ideologies of the authoritarian rulers of El Salvador and Nicaragua, both regimes were founded on their suppression. For fifty years the principal ideological consequence in Central America of the visions of Martí and Sandino was expressed through their denial.

The Communist Party of Costa Rica was banned by the victorious Liberation Army of José Figueres in 1948. Many leading Communists including Mora were arrested and exiled, and others were killed in the civil war or its aftermath. The Communist Party was not legalized again until 1972. Nevertheless, the social reforms initiated in the tumultuous decade of the 1940s with Communist backing were embraced by the Figueres regime and remain fundamental principles of Costa Rican national politics and consciousness to the present. In El Salvador the Depression crisis added to the order and progress of traditional Liberal ideology a paranoid anti-communism, a deep-rooted fear of change and instability, and a willingness to ally with the most unsavory political regimes and tactics in the defense of privilege. In Nicaragua the heritage of the 1930s was more ambiguous. The coffee elite remained committed to the unrealized Liberal vision of the revolutionaries of the Zelaya era, but at the same time benefited from a regime founded on the ideological suppression of Sandino as a Communist subversive. In all three countries the

Depression added a new element, vehement anti-communism, to the elite's traditional liberal ideology, and in both El Salvador and Nicaragua anti-communism provided the legitimation for a long night of authoritarianism.

The exact way in which the Depression crisis affected elite ideology depended not only on the nature of the alternative vision proposed by the challengers to the coffee elite's Liberal narrative, but on the class relations in the coffee industry and the complex political events set in motion by the challenge in each country. In El Salvador the association of the challengers with an orthodox Communist Party of the Third International profoundly influenced the issues and ideology of the challenge and the nature of its ultimate resolution. The political struggle took place, however, in a social and economic context of acute polarization and class division in the coffee sector that rapidly undermined less doctrinaire positions. In Costa Rica the same orthodox ideology of the Third International became transmuted into a social democratic or Euro-Communist program of "tico" (as Costa Ricans call themselves) or "criollo" (creole) communism, which better suited Costa Rica's democratic traditions and its less polarized class relations in the coffee sector. Finally, in Nicaragua, the United States intervention from 1909 to 1933 and the absence of fully developed social classes in coffee assured that both the central axis of political and economic conflict and the dominant revolutionary vision would be anti-Yankee nationalism rather than class-based communism.

El Salvador: Communism, Class Conflict, and the Insurrection of 1932

During the night of January 22–23, 1932, farmers and agricultural workers in El Salvador launched attacks against several towns in the western coffee-growing districts in response to a call of the Salvadoran Communist Party for a general insurrection. Armed almost exclusively with machetes and hoes, the rebels succeeded in taking the predominantly Indian towns of Juayuá, Izalco, and Nahuizalco in Sonsonante and Tacuba in Ahuachapán, and staged unsuccessful mass assaults on the provincial capitals in both of these provinces and on the towns of Colón and Santa Tecla in La Libertad and the

Llopango-Soyapango area of San Salvador. The revolt had been undermined by the arrest of the Communist Party leadership on the night of January 18 and the disarming of rebels in an army detachment in San Salvador. The military counteroffensive began almost immediately, and the last city to fall, Tacuba, held out for only three days. Military reprisals began with the counteroffensive and lasted for as long as a month in a mass slaughter that has come to be called the *matanza* (massacre) in El Salvador.[3]

During the insurrection the estates of a number of leading planters had been threatened, and many younger members of the elite organized a Civic Guard to assist the army in carrying out reprisals. Anyone with vaguely Indian features, carrying a machete, or dressed like a *campesino* was assumed to be a rebel: a pattern of slaughter by category that would be repeated in the even bloodier massacres of 1980–81. In Izalco groups of fifty were shot at the four corners of the town every day for month; sulfur pits were used to dispose of corpses in Tacuba. Mass graves proved insufficient, and drainage ditches were filled with unburied corpses left for pigs, dogs, and vultures to feed on. One army driver lost his mind for more than two years after being forced to drive his truck over the machine-gunned bodies of the dead and dying. The initial revolt took the lives of at most twenty to thirty civilians, most in pitched battles with the rebels. Responsible estimates of the dead in the *matanza* range from eight to ten to more than twenty-five thousand. If the higher estimates of the numbers dead are to be accepted, the casualties amounted to more than two percent of the total Salvadoran population. In the principal centers of the revolt as much as two-thirds of the population may have perished. Investigators working in the area in the 1970s still found an extreme reluctance to acknowledge the revolt and its aftermath.[4]

The uprising and the subsequent massacre were the defining event in modern Salvadoran political history and in the construction of ruling elite ideology. As Salvadoran poet and revolutionary Roque Dalton, himself murdered in 1975 in a factional dispute in the Salvadoran left, observed, "we were all born half dead in 1932."[5] For Miguel Mármol, a member of the Communist Party central committee in 1932—who survived his own execution to tell his story to Dalton thirty years later—1932 was "for El Salvador what the

Nazi barbarism was for Europe, the North American barbarism in Vietnam, a phenomenon that changed completely, in a negative sense, the face of a nation. . . . After that damned year all of us are different men and I think that from then on El Salvador is a different country." Thomas Anderson, author of the definitive historical work on the revolt, argues that "the whole political labyrinth of El Salvador can be explained only in reference to the traumatic experience of the uprising and the *matanza*."

The official story of the revolt reverses the role of victims and perpetrators and fosters "a legend of bloodthirsty mobs butchering thousands of middle-class citizens, and of a heroic army that barely managed to turn back a barbarian wave." Miguel Mármol asked in 1966, "Why do our historians and journalists continue going along with giving young people a schematic, false and criminal view of 'the massacre' that the communists caused in 1932?"[6] The official view is well presented in the contemporary account of anti-Communist journalist Joaquín Méndez, who accompanied the military forces retaking the western coffee town to describe "the devastating work realized by the indigenous masses excited by Communist agitators."[7] Each civilian casualty of the revolt is described in detail, but military reprisals are not even mentioned. In a mock interview with a typical representative of Salvadoran public opinion in 1972, Dalton is told that the slaughter perpetrated by the *communists* in 1932 "was tremendous." "The Indians took up their machetes against the rich and wound up cutting off everybody's head."[8]

Elite ideology was profoundly influenced by the revolt and the massacre and by their subsequent reinterpretation in official and unofficial history and memory. To understand elite ideology requires an exploration not only of the actual social and economic basis of the revolt but of the interpretations that have been placed on the revolt and its aftermath. The revolt occurred in response to the deep economic and social divisions in Salvadoran rural society created by the coffee agro-export economy, but it was also influenced by the failure of efforts to implement a moderate social reform, the rise of the Communist Party as the leading voice of the left, and the persistence of divisions between Ladinos and Indians dating to the conquest. Each of these features of Salvadoran society influenced both the revolt itself and its subsequent interpretation in the minds of the elite.

Coffee and Class Conflict: The Agrarian Origins of the Insurrection

There is little doubt that the acute class polarization created by the successful rationalization of coffee production in El Salvador was the root cause of the revolt. Indeed, this fact is recognized by both contemporary observers and scholars studying the rebellion. The head of the American legation in El Salvador wrote to his government in February 1932: "The conditions which have permitted this rather sudden rise of so-called communism are well known. Farm workers have been often miserably underpaid and have been working under conditions on some fincas which have been certainly intolerable. On the fincas of many of the richest landowners in Salvador, conditions have been the worst. . . . Frequently it has been asserted that a farm animal is of more general value than the worker for there is generally a plentiful supply of the later."[9] The commander of a Canadian destroyer, who briefly landed with a detachment of Marines during the insurrection in response to pleas from the British and Canadian embassies, described rural conditions as "low wages, incredible filth, utter lack of consideration on the part of the employers, conditions not in fact far removed from slavery."[10] Dynasty founder James Hill acknowledged, in his own way, the severity of the agrarian crisis, "Bolshevism? It's drifting in. The working people hold meetings on Sundays and get very excited. They say, 'We dig the holes for the trees, we clean the weeds, we prune the trees, we pick the coffee. Who earns the money then? We do.' Yes there will be trouble one of these days."[11]

The revolution in Salvadoran coffee production between the 1870s and the 1920s had established a situation of acute class polarization unique in Central America. The alienation of communal and public lands that occurred between the formal legal abolition of communal land in 1881–82 and the 1920s created both a resentful, displaced peasantry and a growing proletarianized labor force recruited from this same peasantry.[12] Although Liberal land reform had accompanied the development of coffee production throughout the region, the Salvadoran reforms of 1881–82 were the most radical, reflecting not only the growing influence of the coffee planters in government but the traditional Liberal ideology of the elite. In these two years communal forms of property were eliminated throughout the country as an impediment to agricultural development and economic growth. Private property was imposed as the only legal form of land ownership. Although the process of sorting out individual claims to land continued well into the twentieth century and had actually begun before the reforms, the outcome was the elimination of access to land for much of the population. As much as 40 percent of the arable land had been in communal tenure in 1879, and 50 to 60 percent of the population may have depended on it.[13] The Liberal reforms simultaneously freed the land and the labor.

The effect of the reforms was intensified by the density and distribution of the population. El Salvador was and is the most densely populated country in Latin America and unlike other countries in Central America, it had no agricultural frontier to absorb the displaced population. Furthermore, the most densely settled areas were also prime coffee land, so that coffee directly displaced subsistence cultivators. In the prime belt of coffee land extending from Sonsonate to Ahuachapán, the fields eventually became almost continuous, leaving no room for subsistence cultivators.[14] Coffee estates, unlike traditional haciendas, usually supplied food for their cultivators because the available land was given over to coffee. Much of the western coffee zone had also been an area of strong indigenous communities, and this was particularly true in the central area of the revolt around Izalco in Sonsonate. The coffee area expanded by more than 50 percent in the 1920s, so that by 1929 there were many displaced peasants with vivid memories of the loss of traditional access to community lands.[15] The insurrection was in fact concentrated in those areas in which maximum coffee production overlapped with the maximum concentration of communal land holdings in the past.[16]

The land expropriations created a large proletariat and semi-proletariat of agricultural wage laborers without parallel elsewhere in the region. In the middle of the nineteenth century coffee and indigo producers reported labor shortages, but by the end of the century the land shortage created by coffee expansion made labor freely available and it was unnecessary to recruit it through vagrancy laws.[17] This pattern only intensified in the 1920s with the expansion of coffee production. Two thirds of the total increase of population of 323,000 between 1918 and 1930 was concentrated in the principal coffee-growing departments.[18] By 1929 large numbers of rural workers in the coffee region lacked access to land or had too little land to support their families and depended on permanent or harvest labor on coffee estates for a marginal subsistence income. The 1929 crash removed much of even this meagre income. The Liberal land reform had eliminated subsistence based on traditional agriculture. The crash eliminated subsistence based on the subsequent development of wage labor. The very success of the coffee elite in the expansion and rationalization of production had created a social and economic disaster of immense proportions for much of the population.

The disaster struck with full force in 1930. Coffee prices had already begun to move downward even before the October stock market crash of 1929, but by 1930 they were at less than half their peak levels of the mid-twenties, and by 1932, at less than a third of these levels.[19] Most growers were unable to make mortgage payments and were nominally in default, leaving three large banks as the de facto owners of three quarters of El Salvador in 1931.[20] Wages, which constituted more than two thirds of production costs, were slashed to levels that were less than half of those prevailing in the 1920s. After the government prohibited the export of gold in October 1931, many bankers were reluctant to make loans to growers to cover harvest wages and, according to Thomas Anderson, "coffee rotted in the fields."[21] The harvest of 1931–32 was about 30 percent smaller than the average of the previous two years, and demand for harvest labor declined accordingly.[22] Although, with the exception of that critical year's harvest, growers maintained or even increased production, and the area planted in coffee expanded throughout the 1930s, it is likely that, like other coffee growers faced with financial crisis, the Salvadorans postponed routine maintenance and discharged permanent workers. In the critical harvest of 1931–32, workers were faced with a 50 percent wage cut and massive reductions in employment.[23]

Both the loss of communal lands and firings and wage reductions were principal issues in the revolt. Feliciano Ama, Indian *cacique* of

Izalco and a leader of the revolt, showed Miguel Mármol the scars on his fingers from being hanged by his thumbs and beaten on orders of the Regalado family after they had stripped him of his lands. He pointed out the lands he still controlled and explained how he intended to allot the lands to the poor Indians who had nothing. Ama never managed to carry out his dream of a restoration of indigenous land tenure. He was publicly hanged in the town square in Izalco during the *matanza*.[24] Modesto Ramírez, another leader of the revolt also executed in 1932, had been a Ladino agricultural laborer on various haciendas near Lake Llopango. Shortly before his death he told right-wing Guatemalan journalist Alfredo Schlesinger: "There came a time when we were not given land or work, or if there was land, it was of the worst quality . . . I had to abandon my wife and children. I did not get enough work to be able to give them food, still less clothing, or to educate them. I do not know where they are. Misery has separated us forever. . . . For this I became a Communist."[25]

Miguel Mármol, Communist party member and rural labor organizer who worked in the western coffee regions in 1931–32, found peasants everywhere indignant at "being treated like slaves, by slaveholders on plantations and estates, starvation wages, arbitrary and inconsistent wage reductions, massive unjustified firings, evictions of tenant farmers, systematic refusal to lease land, worsening of working conditions of the tenant farmers, destruction of the crops of unruly peasants by burning the sown fields or letting loose all the livestock on them to graze, to closing of all pathways across the plantations and estates—direct and fierce repression by the national guard in the form of imprisonment, expulsions from homes, burning of houses."[26] The national guard, which had originally been organized in 1912 in a civic-minded effort to contain crime and brigandage, had rapidly become an instrument of rural labor control, and local commanders acted on the orders of local landowners.[27]

A remarkable and unprecedented outpouring of protest and organizing by rural workers in response to their deteriorating economic situation after 1929 was met with direct repression by the army, the national guard, and local landowners. In the spring of 1930 a Mexican farm-worker organizer, Jorge Fernández Anaya, arrived in

El Salvador and began a remarkably successful organizing campaign in western El Salvador, speaking in Náhuatl to growing and enthusiastic crowds of indigenous farm workers. By April 1930 organizers were able to secure fifty thousand signatures for a workers' law that would guarantee contracts and set minimum wages for farm workers. On May Day 1930 an estimated 80,000 farm workers marched through downtown San Salvador to demand better conditions and the right to organize.[28]

On August 12 the government responded by prohibiting organizing and workers' rallies and initiating a reign of "white terror." Continuing strikes and demonstrations by rural workers in late 1930 and throughout 1931 were met with violent repression by units of the army and National Guard, which opened fire on unarmed workers. In May 1931 Indian peasants and rural workers from surrounding towns stormed the provincial capital of Sonsonate, in a preview of events of the insurrection, and were fired on by army and national guard units.[29] By late 1931 groups of hundreds of enraged peasants were besieging army outposts in Ahuachapán in western El Salvador. Miguel Mármol, sent by the Communist party to persuade the peasanrs to stand down, was told that the next such pacific representative was going to have to "face our machetes even before the class enemy."[30]

The Communist Party of El Salvador was not founded until 1930, and the principal Communist labor federation had only 1,500 members, almost all of them artisanal workers in San Salvador, in that year.[31] The Communists had virtually no organizational network in the countryside and relied on loose networks of local leaders rather than any organized structure of party cells.[32] The upsurge in the countryside thus appears to have been largely a spontaneous mass movement with a momentum of its own. The Depression and the deep-rooted class polarization of the Salvadoran coffee sector had already brought the countryside to a situation of open revolt even before the formal declaration of the insurrection in January 1932. Even without political leadership, it is likely that some form of spontaneous uprising would have broken out in the principal coffee regions. But the political situation in El Salvador focused the growing rural discontent on an attempt to overthrow the government in the name of a worker-peasant revolt. The politicization of discontent was in turn a consequence of both the failure of the reformist option in El Salvador and the growing strength of the Communist Party.

Arturo Araujo, Alberto Masferrer, and the Failure of Social Reform

In 1927 Pío Romero Bosque, the hand-picked candidate of the Meléndez-Quiñónez dynasty, assumed the presidency of the republic. He proved to be a surprisingly independent choice, even crushing a revolt organized by Jorge Meléndez in December 1927, when the dynasty found they could no longer control him. Don Pío, as he is universally called in El Salvador, initiated the first, and some would argue the last, era of genuine democracy in the country's history. Faced with growing discontent toward the end of his term of office, Don Pío announced that the election of 1931 would be fully free and open to all and not simply a ratification of the chosen successor of the incumbent, as had been the case for the previous twenty-five years. Six candidates announced for the presidency, and the winner in a free and open vote was Arturo Araujo, candidate of the newly formed Labor Party of El Salvador. Araujo was an aristocratic landowner who had studied engineering at the University of London and had lived with a union shop steward and Labour Party activist while practicing his profession in England. (His Salvadoran Labor Party was modeled after the British Labour Party, which Araujo had come to admire.) On his return to El Salvador Araujo became a model employer, reportedly paying twice the usual wages to his workers, and was a popular figure in labor circles. He was frequently invited to political meetings of workers, and after 1918 was admiringly called "Benefactor of the Working Class in General."[33] In 1920 he attempted to organize an invasion from Honduras to overthrow the Meléndez government, and although the attempt came to nothing, it gained him the reputation as a fighter for progressive political causes.[34]

Araujo was widely distrusted in ruling class circles, and his election was the result of widespread support from urban and rural workers and peasants. He also gained the support of El Salvador's foremost intellectual and social reformer, Alberto Masferrer, whose doctrine of the "vital minimum" became the basis for Araujo's campaign. Masferrer's philosophy combined an anarcho-socialist vision based on the works of Tolstoy, Henry George, Kropotkin, and Marx with a mystical theosophy derived from Eastern philosophy. Although he described himself as a socialist because, in his words, "socialism is the most holy doctrine, it is Christianity in it most advanced consequences," it was clear that his deepest commitment was to social reform based on a change in the collective consciousness.[35] The concept "vital minimum" referred to what Masferrer argued was the moral right of every worker to a decent minimum standard of living, consisting of honest work, adequate food, decent housing, safe drinking water, adequate clothing, medical care, equal justice, free primary education, and leisure and recreation sufficient to "restore the body and the spirit."[36] Although Masferrer outlined no specific economic program, he believed that once the vital minimum had been accepted as a basic right, governments would commit themselves to providing for it in the same way they raised armies and financed public works. He also attacked what he called the "feudal" land-owning structure of El Salvador and advocated a land reform in which every peasant would be guaranteed access to land.[37]

Masferrer was denounced by the right as a "dangerous Bolshevik" and a "criminal agitator," but Araujo embraced his philosophy during the campaign.[38] Araujo supporters made vague promises of land reform during the campaign which the candidate did little to disavow. Araujo was also supported by the radical Partido Proletario Salvadoreño led by Felipe Recinos, although he was forced to disavow Recinos during the campaign.[39] To much of the oligarchy Araujo appeared to be a dangerous outsider threatening the established order, and after his election they boycotted his administration, leaving him with few experienced officials.[40] Once in office, Araujo advanced a modest reform program which included improving education, expanding the supply of potable water, reforming municipal administration, limiting the sale of alcoholic beverages, protecting Salvadoran labor from foreign competition, protecting the status of women, and establishing a free medical aid program throughout the country. He also undertook a limited land reform program based on government land purchases.[41] Together his programs represented a progressive and democratic opening for El Salvador, but they were rapidly overwhelmed by financial crisis and popular desperation.

In a popular view that, according to Alastair White, has "acquired almost the status of established fact in El Salvador," Araujo is viewed as "well-intentioned but inept and ineffective."[42] It is more likely that the popular demands generated by the economic crisis and the conservative structure of the agro-export economy left him with little room for maneuver. There were rumors of a coup attempt shortly after his election, and in part to gain military support, he appointed presidential candidate General Maximiliano Hernández Martínez as his Vice President and Minister of Defense. Martínez had withdrawn his own candidacy and thrown his limited support to Araujo.[43] Two days after his inauguration, Araujo faced a large crowd of workers and peasants outside the presidential palace demanding immediate action. In April and May of 1931 demonstrations and strikes by rural workers were increasingly met by military action, and the President was forced to rely more heavily on Martínez.[44]

Alberto Masferrer, disappointed in Araujo's modest program, withdrew his support and became an outspoken critic of the government from his seat in the National Assembly.[45] The left, led by Agustín Farabundo Martí, kept up a steady barrage of criticism of the government, and attempts to silence Martí by arresting him provoked a successful hunger strike, more demonstrations on his behalf, and growing loss of confidence in the government. A rally in Sonsonate to demand Martí's freedom led to a massacre when troops opened fire; there were more deaths the next day, when peasants from the surrounding towns poured into Sonsonate.[46] On July 11 the National Assembly approved a $1 million loan from American banks to deal with a government financial crisis so severe that even military salaries had fallen into arrears. The next day a student demonstration, organized to protest the loan as a concession to foreign imperialists, was met by army troops, with serious clashes between students and soldiers. Araujo was forced to declare a state of siege.[47] On October 7 the government prohibited the export of gold, causing a near revolt in the banking community.[48] By the end of 1931 the coffee economy was close to financial collapse, and rural protest was reaching alarming proportions.

On December 2 a military coup deposed Araujo after brief resistance by loyal forces, and General Martínez was asked to assume the presidency. There is considerable doubt concerning Martínez's role in the coup, but there is no doubt that he was its eventual beneficiary.[49] Araujo's program of social reform and El Salvador's brief democratic opening had come to an end. Given the polarized nature of the Salvadoran agrarian order and the behavior of other political actors, it is difficult to see what policy Araujo could have followed that would have satisfied the demands of the impoverished rural and urban workers and nationalist students that were his constituency without threatening the coffee export oligarchy and its allies in the military. Demands for unionization and minimum wages for agricultural workers were simply incompatible with the polarized Salvadoran coffee order, and improvements in the school system could not address the urgency of the economic crisis of the workers. Land reform on the scale necessary to address the agrarian crisis would have threatened the proprietary base of the coffee order. If the left had been united, it might have been able to challenge the power of the financial and agrarian interests and their military allies. After all, there had been resistance to the coup attempt, and Araujo had attempted to mount a defense. But the left had been among Araujo's harshest critics, and no effort to save him came from that quarter.

The program of Masferrer and Araujo represented a progressive social democratic opening for El Salvador, and even Araujo's minimum program would have greatly improved the lives of the rural poor. Sixty years later most of the rural population is still illiterate, still lacks potable water, and even minimal medical services. A similar modest beginning by another upper-class reformer in Costa Rica led to the founding of one of Latin America's most successful welfare states. But in El Salvador acute class polarization and a long tradition of oligarchic rule made such an outcome unlikely. The moderate social democratic program of Masferrer and Araujo rapidly lost ground to the growing influence of the militant left represented by the Communist Party of El Salvador. It was the Communists, not Araujo, who defined the terms of the final resolution of the Depression crisis in the insurrection that ended in the *matanza* of 1932.

The Communist Party of El Salvador, the Communist International, and the Insurrection of 1932

The leaders of the Communist Party apparently made the decision to launch the 1932 insurrection without consulting the Communist International or anyone else,[50] but the influence of the International on the Salvadoran Communists was nonetheless profound. The ideology and strategy of the Party from its earliest activities in the 1920s to its virtual extermination in 1932 were closely modeled after the theories and dictates of the International. Thirty years after the insurrection, Miguel Mármol continued to insist that the Party had followed a "correct" line based on "fundamental Leninist norms," although he conceded that the "sectarian tendency" of the Communist International had influenced the thinking of the Salvadoran leaders. According to Mármol, the failure of the insurrection was a result of vacillation and disorganization in the application of a fundamentally correct line.[51]

The Salvadoran Party leadership was closely following developments in the international Communist movement, although it had only weak ties to the Communist International.[52] Farabundo Martí, the informal leader of the Party, was the Salvadoran representative of the Caribbean Bureau of International Red Aid closely allied with the International. When Martí was deported to the United States in December 1930, he was met by the members of the Labor Defense Committe of the International.[53] Jorge Anaya, the Salvadoran Party's most successful peasant organizer, was a representative of the Mexican Communist Party with close ties to the International.[54] Miguel Mármol and Modesto Rodríguez, both leaders in the 1932 revolt, went to the 1930 World Congress of Red Trade Unions (Profintern) in Moscow and were vigorous participants in its debates on Latin America.[55] Two Salvadoran delegates attended the most important meeting of the Latin American Section of the Comintern, the conference in Buenos Aires in June 1929.[56] The Secretary General of the Party had been a delegate to the founding meeting in Buenos Aires of the Latin American Trade Union Confederation, strongly influenced by labor leaders associated with the International.[57]

The impact of the Russian Revolution and of the Third International on the Salvadoran Communist Party was greater, however, than any strictly organizational ties. An underground publication called the *Bolshevik Submarine* circulated in San Salvador, and the popularity of the Revolution led to crazes for "Bolshevik bread," "Bolshevik shoes," and "Bolshevik sweets" in local markets.[58] In 1917 Alfonso Quiñónez of the ruling dynasty actually founded a labor organization called the Red League (Liga Roja), with a red flag as its banner, to further his own (conservative) political ambitions.[59] The leading intellectuals of the party, Martí and his student followers, Alfonso Luna and Mario Zapata, read *Capital* in French translation, typewritten and even written out by hand, but it was the influence of Lenin, according to Miguel Mármol, that was decisive with party activists. He mentions Lenin's "Left-wing Communism: An Infantile Disorder," and "Proletarian Revolution and Renegade Kautsky" as particularly important.[60]

As was the case throughout Latin America, the most profound effect of the International was theoretical. As Manuel Caballero notes, "Marxism, or even socialism, arrived wrapped in Leninism not to say Stalinism."[61] In Europe Communist parties emerged in opposition to powerful and long-established socialist trade unions and parties that remained major competitors to Leninist ideas. El Salvador lacked any tradition of democratic socialism or trade unions; the only other significant force on the left, Araujo's Labor Party, was itself only two years old when the Communist Party was founded in March 1930. For better or for worse the ideas of Lenin and the organization he founded, the Third Communist International, defined the Salvadoran Communist Party, which emerged as the dominant factor on the Salvadoran left. The consequences for both the Salvadoran left and the ideology of its elite opponents were profound.

Given the immense influence of Leninism and of the Third International on the Salvadoran Communists and the doctrinaire policies of the Salvadoran Party, it is important to review the key theoretical ideas of the Third International. Founded in March 1919 in the flush of Bolshevik victory, the organization was dedicated to spreading the Revolution throughout the world. Whatever twists and turns the International's policies may have taken, this remained its only goal from its founding in 1919 to its dissolution by Stalin in 1943. Even though tactical alliances and popular fronts may have been permitted at various times, they were seen only as temporary expedients on the road to violent and worldwide proletarian revolution. Democratic socialism and reformism were decisively rejected, and indeed the Third International had been explicitly founded to oppose the "social chauvinism" of the parties of the Second International, which, it was claimed, had led to failure and world war.[62]

Whatever changes of direction may have been imposed by his successors, the central direction of the International was set by Lenin in his lifetime. In particular, it reflected his obsessional anti-Menshevism and contempt for bourgeois reformers and democratic socialists of any stripe. This was the unequivocal message of those manuals of political action, "Left-Wing Communism" and "Renegade Kautsky," which were studied carefully by the founders of the Salvadoran Communist Party. Despite its title, "Left-Wing Communism" actually designates the "opportunism" and "social-chauvinism" of social democratic parties as the principal enemies of the working class movement, compared to which "left doctrinairism" is "one thousand times less dangerous."[63] In the savage invective characteristic of his polemical work, Lenin accused "renegade" Kautsky of "civilized belly-crawling and bootlicking before the bourgeoisie," and declared "merciless war against the desertion of principles" represented by Kautsky and other social democrats, who would "castrate Marxism" by purging it of its revolutionary soul.[64]

These principles were faithfully followed by the International, particularly after the Sixth Party Congress in 1928, when the Comintern proclaimed a so-called "third period" of intensified class conflict and revolution and adopted a radical "class against class" line that rejected any cooperation with the "social fascism" of social democratic parties. The disastrous consequences of this policy in the Western European socialist movement, notably in Weimar Germany, are well known. The consequences in El Salvador were to place the party in defiant opposition to the reformism of Araujo and Masferrer and to the non-Communist labor movement. As Martí biographer and Party member Jorge Arias Gómez noted in 1972, Araujo's "laborism" was regarded by the Party as "a screen of reformism fabricated by a wing of the oligarchy."[65] Alberto Masferrer was denounced as a class traitor, a right-wing socialist, and a naive utopian.[66] Miguel Mármol asserted with pride that the labor movement had followed Lenin in purging "reformists and anarcho-syndicalists."[67] The Party newspaper *Estrella Roja* announced that the "blunders of Araujo" had imposed on the military "the moral obligation of overthrowing him."[68] Martí apparently believed that the chances for a successful insurrection were actually better under a military regime.[69]

Although Martí, who wore a red star with a picture of Trotsky in his lapel, was no Stalin or even a Lenin, he was nonetheless known for his rigid adherence to Marxist-Leninist principles and his fiery anger at those he regarded as the class enemy. According to Miguel Mármol, Martí used to observe that "a leader of the poor must be the angriest one, the most outraged in the face of the class enemy." "A born fighter," according to Mármol, "with an aggressiveness that would distress anyone," Martí lived up to his own dictum.[70] In college he had challenged his sociology professor to a duel after a philosophical argument ended in personal abuse. He was exiled for the first time after he denounced President Jorge Meléndez to his face.[71] A meeting with Araujo at the height of the 1930s crisis ended when Martí became furious and insulted the President.[72] His failure to convert Sandino to his own uncompromising Marxist-Leninist line led him to break with the Nicaraguan revolutionary and denounce him for "betraying the world anti-imperialist movement in order to make himself into a liberal petty bourgeois caudillo."[73] The radical "class against class" line of the International fit Martí's own combative and uncompromising nature.

The Salvadoran Communist Party also followed the International's prescription for revolution in backward societies. The International called for revolutionaries to strike at the "weakest link" of the world capitalist systems in backward societies termed "dependent, semi-colonial or colonial," lacking industry, and hence without a developed proletariat or bourgeoisie. The vanguard of the Communist Party was to substitute itself for the absent bourgoisie, and on behalf of the workers and peasants carry out a "bourgeois-democratic" revolution that was both "agrarian" and "anti-imperialist." The "bourgeois-democratic" revolution would not only clear out the feudal agrarian relations, authoritarian political structures, and foreign economic domination that were the obstacles to the development of a national bourgeoisie, but would then "grow over" into "a proletarian-socialist" revolution in which power would pass to "worker-peasant soviets" in the manner of the Russian Revolution. The "bourgeois-democratic" revolution led by the Party vanguard would therefore jump directly to socialism without passing through a stage of industrial capitalist development.[74]

As Rodolfo Cerdas Cruz has pointed out, the Salvadoran Communists put into practice almost every component of the International's revolutionary strategy, including "the slogans of class against class, of transformation of the bourgeois-democratic revolution into a socialist revolution through the hegemony of the proletariat in the former, by means of the democratic revolutionary dictatorship of the workers and peasants, . . . to leap over the epoch of capitalist development . . . toward the formation of a federation of republics of worker peasant soviets."[75] The Salvadoran Party's final call to revolt on 21 January ended with the words, "All Power to the Soviets of Workers, Peasants and Soldiers."[76] Indeed, worker-peasant soviets were briefly proclaimed in towns taken by the Salvadoran rebels and lasted for three days in Tacuba, where efforts were made to carry out the "agrarian revolution" through land reform.[77] Forty years after the great insurrection, Miguel Mármol still stated its objectives in the language of the International. "Our party proposed to lead the people united around one great objective: the realization of bourgeois-democratic revolution."[78]

The failure of the 1932 insurrection set off an unseemly scramble to dissociate the International and the party line from the "leftist sectarianism" and "adventurism" of the Communist Party of El Salvador, even though the Salvadorans had followed the International line exactly.[79] The insurrection provided no real test of the viability of the International's revolutionary strategy, however, because of the extraordinary organizational and tactical failures of the Salvadoran Communists. The entire Party leadership was betrayed and arrested four days before the revolt, and sympathetic military units were also exposed and disarmed. Party activists had neglected even to arm themselves, let alone seek military training, and the Party apparatus scarcely existed in most areas. Finally, the military was informed in advance of the revolt by the Party itself, when a delegation called on General Martínez to negotiate calling off the revolt in exchange for an end to the repression.[80] As Miguel Mármol ruefully observed of the insurrection, "we did it too late, like assholes, we did it after the enemy had begun his repression and delivered devastating blows to our leadership apparatus, to the basic military nucleus, putting us totally on the defensive."[81]

Even if the Salvadoran Communists had created a disciplined Leninist organization and avoided their tactical blunders, the fundamental question of the viability of the overall Leninist strategy of the International would remain. Certainly the "class against class" line split the left, contributed to the collapse of Araujo's government, and foreclosed a further democratic opening. But Lenin himself had denounced Kerensky and "bourgeois democracy" and triumphed with scarcely more support than the Salvadoran Communists commanded in 1932. In a later period revolutionary Leninists with more sophisticated military organizations, derived from Mao's doctrines of people's war, did succeed in Latin America—in Cuba and Nicaragua but, once again, not in El Salvador. If the Leninist strategy of the International is to be blamed for the disastrous collapse of the democratic left in that country, it must also be given credit for the later triumphs of Communist revolutions inspired by these doctrines.

There is little doubt, however, that the narrow base of the "bourgeois-democratic" revolution in El Salvador severely limited whatever prospects the revolution enjoyed for wide popular acceptance and eventual success. The "class against class" line and the "worker-peasant soviets" excluded not only the considerable number of supporters of Araujo's reformism but also much of the property-owning peasantry and small merchants and professionals of the towns, to say nothing of progressive members of the bourgeoisie or landowning elite like Araujo himself. The Communists' revolutionary appeals to the rural proletariat and poor peasants gained a popular following because these groups were a major force in El Salvador, particularly in the western coffee regions. But this message also limited their appeal elsewhere in the country, and it terrified property owners and defenders of the established order everywhere. Many of these groups not only did not support the revolt but enthusiastically supported its suppression, leaving the Salvadoran Communists and their supporters fatally isolated.

It is difficult to avoid the conclusion that the 1932 catastrophe was not simply a failure of organization and tactics but a failure of the Communist International's strategy of revolution. Even a better-organized revolt would have been handicapped by the narrow social base and sectarian political isolation dictated by the Communists' revolutionary dogma. On the other hand, it is not clear that a more inclusive social democratic strategy along the lines of Araujo's reformism could have prevailed, given the extraordinary class polarization and agrarian discontent in the country. The options available to the left in 1932 were in fact extremely limited. The strategy of the International, however, turned out to be a recipe for disaster not only for the victims of the *matanza* but for the political future of El Salvador.

The fact that El Salvador's only experience with social reform and popular mobilization ended in insurrection led by sectarian followers of the Communist International profoundly influenced popular and elite attitudes toward reform and social change. As Thomas Anderson has pointed out, ever since 1932 a "paranoid fear of communism . . . has gripped the nation," expressed in "the continual labeling of even the most modest reform movements as communist or communist inspired."[82] In 1932 the revolutionary thesis of the Communist International generated its ideological antithesis in the anticommunism and hostility to social reform that dominated popular and elite thinking thereafter. These attitudes were reinforced and deepened by a factor unacknowledged in the doctrines of the International but critical in the actual unfolding of the insurrection — race.

Indians, *Cofradías*, and Communism

The center of the revolt, the towns of Juayuá, Izalco, and Nahuizalco in Sonsonate, was a region of strong Indian cultural identity and organization. The Indian political leaders or *caciques* of these towns were the principal leaders of the revolt in Sonsonate, and Indian community and religious organizations were critical to mobilizing the local population. *Cofradías,* religious organizations based on the festival worship of particular saints or holy figures, were central to the local Indian life. In fact these traditional organizations substituted for the almost entirely absent Party organization in these areas, although local Communists were also prominent in the revolt. Most of the participants in the revolt were culturally Indian, and it is clear that racial tensions and conflict between Indian communities and

Spanish landowners over rights to Indian communal lands were fundamental issues in the revolt. The leader of the revolt in Izalco, José Feliciano Ama, was the cacique of the Indian town of Izalco, head of the most important *cofradía,* Espíritu Santo, and a local landowner with a long-standing dispute with the aristocratic Regalado family over communal lands.[83]

The Indian leadership supported the Communists, however, and the revolt combined Indian and Communist leadership and class and racial issues. The *caciques* of Izalco, Juayuá, and Nahuizalco all backed the Communists and worked closely with them. In Tacuba leadership was provided largely by the Cuenca family, who were Ladino Communists, and racial issues do not seem to have played a central role in the revolt, although here as elsewhere in western El Salvador in 1932 the poorest agricultural laborers were likely to be Indian. Similarly, the revolt in the Santa Tecla-Colón area and around Lake Llopango seems to have depended not on traditional Indian religious or community organizations but on local Communist organizers, most of whom were Ladino.[84] Economic issues clearly underlay the revolt, although the conflict over community land was both cultural and economic. The fusion of class and race in western El Salvador in 1932, and the strong ethnic component in the revolt, however, have led most observers to conclude that it was as least a much an Indian rebellion as a Communist insurrection.[85]

This was certainly the perception of the Ladino upper classes and their supporters in the military, who were the principal targets of the revolt. A ferocious racism underlay the repression. In the aftermath of the revolt, anyone who looked or dressed as an Indian was automatically considered to be a supporter of the revolt and became a target. In some areas the *matanza* approached genocide, with the majority of the Indian population of some communities massacred.[86] As one *hacendado* from Juayuá wrote in a Santa Ana newspaper, "They did it right in North America, getting rid of all of them with a bullet before they could impede the progress of the nation. First they killed the Indian because they will never have sympathy for anything . . . They have fierce instincts."[87] The *matanza* forced the permanent abandonment of Indian dress, language, and identifiable cultural traits in much of western El Salvador.

For the elite, then, the revolt combined their two worst nightmares, Indian rebellion and Communist revolution. As the same *hacendado* observed, "There is not an Indian who is not a Communist." In the aftermath of the insurrection, racism and anti-communism merged into a single powerful ideology to justify repression and permanently block social change. The combined power of these images and their association with popular mobilization and social reform made it possible to view even moderate advocates of change as dangerous and subhuman. Furthermore, leading members of the aristocracy had been directly involved, as Civic Guards, in assisting the army in the *matanza* and in financing the military repression. The ideological consequences of 1932 for the elite were paranoid anti-communism, dread of social reform, and dehumanization of the left. The revolt and its aftermath compelled the elite to rationalize mass slaughter as a political tactic or to deny that it happened, and created a long-lasting coalition with the most repressive elements of the military. It also reinforced the belief that the poor were a separate species, ignorant, ferocious, and credulous, easily "excited" by "Communist" agitators. These attitudes were still widespread among the elite half a century later and were vividly expressed in a remarkable contemporary statement by the Coffee Association of El Salvador on the causes of the revolt.

The Coffee Elite and the Causes of the Insurrection

In the July 1932 edition of its journal, *El Café de El Salvador,* the Coffee Association of El Salvador (Asociación Cafetalera de El Salvador) provided it own analysis of the causes and consequences of the insurrection in a response to a questionnaire sent them by an organization called the Association for the Study of Social Reform.[88] The Cafetalera leadership in 1932 represented a *Who's Who* of the Salvadoran elite, and the statement itself was signed by two leading coffee producers, Agustín Alfaro and Enrique Alvarez. It provides a revealing insight into the coffee elite's view not only of the causes of the insurrection but also of the structure of Salvadoran society.

Class divisions are regarded by the Cafetalera as an inevitable and immutable part of the social order. Attempts to change the class structure are regarded as utopian and can lead only to chaos and anarchy. In phrases that sound as if they had been taken from the *Communist Manifesto* the elite proclaims, "In the general history of humanity one constant fact is recorded: the domination of man by man . . . there have always been two essential classes in every society: the dominators and the dominated . . . the strong and the weak, later the noble and the plebeian, today they are called the rich and the poor." But efforts to eliminate these class divisions are "impossible and fatal," because they "break the equilibrium and cause the disintegration of human society."[89] The elite rejected any fundamental change in the structure of wealth and power in El Salvador, a position that it continues to hold sixty years later.

The poor are described as a "primitive mass" who have failed to enter the twentieth century, living and thinking like "Roman slaves." According to the elite, the poor are a class that is "infinitely low and remote, that feels not the need to clothe themselves, educate themselves, care for themselves . . . that is, they have no civilization."[90] The coffee growers traced the cultural inferiority of the poor to the racial divisions established at the time of the Conquest and subsequently reinforced by governmental failure to incorporate the indigenous population into "civilization." Despite the fact that coffee growers had controlled the Salvadoran government for the previous fifty years, the elite denied any responsibility for the barbarism of the poor. After all, they argued, how could they be held responsible for a situation that had developed over "hundreds of years."[91]

Nor did the elite accept any responsibility for the agrarian conflicts that had led to the insurrection. According to the Cafetalera, there were classes in El Salvador, to be sure, but no class exploitation and, despite the apparent evidence of bad feelings between the classes in the insurrection itself, no class conflict. "Exploitation" is the extraction not of profit but of unreasonable or excessive profit; not through the payment of low wages but wages lower than those dictated by the market. Class conflict is associated with the large bureaucratic unions and corporations of the United States or the backward Russian autocracy, not with the close personal relations that, according to the elite, exist between patron and worker in El Salvadoran coffee estates. As evidence, the Cafetalera pointed out that during the insurrection itself patrons continued to live safely in the midst of their workers and had to fear attacks only from strangers. A benign paternalism, not class exploitation, was, according to the elite, the true structure of class relations in the Salvadoran countryside.

If there was no class exploitation or class conflict in El Salvador, then why was there an insurrection? The elite's answer to this question follows directly from its concept of the primitive and uncivilized nature of the Salvadoran masses and the utopian nature of fundamental social change. The "Communist threat" was simply "a dangerous lunacy in the simple minds of the peasants caused by the preachings of the Communists that tricked them."[92] These "preachings" included the promises of a life of luxury without "suffering, privation or effort," and a vision of a future Communist society as a "happy Arcadia in which the ex-rich and the ex-poor, crowned with roses, would sing, in an apotheosis of human fraternity, the virile strains of the anthem of the Third International."[93] Foreign ideas of class struggle imported into El Salvador, "as one would import luxury items," caused the "disorientation" in the minds of simple folk that led to the insurrection.[94] There was nothing fundamentally wrong with Salvadoran society that the purging of these foreign ideas would not cure.

Policy prescriptions in the aftermath of the revolt reflect this view of its causes. Education is essential to raise the low cultural level of the masses and to defend the peasants against "the invasion of anarchic and subversive ideas." But the principal solution is to free the coffee planters from onerous taxes and export duties so that they may adequately provide for the needs of the poor. Only a revival of the coffee economy will solve the economic questions that "the school of Karl Marx" has emphasized. And as the Cafetalera leadership notes, the "serene severity" of the government has already "drowned" the insurrection and restored the normal cordial paternal relationships in the countryside.[95] Left to its own devices, perhaps aided by a better public education system, the coffee economy will raise the primitive masses if not to civilization at least to a modicum of material and financial security. The Liberal vision of gradually improving living standards through export agriculture remains the core of the elite's belief to this day.

The Heritage of 1932

Although the ideas of the Coffee Association seem to verge on self-parody, they not only accurately reflect the official view in 1932 but were still widespread among members of the elite when they were interviewed by the author in 1990. The poor were still regarded as a separate species "infinitely remote" from the lives and consciousness of the elite. Structural change was still regarded as a dangerous subversion of the social order promoted by foreign agitators at the command of international communism. And economic growth through export agriculture was still regarded as the surest route to raise the standard of living of the masses, still living in poverty more than fifty years after the great insurrection of 1932. The "serene severity" of the government was still implicitly endorsed as a necessary condition for purging "subversive and anarchic" ideas that threatened the future of the Salvadoran export economy and society. And the elite continued to deny that the real causes of the Salvadoran insurrections of both the thirties and the eighties were the agrarian inequalities and repressive governments they had done so much to create. The Communist agitator and the fierce Indian have became mythical images that absolve the elite from its responsibility for either the conditions that caused the revolt or the bloody slaughter that followed.

In 1932 there was no open break between the agrarian and agro-industrial fractions of the elite. Nor, for that matter, was there a division between them and the military that they had relied on to suppress the great insurrection. Nor was there any ideological deviation within the elite from the paranoid anti-communism that was the principal ideological heritage of 1932. The Coffee Association at that time was an organization of both growers and processors, and its views of the 1932 crisis can be seen as representative of the elite as a whole. The divisions between the two fractions of the elite deepened, however, with the development of the industry, and particularly with the post-World War II expansion of the agro-export economy. So too did the tensions in the always uncomfortable alliance between the elite and the military. Nevertheless, no open break occurred in either alliance before the 1980s, when once again the elite was faced with a revolutionary challenge from below. For almost sixty years the oligarchic-dictatorial alliance that was the heritage of the Depression continued in power. Anti-communism, the ideological consequence of that crisis and the justification of the system that emerged from it, became enshrined as the central element in the elite and the national ideology.

If in 1932 the views of the coffee elite sound like the ideas of an earlier century, they were even more anachronistic during the civil war of the 1980s. In an important sense, time stopped in 1932. Fifty years of military regimes insured that there would be no need for the elite to face the demands from below that were reshaping much of the rest of the world in the tumultuous twentieth century. When the second Salvadoran insurrection began in 1980, the elite remained committed to an ideology forged in the first. The paranoid anti-communism, fear of social reform, remoteness from the poor, dehumanization of the political opposition, and willingness to tolerate the most severe repressive measures in defense of the agro-export order were the ideological heritage of 1932. Any vision of an alternative social order, of a fundamental redistribution of wealth and power, remained inextricably bound up with the ghosts of the long-dead Communist rebels of 1932. This, even more than the horrendous loss of life, may have been the ultimate tragedy of 1932 for El Salvador.

4

Manuel Mora and the Rise of Euro-Communism

The Depression hit Costa Rica at the same time and with the same severity as it did El Salvador. The political consequences in Costa Rica were very different, however, not only because the class relations in the Costa Rican and Salvadoran coffee economy were very different, but also because in Costa Rica a second export crop, bananas, also influenced political developments. Indeed, the rise of the Costa Rican Communist party is intimately linked to the Depression crisis in the banana industry, just as the triumph of social reform is linked to the absence of any acute class polarization in the coffee industry. Both developments were also influenced by a tradition of institutional legality and democratic politics which was itself closely related to the pattern of class relations in the coffee sector. Only the coffee sector was under the control of the Costa Rican political and economic elite. Hence when Communist popular mobilization came to Costa Rica, it affected the foreign-dominated banana sector, not the coffee sector, where it might have threatened the interest or even survival of the coffee elite.

There was no mass Communist rebellion by coffee pickers or anyone else in Costa Rica in the 1930s, and even the civil war of 1948 was not a mass revolt but a counter-revolution spearheaded by dissident members of the Costa Rican middle and upper classes. Costa Rica escaped the revolutionary violence in the 1930s, just as fifty years later it would be spared the decade of revolution in Central America. This outcome is all the more remarkable given that the principal force on the Costa Rican left during the Depression crisis was, as in El Salvador, an orthodox Communist Party affiliated with the Third International and dedicated, at least in theory, to the same principles of worldwide proletarian revolution. The Costa Rican Communists, however, under the leadership of Manuel Mora Valverde, largely abandoned the sectarian orthodoxy of the International and pursued what for the most part amounted to a social democratic policy, thus profoundly influencing the subsequent interpretation of Costa Rica's resolution of the Depression crisis in both elite and popular memory. The pattern of class relations in the Costa Rican coffee sector interacted with the policies of the Communist Party to prevent an insurrection like the one in El Salvador. Instead, the elite faced only the most moderate and gentlemanly of protests.

Coffee: Agrarian Protest and Social Peace

As it had been almost from its origins, the Costa Rican coffee sector in 1932 was divided between an aristocratic class of coffee processors, some of whom were owners of large coffee estates themselves, and a large number of small and medium producers from whom the processors purchased much of the cherry coffee they milled and exported. Although in some areas, notably around Turrialba, there were enough large estates to create a nascent rural proletariat, in most of the coffee zone small holders were the most important lower-class group, and members of their families supplied much of the harvest labor force for the large estates.[1] But some small coffee farmers were also employers of hired labor. The massive agrarian proletariat that had been the basis for the Salvadoran Communist Party's most successful organizing efforts was absent in the Costa Rican coffee sector. There had been no large-scale displacement of small holders from the land, although, as in El Salvador, government officials and others with political and social influence managed to gain control of much of the best coffee land. Unable to dislodge the small holders from their plots, the Costa Rican elite found an even more lucrative economic niche in processing and export, where the greatest profits were always to be made. At the onset of the Depression, then, class relations polarized not along lines of proletarians versus agrarians but of small farmers versus agro-exporters and processors.

As in El Salvador, the worldwide drop in coffee prices at the outset of the Depression was felt immediately. In 1930 prices for Costa Rican coffee dropped by a third from their highs of the late 1920s, and by 1932 prices had fallen to less than half their peak levels. Small growers may have lost as much as a third more, because the processors were able to pass on their losses.[2] The price of coffee at the mill became the central issue in a social movement of small producers against the processing elite. In distinct contrast to El Salvador, however, there was no protest movement among coffee wage laborers, either resident or migratory, nor was any effort made to organize rural unions among these workers by the Communists or anyone else. The Communist Party did successfully organize the proletariat of the banana plantations in the great strike of 1934, but had no role whatsoever in the small coffee producers' protest movement.[3]

Indeed, the small producers' movement was characterized by its moderate tactics, its limited goals, and its remarkable ideological convergence with the views of the large processors.[4] In March 1932, only two months after the great Salvadoran insurrection, the small producers organized the National Association of Coffee Producers and launched an ultimately successful campaign to regulate the price of coffee purchased by processors. In contrast to the revolutionary violence of the Salvadoran coffee workers, the Costa Rican small producers held public meetings, mass assemblies, and conferences, lobbied and petitioned legislators, and publicized their views through the column of their best-known leader, Manuel Marín, in a San Jose newspaper. On only one occasion did they so much as hold a demonstration without a legal permit. Despite occasionally fiery rhetoric about "capitalist exploitation" by the "trust of the processors," the movement was entirely peaceful and legal, if not legalistic, in its respect for institutional channels.[5]

Neither the goals nor the tactics of the protest movement challenged the fundamental interests of the processors. And the ideology of the movement not only advocated class collaboration instead of class conflict but converged to a remarkable degree with the ideology of the large processors (see Chapter 7). This was particularly true with respect to two central elements of the small holders' ideology: their belief that harmony, equity, and social justice should and could reign in relations between small holder and processor, and their firm conviction that the small coffee producer was the bulwark of Costa Rican democracy and, therefore, of the nation. These beliefs of the small coffee producers of the 1930s are echoed, often in identical words, by the large processors interviewed for this study sixty years later. They are widely shared by Costa Ricans within and outside the coffee sector and amount to what Víctor Acuña has called the "Costa Rican ideology" of an egalitarian agrarian democracy where harmony and social peace reign supreme.[6]

During the thirties, this harmonious world was threatened by conflict between the small producers and what they called the "trust of the processors." The processors were seen as holding an illegitimate, parasitic monopoly over the hard-pressed small producers that was driving them to ruin if not to communism. Manuel Marín Quirós even compared the processors to "wolves," and his fellow producers to "serfs." Even in the heated rhetoric of their most impassioned pronouncements, however, the small holders always distinguished between honest, decent patriotic processors like Julio Sánchez Lépiz, who paid fair prices, and the anonymous "trust of the processors" conspiring against them. Remarkably, the rhetoric of today's processors echoes that of the small holders' critique of their predecessors in the thirties. They too now complain of capitalists who pursue gain without limit, like the coffee growers of El Salvador who, they claim, brought ruin on themselves by their unrestricted exploitation. The rhetoric of the small holders, on the other hand, has cooled significantly since the thirties, and there are now few complaints about capitalist exploitation even at times of adverse coffee prices.[7]

The principal reason for the reversal of the rhetorical evaluation of the processors' oligopoly is the legislative class compromise embodied in 1933 legislation establishing a national coffee institute and regulating relations between growers and processors. Demand for such regulation was the principal issue of the 1930s protest movement, and the passage of the legislation defused the issue and led to the movement's demise. An initial version of the legislation had been introduced by Manuel Francisco Jiménez, president of the processors association, father of the most influential and probably the wealthiest member of the contemporary coffee elite, Manuel Jiménez de la Guardia, and grandfather of one of the leading processors interviewed for this study. The "organic intellectuals" of the coffee elite, principally the two presidents and so-called Olympians, Cleto González Víquez and Ricardo Jiménez Oreamuno, did not actively support the legislation, but they eventually accepted it. The legislature voted overwhelmingly for the laws.[8]

The relations between the processors and the small producers as expressed in the 1933 legislation actually reflect a much wider and deeper set of economic, political, and institutional relations that Gloria Rodríguez has called the "coffee pact." The institutional order of the coffee pact established after Tomás Guardia's military coup of 1870 was dominated by the coffee processors and expressed ideologically and politically in the ideas and careers of the members of the generation of 1888, "the Olympians." In distinct contrast to their counterparts elsewhere in the region, the Costa Rican elite did not use the legal and political orders to expropriate the land and labor of the rural population but sought instead to incorporate the lower classes gradually into the Costa Rican nation through legal citizenship and the extension of education and the franchise. By the time of the Depression, the fundamentally symbiotic economic relations between producer and processor had been institutionalized in a set of legal and political relations that made the institutional tactics of the small producers possible, and the moderate response of the large processors expected.[9]

The 1930s protests and the resulting legislation consolidated the interdependent relationship between the small producer and the aristocratic processor, and resolved the remaining point of conflict over the price of coffee at the mill. Complaints about capitalist exploitation and the "trust of the processors" disappear from small-holder protest rhetoric, and elite discourse enshrines the basic law of 1933 as another example of the Costa Rican genius for harmony and social peace. The resolution of the 1930s coffee crisis contributed further to the remarkable convergence of the ideologies of the small producers and the processors. Both enthusiastically endorsed the Costa Rican national ideology of rural egalitarianism, democracy, harmony, and social peace. As in El Salvador, the agrarian protest of the 1930s shaped elite ideology in the 1980s. But in Costa Rica the memories were of class collaboration, cooperation, and ideological convergence rather than polarization. Fifty years later coffee processors were convinced that the 1933 legislation (subsequently amended in 1961) was a fundamental element in the harmony and social peace that, as they saw it, reigned in the coffee sector.

The processors and the small producers agreed on one other element of what would become a central element in the Costa Rican national ideology—anti-communism. As Víctor Acuña notes, it was probably in the decade of the forties, rather than the thirties, that the anti-communist consciousness of the small producers was formed in the common struggles of the entire coffee sector against the social legislation, the labor code, and the alliance between social reform and communism.[10] But anti-communism also had its roots in the fear of proletarianization stimulated by the economic crisis of the Great Depression. As John Patrick Bell has perceptively observed, the fact that the threat to the small property owner in the Costa Rican countryside came from capitalism, not communism, "made the rural areas of the nation no less vulnerable to hysterical anti-communism." Communism, he notes, came to be perceived as "a challenge to the nation's heritage of stability, order, and peaceful solutions to conflicts."[11]

Communism came to symbolize any challenge to the rural way of life of the coffee pact and its ideological representation in the Costa Rican national ideology of harmony and democracy. That there was and is a real threat to that way of life from capitalism itself made the appeal of anti-communism that much more persuasive. Anti-communism in Costa Rica, even among the coffee elite, never took on the paranoid fanaticism of the coffee growers of El Salvador, but it remains an article of national faith. In both countries the resolution of the Depression crisis enshrined anti-communism as a key element in national ideology, but for different reasons. In El Salvador paranoid anti-communism was a product of class polarization and murderous repression; in Costa Rica anti-communism was a product of class collaboration and ideological unity. Costa Rican national ideology symbolically buried communism as deeply as did the Salvadorans. But it did not bury the actual policies and programs of the real Communist Party of Costa Rica, whose effect on both elite ideology and national life was profound.

The Communist Party of Costa Rica and the Great Banana Strike of 1934

The Communist Party of Costa Rica was founded on June 16, 1931, a little more than a year after the founding of the Communist Party of El Salvador, and its early rhetoric shared the sectarianism and revolutionary maximalism of the Salvadoran Party and of the Communist International. An early issue of the Party journal, *Trabajo*, called for "the annihilation of the bourgeoisie as a dominant class, absolute control of the administration and economy of the nation by a government of workers and peasants," and proclaimed that "violence and revolution are indispensable." Party leader Manuel Mora called for the "exploited working population" to wage the final battle against the "capitalist assassins." The Party rejected social democracy, denounced the principal reformist leaders of the day, and steadfastly defended the Soviet Union as "the first glorious citadel raised against capitalist exploitation." In 1934 Mora even denied that there was any sentimental attachment to property or even a class of small property owners with feelings for property in Costa Rica, since "there can be no sentiment for that which does not exist."[12]

But from its beginnings the Party was much more flexible in its policies than in its rhetoric, and within a few years the rhetoric changed to fit the practice and the realities of Costa Rican political and economic life.[13] The result was an early form of Euro-communism whose policies in practice were for the most part indistinguishable from those of European socialist parties or the reformed Communist parties in contemporary Eastern Europe. The Party's "minimal program," proclaimed in 1931, begins by arguing that revolution cannot be realized in a dependent or semi-colonial society like Costa Rica unless revolution succeeds in the developed world, and the Party will, therefore, strive for immediate improvements in the life of working people. The program calls for a social security system, a national health plan, the eight-hour day, minimum wage laws, union organization laws, nationalization of natural monopolies, civil service legislation, and national development planning. Remarkably, almost every point of the Party's "minimal program" was in fact achieved—but through parliamentary alliances, not revolutionary action.[14]

Most important for its relations with the coffee elite, the Communist Party never developed any policy to break elite domination of the agro-export economy, nor was it able to gain any mass base among the rural workers of the coffee zones. The "minimal program" confines itself to calling for redistributing either land held by the state, or "idle" land. In 1934 the Party declared that it did not propose the "suppression" of large agrarian property but rather believed that "it can be regulated for the benefit of the people," a position almost identical to that held by Manuel Marín Quirós and his army of small property owners.[15] The "popular universities" of the Salvadoran Communist Party had been concentrated in rural areas. The Costa Rican Party's popular universities had no programs at all in rural areas. The Party was unable to break the ties of paternalism that bound peon and coffee grower in the countryside. Farm workers in the coffee areas of Costa Rica did not organize mass protests and demonstrations as they had done in El Salvador. The closest parallel to the militant proletariat of the Salvadoran coffee districts was the work force of the Atlantic Coast banana plantations. Here the policies pursued by the Costa Rican Party were in distinct contrast to those pursued by the Salvadoran.

The great multinational enterprise that was to become the United Fruit Company was founded in Costa Rica by Minor Keith. The Soto-Keith contract of 1883 ceded to Keith approximately seven percent of the national territory in exchange for his efforts in the construction of the Northern Railway connecting the coffee districts with the Atlantic Coast port of Limón. Keith began planting bananas along the rail lines and expanded his operations into what became a state within a state, a banana empire in the coastal lowlands.[16] Even before the Depression crisis, economic and social conditions in the banana zone were very different from those prevailing in the coffee regions of the central plateau. A large and impoverished rural proletariat, many recruited from Jamaica, Nicaragua, or the poorest regions of Costa Rica, lived in unbelievable squalor and privation in primitive encampments throughout the banana zone.[17] There were no coffee growers and few small holders in the region. The class structure presented a stark contrast between a multinational corporation, more powerful than the Costa Rican state in some respects, and a racially mixed proletariat of banana pickers and dock workers. The entire region was among the poorest in Costa Rica, and the Communist Party had been active there even before it had been formally founded.[18]

After a miraculous rise in the first decades of the twentieth century, the banana industry had already begun to decline as a result of plant diseases even before the Great Depression. But the Depression was the final blow. Exports fell from a high of eleven million stems in 1913, the peak year, to just over three million in 1934, with most of the decline occurring after 1929.[19] The company attempted to pass on the costs of the Depression-induced decline in demand for bananas by lowering prices and refusing advance contracts with Costa Rican producers, or simply by refusing to accept deliveries and allowing the fruit to rot on the piers. The producers as well as the company's own plantations responded with massive firings of workers, reductions in wage rates, and a shift to payment not for fruit collected but for fruit accepted by the company.[20] The company threatened to abandon the zone entirely and move its production to the virgin lands on the Pacific Coast, leaving the workers behind. Since the company owned not only many of the plantations but the docks, rail lines, roads, and retail establishments, the move, when it was eventually carried out, devastated the region.

The economic crisis in the banana zone made some sort of protest likely, but the Communist Party played an indispensable role in organizing the protest into a disciplined mass strike of some 10,000 workers. The Party's success rested in no small measure on the efforts of its chief organizer, Carlos Luis Falla ("Calufa"), who also became Costa Rica's greatest literary figure of the twentieth century. His best known work, the novel *Mamita Yunai* (Mama United), chronicled the privations of the banana zone that he knew well as a worker himself.[21] Born to a peasant family in Alajeula in the central plateau, Falla first went to the zone at age sixteen and worked at a variety of jobs before returning to Alajeula at age twenty-two when his mother died. There he sought employment as a shoemaker, one of the militant trades that were most active in founding the Communist Party.[22] After giving an inflammatory May Day address in 1933, Falla was sent into internal exile in Limón—a singularly ineffective act of political repression.[23] There he found an industry he knew at first hand deep in economic crisis. On the 9th of August, 1934, Falla and other Communist Party organizers led the banana workers out on the largest strike in Costa Rican history up to that time.

Despite the Party's rhetorical commitment to proletarian revolution, the strike was a conventional labor action, not an insurrectionary mass movement. There was almost no violence in the first phase of the strike, which lasted from the 9th to the 28th of August, when an accord was signed with Costa Rican national producers. On the 31st of August United disavowed the settlement, precipitating an immediate resumption of the strike, this time accompanied by sabotage of company transport facilities, but still free of violence against persons. On the 10th of September police were sent in. They fired on fleeing strike leaders and arrested others, effectively ending the strike through official repression.[24] No attempt was made to oppose the police action, and in typically Costa Rican fashion all of the leaders were eventually released without punishment, thanks in part to the discreet efforts of Olympian President Ricardo Jiménez to delay the proceedings. During the first phase of the strike, Party leader Manuel Mora contacted this representative of the "capitalist assassins" to seek a negotiated settlement.[25] The government acted as intermediary in the successful settlement of the first phase, before washing its hands of the affair and sending in the police after United disavowed the agreement.

Some militant Party members had apparently called for an insurrection in the banana zone; given the conditions there, an uprising was not beyond the realm of possibility.[26] The actual policies and pronouncements of the Party, however, were in distinct contrast to its own revolutionary rhetoric and to the behavior of the Salvadoran Party when faced with a roughly similar situation among the proletarianized coffee workers. The Party's official view in answer to its internal critics made clear its essentially moderate policy even in 1934: "in the circumstances, to put into practice the slogan of 'Organize the Soviets,' would have had no other result than a senseless suicide, because without arms, without the backing of the workers of the rest of the country, without a skilled previous effort at the 'disintegration' of the capitalist police, the proletariat of the Atlantic would have been cruelly decimated and a united workers' movement in Costa Rica would have been set back who knows for how long."[27] The outcome, in other words, would have been exactly what it had been in El Salvador in 1932.

Manuel Mora Valverde, the Party's General Secretary from its founding in 1931 until his resignation in a factional dispute in 1983, was elected deputy to the national legislature in 1934 and, as his role in the great banana strike indicates, rapidly became the leading voice of a separate brand of communism the Costa Ricans called "tico-comunismo" or "comunismo criollo." Fifty years later some members of the coffee elite still distinguished between this Costa Rican "national" communism and the international communist movement. At times, however, most notably during the civil war of 1948, which coincided with the beginnings of the cold war, many Costa Ricans ignored the distinction, and the Party suffered accordingly.[28] In 1983, however, Oscar Arias praised Mora for the "muy tico" stamp he had put on the party and for his "indisputable nationalism" that always placed the nation ahead of Communist orthodoxy.[29]

Mora's vision of "comunismo criollo" did indeed represent a decided departure from the orthodoxy of the Communist Party of the "third period" and from the Soviet party line in general. In 1937 Mora proclaimed that if the leaders of the Soviet Union established a dictatorship for its own sake, he would denounce them as "traitors to socialism." If it were necessary, he said, to "destroy liberty and all of those attributes of the human personality" in order to realize Marxist doctrine, then he "would be the principal adversary of socialism."[30] In 1939 he declared that violent Communist revolution was not "the order of the day in Costa Rica" because it would violate "the right to think, speak, assemble, organize and propound and achieve the demands of the people" enjoyed by all Costa Ricans. Revolution was not armed action that would "bloody our soil," but "the transformation of institutions blocking and poisoning the welfare of the people."[31] In 1945 he proclaimed that "the class struggle has been replaced by class collaboration."[32]

The moderation of the Communist Party can be traced in no small measure to exactly those factors mentioned by Mora—the institutional guarantees of democratic rights that extended to all Costa Ricans, and most of the time to members of the Communist Party. Although the Party was a major issue in the Costa Rican elections of 1936, 1940, 1944, and 1948, and was perhaps the decisive issue in the civil war of 1948, before that time the Communists enjoyed considerable, if not completely unrestricted, rights to participate in Costa Rican political life.[33] President Jiménez not only negotiated with Mora during the banana strike but resisted pressures to outlaw the Block of Workers and Peasants, as the Party was called.[34] He referred to Mora's presence in the Congress as "honoring" that body.[35] In the 1940 election Jiménez entered into an alliance with Mora against the successful candidacy of Calderón Guardia. Although President León Cortés (1936–1940), who owed his victory to anticommunist scare tactics, took a notably harder line against them, for the most part deviations from electoral legality were minor, and the Communists were allowed to participate in national life. The remaining restrictions on their participation allowed Party members to pose as defenders of electoral probity and democratic rights.

In distinct contrast to the situation in El Salvador, the Communists were the inheritors of a rich tradition of popular social reform movements, some led by members of the elite itself. Although the reformist administration of Alfredo González Flores (1916–1917) was overthrown by Federico Tinoco (1917–1919) in a coup backed by most of the coffee elite, the ousted president had established a tradition of upper-class reformism that was carried forward by another member of the elite, Jorge Volio, in the 1920s. Volio's Reform Party, based on social Christian doctrines, achieved a notable success in the 1924 national election before losing ground after Volio made a deal giving the presidency to Jiménez.[36] In the 1920s some members of the "Olimpio" formed the anti-imperialist Liga Cívica (Civic League) to protest the role of foreign corporations, particularly the United Fruit Company and its Northern Railway subsidiary, in the national economy.[37] Many Communist Party founders had been veterans of the successful struggles against the Tinoco dictatorship; many had been militants in Volio's Reform Party; and others had been members of the Civic League.[38] Successful popular reformist movements were the first political experience of the founders of the Communist Party of Costa Rica.

Indeed, given the institutional incorporation of the Communists and popular support for many of their principles, what is surprising is that a revolutionary Communist rather than a democratic socialist party was the eventual inheritor of Volio's failed Reform Party. Just as in El Salvador, the initial radicalism of the Party owed much to its roots among the impoverished artisanal workers, particularly the carpenters, shoemakers, and bakers.[39] In addition, many of the Party founders were anti-imperialist student radicals of the University of Costa Rica's law faculty.[40] The absence of any industrial proletariat in Costa Rica eliminated the possibility of a European-type mass-based socialist party among unionized workers with a stake in the existing system. The only proletariat organized by the Party was that of the marginalized and oppressed workers of the semi-colonial banana zone. Finally, Volio's compromise with the elite after 1924 served to discredit social reform and made radicalism more attractive. The Party's initial social base predisposed it to radicalism. But Costa Rica's institutionalized democracy and tradition of elite reformism eventually pushed the Party in the direction of Euro-communism.

As Ana María Botey and Rodolfo Cisneros note, Manuel Mora Valverde's personal biography incorporates many of the experiences that created both the initial radicalism and the ultimate reformism of the Costa Rican party.[41] His father was a skilled artisan, a cabinet maker, and the family suffered extreme economic hardship when the father was exiled for his role in opposing the Tinoco dictatorship. Mora's father had been a great friend of the upper-class reformer Alfredo González Flores and an admirer of the Russian Revolution. As a young man, Mora was an ardent supporter of another elite reformer, Jorge Volio, and was subsequently disillusioned by Volio's compromise with Jiménez. He was a member of the anti-imperialist law students association at the University of Costa Rica and an organizer of the unemployed. During his own career as Communist Party General Secretary and congressional deputy, however, he worked closely with members of the elite, including not only Jiménez but, more importantly, the leader of the reform wing of the ruling National Republican Party, Rafael Angel Calderón Guardia. When Mora finally left the Party in 1983, it was because revolution, rather than reform, seemed to be on the agenda for the Costa Rican left.

Mora and his associates were, nevertheless, Communists; this fact, along with the rise of a social reform movement allied with the Party, divided the elite and terrified some of its members. One consequence of the great banana strike of 1934 was the organization of the Anti-Communist League, a group of banana and coffee growers united against the perceived Communist menace. As John Bell notes, many members of the elite were "horror struck at the possibility that the *Bloque de Obreros y Campesinos* might grow to a position of influence in Costa Rica."[42] León Cortés, the champion of anti-communism, successfully rode the issue to the presidency in 1936. The thirties brought increasing ideological and political convergence within the coffee sector, but increasing polarization between that world and those social groups not included in its vision of harmony and rural egalitarianism. To the coffee producers communism—the symbol, not Mora's actual "tico" Communists— came to represent all those forces threatening changes in the coffee order: the poor, the unemployed, city workers, dock and banana workers, even the forces of capitalism itself.

The growing polarization between the coffee order and the forces of social reform symbolized by the Communists did not lead to a breakdown of the coffee order in the 1930s. It was in the decade of the 1940s, following the election of aristocratic reformer and heir to the tradition of González Flores and Volio, Rafael Angel Calderón Guardia, and his subsequent alliance with the Communist Party, that the growing polarization in the country came to the point of civil war. In Costa Rica the Depression-era crisis did not end until 1948, with the triumph of José Figueres's counter-revolution, the suppression of the Communists, and the exile of Calderón. Paradoxically, the defeat of the reformers signaled the victory of their reforms. Communism was expunged from Costa Rican national life and ideology, but the reforms of the Party's minimal program became a fixture of that same ideology. How this strange resolution came about requires a brief consideration of the complex events of the 1940s crisis and civil war.

Calderón, Communists, and the Coffee Elite: The Revolutionary Decade of the 1940s

On May 1, 1933, the Communist Party participated in a Costa Rican May Day celebration for the first time. Three weeks later, after a violent confrontation between Communist-led unemployed workers and the police, most of the Party's Central Committee were jailed, several foreign-born leaders (including future Venezuelan President Rómulo Betancourt) were expelled from the country, and Carlos Luis Falla was sent into his fortuitous internal exile in Limón.[43] Ten years later, on September 15, 1943, the Secretary General of the Party, Manuel Mora Valverde, rode through the streets of San José in an open car accompanied by the President of Costa Rica, Rafael Angel Calderón Guardia, and the Archbishop of San José and titular head of the Costa Rican Catholic Church, Monseñor Víctor Sanabria.[44] This remarkable reversal of the Party's fortunes as well as the incongruous alliance between the aristocratic President, the Catholic Church, and the Communist Party created a social revolution. Neither the alliance nor the Party's change in fortune were as strange as they seemed.

As we have already seen, the Party's evolution from its sectarian beginnings to its mature moderation made such an alliance neither unlikely nor undesirable. The Catholic Church too had a long tradition of social concern and conflict with the Liberal aristocrats that made its entry into the alliance possible. The key figure, however, was Calderón. A direct descendent of the seventeenth-century Spanish nobleman Cristóbal de Alfaro and of the founder of the Liberal order, General Tomás Guardia, he was also closely related by blood and marriage to many other leading families of the coffee elite. Calderón was hand-picked by President León Cortés (a staunch anticommunist) as his successor, and was elected in 1940 with the overwhelming support of the coffee elite and most of the rest of the population, receiving over 86 percent of the vote. He carefully avoided concrete references to social reform during the campaign and presented himself as a progressive alternative to communism. His election did not appear to represent a break with the Liberal coffee order that had ruled Costa Rica since the days of Calderón's great-grandfather, General Guardia.

In fact Calderón was the inheritor of the tradition of aristocratic reform pioneered by Alfredo González Flores and Jorge Volio. Like Volio, Calderón studied at the Catholic University of Louvain in Brussels where he was likewise deeply influenced by the social Christian doctrines of Cardinal Désiré Mercier and the 1891 encyclical of Pope Leo XIII, "Rerum Novarum."[45] Leo's encyclical, reaffirmed by Pius XI in "Quadragesimo Anno," issued on the fortieth anniversary of "Rerum Novarum," represented the Church's attempt to come to terms with the growing European working-class movement and find a middle way between socialism and capitalism. On the eve of his election Calderón announced that the two encyclicals and Cardinal Mercier's "Social Code of Malinas" would be the basis of his administration.[46] Calderón's social Christian principles led him to reject class struggle, since "the only differences were between men who suffered and men whose duty it was to alleviate that suffering."[47] He rejected both Marxist materialism and Liberal individualism and sought to incorporate workers into a Christian notion of community through state action.

Calderón's social Christian principles had been deepened by his own training and experience as a physician. Himself the son of a distinguished physician of deep Catholic convictions, Calderón was trained in medicine at the University of Brussels, a considerably more liberal institution than the Catholic University of Louvain. He returned to Costa Rica to occupy important positions in medicine and medical administration—Chief of Surgery of the San Juan de Dios Hospital, Vice-President of the Anti-Cancer League, Member of the Board of the Duran Sanatorium—that did much to solidify his reputation as an individual concerned with the well-being of his fellow Costa Ricans and explained much of his popularity.[48] Manuel Mora, who regarded Calderón as a decent and progressive man if a bit "romantic" and "unscientific," attributed his social concern to his first-hand exposure as a physician to the privations of the poor.[49]

Calderón therefore combined the paternalistic but progressive tradition of the reform wing of the Costa Rica aristocracy, the social Christian philosophy of reform Catholicism, and the instincts and experiences of a socially concerned physician. Unlike earlier aristocratic reformers, however, he was a successful politician who put his ideas into practice and in the process created the modern Costa Rican welfare state. His three most enduring achievements are the Costa Rican social security system, enacted by the Congress in November 1941; a social bill of rights, "the social guarantees," passed in June of 1942; and a set of constitutional revisions, the Labor Code, greatly extending workers' rights, passed in August of 1942.[50] The social security system, which included medical care as well as old age, unemployment and dependent benefits, was initiated from above by Calderón and his closest advisors, although it had been an early demand of both Volio's Reform Party and the Communists.[51] The other reforms were passed with the active support of the Communist Party and the Catholic Church, support that became indispensable to Calderón after 1942.

Calderón was apparently unprepared for the storm of opposition in upper-class circles created by his social security proposals. This opposition was further inflamed by Costa Rica's declaration of war on the Axis powers on December 11, 1941, and the subsequent internment and confiscation of the properties of members of the German, Italian, and Spanish communities suspected of being Fascist sympathizers. The Germans in particular had been among the wealthiest and most influential members of the Costa Rican business community and held key positions in the coffee export trade. Their arrest, and even more so the confiscation of their properties, were seen as an attack on property rights.[52] In February 1942 a poll of the Club Unión, the principal social forum of the coffee elite, found only one member still supporting Calderón. By 1942 Calderón was writing that he had "burned his bridges" and feared that his political career had been irreparably damaged. Rumors of a coup circulated in San José, and Calderón's erstwhile mentor, León Cortés, organized a new party to defeat him.[53]

The alliance between Calderón and the Communists apparently dates to early in 1942. According to Mora, he had been approached by right-wing members of the elite seeking his support in a coup and the formation of a national unity government. Mora rejected the offer and went directly to Calderón and offered his and his Party's support in exchange for deepening and quickening the pace of reform.[54] According to Calderón, he welcomed the Communists' support for policies he and his National Republicans had already put in motion.[55] In 1942 the Communists were at the peak of their popularity and achieved 16 percent of the vote in the midterm election of that year. They brought to the alliance a reputation for electoral probity and fierce opposition to fascism and imperialism.[56] They also brought dedicated militants and mass support in urban working-class districts that could play a critical role in defeating any attempt at armed uprising. For Calderón they represented a crucial substitute for his vanished elite support.

There remained the problem of the Catholic Church. Early in his administration Calderón had gained favor with the Church by abrogating anti-clerical legislation enacted by the ruling Liberal elite in the nineteenth century. In 1940, the year Calderón took office, his long-time friend and supporter of social Christian doctrines, Monseñor Víctor Sanabria, was appointed Archbishop of San José. Alarmed by the growing strength of both communism and Protestantism in Costa Rica, Sanabria embraced Calderón's program and actively cultivated the support of the urban working classes while remaining adamantly anti-communist. The conflict between Calderón's incongruous allies was resolved in June of 1943, when the Communist Party announced that it would dissolve itself and form a new party, Vanguardia Popular. In a letter to Mora, Monseñor Sanabria announced that he found nothing in the new party's doctrines that would preclude membership by practicing Catholics. The alliance was sealed.[57] The appearance of the three men, Calderón, Mora, and Sanabria, in the 1943 Independence Day motorcade celebrated the passage of the labor code and announced the formal alliance. The alliance was critical to the success of Calderón's reform program. It also led directly to the civil war of 1948.

The Revolution of 1948: José Figueres and the Coffee Elite

After the death of León Cortés, opposition to Calderón and the Communists rapidly crystalized around two men, aristocratic publisher Otilio Ulate and self-made man José Figueres. Ulate had originally been involved in reform circles himself but after Calderón's alliance with the Communists, his newspaper, *Diario de Costa Rica*, became increasingly outspoken in its opposition to the government. Ulate denounced the social guarantees as the "opium of the people."[58] Figueres first came to national prominence when he was arrested in the midst of a radio address in which he denounced the government's handling of anti-foreign rioting that had broken out after the torpedoing of a United Fruit Company ship at the docks in Limón by a German U-boat. He became an implacable opponent of the popularly elected Calderón, whom he incongruously denounced as a dictator.[59] Ulate, true to the traditions of the Costa Rican upper class, favored compromise and electoral politics. Figueres dedicated himself to armed insurrection.

The Bloque de Victoria, as the Calderón-Communist alliance was called, found its support among the urban poor and working classes, the proletarians of the banana zones and other rural poor, devout Catholics of various classes, and some progressive members of the aristocracy.[60] Ulate initially represented moderate professionals and small businessmen, but as the 1940s crisis deepened, the oligarchy, including the coffee elite, rallied around his party.[61] Figueres's initial base of support was the growing Costa Rican middle class as represented by the young intellectuals in the Centro de Estudios Nacionales, who rapidly emerged as a leading source of oppositional ideology.[62] Figueres and the intellectuals of the Centro shared Calderón's social democratic ideology, supported his reforms while criticizing their administration, and in some respects were even more radical than Calderón. Calderón was a firm supporter of liberal capitalism and the coffee-based Costa Rican agro-export economy. Figueres and the young men of the Centro wanted an economic revolution led by the state to create an industrial Costa Rica.[63]

Although Figueres and the Centro agreed with the principles, if not the practice, of Calderón's social reforms, they broke sharply with him over the role of the Communists. Given this fundamental agreement on social democratic principles, if not on development policy, the emerging anti-Calderón alliance was at least as strange as the alliance backing Calderón himself. Conservative members of the coffee elite and their rural followers, led by Ulate and outraged by Calderón's social democratic reforms, joined forces with middle-class social democratic reformers outraged by the closed coffee economy of the Liberal prewar era. United only by militant anti-communism and opposition to Calderón, they combined first to destabilize and then to overthrow the regime. The precipitating incident was the disputed election of 1948 that pitted Ulate against Calderón running for a second non-consecutive term.[64] Amid growing political tension and widespread charges of fraud, Calderón used his power in Congress to overturn the results and declare himself President.[65] Figueres, ever the man of action, seized the moment to launch his long-threatened armed rebellion.

After several sharp engagements in which the government and its supporters suffered heavy losses at relatively little cost to the insurgents, Figueres prepared to march on San José, which was held by government forces and a Communist workers militia led by Mora. Many of the workers defending San José were veterans of the struggles in the banana zones in the thirties. A final battle and potential bloodbath was avoided by negotiations at the Mexican embassy and informal consultations between Figueres and Mora in the no-man's-land of the Ochomongo heights. Figueres assured Mora that he intended to preserve the social reforms of Calderón and respect the rights and property of the defeated parties, including the Communists. On April 19, 1948, all parties signed the Pact of the Mexican Embassy ending the forty-day civil war. Figueres marched triumphantly into San José and initiated his social revolution.

Although the revolution had ostensibly been fought to defend the election of Otilio Ulate, the immediate assumption of the presidency by the conservative publisher did not suit Figueres's plans for social transformation. Instead, Figueres suspended the Constitution and appointed an eleven-man junta that ruled by decree for 18 months before permitting Ulate to assume the presidency. To the horror of the coffee elite, Figueres soon proved himself to be even more radical than Calderón. True to his word he preserved Calderón's social reforms but also embarked on a plan to transform the Costa Rican economy. His most controversial moves were the nationalization of the banking system and a ten-percent tax on wealth.[66] The bank nationalization struck at the heart of the economic power of the coffee elite, which had controlled much of the bank capital, and, together with the tax on wealth, that action split the incongruous alliance of the civil war victors. Conservative Minister of the Interior Edgar Cardona launched an abortive coup against Figueres.[67] *La Nación,* traditionally the voice of the coffee elite, denounced the junta's rule as a "storm of hatred."[68]

The criticism did not deter Figueres from his plans for economic transformation. He rejected socialist state ownership but also laissez-faire capitalism, and sought a middle road through the establishment of state-sponsored autonomous entities to manage key sectors of the economy. During the period of the junta the principal achievement of this policy was the establishment of the Costa Rican Electricity Institute (ICE) to control the nation's hydroelectric power and electrical grid.[69] Figueres also succeeded in including the idea of the autonomous entities in the revised Constitution that was to provide the basis for his Second Republic.[70] When he turned the government over to Ulate in November 1949, the ground had been laid for his economic revolution. The basic fault lines of postrevolutionary Costa Rican politics had also been established. The division between the erstwhile allies of the civil war superseded the conflict between Calderón and the opposition.

Figueres and his allies in the Centro founded their own political movement, Liberación Nacional, to promote his development programs through electoral politics. The remnants of the Cortesista old guard and supporters of Ulate formed the core of the opposition. In the 1952 presidential election it was Figueres, not Calderón, who was attacked by the opposition as a "communist," despite his impeccable anti-communist credentials.[71] The contest, however, remained in the electoral arena. One of Figueres's first acts had been the abolition of the Costa Rican national army. By so doing he removed a potential ally of the oligarchy and, with the demobilization of the army of National Liberation, eliminated the possibility that the division between the victorious factions in the civil war would lead to renewed military conflict or another coup attempt. Figueres won the 1952 election handily, and he and later Liberación administrations continued his policies of reform.

Government control over credit through the bank nationalization and the establishment of autonomous economic entities were the core of the Liberación economic program. The autonomous entities came to control such basic economic functions as electricity, telephones, insurance, aviation, and petroleum refining. State entities also encouraged economic development in such areas as fisheries, tourism, sugar refining, cement, and fertilizer production. They also transformed the traditional coffee economy through an ambitious program of credit, technical assistance, and state sponsored cooperatives.[72] In the years after 1948 Liberación succeeded in forming a new state-initiated economy that created a new class of capitalist entrepreneurs as well as a substantially expanded state sector. These Liberación policies became the central issue in the political disputes of the post-1948 period and the focal point for coffee elite discontent.

The revolution of 1948 and the rise of Jose Figueres and Liberación put an end to the crisis initiated in Costa Rica by the Great Depression and created a new economic, political, and ideological order. In El Salvador the new order emerged out of the Depression itself and weathered the economic dislocations of World War II. In Costa Rica the unresolved social and economic issues of the Depression were exacerbated by the political and economic strains of the war before the system broke down in 1948. In El Salvador the formative period of elite ideology was 1932, with the insurrection, the rise of the Martínez dictatorship, the massacre of the Communists, and the entombment of any oppositional currents. In Costa Rica the role of the Communist Party and its oppositional ideology was not settled until 1948, and the outlines of the new order did not emerge until Figueres's policies became clear during the junta. In El Salvador the Depression crisis ended with the suppression of oppositional ideology and the restoration of the coffee elite. In Costa Rica the outcome was much more ambiguous.

Ideological and Political Consequences of the Depression Crisis in Costa Rica

As the interviews reported in Chapter 7 indicate, the events of the 1932–1948 period in Costa Rica continue to influence coffee elite ideology. Several important consequences of these historical events warrant emphasis. The Depression-era protests in the coffee sector did not lead to ideological polarization, insurrection, or civil war, but rather to a consolidation of the Costa Rican national ideology shared by both small coffee producers and the coffee elite. While the conflict over the price of coffee did threaten the coffee pact temporarily, the protest was moderate and gentlemanly and did not question property relations or the market economy. The successful resolution of the conflict through the regulation represented by the basic law of 1933 restored and even deepened ideological consensus and social peace. In the coffee sector itself the resolution of the thirties crisis only confirmed the elite's beliefs in the fundamental virtues of the national ideology of rural egalitarianism, harmony, and social peace.

The oppositional ideology of the Communist Party and Calderón did challenge both the elite ideology of the coffee culture and the elite's role in Costa Rican society. And unlike the conflict in coffee, this conflict could not be resolved short of civil war. The Communists and communist ideology were both expunged from Costa Rican life, and the anti-communism of Figueres and his coffee elite allies in the civil war was enshrined as a tenet of the national ideological consensus. Figueres ignored the promises he had made in the Pact of the Mexican Embassy and Ochomongo. After the civil war Communists were imprisoned, exiled, and murdered. The Party was declared illegal and remained so until 1972.[73] By that time it had lost much of its influence over national political and ideological life. The fundamental class divisions in Costa Rican society emphasized by the Communists disappeared from political discourse along with any fundamental challenge to those divisions. Figueres's pro-capitalist developmentalism and welfare-state reformism prevailed over any ideological challenge to the economic inequalities of peripheral capitalism.

Curiously, although communism was defeated, its minimum program was not. Mora lived to see almost the whole of the Costa Rican Communists' reform agenda enacted into law under Calderón, and the Party elevated to a position of national respect and power. It is a paradox of contemporary Costa Rica that despite the prevailing ideological anti-communism, the Communist Party had more influence on the formation of the Costa Rican welfare state and welfare state ideology than any political force except Calderón himself. As John Patrick Bell has observed, after the civil war, when Figueres embraced Calderón's reforms and initiated his own developmentalist program, the reforms of the Calderón era came to seem a settled matter of national consensus, a part of the Costa Rican national ideology.[74] The axis of political conflict and cleavage revolved around the reforms of Figueres, not of Calderón. As we shall see in Chapter 7, acceptance of the welfare reforms of Calderón and the Communists even extends to the coffee elite itself, which has made them an essential part of its own world view. The reform program of "comunismo criollo" therefore significantly influenced both elite and mass ideology.

The civil war also reinforced elite commitments to democracy and once and for all eliminated the possibility of an elite coup of the Tinoco variety through the abolition of the military. The civil war had been fought to preserve the apparent electoral victory of the elite in the person of Otilio Ulate, and the sanctity of electoral democracy became a tenet of the national faith and a founding principle of the Second Republic. The Constitution enshrined a powerful electoral tribunal as the ultimate arbiter of the voting process, and some members of the elite came to view the civil war as a defense of democracy, despite the long prior tradition of electoral fraud by both the elite and its opponents. Having fought a civil war in the name of democracy, the elite could hardly fail to abide by democratic election results, even if it gave them Figueres and his economic program. One of the members of the coffee elite interviewed listed as one of his proudest accomplishments his role as a member of the electoral tribunal. The crisis of the thirties in Costa Rica simply reinforced the democratic ideology of the coffee elite that was already highly developed in the generation of 1888.

The practical consequence of Figueres's victory in the civil war was the political marginalization of the coffee elite. Although they remained the core of the opposition, they never again gained the hegemony in Costa Rica society that they enjoyed in the days of Don Cleto and Don Ricardo. Figueres and his middle-class revolutionaries, not his conservative allies in the coffee elite, defined the political and economic agenda of post-1948 Costa Rica. This did not mean that the aristocratic traditions of Costa Rican politics were fundamentally changed. Even Liberación presidential candidates like Oscar Arias continued to be descendents of the colonial nobility. Nevertheless, Figueres's civil war victory changed the face of Costa Rican politics. He created both a new political party with an agenda opposed to the coffee elite and new social groups, particularly the rising middle classes in the state sector, that challenged the elite agenda.

Figueres's economic revolution also led to the economic marginalization of the traditional coffee elite, but it greatly strengthened the economic if not the political power of the agro-industrialists. Bank nationalization transferred control over the direction of the national economy from capital associated with the coffee export economy to the state. It also deprived the coffee elite of control over capital—control which in El Salvador became the basis for elite domination of emerging sectors of the agro-export and industrial economy. The coffee elite in Costa Rica, to a remarkable degree, stuck to its own industry. The new industries developed by the Liberación economic program and later export-platform industrialization in the 1990s were in the hands of others. The coffee economy thrived under Liberación development policies, enormously enriching some members of the coffee elite. The net effect of Liberación economic policies was to greatly strengthen the agro-industrial fraction of the Costa Rican elite both in coffee, where the reforms created a new class of mega-processors, and in new agro-industrial exports. The agrarian fraction of the elite, always weaker in Costa Rica than elsewhere, went into nearly total eclipse as a result of Figueres's political actions and economic reforms.

The Depression crisis had deepened and solidified the coffee culture ideology of rural egalitarianism, democracy, harmony, and social peace both through the resolution of the small-holder/processor conflict and through the civil war commitment to democratic restoration. The crisis also sharpened and solidified elite opposition to communism, although never to anything like the degree of fervor of the Salvadorans. The principal change was the assimilation of notions of social citizenship as a result of the reforms of Calderón and the Communists. Since the coffee elite unequivocally opposed these reforms at the outset, this is clearly an example of profound ideological change brought about through historical struggles. Opposition to the statism of Figueres replaced opposition to Calderón as the elite's chief concern. While anti-communism became enshrined as an article of national faith as in El Salvador, the policies of the banished Communists were adopted by Figueres and incorporated into the national ideology.

Alone in Central America the Costa Rican elite emerged from the Depression crisis with a commitment not only to the extension of the franchise to all (including, after 1948, women), but also to the notion of social citizenship and the welfare state. They also emerged with their political and economic power much diminished. When Costa Rica entered the Central American crisis of the 1980s, it did so with an elite vastly more open than those of El Salvador or Nicaragua and a society much less polarized, thanks to the reforms of Calderón and the Communists. The elite had come to embrace attitudes that were far different from those of the Liberals of the days of Don Cleto and Don Ricardo and the generation of 1888. Alone in the region Costa Rica incorporated the working and middle classes into an expanded welfare state, and the elite assimilated the ideas of the extended franchise and social welfare into its own ideology. And alone in the region the elite escaped the tumult of the 1980s.

Despite the diametrically opposed policies favored by the Communist parties in Costa Rica and El Salvador, anti-communism became firmly entrenched in both countries. This had more to do with the uncomfortable issues the parties raised than any fictive international Communist conspiracy or even the exact policies pursued by the parties. In both countries the parties challenged the immense disparities of wealth and power that were the inheritance of both societies since the days of the conquest. In both countries the parties were voices for the dispossessed and excluded, not simply the industrial proletariat of Communist orthodoxy but the rural laborer, the urban unemployed, the dispossessed Indian, the dark-skinned banana worker. In both countries the parties represented a voice for labor and a voice against foreign economic domination. They raised issues that had no part in the Liberal orthodoxy of the coffee elite and have only been weakly represented since their demise. The central role of anti-communism in elite and national ideologies insured that these issues and the contradictions in the agro-export order on which they rested would be buried with the Communist parties of the 1930s.

5

Augusto César Sandino and the Failure of Revolutionary Nationalism

In Nicaragua the Depression deepened but did not initiate a revolutionary crisis that had its origins in military intervention and the failure of Liberal revolution. By the time the Depression began to be felt in Nicaragua in 1930, General Augusto César Sandino and his Army for the Defense of National Sovereignty had already been fighting to expel the United States Marines for three years. The economic crisis, particularly as experienced on the Atlantic Coast, provided new recruits and energy for the movement, and Sandino's war reached its maximum extent between 1930 and 1933, when his forces moved out from their base in northwest Nicaragua to launch attacks throughout the country.[1] As in El Salvador and Costa Rica, however, the resolution of the Depression crisis created the political system that endured until the 1980s and shaped both elite ideology and popular response to the latter crisis. The Somoza dynasty was founded on the physical and ideological liquidation of Sandino and his legacy.

The oppositional ideology was not communism but another revolutionary ideology—Sandino's pan-Latin American, anti-Yankee nationalism. It was Sandino, not the Communists, who led a successful six-year military campaign (1927–1933) to expel the Marines from Nicaragua. Although Somoza denounced Sandino as a "communist," orthodox Communist thought played no role in Sandino's movement or in Nicaragua in the 1930s. Neither did democratic social reform movements. The Communist Party was not founded until 1943, although clandestine Party organizers operated on the Atlantic Coast as early as 1931–32.[2] It played no role in the resolution of the Depression crisis. No aristocratic reform movement such as those led by Araujo or Calderón emerged in Nicaragua; the country went directly from oligarchic rule to dictatorship with no reformist interlude. The language of class, so prominent in both El Salvador and Costa Rica, was also entirely absent in Nicaragua, where the revolutionary challenge was expressed through nationalism, not communism. This was Sandino's greatest strength and, as it turned out, his fatal weakness.

Three factors in particular stand out as determinants of the rise of nationalism and the parallel eclipse of class in the rhetoric of opposition in Nicaragua. First, the Liberal revolution of the coffee elite, which had succeeded in both El Salvador and Costa Rica, failed in Nicaragua. The overthrow of President José Santos Zelaya (1893–1909) by a United States-backed revolt in 1909 ended the Liberal revolution and coffee elite power. Zelaya's Liberal nationalism, therefore, became the starting point for the resistance movement. Second, the United States intervention and subsequent informal protectorate from 1909 to 1933 insured that the main axis of conflict would be the struggle against foreign domination, not internal class cleavage. Third, the peculiarities of Sandino's own mystical vision of national liberation and the social base of his movement interacted to push the movement in the direction of Indo-Hispanic nationalism. The three factors are closely related and tied to class relations in the coffee sector. The end of the Liberal revolution and the United States intervention prevented the development of well-defined classes of agro-industrialists, proletarians, and commercial small farmers and therefore provided scant basis for class-based, as opposed to national, appeals. Each of these factors requires more detailed consideration.

The Failure of Liberal Revolution: The Rise and Fall of José Santos Zelaya

Sandino's war of national liberation began with the Nicaraguan civil war of 1926–27, in which he rose to prominence as military leader of the Liberal faction. That civil war in turn was a renewal of the civil war of 1912, in which the insurgents sought to reverse the overthrow of Liberal President José Santos Zelaya in 1909. Although there are profound differences between Sandino's revolutionary nationalism and the Liberal nationalism of Zelaya, it is important to note that the movement of the former had its origins in the struggle to reverse the defeat of the latter. Liberal Zelayist General Benjamín Zeledón, killed during the struggle against the United States intervention of 1912, was one of Sandino's heroes and an inspiration for his own struggle. Given the importance of Zelaya's Liberal nationalism in the origins of Sandino's movement, it is well to consider what that nationalism represented.[3]

Liberal revolution and the rise of coffee production went hand in hand throughout Central America, and Nicaragua was no exception. Coffee production began much later in Nicaragua, and the Liberal revolution was correspondingly delayed until 1893. Nicaragua's late start in coffee was a result of continuing civil strife surrounding the traditional rivalry between the Conservatives of the city of Granada and the Liberals of León. In 1855–1857 this rivalry provided an opening for the American soldier of fortune, William Walker, to seize power and make himself the only American ever to hold the presidency of a Latin American republic.[4] Military action by combined Central American armies finally defeated Walker, but at the cost of further economic disruption. By the time stable government had returned, Nicaragua was far behind its Central American rivals in the transition to coffee. The rise of a new class of Liberal coffee growers interjected a new and decisive element into the traditional Conservative-Liberal rivalry between Granada and León.

The economic bases of the Conservatives of Granada on Lake Nicaragua were ownership of vast cattle ranches in the provinces of Boaco and Chontales along the shores of the lake, control of foreign trade across the lake and down the Río San Juan to the Caribbean, and colonial exports such as cocoa and indigo grown on the Rivas Isthmus between the lake and the Pacific. Like Conservatives elsewhere in Latin America, they appreciated the special monopolies and protections of the colonial order and the dominant role of the Church in colonial society. In the republican period they attempted to preserve their traditional advantages under colonial rule and were skeptical of unrestricted free trade, free enterprise, secular education, and egalitarian judicial and political institutions. Satisfied with the rents extracted from their traditional mercantile activities and incomes from their extensive cattle ranches, they generally opposed expensive government initiatives to improve the economic infrastructure and expand the agro-export economy. Their goal was the traditional colonial society ordered by Church and family. Their nineteenth-century slogan of "Legitimidad o Muerte" (Legitimacy or Death) gave way in the twentieth to "Orden, Iglesia, Familia" (Order, Church, Family).

Liberals had their traditional base of support among artisans, small merchants, and landowners in the city of León, who chafed under the dominance of the colonial merchants of Guatemala City and Granada. In the republican period they generally favored free trade, free enterprise, parliamentary institutions modeled after those of Western Europe and the United States, secular education, and a more egalitarian judicial and political system. They were often violently anti-clerical. In contrast to both the Conservatives and nineteenth-century European Liberals, the Central American Liberals saw a role for a strong state to facilitate agro-export-based development through investment in infrastructure, particularly railroads, roads, and ports, and direct subsidies and special concessions to new industries. In Nicaragua (and elsewhere) their slogan was "Paz, Progreso, Libertad" (Peace, Progress, Liberty). The conflict between Liberals and Conservatives continued (and continues) well into the twentieth century.[5]

The disastrous Walker episode had been initiated by the Liberals in a desperate attempt to gain an advantage over their Conservative rivals. Walker's defeat ushered in a period of Conservative dominance and relative political stability (1857–1888) known in Nicaragua as "the thirty years." Despite their economic traditionalism, the Conservatives facilitated the development of a coffee export economy by paying modest premiums to coffee growers, establishing agricultural judges to coerce labor, and, most significantly, beginning the alienation of the communal land of indigenous Indian communities.[6] The rise of the new class of coffee growers, first in the sierras of Managua halfway between Granada and León, and then in northwestern Nicaragua, inland from León, upset the balance of power and the dominance of the Conservatives of the thirty years. The new coffee Liberals were satisfied neither with traditional Conservative philosophy nor with the pace of agro-export development. After a period of increasing instability, in July of 1893 José Santos Zelaya, Liberal politician and son of a prominent coffee grower from Managua, seized power in an armed uprising and initiated a sixteen-year period of Liberal rule.[7]

Although the Conservatives had hardly been hostile to the development of the coffee agro-export economy, the pace of change increased markedly under Zelaya and the Liberals. The money, land, and labor that coffee growers needed were obligingly supplied by the government. Cash subsidies to coffee growers and others engaged in export agriculture were greatly expanded. Coffee was guaranteed free shipment on government-controlled railways. Harsh labor codes were enacted that forced workers to choose between military service, work on public projects, or paid labor in the agro-export economy. A special force of agricultural guards was recruited to enforce what was essentially a system of forced labor. Debt servitude was institutionalized through the rigid enforcement of unequal labor contracts. In 1909 all titles to communal lands were abolished, completing the process of alienation that had begun with the Conservatives in 1871. Vast tracts of public lands were auctioned off at minimal prices or granted outright as concessions to those willing to plant coffee or other export crops. The result of this whirlwind series of reforms was the doubling of coffee exports under Zelaya's administration.[8]

The government agro-export program benefited an extremely small number of Liberal and some Conservative families of the colonial and republican elite. Fifty percent of all land sales under Zelaya went to only 30 families, all of them Liberals.[9] In 1900 just 57 growers received the bulk of government agricultural premiums paid in that year. Among them were leading Conservative as well as Liberal families.[10] In all, during the Zelaya period, 1,300,000 hectares were transferred to private owners, almost all of them members of the elite. Fifty years later, these lands still constituted a third of all agricultural land in Nicaragua.[11] The Liberal reforms created the pattern of monocultural agro-export production by large landed estates dependent on impoverished wage laborers that was a characteristic feature of twentieth-century Nicaraguan agriculture and a principal cause of the Sandinista revolution in 1979.

The greatest losers were the lower classes. They lost control of their lands, were recruited for forced labor, and received no benefits at all from premiums or concessions to elite coffee-growing families. Under Zelaya virtually the entire cost of agro-export development was paid by them. In 1881 the Indians of Matagalpa rose up in general insurrection—in Nicaragua called "the war of the communities"—against the Conservatives' communal land and forced labor policies. The insurrection was savagely repressed by the Conservatives. In 1895 a millennial movement broke out in the same region and was once again repressed, this time by the Liberals.[12] Zelaya himself saw communal lands as an "anachronistic" barrier to modernization and economic development, and his agrarian policies removed the communal economic base of an autonomous Indian culture.[13] Indian artifacts were appropriated to "enrich foreign Museums," and a new National Museum was established in Managua to provide enlightened citizens with a scientific view of the cultures Conservative and Liberal policies had destroyed.[14]

Liberal nationalism was based on an extremely circumscribed view of the nation essentially limited to the leading Liberal and Conservative families.[15] National development meant agro-export development under the control of this class, accompanied by the mobilization of the rest of the population as a dependent labor force. True to his Liberal philosophy, Zelaya embarked on a series of infrastructure improvements including an extensive railroad- and road-building program to facilitate the transport of coffee and other agro-export products. In 1906 he negotiated a $6 million dollar loan to be used in part to finance the construction of an Atlantic railroad linking the coffee regions of western Nicaragua with the Caribbean and from there to markets in New York and Europe.[16] He diligently negotiated with the United States to establish an interoceanic canal in Nicaragua.[17] He dramatically expanded the education system in Nicaragua and founded the first lending library in Managua, stocked with the works of French Enlightenment thinkers.[18] But Zelaya's liberalism, inspired by Enlightenment ideas, still defined the nation in terms of the economic development of a narrow agro-export elite.

Zelaya's assertive nationalism extended to foreign as well as domestic policy, and he brought to Nicaragua a degree of regional and even international power and prestige that it would not again attain until the Sandinista revolution in 1979. Like all Central American Liberals, Zelaya was committed to the idea of union. He established, but failed to sustain, a formal political union of Nicaragua, El Salvador, and Honduras. His efforts at union were opposed by Conservative Guatemalan dictator Manuel Estrada Cabrera. The conflict between the two strongest powers in Central America, one Liberal and the other Conservative, kept the region in turmoil and led to increased United States involvement. In 1907, prompted by the United States and Mexico, the Central Americans established a Court of Justice in Costa Rica to settle future regional disputes. Zelaya respected the court's authority, and regional tensions declined markedly in the last two years of his rule.[19]

Paradoxically, despite Zelaya's assertive nationalism, he welcomed foreign investment and turned over wide areas of the economy to foreign control. His instrument was the granting of exclusive rights or monopolies, called "concessions," in exchange for promises to develop a particular industry or resource. As Benjamin Teplitz notes, "Zelaya had a reputation for bestowing concessions on foreigners. Among such contracts were timber cutting to an Italian, government printing to a Spaniard, ice making to an American, publishing to a Panamanian, telegraph repair to an Austrian, rubber extracting to a Swiss, and aguardiente distilling to a syndicate of Englishmen, Italians and Spaniards." According to Teplitz, Zelaya showed "greater friendliness to Americans than did any other Central American president of his day."[20] In 1904, for example, he granted exclusive rights of navigation on the Escondido River, and thus a monopoly of the shipment of Nicaraguan bananas, to a subsidiary of the United Fruit Company.[21] Domestic critics charged Zelaya with selling out the country to the Yankees.

Despite Zelaya's partiality to foreign and especially United States investment, he was above all devoted to the economic development of the Nicaraguan nation, as he defined it, and in the end this brought his policies into collision with the expanding commercial and military empire of the United States. The point of friction was the Atlantic Coast of Nicaragua, a vast region of tropical lowlands which had been dominated by British interests through the largely autonomous Kingdom of Mosquitia. Although Britain had ceded nominal control of the Mosquitia to Nicaragua through the Treaty of Managua in 1860, the British-backed government of the Mosquitia still functioned as a informal protectorate when Zelaya seized power. Geographically and culturally remote from the centers of Hispanic Nicaragua, populated by Miskito and Sumu Indians and Afro-Creole settlers from the British Caribbean, and influenced by English language and religious institutions, the Mosquitia was always the weak link in Nicaraguan sovereignty.[22]

The weak government of the Kingdom of Mosquitia proved a compliant instrument in the hands of foreign investors, who rapidly developed the region into Nicaragua's most economically dynamic in the late nineteenth and early twentieth centuries. The Kingdom of Mosquitia readily granted concessions to foreigners, winked at customs regulations and taxation, and provided a congenial legal environment for foreign business enterprises. By the 1880s the Atlantic Coast port of Bluefields in the Mosquitia had become a world leader in the export of bananas, rivaling the Costa Rican banana port of Limón. The United Fruit subsidiary, the Bluefields Steamship Company, dominated the nineteenth-century banana trade. Gold mining also began in the 1880s and was controlled by American and German firms. Of these firms the most important one was the La Luz and Los Angeles Company, owned by the Fletcher family of Pittsburgh. The John D. Emery Company of Boston in 1894 obtained a concession in the Mosquitia to cut and export mahogany. By 1894, 90 to 95 percent of the commerce of the Mosquitia was under American control, and Bluefields had become an American town.[23]

After taking power in 1893, Zelaya moved rapidly to establish Nicaraguan sovereignty in the Mosquitia. In January 1894 Nicaraguan troops landed at Bluefields in response to a Honduran invasion of the Atlantic shore and initiated a complicated struggle to establish Nicaraguan control. Reluctant to give up their privileged position under the lax rule of the Kingdom, the American colony in the Mosquitia vociferously opposed Nicaraguan authority. In a development that R. L. Murrow has called "one of the few conflicts between United States government policy and United States businessmen," the United States backed Zelaya and the Nicaraguans against the American businessmen and their Miskito and Creole allies.[24] The reason for this departure from conventional foreign policy was the interoceanic canal which the United States still hoped to build in Nicaragua with the blessings of the Nicaraguan government. Continued British influence on the Mosquitia shore threatened U.S. control of a potential canal. After a complex struggle the British relinquished their remaining rights on the Atlantic Coast and the United States backed Zelaya's successful assertion of Nicaraguan sovereignty.[25]

American business, however, remained unreconciled. In 1899 a revolt by dissident Conservatives allied with the American business community failed when the United States, once again, refused to back the American businessmen. Given Zelaya's solicitude to foreign and especially U.S. interests, one can well wonder what so agitated the American business community. Although Zelaya did grant generous concessions to foreigners, he did not hesitate to cancel them when the terms were not fulfilled, and always placed the economic development of Nicaragua ahead of the interests of individual concessionaires.[26] In January 1907, for example, Zelaya canceled the Emery mahogany cutting concession, charging that the company had not reforested cut areas as promised and was abusing its duty-free import privileges. The Emery firm brought a claim against the Nicaraguan government. Zelaya, under intense pressure from the State Department, eventually settled the claim on terms the Nicaraguans regarded as extortionate. The settlement, however, did not reduce American business hostility to Zelaya.[27]

In 1909 another revolt in Bluefields broke out, once again led by a coalition of United States businessmen and Conservative opponents of Zelaya. But this time the United States did not remain neutral. After two American soldiers of fortune serving with the rebels were executed by Zelaya for attempting to blow up a government troop transport, Secretary of State Philander Knox sent a letter to Nicaragua's chargé d'affaires in Washington denouncing Zelaya and all his works and severing diplomatic relations with Nicaragua.[28] In the face of uncompromising United States hostility, Zelaya resigned. The Nicaraguan Liberal revolution had been ended by a note from the United States Secretary of State. It would prove to be the decisive act in twentieth-century United States-Nicaraguan relations. The

"Knox Note" began a prolonged United States diplomatic and military intervention in Nicaragua whose outcome is still uncertain 85 years later. It was the ultimate cause of the Sandinista revolution, the contra war, and the current shaky peace in Nicaragua. The reasons for the United States intervention have been debated ever since. As might be expected, its causes lie as much in the United States as they do in Nicaragua.

From the "Big Stick" to "Dollar Diplomacy": United States Imperial Ambitions and Nicaraguan Reality

On November 20, 1906, Theodore Roosevelt's Secretary of State, the corporate attorney Elihu Root, declared the end of one era of United States development and the beginning of another. In an address to Western businessmen he announced that the United States had now come to a point of "distinct and radical change in their economic relations with the rest of the world." No longer a debtor nation concerned with its own internal development, as it had been for three centuries, the United States was now accumulating a surplus of capital "with extraordinary rapidity." This surplus would cause the United States to search throughout the world "to find opportunity for the profitable use of our surplus capital, foreign markets for our manufactures, foreign mines to be developed, foreign bridges and railroads and public works to be built." The United States, he said, had taken the place of England, Germany, and France as the leader of the industrial enterprise of the world.[29]

As he spoke, North American "surplus capital" was already revolutionizing the Atlantic Coast of Nicaragua and building the greatest public work of the time in the Isthmus of Panama. Roosevelt had already used the "big stick" of United States naval power to "take the Isthmus [and] start the canal," as he would triumphantly declare a few years later.[30] A year before Root's address his President had added the Roosevelt Corollary to the Monroe Doctrine—the United States not only opposed foreign involvement in Latin America, but would intervene to prevent the political instability that might lead to such involvement. The policy had already been put into effect in the Dominican Republic, where financial instability threatened to lead to British intervention.[31] In Nicaragua Root and

Roosevelt followed a more cautious policy, pursuing negotiation and international agreements rather than direct intervention. Root refused to become involved in the machinations of American businessmen on the Atlantic Coast. The fundamental principles justifying United States intervention in Central America had, however, already been established by Roosevelt and Root, and the underlying causes of that intervention had been perceptively outlined by Root in his address.

United States policy in Nicaragua in the Zelaya era was actually governed by two initially contradictory objectives, both of which served North American commercial expansion. As John Findley has observed, "the first and most enduring American interest in Nicaragua was in the construction of an Isthmian canal."[32] The other objective was the American "surplus capital" rapidly accumulating on Nicaragua's Atlantic Coast. When the two objectives came into conflict, as they did in 1894 and 1899, the United States placed good relations with the Nicaraguan government and the potential Nicaraguan canal route above the interests of American businessmen. After 1903, when the Panama route became a reality, the interests of American businessmen on the Coast assumed greater importance in the State Department. As Findley notes, "from 1903 to 1909, the question of American claims against the Nicaraguan government reached an importance in the State Department rivaled only by the Department's concern with Zelaya's meddling [sic] in the affairs of his neighbors."[33]

Despite these concerns Root and Roosevelt pursued a generally conciliatory policy toward Zelaya, even after 1903. The election of the much more conservative William Howard Taft in November 1908 brought a distinct change in United States policy and began the era of dollar diplomacy in Central America. As Taft forthrightly declared, this diplomacy was based on "the axiomatic principle that the government of the United States shall extend all proper support to every legitimate and beneficial American enterprise abroad."[34] Dollar diplomacy intended to substitute "dollars for bullets" by extending North American bank loans to indebted Latin American countries to bind them close to the United States and avoid giving a pretext for foreign governments to intervene militarily, as they customarily did in the period, to collect unpaid debts. In practice, extending "all proper support . . . to American enterprise abroad" frequently included sending in the Marines when foreign governments resisted North American management of their financial affairs.[35]

Taft's election was accompanied by a series of sensational articles in the *Chicago Tribune* and other conservative Republican newspapers describing the supposed outrages of the Zelaya regime, most of which seem to have originated with his Conservative opponents or the United States Ambassador to Nicaragua. The Knox Note described the Zelaya government as a "blot on the history of Central America." Knox accused Zelaya of "keeping the entire region in turmoil" through "flagrant violations" of the peace accords of 1907, and denounced him as a tyrant who had destroyed republican institutions in Nicaragua. No evidence was advanced in support of any of these extraordinary assertions. Even though as late as 1908 Roosevelt had declared Zelaya "his great and good friend," the Taft administration and its allies in the press created an image of a vengeful tyrant bent on the destruction of his neighbors and political opponents. Needless to say the image had little basis in reality.[36]

Zelaya's real problem was that his economic nationalism represented an obstacle to "the profitable use of [U.S.] surplus capital" in Nicaragua and Central America. As Karl Berman has perceptively observed, "Zelaya's tampering with the concessions of United States companies and other nationalistic economic policies conflicted with the Taft Administration's plans to promote greater US investment in Central America and the Caribbean while his prestige challenged US political hegemony in the area."[37] United States foreign policy in the age of the "big stick" and "dollar diplomacy" was less concerned with the specific interests of particular firms than with the general issue of the economic and political hegemony of the United States in competition with declining European empires. Efforts to link Secretary Knox to direct U.S. investment in Nicaragua (he was the attorney for the Fletcher family, owners of the La Luz and Los Angeles gold mining firm, and reputed to be a stockholder) miss the point.[38] It was the general principle of United States investment, not the particular investments in Nicaragua, that agitated Knox and the State Department.

On the other hand, it is inadequate to argue that strategic and military concerns related to the security of a canal route or defense of the approaches to the Panama Canal once it was built were the primary issues in United States intervention. Zelaya was anxious to come to terms with the United States on a canal route and in 1901 accepted the outline of an agreement that was not too different from that finally agreed to by Nicaragua in 1914 after his overthrow.[39] And while the United States was concerned about its military and political dominance in the region and the defense of the canal, these concerns were inextricably tied with its emerging economic power, as the sage Elihu Root assuredly understood. A new era had begun in the United States: the age of American imperialism. The long-term consequences of the policies of this new age, however, were not even dimly understood at the time. In Nicaragua they created a political and human catastrophe from which neither Nicaragua nor the United States has as yet extricated itself.

The Fruits of Dollar Diplomacy: The United States Protectorate and the Rise of Sandino

The United States intervention had three related consequences with immense long-term significance to Nicaragua. First, it led to a prolonged and unsuccessful search for regimes friendly to the United States that could maintain political stability while excluding Zelayist Liberals. In practice this meant support of Conservatives or compliant Liberals, neither of whom were able to gain much popular backing. Second, true to the principles of "dollar diplomacy," the intervention created a financial protectorate that took key sectors of the economy out of the control of either the Nicaraguan government or the Liberal coffee elite and placed them in the hands of North American bankers. Third, in order to end the instability created by its own intervention, the United States created a new constabulary, the Nicaraguan National Guard, organized and initially officered by United States Marines. Eventually these three initiatives became institutionalized in the Somoza dictatorship. In the meantime, however, they generated a ferocious opposition movement led by dissident Liberal General Augusto César Sandino.

The victorious anti-Zelaya rebels, led by Juan Estrada, the renegade Liberal Governor of the Atlantic Coast, Adolfo Díaz, a Nicaraguan executive of the La Luz and Los Angeles mining concern, and Emiliano Chamorro, Nicaragua's eternal Conservative caudillo, soon fell to fighting among themselves. When a 1912 revolt by Minister of War Luis Mena, a member of the victorious Estrada coalition, was joined by Liberal Zelayists, the United States once again sent in the Marines. The force eventually reached 3,000 men. Mena surrendered, but Liberal General Benjamín Zeledón, holding the fortress of Coyotepe in Masaya, refused to lay down his arms. The Marines assaulted the fortress and captured Zeledón after a pitched battle. Zeledón was murdered, apparently by Nicaraguans, after studied inaction on the part of the Marine commander. Zeledón's body was paraded through the streets lashed to the back of a horse. The Marines remained in Nicaragua, except for a brief period from August 1926 to June 1927, until 1933. Most of this time the force consisted of a legation guard of 100 men, but it was enough to insure United States control. Nicaragua had become an occupied country.[40]

According to the precepts of dollar diplomacy, political stability was to be insured by extending loans underwritten by North American banks. As a condition of diplomatic recognition and continued support, the anti-Zelayist rebels agreed to accept a loan from two American banks secured by custom house receipts and the revenues of the Pacific railway, which also controlled steamships on Lake Nicaragua. Part of the loan was to be used to establish a National Bank, controlled by North American bankers, to manage Nicaragua's financial affairs.[41] North Americans also established a merchant company to export coffee. Because the National Bank also controlled loans to coffee growers, the North Americans gained complete control over Nicaragua's principal export.[42] Having given up its railroad, its custom house, its bank, and its major export commodity, Nicaragua then signed away its rights to any future canal as well as to strategic points in the Gulf of Fonseca and the Corn Islands, in the Bryan-Chamorro Treaty of 1914. Both the loan and the treaty were met with rioting in Managua. The Board of Directors of the Bank of Nicaragua, the ultimate power in the financial protectorate, continued to meet in New York as late as 1938.[43]

The Zelayist economic revolution had been reversed and the Liberal coffee elite had been dealt an economic blow from which it would never recover. The coffee economy stagnated and would not resume sustained expansion until the 1950s and 1960s. The rolling stock of the railroad deteriorated, road building slowed, and Zelaya's efforts to build the Atlantic railroad were abandoned. Coffee was brought to market on mule back.[44] Deprived of control of the banking system and the export trade, which had been the key to the success of the Salvadoran coffee elite, the coffee growers never became the nucleus of an important financial group. When private banks were finally formed in the 1950s, they were financed by León cotton growers and traditional Granada Conservatives, not by coffee growers.[45] In 1910, under the momentum of Zelaya's modernization program, Nicaragua held its first coffee census. It would not hold another until 1957. The Liberal and bourgeois revolution of Zelaya and the coffee elite had been destroyed by the world's most powerful liberal bourgeoisie. The coffee elite never again played an important political role in Nicaragua.

Because the United States intervention destroyed the local coffee bourgeoisie that might have supported a stable political system under capitalist auspices, the search for stability under the Conservatives was inherently doomed to failure. In 1925 the system again collapsed when hard-line Conservative Emiliano Chamorro launched still another rebellion, this time against the Conservative-Liberal coalition that had won a U.S.-supervised election in the previous year. Chamorro's successful coup was followed by a revolt by Liberals fighting in the name of deposed Liberal Vice President Juan B. Sacasa. Led by anti-Zelayist Liberal General José María Moncada, the Liberal armies defeated Chamorro's forces and were advancing on Managua when the United States once again intervened to prevent a Liberal victory. U.S. envoy Henry Stimson, dispatched by the Coolidge administration, negotiated a peace agreement under the threat of United States military intervention. Moncada and all his Liberal generals agreed to the accord. All but one.

Liberal General Augusto César Sandino rejected the Stimson agreement and accused Moncada of selling out the Liberal revolution to the Americans. He announced his intention to expel the Americans from Nicaragua by force of arms. Stimson was not dismayed. There were, he said, "general manifestations of gratitude to the United States" for its role in negotiating the peace agreement.[46] According to the terms of the peace agreement, negotiated at the town of Tipitapa in May 1927, the Liberals would lay down their arms in exchange for the right to participate in a U.S.-supervised election in 1928 (which they confidently expected to win). Conservative and U.S. favorite Adolfo Díaz would remain in power until that time. One other provision of the Tipitapa Accords (as they are called in the United States), which seemed less significant at the time, had much greater long-term significance. A non-partisan constabulary would be established—trained, organized, and led by United States Marine officers—to put an end to partisan armies and political revolts. The constabulary, called the Nicaraguan National Guard, would grow to become the decisive arbiter of political power in Nicaragua for the next fifty years.[47]

Despite the "friendly good will" that Stimson perceived as he sailed away from Nicaragua in May of 1927, the American intervention had left enough resentment and anti-American feeling to sustain a bitter six-year struggle against the American Marines, as well as to fuel the Sandinista revolution a half century later. The cycle of intervention fed on itself, as each new American involvement generated more resentment and instability that required ever deeper American involvement. In the end, as the Marines were drawn more deeply into the struggle, their presence became its principal motive force. The expulsion of the Marines would end the national humiliation that had begun with the overthrow of Zelaya in 1909—or so the predominantly poor Nicaraguans who followed General Sandino into battle thought. That the movement took the form it did was strongly conditioned by Zelaya's defeat and the American military, political, and financial intervention. But it also had much do with the ideas of General Sandino and his followers.

Sandino and the Failure of Revolutionary Nationalism

Born in the town of Niquinohomo in the sierras of Managua in 1895, Augusto Calderón Sandino was the illegitimate son of a wealthy coffee planter and Liberal. His mother, Margarita Calderón, was a coffee picker and domestic on his father's estate. His father nevertheless raised him as his own son, passing on to him his Liberal philosophy and love of the classics. Augusto was delighted to find that his first name was the same as the Roman emperor's and gradually began using César instead of Calderón as his middle name.[48] As the editor of his papers notes, Sandino personally witnessed many of the events surrounding the United States intervention, including the body of Benjamín Zeledón tossed over the back of a horse, and the arrest of his own father for protesting the Bryan-Chamorro treaty.[49] Sandino was a leading participant in the events of the 1926–27 civil war and Stimson intervention, and considered his war to be a continuation of the struggle of Zeledón to reverse the American intervention of 1909.[50] The national humiliation imposed by the North American intervention and the principal historical events of that era run like a thread throughout Sandino's writings and manifestos.

Sandino traced the humiliation of Nicaragua to the overthrow of Zelaya in 1909, which he wrongly, if patriotically, attributed to Zelaya's resistance to North American plans for a canal and efforts to gain German and Japanese support for a competing canal in Nicaragua. According to Sandino, Zelaya's efforts were frustrated by the treason of Chamorro, Díaz, and Estrada, who ended legitimate constitutional rule in Nicaragua and turned the country over to American Marines and Wall Street bankers.[51] "Vendepatria," literally "country seller," or, more idiomatically, "sell-out," became one of Sandino's (and later the Sandinistas') most popular epithets. It applied not only to those Conservatives who, like Chamorro and Díaz, betrayed Zelaya and consented to the humiliating Bryan-Chamorro Treaty and the U.S. financial protectorate, but also to Liberals like Moncada who had sold out the country once again at Tipitapa.[52] For Sandino the history of Nicaragua from 1909 to 1927 was one of unconstitutional betrayal. Reversal of the Bryan-Chamorro Treaty became one of his most frequently enunciated demands.[53]

Not only the historical figure but also the myth of Sandino have been the subject of heated scholarly and political debate.[54] There is almost unanimous agreement that, as Michael Schroeder concludes, Sandino's principal goal was "to free the Nicaraguan nation, and indeed all the Indo-Hispanic race, from the clutches of Yankee imperialism and its natural allies, the vendepatrias."[55] As latter-day Sandinista and Nicaraguan Vice President Sergio Ramírez noted, "Sandino's deeds were shaped by one fundamental contradiction: the contradiction between the Nicaraguan nation and North American

Imperialism."[56] Sandino called his army the Ejército Defensor de la Soberanía Nacional de Nicaragua (Army for the Defense of the National Sovereignty of Nicaragua) and his red and black colors symbolized, he said, a free country or death.[57] His slogan, placed in all official communications, was "Patria y Libertad" (Fatherland and Liberty).

Sandino's official shield showed a soldier of the Army for the Defense of National Sovereignty about to decapitate a prone, defenseless United States Marine. An "uncontrollable anti-Yankee phobia" verging on racism was one of the constant themes in his speeches and writings.[58] North Americans were frequently referred to as "machos," which had connotations of its contemporary meaning, but in Costa Rica and Nicaragua also means "blondes." It is usually translated as "blonde beasts." The invaders were also called "degenerate pirates," "paid assassins," "hired thugs," "morphine addicts," "murderers," "criminals," and "the enemy of our race and language." "The Yankees," Sandino wrote, "are the worst enemies of our people." No similar opprobrium was heaped on Spanish colonialists, since they had mixed their blood with that of Indians to create what Sandino called "the Indo-Hispanic race." In his first manifesto Sandino defended the Indo-Hispanic race against the "claws of the monstrous eagle with curved beak that feeds on the blood of Nicaraguans."[59]

As Michael Schroeder points out, such extravagant and venomous language was characteristic and was applied equally to the "barbarian colossus of the North" and the "vendepatrias" of Nicaragua. "Sixteen years ago [in 1909] Adolfo Díaz and Emiliano Chamorro ceased to be Nicaraguans," writes Sandino in his first manifesto. They and Liberals like Moncada were "traitors," "deserters," "cowards," "eunuchs," "swamp geese," "shameless hired assassins who have committed the crime of high treason." "My greatest honor," he continues, is "that I come from the lap of the oppressed, the soul and spirit of our race," and he claims "the bond of nationality" as justification for his actions.[60] The Indo-Hispanic race and the oppressed, not the traitorous oligarchs and sell-outs, were the Nicaraguan nation for which he fought. In a famous phrase that sums up the racial and pan-Latin American basis of his nationalism, Sandino declared, "Sandino es Indohispano y no tiene fronteras en América Latina" (Sandino is Indo-Hispanic and has no frontiers in Latin America).[61]

Although Sandino at times described himself as a "socialist" dedicated to a coming "proletarian explosion," and he actually did say, as the later Sandinista slogan claims, that "only workers and peasants go on to the end," there is no evidence that he ever developed any systematic class-based ideology or any socio-economic program beyond anti-Yankee nationalism.[62] There are no references to any writings by Marx or any Marxist in any of his published writings, speeches or interviews. Sandino's great hero was Bolívar, not Lenin.[63] Although he numbered among his lieutenants Salvadoran Communist Farabundo Martí and Peruvian Aprista Esteban Pavlevitch, there is no evidence that he subscribed to either's ideology. As Martí observed after he had been dismissed from his command by Sandino, "I was a Communist and understood that Sandino neither then or thereafter would be a Communist."[64] Pavlevitch too was relieved of his command, and Sandino's most trusted adviser became the Liberal physician Juan José Zepeda.[65] "This movement is national and anti-imperialist," Sandino told Basque journalist Ramón de Belausteguigoitia, insisting that he had "opposed . . . with all my strength" efforts to transform the movement into a struggle with "a more social character."[66]

Representative of Sandino's analysis of class issues is his portrayal of labor relations in the North American-owned San Albino gold mine in northern Nicaragua. San Albino is of particular significance in Sandino's movement. It was here that he worked as an assistant payroll clerk when he first returned to Nicaragua to join the Constitutionalist struggle, and here too that he first discovered his talent for rousing workers to political action. The "original 29" (actually closer to 40) members of his Liberal army in the civil war of 1926–27 were all from San Albino; so was a majority of the second "original 29" (really 29; 30 counting Sandino) with whom he began his war against the Marines. It was to San Albino that he returned after announcing his defiance of the Tipitapa Accords and from here that he dispatched his first manifesto to the Nicaraguans and the Indo-Hispanic race. The gold-mining country around San Albino provided his most consistent base of support for the next six years. Sandino made San Albino an international symbol of exploitation by foreign capital.[67]

In his second manifesto, also issued from San Albino, Sandino denounced the wretched conditions to which workers were subjected (payment in scrip, twelve-hour days, dishonest company stores, starvation wages), attributing them not to capitalism in general or even to a particularly greedy capitalist, but entirely to the national origin of the owners. "He *thinks himself authorized by nationality* [italics in original] to commit such abuses, . . . but being an American does not mean being invulnerable," he said of the mine owner (and his former employer), Charles Butters. In his own peculiarly nationalist version of the labor theory of value, Sandino proclaimed that "gold produced in the bowels of the Nicaraguan earth belongs to Nicaragua, and it is extracted by the hands of Nicaraguan workers." He had seized the mine for Nicaragua to redeem in gold the back wages of workers formerly paid in scrip. There is no suggestion of either a government nationalization or any change in the social relations of production. The debt paid, he even proposed to return the mine to its (American) capitalist owners. For Sandino the problem in Nicaragua was not capitalism, but North American capitalism.[68]

Nor did Sandino have any plan for reversing the land expropriations of the Zelaya era—he had no land reform program whatsoever. When asked by Belausteguigoitia if he planned to give land to those that did not have it, Sandino replied, "Yes, of course, that will not be hard for us to do. We have uncultivated land, perhaps the best in the country." Sandino was referring not to land reform but rather to his plan to colonize frontier lands along the Coco River. Here he favored cooperatives rather than capitalist small holdings, but he never spoke publicly of land reform.[69] "There is not need for class struggle in Nicaragua," Sandino said, "because here the working class lives well; it struggles only against the American intervention."[70] Although he consistently saw himself heading a people's movement with "an advanced position on social questions,"[71] he never advanced any program that would have challenged rural or urban property relations or indeed any specific socio-economic program whatsoever. Class, as opposed to national, issues were almost entirely absent from his thought.

The same appears to be true of his followers. Interviews with surviving members of Sandino's army undertaken by the latter-day Sandinista Party Institute for the Study of Sandinismo (Instituto de Estudios de Sandinismo or IES) and by North American scholars found an almost total absence of class themes. As one of the North American scholars notes, "On the whole there is a deep silence in the IES testimonials with respect to issues of land, labor, and relations between rich and poor—and with respect to ethnicity—issues that fade in comparison to Conservative and Yankee violence."[72] Only a quarter of the interviews even mentioned the subject of property relations, and most of these involved vague promises of land, probably recollections of the Río Coco colonization scheme.[73] According to Richard Grossman, the most frequent motive for joining the Army for the Defense of National Sovereignty was, not surprisingly, nationalism in various forms (82 percent of those interviewed), followed by liberalism (a little more than half), although most could not explain what liberalism was.[74] As Schroeder concludes, "The IES interviews make abundantly and painfully clear that *opposition to the Marine invasion* [italics in original] was far and away the single most important motive force propelling the Rebellion from beginning to end."[75]

Hatred of Yankees was filtered though the prism of Sandino's own anti-Yankee racism, but it also reflected the real presence and atrocious behavior of the Marine occupiers. The famous photo of U.S. Marine Lt. O. E. Pennington holding the severed head of a Sandinista soldier is not a fake and says more about Marine attitudes toward their opponents, whom they invariably referred to as "bandits," than any number of Marine combat reports.[76] The deep-seated racism and arrogance of Marine officers and men in Nicaragua was repaid with the racial hatred of Sandino's peasant supporters.[77] In the countryside it was a war without quarter. Marine documents are filled with reports of prisoners "shot while trying to escape." As would be the case in Vietnam, whole areas of north central Nicaragua were converted into free-fire zones in which any running Nicaraguan was shot. Houses, cattle, and crops were burned to deprive the enemy of supplies. Any "suspicious" group or settlement of Nicaraguans was mercilessly bombed and strafed, killing hundreds of civilians. Although some of the most vivid Nicaraguan memories, such as reports of rapes and the bayoneting of children, are not based in fact, the disgraceful conduct of the United States Marines kindled hatred in the minds of Nicaraguan men, women, and children that still burned brightly fifty years later in the IES interviews.[78]

The Marines themselves became the single most important stimulus to the movement they were sent to end. American Ambassador Hanna himself recognized that the American occupation was "the principal cause of Sandino's belligerency."[79] After an ambush on New Year's Eve 1931, in which eight of a patrol of ten Marines died, Henry Stimson, now Secretary of State, agreed to withdraw the Marines from the combat to which his Tipitapa agreement had committed them five years before. The last Marine was withdrawn on January 2, 1933, one day after Liberal Juan B. Sacasa, in whose name Sandino had launched his Constitutionalist revolt, was sworn in as President. Sacasa immediately negotiated a peace with Sandino. The American intervention over, Sandino signed the peace agreement on February 2, 1933, and his army, numbering some 2,600, laid down their arms. The truce left the Nicaraguan National Guard, created by the Marines but now directed by a Nicaraguan, Anastasio Somoza García, as the only significant military force in the country. On the afternoon of February 21, 1934, "the last Marine," as Somoza was called, ordered the murder of Sandino. Sandino was taken to the Managua airport and machine-gunned to death the same night.[80]

Sandino's murder was the signal for an eight-day orgy of killing in which hundreds of his supporters were murdered by the National Guard in an action reminiscent of the Salvadoran *matanza* of 1932.[81] Sacasa took no action against Somoza or the Guard. Two years later Somoza overthrew Sacasa and in January 1937 assumed the presidency, beginning the dynasty that would rule Nicaragua until the Sandinista revolution of 1979. In 1936 Somoza published a book entitled *El verdadero Sandino o el Calvario de las Segovias* (The True Sandino or the Calvary of the Segovias) to defend the murder of Sandino and the massacre of his followers. Sandino's demobilized forces represented a potential threat to Somoza's continued military control, as Somoza himself obliquely admitted.[82] The murder of Sandino was the basis for Somoza's rise to power. It is not surprising that the rebels of fifty years later would take Sandino's name to challenge the legitimacy of his regime's foundation. On July 17, 1979, Somoza's son exhumed the dictator's body from the family crypt in Managua and flew it and himself to Miami. The Somoza dynasty that had begun with the death of Sandino had ended.

In the end Sandino's greatest strength, his anti-Yankee nationalism, turned out to be his fatal weakness. As Gregorio Selser observed,

"Sandino neither would nor could see beyond his immediate objective, to stop the intervention. That once achieved, he thought Nicaraguans—and by extension Latin Americans—would solve their own problems, the parties would be honest, the military less ambitious, the businessmen more honorable, and the workers and *campesinos* less despoiled."[83] Most of his followers no doubt would have agreed. With the intervention over they too had lost the reason for their struggle, as their leader himself sagely acknowledged.[84] The absence of any social program meant that Sandino was never able to mobilize much support outside of the north central frontier zone of the Segovias where he first called the San Albino miners to arms. He was never able to reach an agreement with the nascent Nicaraguan labor party, which in any event did not have much of a working class to represent.[85] Sandino's ideology offered little to the peons of the great cattle estates of Boaco or Chontales or the coffee latifundia of the sierras of Managua. The estates were, after all, owned by Nicaraguans, and far from the Marines and foreign business enclaves.

Sandino did recruit a substantial following among poor peasants, most of whom had some land, and mine workers in north central Nicaragua, and eventually gained a significant following in the Atlantic Coast banana zone after the Depression crisis stimulated discontent there, much as it had in Costa Rica.[86] These were areas of the greatest foreign economic penetration in Nicaragua: in the gold mining fields around San Albino, the banana plantations and mahogany operations on the Atlantic Coast, and in the coffee country south to San Rafael in Matagalpa.[87] The northwest coffee zone had the largest participation by foreigners, many of them Americans. Sandino's anti-imperialism must have resonated with the poor peasants and workers in an area dominated by foreign business even if economic issues played little role in his ideology. Whatever economic issues were generated by the foreign economic enclave were submerged in Sandino's anti-Yankee nationalism, reinforced by Marine depredations.

Sandino and the Myth of Indo-Hispanic Nicaragua

Sandino was, as he said, the leader of an oppressed people, many Indo-Hispanic, but others just plain Indian. Yet he never developed any notion of an autonomous Indian identity and shared the widespread Liberal belief in the civilizing power of Hispanic culture and economic modernization. In one of his last interviews he described how he hoped, through his plans for the economic development of the Atlantic Coast, "to civilize these poor Indians who are the marrow of our race," but still thought it difficult to instil in them even "the most elementary notions of morality and hygiene."[88] Sandino's racial fiction of the Indo-Hispanic actually concealed the fundamental ethnic and economic divide of northern and eastern Nicaragua—that between the rich upper class largely of Spanish extraction and the poor, predominantly Indian populations of the region recently dispossessed by the Liberal reforms of Zelaya.[89] It was the Hispanic Liberals, not the "blonde beasts of North America," who had despoiled the Indian communities and destroyed their culture to bring them the benefits of civilization.[90] It was the Hispanic Liberals too who granted most of the foreign concessions that brought miners and coffee and banana planters to the Indian lands. A half century later the Indians of the Atlantic Coast were still resisting the civilizing mission of Sandino's heirs, the Sandinistas.

All nationalisms, as Anthony Smith has most persuasively argued, are founded on historical myths.[91] Sandino's Indo-Hispanic race was one; the "blonde beast" was another. Both submerged the primary contradictions within Nicaragua itself, of race and of class (to say nothing of gender), by posing a false dichotomy between a mythical Nicaraguan nation, united (except for a few "sell-outs") by blood and culture, and an avaricious band of Yankee pirates united in their quest for economic and racial domination. That there were avaricious and racist Yankees in Nicaragua lent credence to nationalist myth making, but did not remove ethno-class divisions within Nicaragua. Upper-class Hispanic Nicaraguans, including Liberals like Zelaya and Zeledón, no less than "sell-outs" like Díaz and Chamorro, had less in common with the Indian and mixed-race working people of north central Nicaragua than they did with the "blonde beasts" from North America. Sandino was, as he claimed, the heir of the Liberal national revolution of Zelaya and Zeledón. But his followers had been the principal victims of that revolution.

Sandino was, among other things, a mystic and a spiritualist, although these tendencies have been downplayed by his Sandinista interpreters. He was a devoted follower of the so-called "magnetic-

spiritual school of the universal commune" of the Argentinian Joaquín Trincado, who preached the Zoroastrian god of "Light and
Truth."[92] As José Román observes, Sandino's spiritualism "does not
subtract one whit from his gigantic crusade. On the contrary, perhaps it may not have been possible without it."[93] It may explain the
almost religious hold that, according to Ramón Belausteguigoitia,
he had over his troops.[94] His crusade was as much a millennial movement as it was a national liberation struggle. After the millennium
the God of Love and Truth would bring universal justice to all and
make all men brothers, as Sandino outlined in his notorious "Light
and Truth" manifesto.[95] His proposed Coco River department was
to be called Light and Truth, after the Zoroastrian deity. Only
Hodges and paradoxically Somoza, among the many interpreters of
Sandino, have made this side of his thought central, but his movement can not be understood without it.[96]

Millennial movements, like nationalism, deal with mythical and
mystical events, not with real history. As Marvin Harris has persuasively argued, all millennial movements have a secret that cannot be
acknowledged because it would split the basis of the movement's
support or involve it in fatal confrontations with authorities.[97] What
was Sandino's millennial secret? Although any such judgment is
speculative, in fact Sandino never acknowledged that driving out the
Marines would not necessarily improve the lot of his poor followers,
and might actually make it worse. True, they would be free of Marine
depredations, but they would still be exposed to the tender mercies
of the Liberal Hispanic elite. There is evidence that Sandino sensed
this secret. In one of his last interviews he told José Román that he
would be killed by other Nicaraguans, but by Nicaraguans in the
service of foreigners. He could not acknowledge that the Liberal
Hispanic nation-builders were in the end also his enemies and those
of poor Nicaraguans.[98] This was Sandino's millennial secret. It was
the same hidden contradiction that underlay his anti-Yankee nationalism.

Although later Sandinista interpreters have tried to find in him
an early proponent of post-World War II national liberation movements, the absence of any social, ethnic, or class analysis in his racial
and mystical nationalism separated him decisively from such movements. Such analysis was to be one of the defining characteristics of

his later Sandinista interpreters.[99] Sandino was a pure nationalist with no plan to transform Nicaragua after the Marines were gone, and no solution for or even acknowledgment of the fundamental contradictions in Nicaragua that had existed from the time of the conquest. Sandino's mythical Nicaraguan nation did not in fact exist in 1909 or 1934, although his struggle to incorporate the poor into the existing culture and society might have created such a nation. Sandino's struggle for a mystical and mythical national identity simply concealed exploitation by the *criollo* elite that had always controlled the Nicaraguan poor. Trading Yankee for Hispanic exploiters offered little to the Nicaraguan poor.

This is not to say that driving out the Yankees was not a necessary condition for any social or economic progress. The North American intervention was an economic, political, and social tragedy from which Nicaragua has still not recovered. And the intervention itself was renewed with a vengeance in the 1980s, further damaging the country. But the Liberal revolution of the Hispanic coffee elite in Central America, including Nicaragua, had been as damaging to most of the population. The Liberal revolution in El Salvador, with no direct United States protectorate, created the social conditions that led to 1932. In Costa Rica, of course, the Liberal revolution of the coffee elites had a much happier outcome.

Which way would the Liberal revolution have gone in Nicaragua? Zelaya's reforms certainly were moving in the direction of the Salvador model of lower-class expropriation and upper-class land concentration. At the same time, there was a stronger class of small holders, who persist in the northwest coffee zone into the present (see Chapter 2). Without United States intervention Nicaragua might have moved closer to the Costa Rican outcome—but we will never know. That is perhaps the ultimate tragedy of "dollar diplomacy" in Nicaragua: the country never got to work out its own destiny for better or, possibly, even for worse. In the 1980s too American intervention would work to prevent a Nicaraguan solution to the country's immense problems, inherited as much from Spain as North America. The problems remain unresolved at this writing.

The United States intervention that gave birth to Sandino's mystical nationalism also inhibited the formation of social classes that might have provided the social base for a class-oriented movement. If the Liberal reforms had continued, it is possible that the developing export economy might have created a rural proletariat like the coffee zones of El Salvador or the Atlantic Coast of Costa Rica, or even a class of commercial small holders like the coffee growers of Costa Rica. All three groups were the social base for important class-based movements, the Communist Party of El Salvador, the Communist Party of Costa Rica, and Manuel Marín's National Association of Coffee Growers in Costa Rica, and could have played the same role in Nicaragua. The American intervention, however, both financial and military, weakened the coffee economy and much of the banana industry as well. The Atlantic Coast was never a dynamic region of Nicaragua after the 1920s. The lack of export development also inhibited the development of the urban artisanal working class that was so important in class-based movements in both El Salvador and Costa Rica. The weakness of class-based appeals in Nicaragua reflected the weaknesses of capitalism and capitalist class relations themselves.

Similarly, the North American intervention and the defeat of the Liberal revolution of the coffee elite prevented the emergence of a cohesive agrarian bourgeoisie in control of the state, as was the case in both El Salvador (before 1932) and Costa Rica (until 1948). The Nicaraguan bourgeoisie continued to be divided between Liberal and Conservative factions, and the state remained a tool of prominent families, including finally the Somozas, rather than the expression of domestic class interests. This inhibited the formation of class-based oppositional alliances and restricted the development of the bourgeoisie itself. The Nicaraguan elite remained a frustrated, fragmented bourgeoisie in the making. In the 1970s it was still awaiting the return of the bourgeois revolution initiated by José Santos Zelaya in 1893. Some of its members, as we shall see in the Chapter 9, thought they had found such a revolution in 1979. They were once again to be disappointed. The ideology of the Nicaraguan agrarian bourgeoisie in the 1970s cannot be understood without understanding the failure of bourgeois revolution in 1909. Their hopes and dreams remain the same now as then—"Paz, Progreso," and, above all, "Libertad."

The Dead Hand of the Past: The Legacy of the 1930s in Central America

The crisis of the 1930s in Central America removed the coffee elite from direct rule in El Salvador, Nicaragua, and finally, in 1948, in Costa Rica. In place of the elite in El Salvador and Nicaragua were dictators who had seized power to control the social forces set in motion by the Great Depression. These narrowly based dictatorships were to come apart with stunning speed in the next great world economic crisis in the 1970s. Only Costa Rica, with a broadly based popular government that extended not only democratic but social citizenship to most of the population, avoided the revolutionary decade of the 1980s. These political outcomes depended not only on differing class relations in the coffee export economy of each country, but also on the nature of the oppositional ideologies, themselves closely related to these class relations. Proletarianization and class polarization in El Salvador restricted reform and facilitated revolutionary communism, just as family farmers and class collaboration encouraged Euro-communism in Costa Rica. The absence of well-defined classes in Nicaragua, except for a clearly defined group of foreign capitalists, inhibited class-based ideologies, and together with the Marine presence, favored Sandino's nationalism.

The new ideological order of the coffee elite that emerged in response to these oppositional movements had changed markedly from nineteenth-century Liberal orthodoxy. In El Salvador the elite remained committed to order and, above all, progress, but embraced a new and more savage authoritarianism, a fear of change, and a contempt for Liberal principles of legality and humanity that belied the Enlightenment origins of their thought. At the core of these new beliefs was a paranoid anti-communism that had become an item of national faith. In Nicaragua liberalism, like Sandinismo, remained as a suppressed undercurrent without practical effect in the Somozas' tyranny. In the 1970s this liberalism fused with a reborn Sandinismo to destroy the Somoza regime. In Costa Rica the positivist Liberal ideology of the Olympians was substantially modified by the reform Catholicism and socialism of its opponents. At the end of the tumultuous 1980s the Costa Rican elite would pride itself on how its

Liberal ideology had been "socialized" and how it had, therefore, avoided the terrors of El Salvador and Nicaragua. Nevertheless, the civil war of 1948 had enshrined anti-communism as an article of national faith while at the same time incorporating Communist programs. The Liberal vision of order, progress, and liberty had been modified to include a much more violent authoritarianism justified by the ideology of anti-communism.

None of the oppositional ideologies that emerged in the 1930s to challenge the Liberal order of the coffee elite was wholly successful, and two were complete failures. Neither the Salvadoran Communists nor the Nicaraguan followers of Sandino recognized the actual complexities of Central American class structure. Martí's "worker-peasant soviets" and Sandino's "Indo-Hispanic" race were both fictions that concealed the fact that workers, even rural ones, were a minority in El Salvador in the 1930s, or that the Hispanic upper class held a monopoly of national power in Nicaragua. Martí's vision never encompassed small holders, professionals, progressive members of the elite, the Church, or other important social forces in the real, as opposed to the ideological, construction of El Salvador. Sandino, faced with a weak or non-existent working class and a fragmented and weak bourgeoisie, tried to carry through in the name of the poor and oppressed a bourgeois nationalist revolution of the rich. This contradictory mission was his undoing. The fate of millennial dreams—both Communist and nationalist—in Central America was the same. Both ended in murder and massacre.

Manuel Mora and Costa Rican Euro-communism were the only leader and ideology to survive the Depression crisis. Costa Rican communism was the only oppositional ideology to come to terms with the realities of its national class and social structure. Mora and the Costa Rican Communists, in contrast to Martí and Sandino, never threatened the established order, particularly the established institutions of property. They were strong enough to make change necessary, but not so threatening as to make it impossible. The result was a social democratic society and ideology that left Costa Rica's social structure and position in the international division of labor unchanged. After the 1948 revolution Costa Rica remained what it still is today—a small, peripheral agro-export economy with the most aristocratic political elite in Central America. Both Martí and

Sandino dreamed greater dreams of class and national transformation. The Costa Rican Communists dreamed less and accomplished more. But they left for another day the transformation of Costa Rica into an egalitarian autonomous society. That day has still not come in Costa Rica.

The visions of Martí, Mora, and Sandino continued to exist in each national consciousness as suppressed undercurrents and alternative discourses for the construction of Central American reality. Sandino, however uncertainly, spoke for the poor, the oppressed, the ethnically distinct, those left out of the Nicaraguan state and the Liberal revolution that he fought so vigorously to defend. He provided a powerful image of national struggle against the North American colossus that seized the imagination of Latin Americans everywhere. Somoza and Sandino became powerful symbolic poles of national humiliation and redemption. Martí and Mora spoke the language of internal class oppression eschewed by Sandino and entirely absent from the ruling discourse of El Salvador after 1932 and Costa Rica after 1948. The language of class remained (and remains today) a powerful and threatening force in El Salvador and an unspoken rebuke to the inequalities of the Costa Rican agro-export order. These currents of national and class-based liberation would emerge and fuse in the national revolutionary struggles in the 1980s. To choose the name "Martí" or "Sandino" for a movement struck at the heart of the new ideological order of the coffee elite that emerged from the Depression crisis.

It was with the ideologies forged in the Depression crisis that the coffee elite faced the next great systemic crisis in world capitalism in the 1970s. The Liberal faith in progress, liberty and, in the case of Costa Rica, democracy, fused with the anti-communist authoritarianism that was the heritage of the 1930s, proved inadequate in response to new challenges both to that belief system and the political order on which it rested. When members of the elite were interviewed between 1986 and 1990, they were in the midst of a revolutionary crisis even more profound than that of the 1930s. They were struggling to construct a new system to make sense of that crisis. The four chapters that follow examine these beliefs as they emerged in the interviews. They do not constitute a formal ideology like that of the Communist International in the 1930s or nineteenth-century liberalism, but take the form of narratives, stories told by a class about itself. These stories, as they were told to the author in the 1980s, were shaped by the events of the 1930s which had touched the families or even the persons of many of those interviewed. They were not the stories of Martí and Sandino, which existed only as silences and elisions in the narratives of the coffee elite. This silence was established at great human cost, as this section makes clear. It also proved costly to maintain. In the 1980s the coffee elite found out exactly how costly. The suppressed voices of the 1930s returned to speak in the symbolic language of those two long dead heroes of the 1930s, Agustín Farabundo Martí and Augusto César Sandino.

III

~

*Narratives of Class:
The Crisis of the 1980s*

6

Agro-Industrialists versus Agrarians in El Salvador

In the crisis of the 1930s the Salvadoran elite presented a united front in opposition to both the reformism of Araujo and the communism of Martí. When the ideological descendents of Martí renewed their struggle in the 1980s, the response of the elite was once again to close ranks in support of the hard-line policies of the army and Roberto D'Aubuisson and his ARENA Party. As the revolutionary decade and the civil war continued with no end in sight, however, differences emerged between the two powerful fractions of the Salvadoran coffee elite—the agro-industrialists and the agrarians. Increasingly, the agro-industrialists looked for a way out of the crisis even at the expense of abandoning significant elements of the authoritarian order or reaching an accommodation with the FMLN. Some hard-line members of the agrarian fraction, on the other hand, continued, and continue, to resist the democratic opening in El Salvador. The disunity, particularly apparent after the last great offensive of the FMLN in 1989 convinced many members of the elite that the war was unwinnable, followed fault lines that had already developed within the coffee sector between processors and producers.

As early as 1961 the separation of interests had become sufficiently pronounced to occasion the founding of a new organization that would represent the miller-exporters. The Asociación Salvadoreña de Beneficiadores y Exportadores de Café (ABECAFE) was established

187

as an alternative to the traditional organization of Salvadoran coffee growers, the Asociación Salvadoreña de Café (ASCAFE, often known in El Salvador as simply La Cafetalera).[1] The older group, founded in 1929, had been the main economic-interest group of the Salvadoran coffee elite, and its early boards of directors read like a "who's who" of the Salvadoran elite—Alfaro, Hill, Dueñas, Magaña, Alvarez.[2] In the area of economic policy-making the Cafetalera became a virtual state within a state, and after the founding of the Banco Hipotecario in 1934 and the Companía Salvadoreña del Café in 1942, a major factor in the large-scale management of the coffee economy. The Cafetalera was the major stockholder in both groups, and together the three interlocking organizations brought the coffee economy out of the Depression and began the postwar transformation of the industry that made it a world leader in coffee during the 1970s.[3]

Leading coffee families, millers and producers alike, continued to serve on the Cafetalera board of directors through the 1950s, but after ABECAFE was founded in 1961, the milling and exporting elite focused on its own organization. By the 1970s, few names of large processors or leading coffee families appeared on the Cafetalera board, and the organization increasingly was dominated by non-elite producers.[4] Nevertheless, ABECAFE represented only a fraction of the leading families, in particular such immigrant coffee millers and exporters as the Hills, Daglios, and Borgonovos as well as members of the traditional elite like the Salaverrías and Llaches, who had made the transition to the industrial phase of the industry. Notable coffee-growing families of the republican period such as the Dueñas, Regalado, Quiñónez, and Meléndez clans have been underrepresented in ABECAFE and other institutions of the milling elite.[5] Although the interests of all of these families extend beyond coffee, the division in the coffee economy between ABECAFE and the Cafetalera is one manifestation of the division between the agro-financial and agro-industrial factions at the heart of Salvadoran elite politics.

The election of Alfredo Cristiani—a descendent of Italian immigrants, past president of ABECAFE, and heir to the Cristiani-Burkard coffee-processing fortune—as President of El Salvador thus represented less a return to the "coffee republic" of the Meléndez-Quiñónez dynasty (1911–1927) than the emergence of the agro-industrial faction of the coffee elite (among them the coffee processors belonging to ABECAFE) as the leading contender for power. In 1980–81 Cristiani's family firm ranked as the tenth-largest coffee processor in El Salvador. The eminence grise of the administration, Cristiani's brother-in-law, Roberto Llach Hill, is the fifth largest processor. For the critical diplomatic post in Washington, Cristiani chose his friend Miguel Angel Salaverría, then general manager of Prieto, S. A., the eighth largest processor. These three men and two of their first cousins together controlled five of the fifteen largest coffee-processing firms in El Salvador.[6] All five men belonged to ABECAFE, and Salaverría as well as Cristiani had served as president of the organization. All five were founding members of the Fundación Salvadoreña para el Desarrollo Económico y Social (FUSADES), an influential policy-research center closely tied to the U.S. Agency for International Development and the U.S. Embassy, and two served on its critical coffee committee.

From the era of General Gerardo Barrios in the nineteenth century to the overthrow of President Arturo Araujo by General Maximiliano Hernández Martínez on 9 December 1931, the coffee elite had ruled El Salvador almost without interruption. For the following sixty years, however, no member of the coffee elite occupied the Salvadoran presidency. Formal state power was held first by a succession of military juntas and dictatorships and then by the elite's arch-opponent, Christian Democrat José Napoleón Duarte.

Election of a member of the agro-industrial fraction of the coffee elite to the presidency in 1989 did not necessarily imply a major change in political direction. The army remains a formidable political force and has been an important ally of the coffee elite in the past. The hard line of the agrarian fraction, represented in the ruling ARENA Party by the late Roberto D'Aubuisson, retains substantial influence. Nevertheless, the election of Cristiani and even more the acceptance of the Chapultepec peace treaty represent a sharp break with the authoritarian past and an implicit rejection of the hard-line agrarian fraction. At the time of the interviews the elite was in the midst of this transition.

The interviews analyzed here reflect the divisions within the Salvadoran elite. Most of those interviewed belonged to the ABECAFE faction of the milling and exporting agro-industrial elite, including

President Cristiani and Ambassador Miguel Angel Salaverría. A substantial minority of those interviewed were growers associated with the Cafetalera. That group itself was split into two antagonistic factions, one sharing broad areas of agreement with the ABECAFE elite and the other dissenting, often vehemently, from the views of what one of them dismissed as the "Red millionaires" of ABECAFE-FUSADES. The views of the ABECAFE members and their allies in the Cafetalera may be understood as reflecting the views of the agro-industrial fraction of the coffee elite. The dissenters in the Cafetalera represent the views of the traditional agrarian fraction of coffee growers.

Given the number of officers of both ABECAFE and the Cafetalera among the interviewees, the views expressed can be taken as reasonably representative of both fractions. Understanding the relationship between the apparently hegemonic agro-industrial fraction of millers and exporters in ABECAFE and the dissenting agrarian fraction of the Cafetalera is central to understanding the chances for authoritarianism or democracy in El Salvador. The views of the agro-industrial ABECAFE elite, now formally in political control, are crucial to prospects for democracy and peace in El Salvador. Both they and their opponents in the Cafetalera told stories about the Salvadoran present and past that reflected their own well-defined viewpoints. Topics that did not fit into these narratives could be raised with difficulty, if at all. The central themes of these narratives, as well as the denials, elisions, and tensions surrounding them, provide insights into the elite's thinking at the precise historical moment of fission between the agro-industrial and agrarian fractions.

The View from ABECAFE

Coffee, Gift of God

Whatever the differences of opinion within the coffee elite, none of its members doubt the centrality of coffee to El Salvador's past, present, and future. Several of those interviewed pointed out that coffee will remain "the backbone" of the Salvadoran economy. Any questioning of this idea was met with incredulity. One former ABECAFE president explained, "If coffee is good, the economy is good;

if it is bad, the economy is bad." President Cristiani made it clear in a pre-election interview that reviving the coffee economy was the main plank of his economic and social policy and a key component in his military policy as well. He pointed out that coffee production under the Christian Democrats had totaled less than half its pre-1979 levels, and that at late-1970s prices, the earlier level of production could have brought in foreign exchange approaching one billion dollars, more than twice the current level of U.S. aid. According to Cristiani, reviving the coffee economy would deprive the guerrillas of their oxygen—social and political discontent—and permit ARENA to pursue a military policy independent of U.S. restraints.

All those interviewed regarded efforts to diversify or reorient the Salvadoran economy as ill-conceived at best, and many found the idea preposterous. Another ABECAFE president scoffed, "What are we going to export—hammocks?" The president of a major coffee co-op quoted a conversation with former U.S. Vice President and Secretary of Agriculture Henry Wallace, whom he met when Wallace traveled to El Salvador. Wallace told him that those saying "diversify" never told you what to diversify into. They were, according to Wallace, charlatans. The co-op president repeated the word "charlatans" with evident satisfaction. A leading miller noted with some dismay that U.S. AID had emphasized diversifying into ornamental plants, flowers, and fruits, and he decried the lack of research on coffee cultivation. Even one of the main beneficiaries of such diversification, the owner of a multimillion-dollar melon farm, still regarded coffee as the main pillar of the Salvadoran economy in the foreseeable future. Another ABECAFE president, in a sophisticated analysis of the Salvadoran economy, emphasized that even domestic industry like the Phelps Dodge wire factory required imported copper, and that such imports could only be purchased with funds generated by coffee exports.

No member of the coffee elite perceived any contradiction between an agricultural economy based on coffee and industrial development. On the contrary, most viewed the former as indispensable for the latter. When asked about coffee's role in the economy, one member of the ABECAFE board replied, "Are you kidding? The banks—everything—depends on it." He then used a hand-held calculator to compute the effective demand generated by wages paid during the coffee harvest and pointed out that without those wages, little demand would exist for industrial products. Several growers made identical arguments. None seemed to see a low-wage rural economy as an obstacle to the development of adequate internal markets. Those interviewed did not exaggerate rural wage levels but argued that they were generally high when compared with the earnings of urban unskilled labor in El Salvador, and argued that without coffee the rural economy would collapse. Several even claimed that mismanagement under the Duarte regime had caused the rural coffee economy to collapse, and that this debacle had played a major role in the Christian Democrats' defeat.

Those interviewed were certain that once the constraints imposed by government intervention in the coffee economy were eliminated, coffee would lead El Salvador into a balanced industrial development with broad benefits for all Salvadorans, including the poor. None saw any need to change the agrarian export model that had dominated El Salvador for a century and a half without producing any significant industrial development. Rather, they argued, El Salvador had reached the point of industrial takeoff just when the civil war intervened. One past president of the Cafetalera asserted that Brazilian and Colombian development demonstrated that coffee could lead directly to industrial development. In a series of paid announcements in leading San Salvador newspapers, ABECAFE had claimed during the 1984 election that a decline in coffee production would lead to numerous prejudicial outcomes: a dramatic drop in foreign-exchange earnings, insufficient tax revenues to pay for public services, increased rural unemployment, bankruptcy for thousands of businesses, difficulty in importing primary materials for manufacturing, difficulty in purchasing imported medicines for the general public, and budget cuts for education and health services.[7]

Whatever the merits of these arguments—and it is far from clear that any other crop is as well adapted to El Salvador's climatic and geological conditions as coffee—the vigor, enthusiasm, and sincerity with which these claims were put forth were striking. All those interviewed would undoubtedly agree with the role assigned to coffee growers in the following excerpt from an ABECAFE position paper entitled "Coffee Culture, Gift of God":

Coffee has made it possible in a tiny densely populated territory, devoid of such natural resources as forests, petroleum, natural gas, metals, and precious stones, to find work and to achieve economic development.

People from various countries journeyed here decades ago to live and work with us. Those who dedicated themselves to coffee experimented with different cultivation methods and new varieties of coffee and shade trees, identified pests and diseases and combated them, improved processing, invented drying equipment, opened markets in the exterior, and taught us how to compete. To mention some of the names that were new at first and are now our own and make up a cosmopolitan mosaic representing different nationalities that have fused with ours—Choussy, Alvarez, Hill, Meardi, de Sola, Daglio, Duke, Soundy, Deininger, Llach, Ferreiro, Cristiani, Borgonovo, Ruffatti, Parker, Shonenberg, Dalton.

Coffee cultivation has not been an improvised thing. The ability to produce, wash, dry, classify, and sell coffee has been an undertaking pursued for more than a century. A hardworking people has known how to take advantage of these lessons and has put El Salvador in fourth place among coffee exporting countries.[8]

This comment expresses the sentiments of almost all those interviewed, including members of several of the families it refers to by surname. The members of the ABECAFE elite, many of whom are descendents of immigrants, clearly think of themselves as the key to Salvadoran economic development and the best hope for the future for themselves and the "hardworking" Salvadoran people whom they taught to be world-class coffee producers. It would be a serious mistake to dismiss these views as merely the natural enthusiasm of entrepreneurs for their own industry. For them, coffee is all but synonymous with the nation of El Salvador or at least with the economically competitive nation they feel they have created. It is not surprising that they reject what the ABECAFE position paper calls the "black legend" of "exploitation" of agricultural workers. These leaders believe that their efforts have provided meaningful work and hope for development to those who lack their special talents for technological and economic innovation.

If coffee is the nation and the fourteen families are the key to coffee, then these families are in essence the nation. Yet virtually all the producers who chose to comment on this issue vehemently denied this implication. As one ABECAFE board member (and a member of the one of the families) said, "You know, it's not just the fourteen families—there are five million of us Salvadorans." Most went to great lengths to emphasize the large number of coffee growers, whom they variously estimated at from thirty-five to forty thousand. In fact, 10 percent of all producers control 80 percent of all Salvadoran production, and most millers individually control the production of hundreds of small growers.[9] The division between processors and workers, between the rural poor and the economic elite, was treated as a fact of nature by all those interviewed. But they clearly regard themselves as the best hope for bringing the rest of the population out of poverty and backwardness through coffee-based economic development. Many named as their great historical hero Gerardo Barrios, who is credited with having brought coffee to El Salvador.[10] Indeed, their ideas on economic development are virtually identical with the positivist philosophy of Barrios and other nineteenth-century Liberal revolutionaries who ushered in the Salvadoran coffee era. As Ralph Lee Woodward has described this philosophy in nineteenth-century Central America: "The positivists believed that expanded productivity and exports would spark an industrial revolution which would lead them into the same sort of sophisticated economies enjoyed by western Europe and the United States. With the greater revenues from exports, they expected the general standard of living to rise and secondary industries to spring up to satisfy the needs of the people."[11] A century and a half after Barrios's era, no better description could be found of the views of the present-day coffee elite on economic development. Members of this elite have viewed themselves as the heirs of cosmopolitan entrepreneurs who taught the country how to compete, raised the general standard of living, and made possible an industrial future for El Salvador. Thus they viewed the "structural reforms" of 1979–80 as an unreasonable assault on themselves and their principles.

"War to the Death against INCAFE"

On 6 March 1979, the Third Revolutionary Junta issued Agrarian Reform Decrees 153 and 154, and troops moved immediately to occupy estates affected by the first phase of the reform (those larger than five hundred hectares). The next day the junta nationalized banks and savings and loan institutions in El Salvador. In just two days, the junta struck at two key elements of the power base of the agro-financial elite. Less known but at least as important for the fortunes of the coffee elite was an earlier Decree 75, promulgated on 20 December 1979, which nationalized the export trade in coffee and established the Instituto Nacional del Café (INCAFE) to manage the resulting government monopoly of El Salvador's major economic activity. Because most coffee holdings were not affected by the first phase of the agrarian reform and the majority of coffee growers were not bankers (although almost all banks were controlled by coffee capital), export nationalization had a greater immediate economic effect on coffee growers than the other two reforms. A study published in *Estudios Centroamericanos* argued that of the major "structural reforms," nationalizing the coffee trade had the largest effect on the fortunes of Salvadoran capital in general and the agro-export sector in particular.[12]

The establishment of INCAFE led to a ten-year struggle between the government and coffee growers which one of them called a "war to the death against INCAFE." As one past president of ABECAFE said in 1987, "The basic position of all coffee producers is the same—get rid of INCAFE!" The struggle was waged in paid advertisements in San Salvador's leading newspapers, in the National Assembly, in petitions and meetings with Christian Democrats, and in an ultimately successful legal battle to have INCAFE declared unconstitutional. The most outspoken disapproval came from the coffee growers in the Cafetalera, but opposition to INCAFE united all sectors of the coffee industry. In its position papers, ABECAFE argued that INCAFE's continued existence would cause the "collapse of coffee cultivation," "reduce our people to new levels of poverty," and "jeopardize the future of democracy."[13] Leading members of the Cafetalera charged that the reform was Communist-inspired and at one point even contended that they had conclusive proof that the law had been copied directly from the one establishing the Empresa Nicaragüense del Café (ENCAFE) after the Sandinista Revolution.[14]

All those interviewed held INCAFE responsible for what they viewed as the collapse of the coffee industry. The key economic issue for most was price. INCAFE had sold coffee at the international price in dollars, while what it paid producers was at a price in local currency equivalent to one-half to one-fourth of the international price. The difference between the international and the local price showed up as a government foreign-exchange surplus.[15]

Those interviewed were well aware of the differential exchange rates and blamed INCAFE for paying low prices and causing the collapse of their industry. One member of the Consejo Salvadoreño del Café (the CSC, which replaced INCAFE after it was declared unconstitutional) explained, "The problem with Duarte was that the price of coffee was a political price. When coffee reached 200 dollars per *quintal*, Duarte said that was too much money. . . . He said we would just spend it on cars." Most of those interviewed believed that the foreign-exchange surplus, which should have gone to them, was wasted through government inefficiency and corruption, particularly in INCAFE. As one of the most outspoken critics said, "What do they do with the money? They steal it. It all goes to private individuals associated with INCAFE. They spend it on houses costing four million colones. . . . Nobody knows what happened to the funds." Those interviewed argued that the resulting low domestic price made coffee production unprofitable and that growers consequently stopped applying fertilizer, abandoned replantings, and maintained their groves only minimally in an effort to survive at a loss. One ABECAFE president stated, "Nobody has planted a single tree since 1979." Normally 10 to 20 percent of a grove must be replanted each year, and he therefore estimated that it would take ten to twenty years to recover. Another ABECAFE president said that growers had basically been operating at a loss throughout the period and also estimated that it would take ten to twenty years to recover. All attributed the recent low harvest, especially in 1988–89 (the lowest in thirty years), to INCAFE's baleful influence, particularly on prices. Several growers provided illustrative price calculations to demonstrate the differential exchange rate and its effects.

Some of those interviewed also argued that the agrarian reform played a substantial role in the decline in production because it had created an atmosphere of insecurity that discouraged reinvestment. As one leading miller explained, "Government ministers went on television and threatened confiscation for the land reform." One co-op president who had lost his lands in the reform said that the primary reason for the decline in production was lack of confidence resulting from the reform, "You can't invest unless you have confidence that you will be able to realize profits from your investment." But most of those who blamed the agrarian reform also cited the monopoly price system, and all opposed INCAFE adamantly. At times it seemed that INCAFE had become a symbol of all the structural reforms of the 1979–80 period.

The specific failures of INCAFE were attributed to politics, corruption, and incompetence stemming from a lack of technical knowledge of the coffee industry. As one member of an elite family with long experience in the industry said, "The coffee growers think they have a monopoly of technical knowledge of the coffee industry just because they are coffee growers. . . . They think Rubén Pineda [head of the Consejo Salvadoreño del Café] is doing a good job just because he grows coffee, not because he is well informed about coffee." An official on the coffee council pointed out that one head of INCAFE had said on television that all he knew about coffee was how to drink it.[16] Those interviewed thought that political influence had determined appointments to INCAFE, leading to widespread incompetence and corruption. One coffee grower commented, "There were too many people who came without shoes and left millionaires." Another asserted that the monetary difference between the international price and the producer price was diverted to other organizations, such as the military. One ABECAFE president said, "Everything was based on corrupt politics rather than on competence, and the result was disaster. . . . The corruption was terrible— Duarte and the others loaning themselves money."

In a pre-election interview, candidate Cristiani vowed that, if elected, he would return coffee to the system that existed before 1979. With the help of a Supreme Court decision declaring INCAFE unconstitutional in July 1989, he did just that. INCAFE lost its export monopoly and a new organization, the Consejo Salvadoreño del Café (Salvador Coffee Council), was established to manage the government's remaining limited involvement in coffee. The council was to be administered by a joint government-private sector board.[17] Although the Banco Central and the coffee council retained control over foreign-exchange and export quotas, the processor-exporters got their businesses back, and producers resumed selling directly to exporters at prices based on the international price. As might be expected, those in the coffee elite, particularly the processor-exporters, were delighted. Most had only good things to say about the Consejo Salvadoreño del Café and its limited regulation. The consensus was that the coffee industry was back in the hands of those who could run it best—the technical leaders who had built the industry in the first place and who continued to offer the best hope for the economic future of El Salvador.

If anything, the INCAFE episode reinforced the elite view that management of the coffee economy should be left to them and to free enterprise. It also confirmed their long-held assumptions that economic development and a rising standard of living for all Salvadorans depended on their economic leadership, and that structural change was prejudicial not only to themselves but to Salvadoran society as whole. As one former INCAFE president who belonged to a leading coffee family explained, "The reforms alienated the small growers and the middle sectors of society, and that's why the last election came out the way it did."

Dictatorship and Democracy

Barrios and other nineteenth-century Liberal coffee growers had shown a marked lack of interest in parliamentary democracy, preferring instead Auguste Comte's concept of "republican dictatorship." In fact, the coffee elite in El Salvador had tolerated a military dictatorship without evident dissatisfaction for more than fifty years. As one leading processor said, "It wasn't like the situation in Eastern Europe, where the economy was a shambles. Here people were basically satisfied with the economic situation. So there was no revolt." Another prominent processor noted, "It wasn't like the situation in Nicaragua, where Somoza intervened directly in the economy. Here they [the military dictatorships] left the economy strictly alone." Most members of the coffee elite pronounced pre–1979 economic policy distinctly preferable to that of the Duarte period, although some expressed limited criticisms of past military regimes. Nevertheless, as one past president of ABECAFE explained, "We needed the military to protect us from the left." The positivistic doctrines of order and progress well describe the Salvadoran system existing prior to 1979, a system supported explicitly or implicitly by members of the coffee elite.

Earlier interviews by journalists found a grudging respect for the hard-line policies of General Hernández Martínez, and one ABE-CAFE press release even referred approvingly to the "leader of our country who had the wisdom to put the social peace and order of our country above all else," an obvious reference to the 1932 massacre he initiated.[18] At that time the coffee elite had enthusiastically backed Martínez and helped finance his bloody vengeance against the rebels. Among the contemporary coffee elite, the extreme right has been represented by Orlando de Sola, the outspoken conservative member of a relatively liberal Salvadoran family. De Sola openly backed the death squad massacres of the early 1980s and urged a return to a 1932-style *matanza* to settle things. Such views are not uncommon in El Salvador, although de Sola by no means represents elite opinion in general or the ABECAFE perspective in particular.

Support for the hard-line approach was not expressed by ABE-CAFE members in the 1987 and 1990 interviews. Whether this represents a change of opinion (as suggested by some of those interviewed) or whether the ABECAFE faction was never as enthusiastic about the hard line as the public comments of some made it seem is difficult to determine. It is nevertheless clear that respect for democracy has replaced "republican dictatorship" as the party line at ABECAFE. It is also evident that these elite conceptions of democracy do not correspond to those held by most citizens in industrial democracies like the United States. Although general support now exists for less authoritarian and more democratic political forms, they are conceived, as López Vallecillos has noted, "within the framework of liberal democracy, representative but restricted and controlled."[19]

Given the intransigent public image of the coffee elite, the views expressed by some of its members are surprising. One of the most liberal of those interviewed, a leading miller and banker, referred to Shafik Handel (head of the Salvadoran Communist Party and chief negotiator for the rebels) as "a great democrat." He also described the political role played by Rubén Zamora, leader of the guerrillas' civilian allies (the Frente Democrático Revolucionario or FDR), as "constructive" and argued that the conflict would be resolved by opening up democratic political space in El Salvador to include both rebel leaders. One past president of the Cafetalera who supported the ABECAFE viewpoint on most issues asserted that complete freedom of speech and electoral freedom were a necessity: "If the people vote for the Communists, then a Communist government it is. It's the people's choice." A member of the ABECAFE board of directors said, "Look, if you're a Communist and I support some other party, the way to do it is fight it out in the election campaign." Another coffee grower said that the rebels "couldn't demand that we replace Cristiani with Shafik Handel, but within reason there has to be give and take on both sides." A co-op president listed three conditions for ending the war: a general amnesty covering all crimes associated with the war, a guarantee of absolutely no reprisals (against the rebels), and rebel participation in political parties in an election.

Orlando de Sola's harsh stance was thus a distinct minority view among those interviewed, and it was not shared by any member of the ABECAFE faction. One prominent grower dismissed de Sola as "a very angry person" who was paid by his family to stay out of the family business. This interviewee even volunteered that de Sola was said to be involved in death squad activities and that his radical ideas "could get him killed." An ABECAFE president noted that the only real choice for Third World countries was between capitalism and socialism. "There's fascism," he added, "but the cost in human freedom is too high." Although they were not asked directly about the killing of the Jesuits at the Universidad Centroamericana three months earlier, several of those interviewed took the occasion to condemn it. One member of a prominent miller family referred to the murderers as "savages," while another pointed out that his cousin had been one of those killed. The same liberal miller who thought Shafik Handel was a democrat was delighted at the arrest of the murderers and seemed incredulous that it did take place. A prominent grower, reacting to charges made by retired colonel and ARENA leader Sigfredo Ochoa implicating members of the army's high command in the killings, said, "Well, if we are going to have peace, some people [i.e., members of the army high command] will have to go."

Indeed, the ABECAFE elite's relationship to the Salvadoran armed forces was considerably more ambivalent than their longtime tacit support might suggest. When queried about the oligarchy's role in running El Salvador, one ABECAFE president asked, "Do you think if we had been running things, we would be in the kind of mess we are in now?" The same individual, who had described his position as "chairman of the board of the oligarchy," went on to say, "but I didn't run El Salvador—the army did." Another miller said, "You can't tell the army anything. Maybe you can politely make a suggestion." Another grower claimed that funds had been diverted from the government coffee board (INCAFE) to the army to pay for troops to guard the coffee harvest. President Cristiani went so far as to blame the army for the mass murders of the early 1980s, although he did so to exonerate ARENA from complicity in the slaughter. Another ABECAFE board member asked, "Why do we need such a big army—to protect us from Honduras?"

Yet the concept of democracy held by most of those interviewed was circumscribed, and their willingness to question military lawlessness was limited. Although all said that the rebels should get involved in the electoral process, almost none saw any particular need for special legal provisions or modifications in the judicial or military structure to insure the rebels' safety once they did so. Indeed, the elite's unwillingness to acknowledge the need for such changes bordered on the disingenuous. One co-op president claimed, "No one has anything to fear from the army—except Joaquín Villalobos and Shafik Handel." In his view, ordinary supporters of the Frente Farabundo Martí de Liberación Nacional (FMLN) could rejoin society without fear.

When asked if it was realistic to expect rebels to simply lay down their arms without fear, another miller responded, "Sure, we have amnesties all the time. . . . The guerrillas have their representatives, the FMLN-FDR—it's really the same thing. They ran in the election campaign. Anybody can say anything. They go on television and denounce the government. They go into the plaza here" (in the central part of San Salvador). When asked if the rebels might fear retaliation, another co-op president suggested that "they could leave the country. Go to Canada or Australia. Many of them are already in Canada." Asked about reprisals against those who stayed, he allowed that such things could occur in some villages where people had lost family members in the civil war. He then added calmly that there were more deaths after the Spanish Civil War than during it, but did not seem concerned that continued killing might threaten rebel participation in the electoral process. One government official, while pointing out that guerrilla representatives like Rubén Zamora could freely participate in elections, proceeded to describe him as "that Marxist-Leninist" (a characterization that can be tantamount to a death sentence in El Salvador) and linked him to Jennifer Jean Casolo, a U.S. religious worker who had been charged with hiding weapons for the guerrillas during their 1989 offensive. Although the charges were later dismissed, Casolo occupied a special niche in the demonology of the Salvadoran elite as a U.S. citizen who first befriended but later betrayed them. Another interviewee from an elite family recounted studying with Rubén Zamora at the Universidad Centroamericana and having had some sympathy for his position. Now, however, this interviewee wanted all rebels locked up. When asked what would happen if the rebels did not accept the electoral terms offered by the government, one miller shrugged and said, "Then our army will simply continue the process of pacification."

On the basis of these comments, it seems fair to say that members of the elite would not be dismayed whether their political opponents ended up in the National Assembly or in their graves. The ability to hold to such seemingly contradictory notions can be understood, however, if account is taken of their view of the rebels' social base and the likely outcome of the democratic process. The collapse of communism in Europe had reached its climax only a month and a half before most of the interviews began, and in the course of the interviewing the Sandinistas lost the presidential election in neighboring Nicaragua. As might be expected, members of the Salvadoran elite were greatly encouraged by these events, and many took heart from what they saw as not only the defeat of communism but the rise of democracy and the decline of revolution as political forms. As one miller joked, "They say there are only 5,001 Communists left in the world—one old guy in Cuba and 5,000 in El Salvador."

Most of those interviewed expected that the rebels would never poll more than the 3 percent of the vote they received in the 1989 presidential election (in 1994 rebel presidential candidate Rubén Zamora actually received 32 percent). All regarded the rebels as an unrepresentative minority who could never be a significant electoral force. The defeat of the Sandinistas simply confirmed this view. As one grower said, "Look at the Sandinistas—they found out when they voted that people were supporting them out of fear. The same thing will happen here." When it was pointed out to another miller that the Sandinistas had received more than 40 percent of the vote, he replied, "It only shows that they had ten years to brainwash the population." One government official argued that the rebels were afraid of elections: "Look what they—Zamora—got in the last election, less than 3 percent. They are losing force." A co-op president was optimistic about the prospects for democracy because the collapse of communism, the Sandinista electoral defeat, and what he called the "loss of force" of Fidel Castro had together deprived the guerrillas of their external support. Without it, he clearly implied, they would have no chance in El Salvador.

In general, the rebels were regarded as a tiny group of terrorists of foreign inspiration if not foreign origin. No one considered them part of a mass movement. In fact, one ABECAFE president indignantly corrected me when I referred to the conflict as a civil war: "It's really not a war like the Civil War in the United States. That implies there are two sides, two armies. Here there are just 5,000 terrorists. And they are mostly terrorists supplied by Cuba and Nicaragua." When presidential candidate Cristiani was asked if the problem in El Salvador was not the existence of two armies, he replied with uncharacteristic coldness, "Yes, but one of them is outside the law." Another elite member disputed the interviewer's suggestion that the rebels might have wider popular support: "Who ordered the killings of the Americans in the Zona Rosa [four Marines and two businessmen assassinated in 1985 in a popular San Salvador entertainment district]? Shafik Handel, Joaquín Villalobos—they don't need a mass movement for that." Another said that the idea that the guerrillas have popular support was the greatest U.S. misconception about El Salvador. Another said, "They have a few thousand people with guns. If you travel around the country, you will find most people believe in peace and want the country to move ahead." All those interviewed followed conventional norms of public discourse in El Salvador in using the term "terrorist" for the rebels, often correcting the interviewer's use of the term "rebel." All thought that the changes in Eastern Europe had made the rebels weaker, because "they are having a difficult time explaining these changes to their followers."

If the rebels in El Salvador were an unrepresentative minority of foreign-inspired terrorists without a shred of popular support (not an unfair summation of the nearly universal view among those interviewed), then little contradiction exists between elite support for democracy and its relative indifference to the fate of the rebels once the latter join the political process. The civil war is not a civil war or revolution — it is only a matter of controlling domestic terrorism. According to the elite perspective, the electoral process extends to all Salvadorans "who believe in peace and want the country to move ahead." Whatever the factual merits of this view, it does represent an advance over uncritical support for military dictatorship. But elite ideas of electoral democracy did not seem to include the Salvadoran left in either its armed or unarmed version. Elections without civil rights, including the right to life, are not meaningful contests, and thus the elite conception of democracy is a limited one. The real (as opposed to the rhetorical) incorporation of the left remains an unresolved contradiction in the ABECAFE elite's view of a settlement to the war.

These limited notions of democracy did not extend much beyond support for contested elections and free speech. The ideas that the judicial system might require reform or that the army's record on human rights might be cause for alarm were not prominent themes in elite conversations. Only one elite member mentioned the need for a strengthened judicial system in discussing prerequisites for a settlement with the guerrillas. When human rights were mentioned at all (an extremely sensitive area in the interviews), they were raised only in the context of anti-Salvadoran propaganda in the United States. One relatively liberal co-op president, a great admirer of Franklin Roosevelt, complained bitterly about what he perceived as a U.S. double standard in evaluating human rights violations. Why, he asked, was there more outrage at the killings of the Jesuits in El Salvador than at the killing of "your own servicemen," referring to the U.S. Marines killed in the Zona Rosa. Another complained that, in the United States, people always talk about the army when they "make a mistake" and kill someone: "What about all those that the FMLN has killed—assassinated?" A member of a prominent family

who denounced the killers of the Jesuits as savages went on to say
that the FMLN "is using the killings of the Jesuits for propaganda."
One coffee association official acknowledged that there were problems in the army but allowed that they resulted from what he called
"the low cultural level" of the troops: "All we hear about are the
problems of human rights of the army." A prominent miller-banker
was pleased to learn of the indictment of army officers in the Jesuit
case but immediately added that Salvadoran law made their conviction unlikely. He alone advocated reform of the judicial apparatus.

All those interviewed were committed to a negotiated settlement
of the war and to incorporating the rebels into the democratic process. But almost none seemed inclined to demand changes in army
behavior or reforms in the judicial system that would make electoral
democracy meaningful to rebels and rebel sympathizers after the war
ended. Yet without the promise of such changes the rebels had been
unwilling to accept a negotiated settlement, and the absence of military and judicial reform had much to do with the origins of the war.
Nevertheless, the importance of the shift in views of this key class
toward accepting at least limited democracy should not be under-
estimated. But it remains to be seen whether the elite will challenge
the traditions of military lawlessness that have dominated El Salvador for most of this century. If the military retains its legal immunity, it is unlikely that elite support for limited democracy and
a negotiated settlement will have much long-run significance.

"There's Nothing to Reform"

The ABECAFE elite's view of social reform fits with its view of agro-
exports, free markets, and limited democracy like the final piece in
a puzzle. According to the elite's view, the best way to raise the
general standard of living, including that of the poor, is via agro-
exports. Government-imposed restrictions simply impede the ability
of those in the agro-export business to manage the economy effectively in the interest of all. Democracy is open to all those genuinely
devoted to peace, and only a minority of foreign-inspired terrorists
want war. Thus structural reform must be a contradiction in terms.
There is no reason for social discontent because the proceeds of the
coffee economy are widely distributed and are the major source of

economic survival in rural areas. Structural reforms of the economy would simply impede economic development. The gifted Salvadorans who have built the economy can rescue the country from backwardness through the agro-export industry that they and their workers have built over long years of struggle. All Salvadorans who genuinely want to see the country progress recognize this truth. So, as one elite member concluded, "there's nothing to reform."

Elite opposition to structural reform does not imply, however, that its members oppose social programs that benefit the poor or provide a modicum of education and physical security for their workers. Although the view was not unanimous, a number of those interviewed expressed support for some limited social security and welfare reforms. Many emphasized their personal efforts to provide health, educational, and income supplements for their own workers even when such policies were regarded as communism by less enlightened members of the rural elite. Several had participated actively in forming marketing co-ops that would link large and small growers, and a number of millers had provided credit and agricultural extension services to their small growers. Millers have come to accept labor unions in their mills, although not on their farms, but they distinguish between "real" unions and union "terrorists" who are only interested in politics.[20] Just as the elite's notion of democracy does not cover the left, its notion of social welfare does not generally extend to the structural reforms demanded by the left. The agrarian reform of the Junta, like the establishment of INCAFE, was regarded as a disaster by most of those interviewed. For most elite members, the agrarian reform failed because of the peasants' lack of technical and managerial skills. As one grower pointed out, technical efficiency increases with estate size. One ABECAFE president said that the governing councils of the agrarian reform co-ops were "basically PDC [Christian Democrat] party hacks. None of them knew a thing about finances or the coffee business." One favorite elite story (probably apocryphal) recounts how a group of agrarian reform peasants cut up a prize breeding bull into two-thousand-dollar steaks. A former estate owner claimed that he had provided work for five hundred workers on his estate, but the agrarian reform co-op that replaced his ownership had only eighty members. The "evidence" of the faltering agrarian reform co-ops, as perceived by members of the elite, simply confirmed the justness of their position as technical leaders in the industry.

ARENA succeeded in blocking implementation of the second phase of the agrarian reform, which would have affected many coffee farms. Reforms in the first phase, which established producer co-ops on estates larger than five hundred hectares, were watered down but not reversed under ARENA rule. Politically, as one ABECAFE president noted, the agrarian reform seems to have become "a sacred cow." One high-ranking ARENA government official commented that the point was not to debate whether the reforms are good or bad but to improve the management and technical skills of the co-ops and make them productive. A president of the Cafetalera and founding member of ARENA said that the Cafetalera had excellent relations with the leaders of the agrarian reform co-op organization. This acceptance of limited agrarian reform, although not shared by all those interviewed, represents a significant policy shift for some sectors of the elite.

Yet structural reforms were generally viewed as a disaster by most members of the elite. None saw any further need for fundamental change in the distribution of income, property, or the organization of the agro-export based economy. When asked about rural living standards and poverty (another extremely sensitive subject in the interviews), they usually replied that a healthy coffee economy was the best guarantee of rural social welfare. One miller provided a detailed demographic explanation of poverty but rejected redistributive solutions as "socialism." He attributed massive unemployment to overpopulation, a situation that could only be remedied by "massive industrialization." Another explained that in the United States in the 1920s, "you had sweatshop conditions," but "competition for labor developed and caused conditions to improve." He and other elite members explained with evident pride the provisions they had made for the health and education of their workers, although always within the framework of non-unionized, low-wage rural labor. One of the most liberal of those interviewed seemed puzzled by a question about solutions to rural poverty, and, after some thought, said he thought that improvement in rural administration might help. Another, when asked about the need for structural reforms, replied, "What we need is more work. We need to reform the technology."

Of all those interviewed, only President Cristiani and one other government official even mentioned the connection between social discontent and the civil war. None of the others interviewed saw any connection between economic inequality and revolution; nor did they think that organized workers or the poor had any legitimate collective claim to societal wealth. The poor were discussed as almost a separate nation or species to be assisted, to be led, to be employed, to be helped toward a higher standard of living in an industrial future. Labor organizations might be accepted in the mills, but only as long as they had no political ambitions. Democracy was accepted, but not the notion that democratic power might be used to change the relative balance of social and economic power. The war had touched the lives of many in the elite, but it was not perceived as connected to the discrepancies of wealth and power underlying the Salvadoran system of agro-export agriculture. Rather, the war must have been caused by a small group of terrorists, because there was no reason for people "who wanted the country to move ahead" to resort to revolutionary war.

Yet it would be erroneous to dismiss entirely the elite's commitment to a negotiated settlement, its acceptance of at least limited democracy, or its belief in progress. At the least, these attitudes supported a policy of continued serious negotiation with the rebels and provided a limited but significant political space in El Salvador that made it possible for politicians like Rubén Zamora to operate, although at great personal risk, within the country, and for opposition spokespersons to denounce the government on television (as one elite member pointed out). Although the contradictions in elite attitudes toward human rights and social citizenship handicapped them in searching for a solution to the war, they did not prevent them from finally reaching a settlement. These opinions also represent a considerable shift from the ideas of the traditional Salvadoran right, as they were expressed by a conservative minority in the interviews.

Orlando de Sola and the Cafetalera

On 30 May 1984, two days before Napoleón Duarte began his first and last term as an elected president of El Salvador, a dissident faction of coffee growers led by Orlando de Sola took control of the board of directors of the Cafetalera in a disputed election.[21] Members of the de Sola faction led an unremitting struggle against Duarte, INCAFE, the reforms of 1979–80, and the U.S. Embassy. This faction advocated a hard line toward the leftist opposition, whether armed or unarmed. De Sola declined to be interviewed for this study, but one of his close associates graciously talked at length about de Sola's positions, and at least two others among those interviewed (neither a member of the ABECAFE elite) shared the same social and political views. Although de Sola himself has probably been quoted more often than any other member of the coffee elite, two of his associates were also widely quoted: Cafetalera board member Carlos Raúl Calvo and a former president of the organization, the late Francisco García Rossi. De Sola and Calvo wrote their own newspaper columns, and the faction's views were publicized during a five-year campaign of paid newspaper announcements full of colorful invective and intransigent attitudes.[22]

As noted earlier, de Sola's views are atypical of his progressive family. The one member of the family who consented to be interviewed was among the most liberal of the ABECAFE elite. Nor do the views of his faction represent the views of all growers affiliated with the Cafetalera. This faction's control of the Cafetalera was vigorously contested in the elections of 1984, 1986, and 1988 by a more moderate faction of coffee growers from the war-ravaged eastern departments. These moderates denounced the de Sola faction as "retrograde activists" and "polemicists" who had ignored the association's membership, while the de Sola faction denounced the opposing faction as "servile" and "sell-outs" who would hand the association over to INCAFE and the government. Each group accused the other of dividing the association.[23] The more moderate faction eventually ousted the de Sola board in a controversial unscheduled election in 1989. Nonetheless, the views of the de Sola faction should not be discounted as the views of just one man. This faction was elected to the Cafetalera board with substantial support, especially from growers in Santa Ana and other western departments, and it can therefore be assumed that his positions reflect the views of a substantial proportion of the coffee-growing elite (as opposed to the coffee-milling elite) in El Salvador.[24] Although the de Sola faction shared many of the views of the milling elite, particularly regarding the importance of coffee in the Salvadoran economy and the need to abolish INCAFE, the two groups differed strikingly in two important areas: willingness to compromise with the U.S.-backed Christian Democratic reform program, and tolerance for democratic political forms, including human rights. In both areas, the de Sola faction was uncompromisingly opposed to change.

Duarte and INCAFE

Although all those interviewed vehemently opposed José Napoleón Duarte, the Christian Democratic Party, and the structural reforms they represented (including establishing INCAFE and nationalizing the coffee-export trade), the tone of the comments differed significantly in the ABECAFE faction. Millers spoke of Duarte's "stubbornness," his "pride," or his "need for power." One ABECAFE president said (in English) that Duarte had a "psychological thing" about coffee growers, and a president of the Cafetalera (opposed to de Sola) claimed that Duarte believed that "all of us [the coffee growers] are millionaires, and we had all the wealth of the country, and he was going to take it away." Another moderate Cafetalera president complained that Duarte's pride led him to think he could set coffee prices himself on his computer. Although most members of the ABECAFE faction regarded Duarte as a political opponent, most also thought that the best policy was to work with him. At least two members of this faction had served on a coffee advisory commission appointed by Duarte in 1986, and another had been president of INCAFE in the early 1980s. One coffee grower and member of the coffee commission said, "I felt that you should talk to the government—negotiate—whether you liked it or not." Another coffee commission member complained that the de Sola faction created an atmosphere of constant confrontation with the Duarte government: "There weren't any negotiations, just total conflict." He thought that even with the old [Duarte] government it would have been possible to negotiate something. Another miller and banker said, "When you have been in the industry for five generations, as we have, you take the long view." He reported that he had continued to make money in coffee under Duarte.

In fact, the structural reforms, which all those interviewed associated with Duarte, affected growers much more profoundly than they did processors. The land reform affected millers because most of them were also producers, but it had a major effect on growers, whose only or primary source of income was land. The control of prices and the differential exchange rate affected payments to the primary producers but not to the millers, who were paid a standard fee for processing by the government. Moreover, the greater capital resources of the millers enabled them to take the long view. The growers could not afford that luxury. For them, the reforms were a matter of immediate economic survival. As one grower and a close associate of de Sola commented, "The ABECAFE millers made big money even with INCAFE because they were paid a fee for milling. The big losers were the producers."

Thus it is not surprising that de Sola's policy of confrontation and his vigorous attacks on Duarte and his U.S. backers found support among coffee growers. In a 1981 interview de Sola denounced Duarte as "a Communist who happens to believe in God."[25] One coffee grower who had lost much of his land in the agrarian reform said with evident anger, "Duarte destroyed the nation and destroyed the economy." He urged the interviewer to read a recent article on Duarte in *Diario de Hoy,* a consistent defender of extreme right-wing opinion in El Salvador. The article had indeed made that charge and went on to say that he had done more to damage the country than any president in its entire history. The article also accused Duarte of being "an instrument of the Carter administration" in "destroying the constitutional order" and imposing a regime that "brought the economy to ruin."[26] One coffee grower who was close to de Sola and often contributed to *Diario de Hoy* urged Duarte and his cabinet to resign and take up arms along with their "protégés" in the mountains (the FMLN).[27] In an interview, this same grower called the Duarte administration a "party dictatorship." Total opposition was the strategy pursued by the de Sola faction during the Duarte administration. This strategy, however, was largely rejected by the ABECAFE elite.

Democracy and Human Rights

The most striking differences between the de Sola faction and his colleagues in the ABECAFE elite emerged on the issues of democracy and human rights. As indicated, the ABECAFE faction's support for democracy and human rights was at best conditional. De Sola, however, called for a 1932-style *matanza* to settle matters and stated in a 1989 interview with the *New York Times* that the seventy-five thousand persons killed by army terrorism in the early 1980s were "Communist stooges" who deserved to die.[28] His close associate wrote in a *Diario de Hoy* column, "to hell with the human rights of the Communists. . . . let our army win the war."[29] In an interview he proposed establishing teams of "counter-guerrillas" who would locate and "neutralize" potential guerrillas. He rejected what he saw as the "low-intensity" war strategy of the United States and called for total victory. The widow of a former president of the Cafetalera explained to the interviewer that the problem in her area was priests who had spread guerrilla thinking among credulous rural people. The army had no choice, she said, but to make up lists of these "subversives" and kill them. Her daughter said she believed in death squads because "killing these people made a better life for those who are living." Although such opinions may seem bizarre to outsiders, similar views were frequently expressed by middle-class Salvadorans in casual conversations and thus appear to be widely held in the society. To promote their conservative views, de Sola and a close associate from the Cafetalera founded a controversial organization, the Instituto de Relaciones Internacionales. Clearly, they had become as concerned with political ideology as with the interests of the coffee industry.

It was also evident, however, that such views were embarrassing to the anti-de Sola faction of the Cafetalera and the new Consejo Salvadoreño del Café established after the demise of INCAFE. Shortly after President Cristiani assumed office, a controversial, unscheduled election for the Cafetalera presidency and board of directors was held in a San Salvador hotel. The losers, including Cafetalera President René Domínguez, claimed that the election was illegal and challenged it in the courts. The winners, led by Cafetalera President-elect Eduardo Barrientos, defended their claim and were supported by the Ministry of Interior, which certified the election and declared Barrientos the winner. At the time of the interviews, both Domínguez and Barrientos were claiming the Cafetalera presidency, but Barrientos had effective control.[30] A neutral observer (a member of an elite coffee-growing family and a longtime student of the industry) said that the conflict represented in part tensions over prices arising between ABECAFE and the Cafetalera after the demise of INCAFE. This interpretation was confirmed by a member of the losing faction. Another neutral observer and past president of the Cafetalera said that the conflict also reflected a struggle over control of the Banco Hipotecario, whose president had traditionally been appointed by the Cafetalera board.

But the most important issue was Orlando de Sola. According to partisans of both factions, Domínguez had been backed by de Sola. As one member of the winning faction said of Domínguez, "He's the kind of person who did what he was told. The real power was Orlando de Sola." A member of the losing faction, on the other hand, charged that "Barrientos was put in because he could be counted on to keep his mouth shut and not criticize the [ARENA] government." In his view ARENA and what he called the "Red millionaires" of ABECAFE and FUSADES had promoted the special election. He further claimed that President Cristiani was allied with ABECAFE as a past president of the organization. In fact, a close associate of Cristiani's and a member of the ABECAFE faction did denounce de Sola, charging that his faction represented "a small group that excluded everyone else," and he strongly supported Barrientos as president of the Cafetalera. A leader of the Barrientos faction said he saw no particular problem in the Cafetalera's relationship with ABECAFE. He also stated that the Cafetalera had good relations with the Unión de Cooperativas de la Reforma Agraria de Productores, Beneficiadores y Exportadores de Café (UCRAPROBEX), an organization which was anathema to Orlando de Sola. This leader referred to one of de Sola's close associates in the Cafetalera and the Instituto de Relaciones Internacionales as "a crazy rightist in the style of Adolf Hitler." Clearly, the ABECAFE elite considered the de Sola faction of the Cafetalera to be beyond the pale.

At the time of the interviews, de Sola himself was living in exile in Miami after two of his close associates at the Instituto de Relaciones Internacionales were assassinated, and his own house had been machine-gunned on three occasions by unknown assailants.[31] A de Sola associate strongly suggested that these attacks were linked to the struggle for control of the Cafetalera but provided no evidence to support such a claim (the FMLN denied responsibility). The de Sola faction's candidate for the head of the Banco Hipotecario also became the target of an assassination attempt.[32] Struggle over control of the bank became particularly sensitive because of revelations that a number of prominent ARENA politicians, including Roberto D'Aubuisson, had defaulted on loans with the bank.[33] One analysis made at the Universidad Centroamericana suggested that the assassination attempts reflected tensions surrounding the struggle over the bank presidency between a Cafetalera faction "associated with the figures of Raúl Calvo and Orlando de Sola" and the officially recognized Cafetalera leadership and its ARENA allies.[34] It is clear, however, that the controversial positions of de Sola and his Instituto de Relaciones Internacionales earned his faction numerous enemies outside the coffee industry as well.

While ARENA was out of power and INCAFE was ruling the coffee industry, the interests of the de Sola faction and ABECAFE converged. As one perceptive elite observer remarked, "The producers, who cared most about price, were out in front in newspaper statements, but the big processors were working behind the scenes." Following the election of Cristiani, the demise of INCAFE, and return of the export trade to the miller exporters, the interests of the de Sola faction and ABECAFE increasingly diverged. De Sola wanted to roll back the land reform, while ABECAFE regarded a gradual program of privatization as the best way to deal with this particular "sacred cow." Respect for democracy was the party line at ABECAFE. Orlando de Sola and his faction, however, wanted to go back to the old ways. With ABECAFE (or the international market, as the millers would have it) setting prices instead of INCAFE, producers' resentment at the form and level of payment would be directed at either the millers or the ARENA government. Like Duarte and his administration, Cristiani had to deal with concerns beyond those of coffee growers. As one coffee grower and official on the coffee council commented, "We, the government, are representing five million Salvadorans, not just the growers. The growers have to sacrifice to make it possible to import petroleum." But grower sacrifice for the general good was not part of the de Sola program. As one of the surviving members of the de Sola faction ruefully observed, "We had become a thorn in the side of the government."

Although the ABECAFE faction has triumphed in both the coffee sector and the wider political arena, it is too soon to tell whether this victory represents simply another phase in the alternation between authoritarian and more open policies that has long characterized Salvadoran elite politics, or whether it is a genuine breakthrough for democracy. The agrarian fraction remains a formidable, albeit diminished, force in Salvadoran society, and the military is still an obstacle to democratic change. Defeat of the de Sola faction marked a victory by the agro-industrial elite over a rear guard of the agrarian elite. This victory did not, however, eliminate the other faction or its policies from Salvadoran political life. Nor did the outcome resolve the internal contradictions of the ABECAFE position.

ABECAFE and the Future

Shortly after his election, President Cristiani began to meet with Ignacio Ellacuria, rector of the Universidad Centroamericana in San Salvador, and also with the head of the sociology department and director of its Instituto de Derechos Humanos, Segundo Montes. On 16 November 1989, troops under Cristiani's nominal command entered the university campus and murdered Ellacuria, Montes, four of their colleagues, their housekeeper, and her daughter. Shortly before his death, Montes had written that he found reason for hope in the public pronouncements of President Cristiani on human rights: "If it is not time to sing victory for the observance of human rights in El Salvador, neither is it time for despair."[35]

Montes might well have reached the same conclusion about the views of the members of the ABECAFE elite. Their public commitment to electoral democracy and a negotiated settlement represents a considerable step forward, particularly when compared with the de Sola faction. But the idea of democracy they adopted did not include reforming the armed forces who murdered President Cristiani's partners in dialogue or reorganizing the judicial system required to punish the murderers. Nor did the elite's economic prescription of privatization and agro-export-based economic development include any plan to redistribute economic benefits except through a general rise in living standards. This program will not help the elite in dealing with those who demand such redistribution, including the armed and unarmed left.

These contradictions are inherent in the agro-industrial elite's consciousness of itself and its position in the Salvadoran agro-export economy. The core element of that vision is the theme of "progress" inherited from the Liberals of the nineteenth century. This theme organizes all the elements of the stories told in the interviews. The goal of "progress" is social welfare and economic development, not simply for members of the elite and their class but for all Salvadorans. The chosen route has not varied over a hundred and fifty years: export-led economic growth based on coffee. The theme of "progress" ties together elite views on the coffee economy, structural reform, revolution, and democracy. At the center of their ideology is the elite members' sense of themselves as the vanguard of industrial and social development in El Salvador. Each element of the ideology interacts with and reinforces the others, and each is directly tied to their central view of themselves as the economic vanguard of "progress."

If coffee naturally leads to industrial development (as the elite believes it has done in Brazil and Colombia) and if industrial development is the indispensable basis for any improvement in the living standard of all Salvadorans, then structural reforms are not only unnecessary but prejudicial. They are particularly damaging to the poor. Salvadorans of good will understand this "truth" and want the country to move ahead, hence revolutionary violence must be the work of outside agitators and foreign terrorists. The structural changes they demand are simply a ruse to gain power, not an expression of genuine concern for the lives of most Salvadorans. If the only people involved in revolution are "five thousand Communist terrorists," then there is little to lose in denying them democratic rights and at least some justification for the military's actions against them and their allies. A democracy limited to Salvadorans who want a peaceful country that can move ahead is the only reasonable alternative for El Salvador. And such a democracy will permit the coffee economy and El Salvador to develop fully, free from the kind of government control and political interference that so damaged them under the statist vision of Napoleón Duarte.

This summary is not intended to caricature the perspective of those interviewed, nor is their view entirely without basis in the realities of Salvadoran social and economic history. At the center of the ABECAFE elite's ideology is its self-image as an economic vanguard that not only can but has delivered technical innovation, economic development, employment, and a higher standard of living to the Salvadoran rural population. The fact that the elite did create a successful agro-export economy and that much of the Salvadoran countryside came to depend on it is a major source of its influence in Salvadoran society as well as a central element in elite members' view of themselves. The fact that the Christian Democrats could not, for whatever reason, manage this economy effectively had much to do with their electoral defeat, just as the collapse of Communist regimes has had much to do with their own economic failures.

Yet after a century of export-led growth industrial development has not occurred; most Salvadorans are still living in poverty; and the army continues to operate with complete legal immunity. These observations, however, raise issues that fall outside the particular ideological map of the coffee elite. The poor as an organized social force demanding their fair share of the nation's wealth simply do not fit the elite's vision of a gradually improving standard of living for all. And the army too lies beyond elite critical scrutiny, despite its continued centrality in Salvadoran society. The silences in the conversations of members of the agro-industrial elite are at least as significant as the opinions they express.

Despite the acceptance of democracy and the Chapultepec treaty, elite ideology has changed remarkably little since the Liberal revolutions that ushered in the coffee era a century and a half ago. This ideology is rooted in the agro-export economy and the agrarian order of late nineteenth- and early twentieth-century El Salvador. The agro-financial faction has never broken with the framework of land concentration and low salaries that is the basis of its wealth, and it remains wedded to the authoritarian order that sustained it. Events of the last decade have moved the agro-industrial faction away from its agrarian allies and toward a kind of liberal democracy that is "representative, but restricted and controlled." It remains to be seen whether recent history has moved the agro-industrial fraction far enough to reject the agrarians and their authoritarian order and to accept a broader definition of democracy that would exclude the military and include the left. The outcome is critical for achieving a lasting peace and a successful democratic transition in El Salvador.

7

Democracy and Anti-Communism in Costa Rica

If the organizing principle of the Salvadoran coffee elite stories was "progress," then the parallel organizing principle in Costa Rica is certainly "democracy." In fact the evidence from the 1990 interviews suggests that the ideology of the coffee elite is at the core of what Víctor Acuña has called the Costa Rican national ideology—the values of Costa Rican democratic exceptionalism, explicitly or implicitly shared by diverse groups in Costa Rican society.[1] It was to this myth of a peaceful and democratic Costa Rica that Oscar Arias appealed in his successful 1986 election campaign. Arias's election not only insured that Costa Rica would not be drawn into the revolutionary conflict of the 1980s in Central America but also made it possible for him to propose the plan that ultimately brought peace to the region. Arias's victory was not simply a victory of ideology. He was at the center of the Costa Rican agro-industrial elite. Hence his victory was their victory as well. Nevertheless, the election of Arias represented an affirmation of the values of the Costa Rican national ideology of democratic exceptionalism.

Coffee and the National Ideology of Rural Democracy, Harmony, and Social Peace

Lowell Gudmundson has called the Costa Rican national ideology "one of the most attractive and widely disseminated national my-

thologies of any Latin American nation."[2] This "white legend," as it
has been called by Theodore Creedman, portrays Costa Rica as an
"idyllic democracy without violence or poverty, a so-called Switzer-
land of Central America."[3] Gudmundson prefers to call it the myth
of rural democracy or rural egalitarianism.[4] The basic assumption is
the idea that the unique characteristics of Costa Rica, its democracy
and its social peace, rest on the equal division of landed property
and the values of the independent yeoman farmer. Rural egalitarianism has it origins in the colonial period, was either confirmed or
threatened by the rise of coffee (depending on the political views of
the believer), but was, in the end, the enduring basis of the Costa
Rican way of life. As the following quotations make clear, this view
is widely shared by coffee growers (small and large) and social scientists alike.

> In the midst of this almost Acadian country in which we live, our
> intellectual comprehension or civic conscience cannot be so weak as
> to fail to understand the fundamental reason for the happiness and
> good fortune of the Costa Rican people. . . . the division of real prop-
> erty. (Manuel Marín Quirós, leader, small coffee growers, 1932)
>
> The fortunate distribution of land in small plots had endowed our
> country with a consistency of order, a spirit of peace, a love of freedom
> and a solid foundation for democracy. (*La Nación,* long the voice of
> large coffee producers, 1952)
>
> To understand the special concern for liberty that Costa Ricans
> have always shown, the respect of the country's leaders for law and
> for human life, one must know the yeoman who labored on the land.
> This is the axis, the backbone of our history, the nucleus of Costa
> Rican society. (Carlos Monge Alfaro, *Historia de Costa Rica,* 1950).

Gudmundson's own work has shown conclusively that rural egalitarianism in colonial Costa Rica is more legend than fact, although
like any good myth it has a basis in reality. Despite the existence of
a privileged land-owning elite in the colonial period and its persistence in the age of coffee and beyond, the distribution of land and
property was more equal in Costa Rica than elsewhere in the region
in both the colonial and coffee eras.[5] The coffee age did create a new
class of wealthy processors who controlled not only their own production but that of all other producers. But the class structure was

not polarized between estate owners and free (or unfree) agricultural laborers. There were small, medium, and large producers and the processing elite, some of whom were also large producers. The classless society of the rural egalitarian myth, however, never existed in Costa Rica, before or after coffee.

The myth is not based on historical or statistical realities but—as Rodríguez, Acuña, González, and Gudmundson, among others, have all argued—is a product of the interdependent coffee economy of small and medium producers and aristocratic producer-processors of the late nineteenth and early twentieth centuries.[6] Rodríguez argues that the "white legend" is the legal and ideological expression of the symbiotic relationship between processor and small producer that she calls the "coffee pact." Acuña and González have shown that the rural egalitarian myth formed the nucleus of the ideology of protest movements by small and medium coffee growers throughout the twentieth century, and Gudmundson argues that it bears a strong resemblance to the egalitarian populism of farmer movements in the United States and elsewhere.[7] It was the relations of production in the coffee age, they contend, not the relations of property in the colonial period, that were the source of the white legend.

This ideology was sorely tested by the crises of the 1930s and the 1980s. The prolonged political crisis initiated by the rise of the Communist Party and the election of Calderón added significant elements to the national myth while leaving its fundamental principle unchanged. The myth of rural democracy became the ideological foundation of Figueres's regime, for in Costa Rica, unique in the region, the resolution of the Depression crisis did not lead to the repression of the alternative vision of the 1930s revolutionaries but rather to the incorporation of significant elements of that ideology into the national myth. Figueres's victory in 1948 also set in motion forces that eliminated the agrarian fraction of the coffee elite, always weaker in Costa Rica than elsewhere, from national life and vastly strengthened the agro-industrial fraction. His reforms not only created new agro-industrial sectors but also created a new class of agro-industrial mega-processors, such as Oscar Arias's business partners, the Peterses, who came to dominate the private coffee industry in the 1980s. These historical and economic changes significantly influenced the stories the coffee elite told in interviews in 1990. Yet the central element of those stories, as of the Costa Rican national ideology, remained the myth of rural democracy.

Coffee and Democracy

The white legend of rural egalitarianism and democracy is still at the heart of the coffee processing elite's view of its society and itself. Coffee, said one exporter, was not only the rock on which the Costa Rican economy was built but "the foundation of democracy in Costa Rica." An executive of a leading multinational firm (and member of one of the leading coffee dynasties) described what he called *la cultura cafetalera* (the coffee culture) which, he said, was "part of a long history, a lot of small owners, an egalitarian sense that things are distributed fairly—there has always been an egalitarian sense, a sense of community here." Another scion of a leading family said, in a statement that might be taken as a definition of the myth of agrarian democracy, "The country lives on coffee. It is also the basis for our democracy because . . . the land is divided and in Costa Rica it is a family business—of peasant families I mean."

The more historically inclined commentators traced the origins of Costa Rican rural democracy to the colonial period. "My own explanation [of Costa Rican exceptionalism]," said one leading processor, "is the legacy of the colonization. The original conquerors of San José—the city council—gave out free land to the inhabitants." Another processor explained that Costa Rica didn't need a land reform because "there was nothing to divide . . . we had an egalitarian division of land from the beginning dating back to the colonial period." Most thought that the coffee economy had not only not threatened this tradition of agrarian equality but had, on the contrary, either created it in the first place or been its principal guarantor in modern times. One leading exporter traced rural egalitarianism to early Republican President Braulio Carrillo (1835–1837, 1838–1842), who had given out small plots of land to individual farmers if they would cultivate coffee, creating "hundreds and, eventually, thousands of small growers." But most of those interviewed stressed the large number of individual coffee farmers, variously estimated at from 65,000 to over 100,000 in the contemporary period. "Costa Rica is unique in this respect," said one member of a legendary coffee family. "In El Salvador there are fourteen families, in Brazil four land holders. But we have 80,000 producers . . . family farms operating on small parcels."

Coffee was seen as a guarantor of Costa Rica's peace and democratic stability in part because of the large number of individual family producers, but also because of its redistributive effects on rural wage levels and the standard of living in the countryside generally. Most of those interviewed thought that coffee producers had hit upon a remarkable system for fairly distributing the benefits of an export economy throughout the society, thereby reinforcing Costa Rica's democratic ethos. "It has been fundamental," said one processor describing the role of coffee in the Costa Rican economy, "particularly as a way of redistributing riches. Much of the money earned by coffee finds its way out into the countryside to small producers and workers." "The process of liquidation," said another processor, referring to the government-adjudicated division of the proceeds of export sales between processors and small producers, "distributes the benefits of coffee exports throughout the countryside."

Finally, coffee reinforced Costa Rican democracy by providing the financial basis for upward mobility through education and creating a well-educated middle-class society. "We have many very poor farmers," said another leading processor, "and the extra income they can earn in the coffee harvest enables them to buy things—clothes, school supplies—and students are able to earn money for their studies. So [coffee] contributes not only to economic, but to educational development as well." Another processor pointed out that Costa Rica paid the highest salaries to coffee pickers in the world, so that "you find that the children of even very humble people, who have worked as coffee pickers, are able to earn enough money to send their kids to school, and there are many cases of their children growing up to get good jobs, even becoming professionals." "And," he added, "I'm not talking about the children of processors, but of poor coffee pickers."

The existence of a wealthy elite of producer processors descended from a few families of the conquest period would seem to contradict the elite's own view of coffee-based egalitarianism. But these representatives of the twenty leading families of the coffee elite consistently denied that they, or anyone else, constituted a Costa Rican oligarchy. The "fourteen families" of El Salvador were often used as a point of contrast and a negative example of real oligarchic wealth and power. The office manager of a relative of the current President said, to nods of approval from his aristocratic employer, "In El Salvador there are just a few families—the de Solas, four, six families that control everything. And here we have real democracy." A Costa Rican business partner of one of the Salvadoran fourteen families said, "We are very different from El Salvador. We have 100,000 small producers. Almost a third of our production is in cooperatives. And there is nothing like that in El Salvador." A leading processor and member of a prominent German coffee family asserted: "We don't have the extreme wealth that you have elsewhere. We don't have a de Sola, a Sol Meza, the famous fourteen families of El Salvador, or a Castillo as in Guatemala."

Those interviewed recognized the prominence of their own families in Costa Rican economic and social life, but argued that (a) wealth and capital were much less concentrated in Costa Rica than in El Salvador or elsewhere in Latin America; (b) the Costa Rican elite acted more responsibly and with greater restraint and, in contrast to El Salvador, was more likely to share its wealth; and (c) the Costa Rican coffee elite had little power after the 1930s and, especially, after 1948. The only executive of a leading Costa Rican coffee firm interviewed who was *not* a member of the aristocracy said, "In El Salvador you have great concentration of wealth and concentration of power in the same hands. And there was no sharing or division of wealth. Here there are no great concentrations of capital." The son-in-law of a former President argued that "there aren't any fourteen families as there are in El Salvador—capitalists who pursue gain without limit and produce fertile ground for revolution." A descendent of a former associate of United Fruit Company founder Minor Keith said that in Costa Rica, in contrast to El Salvador, "there were not the grand families. Of course we had a coffee oligarchy, but it was of relatively little importance after the 1940s."

El Salvador also appeared as a negative example of inegalitarian, exploitative, and thoroughly un-Costa Rican class relations. There was remarkably little sympathy for the Salvadoran coffee elite's recent political difficulties, which were attributed to its greed and cruelty. As one aristocratic descendent of an English family bluntly put it, "The fourteen families kept everything for themselves and they got the revolution they deserved." He went on to tell a story, probably apocryphal, of a visit by a Costa Rican friend to a Salvadoran coffee grower's home. The host not only ordered a servant to bring him a drink, but told him to kneel while he served it. "That's the way they are," the Costa Rican processor concluded. A thirteenth-generation descendent of Juan Vázquez de Coronado said simply, "They treat their workers like slaves." "They left their marginal classes with nothing," said a leading exporter, and the result was "a war of ten years." The example of El Salvador served to confirm the virtues and the verities of the Costa Rican rural democratic myth.

"Costa Rica Is Coffee"

The white legend of Costa Rican rural democracy is central to the way elite processors view their world and is, in their minds, inextricably linked to the organization of the coffee export economy. It is safe to say that for most of these processors Costa Rican democracy would be inconceivable without coffee. It is "the foundation of our democracy." If democracy and rural egalitarianism are the essence of Costa Rica and coffee is the source of both, then it follows, as one processor explained, that "Costa Rica is coffee." The equation "coffee equals rural democracy equals Costa Rica" is based on a circumscribed definition of the nation limited to the rural society of the central plateau. "This is a coffee country [un país cafetalero]," said a leading processor. Coffee is "fundamental," said his cousin, another leading processor, "because so many people are involved in it throughout the country. . . . If you drive through the country it looks so nice—like a garden—for miles, and the plots are all sub-divided."

The coffee processors were well aware of the economic changes that had dramatically reduced the role of coffee in Costa Rica's export earnings in recent years, but this did not alter their world view. "[Coffee is] the principal factor in the economy. There's a lot of talk of the agriculture of change, but coffee is still fundamental," said one processor. "I saw a headline recently in *La Nación* that exports of *chayote* [a tropical fruit] are up 150 percent," he continued. "A hundred and fifty percent sounds like a lot, but you read the article and you find out that exports have increased to a million dollars a year. But on the same day the price of coffee dropped $5 on the New York exchange and that cost Costa Rica 10 million dollars. In one day, 10 times more than the million earned by *chayote* in *a year!*" "It's the basic source of tax revenues, the biggest employer, the largest earner of foreign exchange," said another leading processor. "I believe in diversification into other exports, industry, but to my way of thinking you don't give up the basis of your economy. You build on it." "It's been fundamental to our economy for 150 years," concluded another processor.

The centrality of coffee did not rest solely on its contribution to export revenues, however substantial. "Without coffee," said one processor, "the economic and social development of Costa Rica would not have been possible." Coffee was seen as an integral part of the social and political organization of Costa Rican society. It was as important for its social as for its strictly economic contributions. "Coffee underlies our political and social stability . . . it is essential to the social and political tranquility of the country," said another. "Clearly coffee is not as important as it once was," said a third, "but it has carried the weight of the development programs." "You know they say the best minister is a good coffee price" said another processor, himself the son of a government minister, repeating a bit of proverbial Costa Rican lore.

At the core of coffee's indispensable contribution to Costa Rican national life was the way the coffee industry redistributed export wealth and, by so doing, maintained the rural society of the central plateau that was the central element in the elite's image of both rural egalitarianism and the nation. In their view, no other export crop or form of economic activity had this sustaining and redistributive potential. "It affects many more people than the other sectors," said a leading coffee processor of his crop, "not only 65,000 farms but perhaps a million people directly involved. What do you have in the case of bananas—100 farms probably owned by twenty people." "It is fundamental," another processor said. "Coffee is the fundamental source of foreign exchange. And the fundamental mechanism for redistributing the income from exports." Most of those interviewed regarded the putative redistributive effects of coffee as much more important than its direct foreign exchange earnings. Even if coffee exports declined as a percentage of total exports, its absolute importance would remain. Some argued that its absolute importance was actually increasing because of the dramatic increases in production in the previous decade.

Many of those interviewed made quantitative estimates of the number of producers and workers benefiting from coffee, and calculated the effect of coffee-based purchasing power on rural living standards and the economy as a whole. Even agricultural wage laborers were seen as benefiting from the redistributive effects of coffee. "The social dimension [of coffee] is very important," said one processor, "because of the labor power involved—coffee is very labor-intensive. And because of the high salaries we pay in Costa Rica—we are 40 years ahead of El Salvador. And the adjustment of salaries—the worker pays 9 percent and I pay 31 percent [for benefits]. El Salvador, Guatemala, they have nothing like this and this is what makes Costa Rica distinct." Although only permanent farm and mill employees are covered by government-mandated benefits, even temporary harvest workers were seen as benefiting. "We have many poor farmers," said one mill owner, "and the extra income from coffee helps them buy clothes, shoes, extra things for the house."

But coffee's alleged redistributive effects were of greatest value to the thousands of small holders who benefited from the earnings passed on to them by the millers and the exporters. Two powerful images, Costa Rica as equality and Costa Rica as coffee, merged in the image of thousands of family coffee farmers in the central plateau. Conversely, a threat to the coffee system was a threat to the nation itself. A principal adviser to President Calderón and a leading coffee grower and processor explained a new government program to aid small and medium producers as a way of preventing them from leaving the industry. "Land is highly divided," he said, "but the crisis [a dramatic fall in coffee prices] could change the structure by driving out the small producers and leaving it less divided." The result might be greater concentration and less subdivision of land, which, he said, "is undesirable." Another miller, recognizing the demands of what he called "the free market era," said that "we have to join the world economy," but he expressed regret at the loss of "an egalitarian sense, a sense of community" that, he said, had declined markedly in the last twenty years.

"Cobbler, Stick to Your Last!"

The elite's identification of Costa Rican society with the coffee-based rural society of the central plateau is, in part, a reflection of its own single-minded devotion to coffee production and a notable aversion to other forms of agrarian and, especially, industrial activity. While elsewhere in Central America, most notably in El Salvador, the coffee elite has widely diversified into other forms of export agriculture, finance, real estate, industry, and tourism, in Costa Rica, both in word and in deed, it remains loyal to the grain of gold.[8] An executive of one of the most successful coffee processing and exporting firms was asked about plans for diversification. He replied, "¡Zapatero a sus zapatos! [Cobbler, stick to your last!] You can be an expert in this business and a failure in other businesses. So we believe in specialization like this in our own firm. We know all the elements of the business—how to work with small farmers—and they know how we operate." This sentiment was almost universal among those interviewed, and at least one other miller put it in exactly the same words—"¡Zapatero a sus zapatos!"—in response to the same question.

Others explained that coffee was "in the blood." "We have always concentrated on coffee," said one miller. "My grandfather [a famous nineteenth-century grower and Costa Rican President] was one of the first to plant coffee on a commercial scale in 1842 and we have been involved ever since. The family has been involved in coffee for four generations." Another grower, with a similarly distinguished family history, said of diversification: "Sometimes I think about buying some additional coffee estates." Another said that he had been experimenting with macadamia nuts, but "it is difficult. New products are difficult to master in the way we have mastered coffee after years of experience." "The mentality of the typical Costa Rican farmer changes slowly," said a third. "Coffee has been the basis of the economy for 100 years. It's difficult to get a farmer to start growing strawberries after all that time."

Many of those interviewed were distinctly skeptical on the putative virtues of other export crops. "My father always said," said one miller, "that the only people who made any money in bananas were the people who sold out at the right time." Another described fluctuations in the international price for cardamom from $2,500 to $300 a hundredweight and added, "It's madness, a market like that. So we have concentrated on coffee." A third miller, who had in fact experimented with alternative crops, said, "Agriculture is a lot riskier than industry, where you have a roof over your head." He went on to point out that fluctuations in rainfall caused by the inversion in the Peruvian current called El Niño had reduced his experimental rice plantings from 1,000 to 150 *manzanas* in a single year. "I think that Costa Rica will continue to depend on coffee for a long time to come," he concluded.

Several growers in the Turrialba region combined coffee with another traditional crop, sugar, in order to take advantage of the complementary seasonal labor demands of the two crops, but with one notable exception (he was a member of what is reputedly Costa Rica's wealthiest family), none of the others had diversified to any significant extent. The most important non-agricultural investment, real estate, did not so much represent diversification as disinvestment. As the names of some of San José's most exclusive districts (Rohrmoser, Dent, Tournon) indicate, some leading coffee families have taken advantage of the proximity of their farms to the city center to make a killing in real estate. At least one of those interviewed was actively considering following the same path at the time of the interviews. Another had inadvertently become involved in real estate when the land under his mill was condemned for a highway overpass. Active coffee farmers, however, remained exclusively devoted to coffee as they had been for 150 years.

Industry and "los Polacos"

Although a minority of those interviewed thought that coffee aided the development of industry through its injection of purchasing power into the rural economy, most thought that coffee and industry were either independent or actually competitive with one another. Only one person, the same notable exception from Costa Rica's wealthiest family who had diversified into other areas, had *any* investment in industry, although his were in fact extensive. For most of the others industry was *terra incognita*—something best left for foreigners and others outside the charmed circle of coffee families. "There must be one," said one former miller when asked about the relation between coffee and industry, "but I haven't thought about what it is." "I think basically they go their separate ways," said another in response to the same question. "Actually, there are few coffee growers involved in industry. That is something the Poles [los Polacos, a term for Eastern European immigrants generally] get involved in," said a member of one of Costa Rica's most successful and famous coffee families.

When pressed, some suggested that coffee might have had some effect on industry through the development of coffee-processing machinery, but often added that coffee's impact had been limited by multinational control of soluble and processed coffee manufacture. Costa Rica has developed a small domestic industry producing coffee-processing machinery that represents formidable, low-cost competition for the best foreign processing equipment. But these observations served to underscore the limited connection between coffee and industry perceived by most of those interviewed. Coffee's impact on industry was seen as limited to the coffee industry itself.

A number of those interviewed saw coffee and industry as competitors for capital and labor. "It's just the way Raúl Prebisch said it should be done," said one miller, referring to the well-known Argentinian proponent of import-substitution industrialization. "So they [industry] get special privileges . . . and we pay the taxes. Taxes for us, exemptions for them." "[Coffee] has been heavily burdened to help the other sectors," commented another miller and estate owner. "Coffee has been a little overloaded with the responsibility of development," said an executive of a leading multinational firm, while conceding the need for an economy in which people were doing something besides "cultivating a coffee bush."

Many processors complained of a chronic shortage of harvest labor, only temporarily relieved by the influx of impoverished Nicaraguan refugees, and a number said the explosive development of drawback manufacturing plants [*maquilas*] in Costa Rica had exacerbated the problem. "The *maquilas* are creating a great problem of labor power.

The women and children who used to pick coffee—the women prefer to work inside out of the rain where there aren't any worms and bugs." He said that he himself had lost many workers to *maquilas* in his area, but readily conceded that three months of harvest labor could scarcely compete with a year-round job in industry. One socially concerned processor founded a development association to provide year-round work for women on her farms, in part to meet the competition from the *maquilas*. Others said that the *maquilas* were driving wages up to levels that were creating an economic crisis for growers. "It is all to the good for them," one miller said of the workers, "but it has created a big problem for us."

Although the coffee elite no longer argues, as it did before 1948, that workers are actually better off in the countryside than in urban industry, the competition for labor between coffee and industry is still a central theme in its conversations. Similarly, although the coffee elite no longer rejects, as it did before 1948, indigenous industrial development as a national objective, it still believes that it is unfairly bearing the economic burden for this development. Coffee and industry are still seen, as they were before 1948, as separate and often antagonistic realms of economic activity.[9] Despite the remarkable expansion of Costa Rican manufacturing in the last five years, none of those interviewed had any involvement with drawback industry, and only one, the notable exception, had any investment in industry at all. ¡Zapatero a sus zapatos!—the coffee elite has maintained its single minded devotion to coffee and left the development of industry to foreigners, sometimes of Eastern European origin, but, more often, North American corporations.[10] For the coffee elite Costa Rica *is* still coffee. Their personal economic experience, as well as their world view, are still based on the traditional agro-export economy of the nineteenth and early twentieth centuries.

The "White Legend": For Whites Only

The image of Costa Rica as coffee country leaves out not only Eastern European industrialists but anyone not of Western European origin. At the heart of the white legend and the coffee culture is a fierce racial pride that was evident in the interviews even though processors were not directly asked about their racial views. "We are Europeans—just look around you—Spain, Italy—we are an industrious people," said one processor of English descent. "I may be too proud but that's the way I feel." "Basically Costa Ricans are white," said another. "This sounds racist, but I think it's important." "The white race is always dominant," said another, "and there are mostly Europeans here in Costa Rica."

Although there was variation among those interviewed and some younger processors described Costa Rica as a "melting pot" rather than a country of white European immigrants, almost all thought that race was an important factor in accounting for Costa Rica's democratic peace and stability. Many mentioned the absence of a large Indian population as a reason Costa Rica had avoided the colonial caste systems found elsewhere in the region. ". . . We have a largely mixed population and have avoided the division—Spanish versus Indian—of the other countries," said one processor. "The Spanish couldn't find anything here to steal and there were few Indians here and you could really say they killed them off," said another. "The other countries had a large Indian population to deal with and we did not," said still another processor.

As these comments indicate, there was little sympathy for the problems of the racially stratified conquest societies of the Central American North and, for that matter, for the Spanish conquerors themselves. Most of those interviewed nevertheless shared the racist assumptions of the European colonial order even while rejecting unequal colonial societies. For most of those interviewed the racial inferiority of the indigenous population of the Americas was an accepted fact and racial stratification an inevitable consequence of that inferiority. ". . . The white race is dominant over the Indian or the Negro, don't you think?" asked one processor of otherwise liberal social views. "I think all the Indians like to do is drink *chicha,*" said one of the older and more conservative processors. ". . . The Indians don't do much work and they are not very intelligent. And they were very cheap workers," said another older processor. For most of the processors, the absence of what they saw as a racially inferior Indian lower class that would inevitably be exploited by dominant Europeans was the foundation of Costa Rica's rural egalitarianism.

Conversely, the yeoman farmer of the white legend was assumed to be European. It could hardly have been otherwise, given the racist assumptions of most of those interviewed. Only Europeans could carry the spirit of liberty and the talent for industry so indispensable to the mythical yeoman who was "the nucleus of Costa Rican society" and the bulwark of agrarian democracy. It is worth noting too that the yeoman was in fact a man. Women figured in processor accounts as family members of independent male owner-operators, often working in the coffee harvest to supplement income from the family farm. They could, however, be included in the white legend as wives, mothers and harvest workers. Non-whites, male and female, could not. Costa Rican democratic exceptionalism could never rest on such "inferior" races and racial mixtures. A fierce racism was, therefore, an indispensable part of the rural agrarian myth.

Harmony, Integration and Law 2762, "Hymn of Peace"

The fiftieth anniversary of the foundation of the Institute for the Defense of Coffee (now the Institute of Coffee or ICAFE) in 1983 was the occasion for an outpouring of rhetorical reaffirmations of the fundamental values of Costa Rican coffee culture and the white legend. Rising to the occasion, Costa Rica's President Luis Alberto Monge declared that ICAFE was destined to "unite, reconcile, put in order and instill moderation and harmony in the nation and the industry." Minister of Agriculture Francisco Morales spoke eloquently of the importance of coffee in the social integration of the Costa Ricans, a quarter of whom, he said, depended on this activity. At a later celebration a leading coffee processor, Tobías Umaña Parra, lauded Law 2762 of 1961 regulating the relations between coffee processors and producers as "the greatest hymn of peace ever sung by the law's author, President Monge, himself." All agreed that the transcendent Costa Rican virtues of harmony, integration and social peace had been well served by the coffee industry and affirmed and defended by government regulation, especially Law 2762.[11]

Indeed the harmonious interdependence of producer and processor under Law 2762 and its predecessors, like the egalitarian distribution of coffee land, is a central element of both the Costa Rican white legend and the contemporary coffee elite's view of itself, its industry and its country. "The most important thing to understand about the coffee business is the role of the Institute of Coffee in the technical side of the business," said one leading processor. "It regulates completely all the relations between the small farmers, the millers, the exporters, the domestic industry. It is an excellent system and a model for others to imitate. . . . It makes the small producers happy and it protects their interests. It is the main reason for the stability and social peace we have enjoyed in Costa Rica in contrast to other countries in the region like El Salvador or Guatemala."

Another grower said that the most important event in the history of the Costa Rican coffee industry was the passage, in 1933, of the first law regulating the relations between producers and processors. Law 121 of 24 July 1933 established the Institute for the Defense of Coffee as a semi-autonomous entity and gave it responsibility for registering and regulating all transactions between producers and processors. The law was passed in response to the gentlemanly, but militant, protest movement of small coffee producers against the processing elite. The law regulated the margins permitted the processors and guaranteed that the price received by the producer reflected world market prices. Although the processors opposed the legislation, neither President Ricardo Jiménez Oreamuno nor his predecessor and fellow Olympian Cleto González Víquez joined them. After the expulsion of small producer representative Manuel Marín Quirós from the board in 1935, the Institute was, increasingly, controlled by the processors and exporters.[12]

The Institute for the Defense of Coffee was nationalized and renamed the Office of Coffee by the founding junta of the Second Republic in 1948, but the functions of the renamed organization remained substantially the same. Relations between producer and processor continued to be controlled by the rules laid down in the 1933 law. The basic law was modified in 1961 by Law 2762, introduced by Monge when he was still a deputy. This law remains in effect today, although the name of the regulatory agency was changed to the Institute of Coffee in 1985. Law 2762 limited the processor's margin to 9 percent of the freight on rail Costa Rican coffee price. It permitted deductions for mill operating expenses including fuel, electricity, insurance, and salaries, but not maintenance or capital replacement costs. All transactions had to be registered with the Office of Coffee, and the price to be paid the producer was determined by a final settlement of accounts or "liquidation" after the crop had been sold on world markets. The Office, later Institute, also handled negotiations with the International Coffee Organization (ICO) over quotas and negotiated to place Costa Rican coffee in non-ICO markets.[13]

For some processors the law had achieved almost the status of a sacred text. One processor urged me to study the basic law in order to understand the Costa Rican industry and when a search of her office failed to reveal a copy, she called home and asked her maid to bring me one. Another grower urged me to read the law in the proceedings of the Coffee Institute at the Institute's library. "The Costa Rican coffee system is like no other system in the world," he said; "every transaction, every sale, must be registered by law." "It is unique in the world," said another processor, ". . . it's a good system for the producer and since I am a producer as well as a processor it benefits me as well."

Although some processors complained that the margin permitted by Law 2762 was inadequate, all but one of those interviewed described their relations with the Institute as "excellent" and voiced enthusiastic support for the basic law. The one exception denounced the Institute as a "white elephant" that had turned the industry over to "the Germans" who, he said, dominated the export trade. What Costa Rica needed was a "real coffee institute" like those of Colombia or Brazil to return the profits of the trade to Costa Ricans. But for most processors the limited regulation represented by Law 2762 and the Coffee Institute was superior to all other systems ever devised to manage national coffee economies. "I think the way the government, the Institute of Coffee, is organized is the ideal way of handling things," said a leading producer and processor. "In El Salvador a number of years ago they nationalized the coffee trade and it was a big mistake." "I know a number of coffee systems well," said a leading processor and member of the board of ICAFE; "those of Guatemala, of Colombia, of Kenya. In Kenya it is a completely state managed system—everything is under state control. . . . But I favor a free system like the one we have in Costa Rica."

The Costa Rican system is not, of course, completely free: processor margins are fixed and the international price, minus the processor's margin, must, by law, be passed on to the primary producer. The coffee trade, like the processing industry, is, however, entirely

in private hands and the system is, as the processor claimed, substantially less restrictive than the Kenyan or Salvadoran state monopolies. And the Institute is controlled by a board dominated by
the coffee elite. By law the board consists of representatives of producers, processors, exporters, roasters for the domestic industry, and
the government; in this arrangement, as one processor noted, "the
private sector has a majority." But since processors, exporters, large
producers, and roasters are all from the same elite families, the elite
actually controls the Institute and has done so since the 1930s.[14]
"The relationship between the government and the private sector in
ICAFE has been very smooth, very tranquil," said one processor.
"That is because there is ample representation of the private sector
on the board."

Despite elite domination of the board of ICAFE (recently modified
to include representatives of the cooperative movement), the processors believed that the Institute was, as one of them said, "basically
run in the interests of the small producers." For many of the processors ICAFE and Law 2762 were fundamental to insuring the tranquility and social peace of Costa Rica through their defense of the
small producer and their harmonious integration of all sectors of the
industry and hence of the society. "Monge Highlights Harmonious
Relations Among Coffee Producers" read a 1985 headline in *La
Nación,* in an article which also quoted him as saying that these
"harmonious relations" in the coffee sector were "a proof of the social
peace in which Costa Rica lives."[15] The basic law was seen as more
than an instrument of economic regulation. It was viewed as part of
Costa Rican uniqueness—a contributor to the peaceful, harmonious
society of the white legend.

A number of processors, in fact, saw the law as the *principal* guarantor of Costa Rican tranquility. "It has produced tranquility," said
one processor of the original 1933 law. "There is no longer the perception of a group of exploiters—the processors—taking advantage
of the small producers. And this has contributed to the smooth
functioning of the system." "The law forces a redistribution of income," said another processor. "It distributes income to large numbers of small producers and they are all small property owners who
have an interest in defending the system. So we don't have the kind
of desperate poverty that is fertile ground for Communists." *La cul-*

tura cafetalera included, said the processor quoted earlier, ". . . the method of financing, the laws and regulations protecting the coffee industry. It's a way of life." A number of the processors, including the three quoted in this paragraph, saw the basic law as the reason Costa Rica had avoided the problems of El Salvador. In contrast to El Salvador, in Costa Rica there were no "capitalists who pursue gain without limit" because "the capitalists . . . are regulated by the basic law."

Harmony and social peace are as fundamental to the white legend as the myth of rural egalitarianism and both are, in the opinion of the coffee elite, sustained by coffee. Indeed, as the above statements indicate, the two ideas are closely linked. The small coffee farmer, the bulwark of agrarian democracy, is joined to the large processor by the basic law which insures the survival of the former and his peaceful integration with the latter. But the basic law is fundamental to the white legend not simply because of its defense of the yeoman coffee farmer. The existence of the basic law resolves the fundamental contradiction at the heart of the coffee economy and the white legend itself—the fundamental class division between the yeoman farmer and the processing elite. Coffee capitalists there may be in Costa Rica, but no "exploiters" or "capitalists who pursue gain without limit." Export wealth was widely distributed not only because of the thousands of small farmers, but because government regulation forced a just division of the proceeds. "We are basically a middle class nation—the middle class is very strong here," because the basic law "regulates all the relationships."

The Client Is King: Social and Sociable Relations of Production

The relationship that the basic law regulates is that between the producer, often a small- or medium-sized farmer, and the processor, by definition a member of the coffee elite. It is this relationship that is at the heart of the Costa Rican coffee economy and shapes the coffee elite's perception of *la cultura cafetalera* and itself. It is the substructure of the white legend. Almost all the processors interviewed had extensive economic relationships of long standing with small and medium producers. Most produced only 10 to 20 percent of the coffee they processed and purchased the rest from other producers. Although large producers contribute a disproportionate share of this production, coffee from the much larger number of small and medium producers constitutes the bulk of purchases for most processors. Some producer-processors continue to process their own production exclusively, a pattern that was considerably more common in the past, but the most successful members of the processing elite have always relied on others to produce their coffee.[16]

Relations with primary producers are therefore vastly more important to the economic success of a processing firm than relations with its own workers in its mills or with its permanent or harvest laborers on its own farms. Since processing is capital rather than labor intensive few processors employ more than 30 or 40 workers in their mills and the number of permanent (as opposed to harvest) workers on their farms is not much greater. In contrast, most of those interviewed reported that they bought coffee from hundreds or even thousands of primary producers. The proprietor of one of the smaller firms reported 400 to 500 primary producers. A successful medium-sized firm had approximately 2,000 and one the largest firms, more than 5,000 producers. The greater the number of producers, and the greater the production of each, the greater the revenues of the firm. Maintaining or increasing deliveries from these producers is therefore the key to economic success in processing, and the social relations of production are defined by the relationship between capitalist processors and primary producers, not between capitalists and workers.

All processors described competition for coffee deliveries as intense and growing more so. Success depends not only on outbidding other competitive mills on price but also on long established social and economic ties between producers and processor. Mill owners referred to their producers as "clients" and treated them accordingly. Many supplied them with credit or provided advance payment at delivery, and all were concerned with their welfare and productivity on which their own success depended. Personal relationships were as important as strictly economic considerations. Effective management of thousands of micro-transactions with clients required bonds of personal trust and intimate knowledge of the habits, intentions, financial condition, and reliability of hundreds or thousands of clients. As one of the leading processors observed, it requires the "eye of a lover" to "fatten the horse"—constant attention was necessary, he added, to manage client relations successfully. Another leading processor said, "We pay a lot of attention to the producers. Some old guy who has been bringing in his coffee for years likes to be able to walk in the door here and sit down and talk over the prices with Don Ernesto [the aristocratic processor himself]." "The client is king," said another executive of a leading firm; "here, he is king."

These feelings are, for the most part, reciprocated by small and medium producers, especially since the basic law "regulated all the relationships" after 1933. But even before the law, in the depths of the Depression, protest by economically threatened small producers was gentlemanly, though determined, and did not aim at overthrowing the system but at reaching an accommodation with what they nonetheless called the "trust of the processors."[17] Since the basic law, protests and demonstrations by small farmers have continued, but they have been more often directed against government taxation and credit policies than against the processing elite.[18] Even at the height of the Depression, the small producers sought accommodation with "good processors" like Julio Sánchez Lépiz, who earned an enviable following among small producers for his equitable dealings and his populist rhetoric.[19] Accommodation and class collaboration, not class conflict and polarization, were the goals on both sides. The contrast with El Salvador, where, during the Depression crisis, the coffee pickers' Communist-led insurrection was drowned in blood by the military allies of an enraged coffee elite, is striking. Peace, tranquility, and accommodation have in fact, as well as in legend, been the legacy of class relations in the coffee industry.

The white legend can thus be viewed as an idealized reflection of the elite's experience of actually existing relations of production in coffee. The white legend says that Costa Rica is thousands of coffee producers; the processors' clients are thousands of coffee producers. The white legend says that the ownership of property is the basis of Costa Rican democracy; the processors' economic fortunes depend on the good will of these owner-operators. The white legend says that harmony and interdependence are the basis of Costa Rican exceptionalism; the processors' experience is accommodation and interdependence between processor and yeoman producer. The interdependent society of small producers, which is the basis of the white legend, is, in fact, the interdependent society of coffee processors and producers. It is, in the processors' version, Don Ernesto, his door always open, talking over the price of coffee with his old friend the trusted client.

Democracy and Communism: The 1930s Challenge to the "White Legend" and the Elite Response

The white legend of agrarian democracy and social harmony could have been, and was, expressed by members of these same coffee elite families at various times since the 1930s and, excepting the praise of government regulation, any time since the late nineteenth century.[20] But the image of *la cultura cafetalera* obviously leaves out elements of Costa Rican society that became more important as the century progressed. The laborers of the sweltering banana zone, the growing working class and impoverished informal sector of San José, urban industry and industrialists, and the coffee pickers who are the basis of the entire system are all outside the coffee culture. It was precisely from these groups that the popular challenges of the 1930s and 1940s arose. The revolutionary decade and the reforms of both Calderón and Figueres presented the elite with a vision very different from that of *la cultura cafetalera*. The revolutionary decade presented an ideological as well as a political threat to the coffee elite's myth of rural coffee-based democracy.

Although these are the events of forty years ago, they are part of living memory for many of those interviewed and, for the more than half of the sample over the age of sixty, they are part of their political coming of age and young adulthood. Many of the coffee elite fought a civil war against Calderón only to see themselves pushed from power by Figueres. The coffee elite, sometimes the very individuals interviewed, often their fathers or other members of their family, were among the most vociferous opponents of the reforms of both Calderón and Figueres. How have these events affected coffee elite ideology? Those interviewed were asked directly about the historic and contemporary effects of these reforms. Although the coffee elite continues to enunciate the values of traditional coffee culture, they have come to terms with the history of the last half century. Surprisingly, given the coffee elite's positions of a half century ago, they are today more enthusiastic about the reforms of Calderón (although not the man) than about those of Figueres.

Social Guarantees and Social Peace: The Reforms of Calderón

Although members of the older generation among those interviewed could clearly remember the controversy Calderón's social reforms engendered when they were first proposed, they and their juniors now said, without exception, that the social guarantees were a necessary and essential part of the Costa Rican way of life. "Of course they [the guarantees] caused a great conflict at the time—the revolution . . . but they have been very good for the country, very good," said one seventy-year-old who clearly remembered the events of the Calderón era. "Everyone said the reforms would bankrupt them," recalled a former processor, "but of course they didn't." "I think the private sector has completely accepted the reforms," said one member of the younger generation whose father had been among their staunchest opponents. A poll of the Club Unión taken today would find almost unanimous support for the social reforms, instead of the nearly unanimous opposition of 1942, although there is no more enthusiasm for the man now than there was then.

But the support for the social guarantees among those interviewed is much more than a reluctant acknowledgement of a long standing social reality. The social guarantees have become a fundamental part of the coffee elite's view of itself and its nation. Together with rural egalitarianism and the basic law, they have become defining characteristics of Costa Rican uniqueness and core elements of elite ideology. "I think the private sector has been 'socialized,' if I can use the term," said one processor. "It's fair to say that the private sector here has a much greater social conscience." Both he and another processor joked that their counterparts elsewhere in Central America viewed them as "socialists." "But," the first processor added, "I think there is a real commitment [in the private sector] to make things better."

Although there were complaints over the costs and bureaucratic inefficiencies of the social programs, not one person among those interviewed challenged their value to Costa Rican society. Most expressed what appeared to be deeply felt devotion to the reforms and the better life they had brought to people less fortunate than themselves. In a few cases this devotion had become a personal commitment or, in one case, a life's work. One aristocratic processor had obtained a Ph.D. at a United States university and returned to Costa Rica with a desire to aid his country. He devoted the early part of his career to working with a leading dairy co-op to introduce pasteurization and other biological controls to insure a healthy milk supply for Costa Rican children. Another processor handed me a business card listing him as a board member of a recreation program at a local children's hospital. "Try to go there some day and watch the families and the children . . . it is something you should really see to understand Costa Rica. . . . I am a Costa Rican and I am tremendously proud of my country . . . the joy people have in living here." The social guarantees, including the state medical system, were, he said, part of the reason for this happiness.

Although few of those interviewed had this level of personal commitment to social welfare activity, almost all shared the enthusiasm for the social guarantees and the belief in their fundamental contribution to Costa Rican life. "Magnificent!" was the way the one unreconstructed Calderonista (and close relative of Rafael Angel) characterized the reforms. "They provide the welfare of the people." "Indispensable," said a leading exporter and long-time Liberacionista. "Necessary—necessary and just," said another, who also added that they needed some changes to increase their efficiency. "Excellent," said another, of the reforms, "despite the cost." Even the most conservative of those interviewed, who said that the social programs needed "drastic reforms," limited himself to demanding "greater efficiency" when asked what sort of changes he had in mind. If they have not, as their colleagues elsewhere in Central America charge, become socialists, members of the Costa Rican coffee elite have certainly become enthusiastic proponents of welfare socialism. The contrast with their counterparts elsewhere in the region, whose resistance to even modest reform is legendary, is striking.

Furthermore, to the extent that the social guarantees of the Calderón era have been woven into the fabric of elite ideology, they have become another facet of the white legend, and, like the basic law regulating producer and processors, a guarantor of Costa Rican democratic peace and stability. "The reforms of Calderón Guardia, the social guarantees, are the price we pay for our democracy, for our social peace, to be able to live in peace. The weight of the social guarantees is heavy, perhaps too heavy, but social peace depends on health, education, social guarantees," was one eloquent but representative comment. "The social guarantees are the basis of our stability and democracy," said another processor. According to another, "the social guarantees are why we are able to live peacefully without armies or coups." "Social peace" was perhaps the most frequently expressed perceived consequence of the reforms. The peaceful democracy of the white legend could not, in the view of the coffee elite today, exist without the social guarantees. The effect of the reforms, one processor believed, was that "there is a kind of understanding between workers and business. And I think this has helped us avoid the problems of other countries in the region."

The Costa Rican coffee elite is well aware of the fate of their colleagues elsewhere in the region, and recent political events in Central America have served to demonstrate graphically the wisdom and foresight of their own commitment to welfare socialism. El Salvador was, once again, a particularly vivid negative example. "Yes, the reforms of Calderón!" said one processor. "That's why we don't have to live the way they do in Guatemala or El Salvador—driving around in armored vehicles with two bodyguards." "I prefer to pay the cost," said another processor of the reforms. "There aren't any guerrillas like El Salvador. I can sit here in my office with my door open and anyone can just walk in. You can't do that in El Salvador." "Guatemala, El Salvador neglected these things," said another processor of the social guarantees. "People can only stand so much."

A former processor explained the difference between El Salvador and Costa Rica with the following observation: "You know, if some man who struggles to find enough money to feed his family, and he can't afford medical care, and he sees somebody riding down the street in a new Mercedes, he's going to want to kill him. . . . If people have nothing, and if you won't give them anything, they will fight." Another described a firm he knew in Guatemala that had tried to solve its labor problems by sending in a platoon of police. Many workers were killed, he said, and the firm finally moved to Costa Rica where, despite the higher labor costs that resulted from the social programs, the climate was still better for business because of social peace. Another coffee processor, also a major sugar producer, said that at a sugar mill he knew of in Nicaragua the workers diverted the mill output into a river, destroying the entire crop. "If you don't share your profits with others, you're going to have problems. You can't keep it all for yourself."

With one notable exception, none of those interviewed attributed the troubles in the region to outside Communist interference. Almost all saw them as a consequence of deep-rooted poverty and inequality that had not been adequately addressed by short-sighted, greedy, and unresponsive ruling elites. Almost all said that the social guarantees were the principal reason that Costa Rica had avoided these problems and their absence elsewhere had been the proximate cause of revolution. Many believed that unresponsive elites elsewhere had brought revolution upon themselves. As one leading processor and former conservative vice-presidential candidate eloquently summed up the role of the social guarantees in Costa Rica, "In El Salvador they have death. In Guatemala, death. In Nicaragua, death. But here we have life. And the social programs are the reason."

Calderón, Communism and Class Conflict: The Limits of Elite Welfare Socialism

The reforms of Calderón Guardia were adopted with the support of the Costa Rican Communist party and the Communist-led union movement. The coffee elite has wholeheartedly embraced Calderón's reforms while still rejecting the man. They have also accepted the social wage demanded by labor while still expressing a decided lack of enthusiasm for organized labor itself. And anti-communism remains a bedrock of elite and, indeed, Costa Rican national ideology. Their skeptical view of organized labor and the political left defines the limits of the coffee elite's vision of social democracy and the welfare state. The white legend was expanded to include social welfare as a guarantor of social peace and democracy. But organized class conflict in the workplace or in the political system is incompatible with the notion of a harmonious egalitarian society of small property owners. Neither the white legend nor coffee elite ideology has a place for a radicalized working class.

None of those interviewed had had any direct experience with labor unions in their own enterprises since there were no unions in their farms or mills or, indeed, in the coffee economy generally. But the coffee elite did not object in principle to the idea of labor unions with legitimate economic grievances; they were against what they described as the "politicized" labor union movement of Costa Rica. "Real unions don't exist in Costa Rica," said one processor. "The unions had their origins in the Communist party and as a result business has always been hostile and workers have been suspicious." "The unions here are not like unions in the United States—responsible for defending workers' interests," said another. "The leaders are crude people, not well trained." Another miller argued that unions were "important, necessary," but they were infiltrated by "foreign" and "leftist" influences. The departure of the United Fruit Company from Golfito in 1984, after what one processor termed "Communist-led disruptions," was proof for many that "communist" unions were as bad for workers as they were for management.

Although one grower saw some hope for the development of what he called "responsible labor unions," and none suggested that unions themselves were illegitimate, the processors' real enthusiasm was reserved for *solidarismo,* a peculiarly Costa Rican form of company union.[21] *Solidarismo* is a worker credit union supported by voluntary contributions from workers and the severance pay funds that management must by law maintain for each worker. The funds are controlled by a joint management-worker committee and are available for individual loans or community development projects. For most of those interviewed, *solidarismo* represented the ideal form of labor-management relations and was markedly superior to trade unions, responsible or not. "It really is a terrific program," said one miller. "A typically Costa Rican association," said another, "which is a system of workers together for the welfare of the workers." "Our people are not happy with unions," said another, "they prefer cooperative arrangements like *solidarismo.*"

Most of those interviewed argued that trade unions were losing ground to solidary associations for good reason—they performed many of the same functions as unions but served the interests of the workers better. "*Solidarismo* is spreading," said one miller, "not only in Costa Rica, but throughout the region." "*Solidarismo* is a very strong movement," said another, "and the unions are losing much of their strength." "Instead of trade unions we have *solidarismo,*" said another, "which has taken the place of unions. So workers see no need for unions." Some of those interviewed also candidly acknowledged that this system also served the interests of management. "It is very good for preventing unions and putting an end to strikes," as one miller put it. According to another miller, *solidarismo* was "a modern democratic form of unionism. It has many benefits for workers and *there are no strikes*" (italics added).

Solidarismo maintained the kind of harmonious relations between workers and management that the basic law insured between producer and processor. It maintained the peace and tranquility of Costa Rican society and so, like the basic law, contributed to the white legend. When asked about the absence of unions in the coffee sector, a number of millers emphasized the small numbers of workers and the importance of personal relations between worker and employer in coffee. *Solidarismo,* therefore, not only echoed core elements of the white legend but reflected the personal experience of millers with their own employees. It is not surprising therefore that a number of millers provided enthusiastic descriptions of solidary associations on their own farms. This system was more than simply a means of discouraging strikes; it was an expression of the core values of the Costa Rican national ideology. A harmonious interdependent association of workers and mangers was the labor relations equivalent of the harmonious interdependent society of small coffee producers.

In such a society the very notion of class struggle, to say nothing of a political party organized to promote it, was a foreign and discordant notion. Not only did the coffee elite reject "communist-led" unions; they reaffirmed anti-communism as an article of their own and the Costa Rican national faith. After expressing views on the welfare state that would have been welcomed by Marx himself, if not by Lenin, a leading processor observed, "the only good Communist is a dead Communist," and added, "I am a very strong anti-communist." His cousin, another leading processor, alone among those interviewed argued that Cuba was the "basic source of subversion" throughout the region. Castro, he said, would never change his subversive ways. "There isn't going to be any change unless they shoot him."

Although such militant views were the exception, most of those interviewed affirmed their anti-communism as an expression of Costa Rican national character rather than as a personal crusade and one or two dissented even from this more limited view. "Costa Ricans are basically anti-communist—naturally anti-communist. It is a fundamental sense we have," was one typical view. "Costa Rica is very anti-communist," said another processor. "The most they [the left] ever had in fifty years is three deputies." But another miller, whose father had been released from jail in the Calderón period by the intervention of Manuel Mora Valverde, head of the Communist Party, described Mora as "a good Communist, a Costa Rica Communist." And the one remaining Calderonista among those interviewed denounced Costa Rica's leading anti-communist, José Figueres, as an ally of "big business." Despite these minority views, the image of a distinct "comunismo tico" had faded, replaced by an image of communism as essentially foreign and un-Costa Rican.

With the exception of the two outspokenly anti-communist cousins quoted above, none of those interviewed expressed any enthusiasm for the militant and militarized anti-communism of Reagan era America and most affirmed their belief in the wisdom and justice of traditional Costa Rican neutrality. "They always seem to end up on the wrong side of the scenery," said one miller of United States policy makers. "Take Oscar Arias and the peace plan for Central America. They were never enthusiastic about it." Almost all of those interviewed, on the other hand, did express support, sometimes qualified, for the Arias plan, and almost all were glad that it had kept Costa Rica out of the region's civil wars. "It would have been another struggle like Vietnam," said another processor, referring to Nicaragua, "so it is good that Oscar Arias kept us out of it. He earned his peace prize." "It was scary," said another processor, who had accompanied Arias on a diplomatic mission to London. "Little Oscar and his peace plan against the big United States." "There was pressure," said another miller, referring to the U.S. effort to enlist Costa Rica in the contra war, "but we never succumbed to it. We were always able to handle it. . . . Costa Rica is a different country. There has never been support for violent solutions here."

Communism and militant anti-communism both threatened the peaceful, harmonious society of the white legend. There was no need for the former since workers and employers were linked in *solidarismo*. The latter jeopardized Costa Rican neutrality and promoted "violent solutions" for problems which, as the millers had consistently argued, had their roots in social and economic inequality. The social guarantees and labor code of Rafael Angel Calderón Guardia had, according to the elite, helped Costa Rica avoid the problems of the other countries in the region, but they had also made further class struggle superfluous. And politicized unions simply created trouble over issues which were more effectively and harmoniously handled by *solidarismo*.

After half a century, the coffee elite had not merely accepted the reforms of Calderón Guardia; they had made them an essential part of their own world view and a central element in an updated version of the white legend. Social welfare, the labor code, and solidary associations are all now seen as contributing to the harmonious interdependent society of small producers that is the essence of *la cultura cafetalera*. Union militancy, leftist political parties, and the class struggle they represented are not part of this world. Their very existence implied conflict rather than peace, division rather than interdependence, and struggle rather than harmony. The very processes that had created the social guarantees in the first place were now rejected as the guarantees themselves were embraced. The *cultura cafetalera* had expanded to include the social guarantees as a source of peace and harmony. It could not and did not expand to include the idea of a militant organized left. Both welfare socialism and anti-communism had become articles of an updated version of the Costa Rican national ideology.

Despite the continuities between the coffee culture and welfare socialism, the elite did not come to its current enthusiastic acceptance of the latter of its own free will. Those seeking the origins of Costa Rican social democracy in a far-sighted, or even a short-sighted, agrarian elite will be disappointed. The elite initially opposed both the political incorporation of the working class and the enactment of the social guarantees, as its members now candidly concede. These reforms were initially pushed by working class organizations, the Communist Party, the Catholic Church, and an upper-class reformer widely regarded as a traitor to his class. They were preserved, paradoxically, by middle-class reformers who had organized a civil war against their principal author. It was pressure from below, not simply enlightenment from above, that established the Costa Rican welfare state. The elite has, as one of them said, been "socialized" by its experiences into accepting the reforms. Left to its own devices it is unlikely that the coffee elite would ever have gone beyond the limited democracy that existed prior to 1940. In Costa Rica no bourgeoisie, agrarian or industrial, created social democracy. It only learned to accept it.

Costa Rica emerged from the revolutionary crisis of the 1930s and 1940s with an expanded democracy, a pioneering welfare state, and a coffee elite that had come to accept these elements as an integral part of its vision of *la cultural cafetalera*. These developments were rooted in the reality of sociable relations of production between the processor elite and small holders in coffee, but they were substantially extended by the popular mobilizations of the 1930s and 1940s. Only in Costa Rica did the elite incorporate any of the ideas of the rebels into its own thought, and only in Costa Rica were these ideas made part of a reorganized political system before the 1980s. And alone among the major coffee exporters of Central America, Costa Rica avoided the revolutionary crisis of the 1980s. This was the enduring legacy of the reforms of Calderón. Figueres's revolution elevated the ideas of the coffee culture, as modified by Calderón's welfare socialism, to articles of national faith and national policy, creating a social democratic Costa Rica. The events of 1948 also institutionalized anti-communist ideology as an article of that national faith and buried the fundamental critique of the inequalities of the agro-export economy, raised most effectively by the Communists in the 1940s, along with the Party itself.

Anti-communism insured that much of Costa Rican reality would be excluded from the ideology of the coffee culture. The large and growing informal sector of San José and other smaller urban areas is excluded both from the ideology and from the programs of the Costa Rican welfare state. Coffee pickers exist in elite ideology only as part-time workers supplementing incomes from small farms. In reality they are part of the landless semi-proletariat of country and city that is the fastest growing class in Costa Rica and the rest of Latin America. No land reform and no changes in the still vastly unequal distribution of Costa Rican wealth are on the national agenda. Indeed, the core of the white legend denies the very existence of such inequalities, and the coffee elite echoes this belief. Parties of the organized left demanding that these issues be included in the elite agenda are also not part of that agenda.

Figueres's ambitious economic reform program actually increased the discrepancy between the white legend (plus social welfare) and the reality of Costa Rican class relations by vastly increasing both the size and strength of the agro-industrial fraction of the elite and creating greater polarization in the countryside between successful capitalist farmers, small and large, and the growing rural semi-proletariat. These developments represented a fundamental change in the sociable relations of production that had given rise to the white legend in the first place. In the 1980s the new ideology of neo-liberalism emerged to reflect the growing dominance of the agro-industrialists in Costa Rican life. Neo-liberalism challenged not only the ideology of the coffee culture and but the reforms of Figueres that had created the new agro-industrial class in the first place.

8

Neo-Liberalism and Agro-Industry in Costa Rica

Despite the initial outrage of the coffee elite, Calderón's reforms did not threaten property relations directly. He had been satisfied to leave the coffee-based export economy largely intact, while trying to expand the social welfare functions of the state. José Figueres had other plans. He intended nothing less than the industrial transformation of Costa Rica through state-led development programs. Although he failed to achieve the industrial transformation he sought, Figueres and the political party he founded, Liberación Nacional, did succeed in creating a new and much more powerful class of agro-industrialists in new national sectors like sugar, bananas, and meat packing, and also in a transformed coffee economy itself. The aristocratic producer-processors whose paternalism had shaped the myth of Costa Rican rural democracy and social peace found themselves pushed aside, not only politically by Figueres's 1948 revolution but, increasingly, economically, by the agro-industrial transformation of the Costa Rican economy. A new class of mega-coffee processors allied with foreign capital came to dominate the industry. By the 1980s the myths of the coffee culture itself were also under attack from these new mega-processors and other agro-industrialists, who saw in the brave new world of unregulated markets and transnational capital a bright future for themselves. When the interviews were conducted, the elite was in the midst of this ideological transition.

251

Ironically, opposition to Figueres and his developmentalist project was as strong among the mega-processors who were the principal beneficiaries of his reforms as it was among the aristocratic producer-processors who were among the reforms' principal victims. Neo-liberalism placed many members of the elite in opposition to all government regulation or involvement in the economy, including the statist reforms of Figueres. Most of the coffee elite had never been enthusiastic about the reforms in the first place. But after Edgar Cardona's abortive coup in 1948, the elite limited its opposition to electoral support for a series of conservative opposition parties. Today, however, allegiance among the families controlling the twenty leading firms in the coffee industry is divided between the current conservative opposition party, Unidad (Partido Unidad Social Cristiana or Christian Social Unity Party), and Liberación Nacional. Although a clear majority of twelve of the twenty-two processors interviewed continued to support the conservative opposition to Liberación, a sizeable minority of nine expressed varying degrees of allegiance to Figueres's party. One miller both practiced and preached the strict political neutrality required by his role as a member of the National Electoral Commission, although his views would place him in the Unidad camp. Unidad supporters retained the coffee elite's long-standing opposition to Figueres's developmentalism. Even the Liberación supporters had begun to reject Figueres's statism in favor of neo-liberalism.

Supporters of Liberación among the coffee elite fell into three major groups. The first included close comrades-in-arms and early political allies of Figueres in the civil war and immediate postwar period, who remained loyal to the party if not always to its policies. A second group, also dating to the period of the civil war, included German families, some of whose properties had been confiscated by Calderón and who had backed Figueres in response. The third group of more recent recruits had begun voting for Liberación when its reformist zeal had cooled, and the differences between the two parties had diminished. One recent supporter argued in fact that many coffee growers had come to see Liberación as more effective in sustaining business confidence. And a member of the coffee elite, at the time of the interviews one of President Calderón Fournier's principal advisers, observed that under Oscar Arias Liberación economic policies were actually more conservative than were those of Unidad. An unsuccessful Unidad vice-presidential candidate said of the parties, "It's really humorous, but the differences are really questions of emphasis." Arias had launched his peace offensive in the 1986 electoral campaign in part because there was so little difference between himself and the opposition in economic policies. Both parties had been moving in the direction of the laissez-faire principles always espoused by Unidad in its various incarnations. Neo-liberalism appealed to both traditional conservatives and Liberación supporters disillusioned with Figueres's developmentalist program.

Political party affiliation proved a fallible guide to attitudes toward the Liberación program and the reforms of Figueres. Only four of the nine millers who could be reasonably counted as supporters of Liberación were firmly committed to the party's program and Figueres's reforms. One of Figueres's closest friends and comrades-in-arms, still a Liberación Party loyalist, supported almost none of the programs traditionally associated with the party. And some supporters of Unidad had become positively disposed to a least some of the reforms. Nevertheless, since most Unidad supporters expressed a distinct lack of enthusiasm for much of the Liberación program and many Liberación supporters shared these reservations to a greater or lesser extent, overall coffee elite support for the reforms of Figueres was, paradoxically, much weaker than was its support for the reforms of Calderón. Although they accepted the realities of contemporary Costa Rican political life, most of the coffee elite still remained, after forty years, unconvinced of the value of Figueres's state-centered developmentalism. There was some evidence in the interviews that opposition was, in fact, increasing rather than decreasing. Some sectors of the elite were clearly rejecting state intervention and moving toward neo-liberal free-market principles. Others had never deviated from a commitment to these principles in the first place.

The Coffee Elite and the Reforms of Figueres

The principal elements in the original developmentalist program of Figueres and later Liberación governments were: (1) state control over the distribution of credit through the nationalization of the banking system; (2) the establishment of state entities to manage such basic economic functions as electricity, telephones, insurance, aviation, and petroleum refining; (3) state-sponsored industrial development projects in such capital-intensive areas as sugar refining, cement, and fertilizer production; and (4) state-initiated transformation of the coffee economy through credit, technical assistance, and sponsorship of small-holder cooperatives. In the early years of Liberación rule, a 10 percent tax on coffee exports was a critical source of funds for the development projects. All of these reforms were vigorously opposed by the coffee-processing elite when they were first proposed. Most have now become distinctly unpopular, even among the Liberación supporters. Figueres's statist developmental policies are in direct conflict with the emerging neo-liberalism of many members of the coffee elite, including some of his old supporters.

The reform that generated the most controversy in the forties and was a major factor in the Cardonazo (as the coup was called) was the nationalization of the banking system. Indeed, one 75-year-old traced his life-long opposition to Liberación to that event. A Unidad supporter, who was chatting with a member of the Calderón administration by telephone when the interview began, said the national banks were the worst of the Figueres reforms and argued, perversely, that even privatization could not undo the damage. "They're too far gone for that," he said, "nobody would want to buy them." But a member of the Calderón administration and prominent member of the coffee elite was more positive: "We are basically satisfied with the situation as it is. Of course we support the private banks, but we do not believe the deposits of the nationalized banks should be touched." Most Unidad supporters either unequivocally supported a return to a private banking system or supported the current mixed system of public and private banks that had replaced Figueres's state banking monopoly. "The national bank . . . has made a substantial contribution to the development of the country," said one Unidad supporter in a typical comment, "so I favor a mixed banking system."

Only a hard core of three or four dedicated Liberacionistas unequivocally argued the virtues of Figueres's state banking monopoly. "It transformed the economy," said one; "thousands of small peasant producers, cattlemen, sugar growers, they all received credit. And this created the modern Costa Rican economy." Pressures for privatization, he said, were coming from external sources like the IMF and AID, not from Costa Ricans, who wanted the banks to remain public institutions. But one of the most outspoken proponents of bank privatization was an old Figueres comrade-in-arms. Bank nationalization "was an excellent idea and had a very good effect at first," he said, "but then it became subject to abuses—now I think all the banks should be privatized." Another Liberación supporter concluded, "basically I favor a mixed system of enterprises . . . in a state bank no one is responsible for the losses." "At the beginning it was very important," said another Liberación supporter of state bank support for the coffee economy, "but it is much less important now."

Opponents of the state banking monopoly and even some of its supporters complained of inefficiency, mismanagement, and political favoritism in the state banks. Many noted what one called "the world-wide trend to privatization" and argued that economic forces, not political influence, should govern bank lending practices. "The private banks are more efficient," said one opponent of the state bank, "the national banks give out credit on political grounds. You get more credit if you are a Liberacionista." One Unidad party leader strongly suggested that his participation in a previous political campaign had cost him a critical bank loan. "Let's just say the party in power tends to favor its own people," he concluded. "Development projects should be based on technical studies, not on political considerations," said a politically neutral supporter of a mixed banking system. Even one Liberación miller whose father had been a director of the national bank for twelve years acknowledged there were "problems of corruption and politics," although he was one of very few defenders of the state banking monopoly.

With the exception of three or perhaps four solid Liberacionistas, the processors I interviewed were equally divided between those favoring complete privatization, mostly Unidad supporters, and those favoring the mixed public-private system recently instituted in Costa Rica. And again, excepting the committed Liberacionistas, all were clearly uncomfortable with the deviation from free-market principles that the state banking monopoly represented. "I am basically a believer in laissez faire, free markets, free competition," said one Liberacionista who, nonetheless, supported a mixed public-private banking system. The private banks, he said, had created more competition, "which is all to the good." After being assured that he would not be quoted by name, a proponent of complete privatization added, "Let me say this. The state is a bad businessman. It does not run things well because there is no boss." Free enterprise remains the fundamental faith of the coffee elite, even though many of them have been persuaded of the value of state-managed credit for development under some circumstances. Liberación has had only limited success in converting the coffee elite, even its own supporters, to its banking policy despite forty years of trying.

A similar lack of enthusiasm, for similar reasons, was expressed toward the state enterprises organized under the revolutionary junta and later Liberación administrations. The most unpopular was CODESA (Corporación Costarricense de Desarrollo, Sociedad Anónima, or Costa Rica Development Corporation Inc.), a state institution founded to sponsor capital-intensive development projects. Only two of those interviewed, both dedicated Liberacionistas, had anything good to say about CODESA. More typical comments from supporters of both parties ranged from "tremendously inefficient," to "a complete disaster," and "the worst." The miller who served as an adviser to Calderón Fournier noted that "within a few days" their administration would have completed the privatization of all the CODESA enterprises except the cement and fertilizer manufacturing subsidiaries. A Unidad colleague on the board of FERTICA, the fertilizer subsidiary, said, "our current policy is to put it on a solid financial basis so that it can function independently." Calderón's advisor added, "eventually we expect it [CODESA] to disappear completely." If it does, the coffee elite will be delighted.

By far the most popular of the state entities was ICE (Instituto Costarricense de Electricidad or Costa Rican Electrical Institute), the state electricity firm which also manages the phone system. Even in this case opinions were mixed. "It's the least bad," said the one political neutral of ICE. "It's more efficient that the other entities." He then immediately added, "but I am opposed to the papa state. Even in ICE, when they get in trouble they run to father state for help." A life-long Unidad supporter and vehement anti-Figuerista insisted nevertheless that ICE had been very efficient. Another Unidad supporter conceded that "in the case of electricity and phones, where you need a great deal of capital," a state enterprise made sense. A Liberación supporter, on the other hand, while acknowledging that ICE was "the most efficient of the state enterprises," added that it would be better off private. The prominent miller and Calderón adviser, discussing the administration's plans for privatization, said, "some people are talking about ICE, but this would be difficult politically." The elite clearly recognized this political reality and opinion was roughly evenly divided between limited positive and outright negative sentiments. Most would probably agree that ICE is the "least bad" of the state firms.

There was, however, little enthusiasm for other state enterprises and little or none for the idea of the state as entrepreneur. There was widespread agreement in principle that the "papa state" is by definition a bad entrepreneur, and rejection of what several referred to as the "estado empresarial" (entrepreneurial state). "I think all the state monopolies should be privatized," was a typical view from a moderate Unidad supporter. "They have a policy of privatizing profits and nationalizing losses," said one outspoken advocate of privatization of the state enterprises. "It's not my view that the government should be in the business of sustaining losses or running money-losing enterprises that can't survive on their own," said another Unidad supporter. "It's the best thing that could happen to the country," said a Liberación supporter and old Figueres comrade-in-arms of the move to privatization. Only one or two of the most dedicated Liberación supporters continued to resist the rising tide of privatization and the anti-state consensus of the coffee elite.

If the elite had their way, Figueres's entrepreneurial state would vanish, leaving perhaps a national bank and possibly the Electricity Institute. This is not likely to happen in the foreseeable political future. As the miller and Calderón adviser said of the administration's privatization program, "some people are talking about INS (Instituto Nacional de Seguros or National Insurance Institute) and RECOPE (Refinería Costarricense de Petróleo or Costa Rican Petroleum Refinery). They might be possible in the future. But now we are trying to privatize the laundries at INS." But this limited policy, which the adviser preferred to call democratization rather than privatization ("we are trying to make the economy more democratic"), clearly reflected a hard-headed assessment of political realities, not the opinions of himself and his fellow members of the coffee elite. For them free enterprise and privatization remained fundamental principles, and the entrepreneurial state of José Figueres, with perhaps some notable exceptions, the failed experiment of an obsolete statism.

The Coffee Elite and the Transformation of the Costa Rican Coffee Economy, 1950–1990

Figueres and Liberación not only set out to create a new Costa Rican agro-export and industrial economy; they also initiated a profound transformation of the coffee economy itself. Figueres secured his political base in rural areas by diverting agricultural credit to small and medium producers and initiating an ambitious program of technical assistance under the direction of the Office of Coffee. Subsequent Liberación governments encouraged the development of cooperatives for marketing, credit, processing, and (later) export through preferential bank credit and exemptions from taxes on profits and agricultural inputs. The Liberación program in coffee achieved remarkable success. Between 1950 and 1980 Costa Rican yields more than tripled to make the country the most efficient and lowest-cost coffee producer not only in Latin America but the entire world. By 1989 forty percent of the crop was produced and processed by small-holder cooperatives with ample state credit and technical assistance. As a result total national coffee production expanded more than *sixfold* between 1950 and 1980, even though the area in coffee only doubled.[1]

These profound changes had two principal consequences for the coffee-processing elite and the coffee industry. First, the greatly expanded production and the technical superiority on which it rested brought Costa Rica into a prolonged conflict with the International Coffee Organization that controlled world coffee prices and production from 1962 to 1989. Second, the expanded production created a potential bonanza for successful coffee processors, while at the same time the reforms greatly increased competitive pressures on marginal private processors. Together these changes markedly increased the degree of concentration in the coffee industry and threatened to increase it further. By 1990, when the interviews were conducted, these changes had caused many traditional aristocratic producer-processors to abandon the industry and produced a new class of agro-industrial mega-processors, often allied with foreign capital, which came to dominate the industry. The agro-industrial mega-processors thought they could do better with free markets and unregulated enterprise than they could under the tutelage of the National Coffee Office or the international coffee cartel. Their neo-liberal free market principles increasingly brought them into conflict with these institutions and even with their own short-run economic interests. The result was a struggle to abandon the regulated coffee markets that had dominated the international trade for thirty years. Costa Rica was in the forefront of this struggle.

Costa Rica Blockades Brazil: The Collapse of the International Coffee Agreement

Despite the free-market principles of coffee processors in Costa Rica and elsewhere, the international coffee trade has in fact always been dominated by national and international regulation of production in the underdeveloped world and oligopolistic control of roasting and distribution in the developed world. Between 1962 and 1989 the world coffee production, including that of Costa Rica, was regulated by the International Coffee Agreement (ICA), which assigned production quotas to member countries in an effort to regulate price fluctuations by controlling production. Marketing and final consumption were dominated by ten multinational companies, all headquartered in the developed world, which controlled three-quarters of the world trade.[2] The International Coffee Agreement reflected in large part the politics of the world's largest producing nation, Brazil, and the world's largest consumer, the United States. The U.S. market in turn has been and remained before the 1990s a three-firm oligopoly. In 1989, for example, General Foods through its Maxwell House subsidiary, Proctor and Gamble (Folger's) and the Swiss multinational Nestlé controlled 80 percent of the ground coffee market.[3]

The establishment of the International Coffee Agreement in 1962 was the product of a coincidence of interests among these major actors. Brazil and other large producers were faced with a potential glut from burgeoning African production. The United States feared continued political instability in Latin America in the wake of the Cuban revolution. The International Coffee Agreement, like the Alliance for Progress, was seen by Kennedy-era liberals as a means of fighting communism at its social and economic roots. The ICA also had the enthusiastic backing of the major American roasters. The U.S. market had reached saturation, if not satiation, in 1962 when three-quarters of all Americans consumed a cup or more a day, and the purveyors of an addictive substance with an inelastic demand seemed to have little to fear from higher prices. The agreement offered the roasters guaranteed supply at a fixed price, and the added cost could be passed on to the consumer. A combination of patriotic and economic motives seems to have convinced the roasters to support the accord.[4]

Although the accord kept the peace in the coffee industry for nearly thirty years, eventually economic and political pressures generated intense internal conflict over the assigned quotas that were the heart of the scheme. Successful producers like Costa Rica, with rapidly increasing production, complained bitterly that their assigned quotas reflected economic history, not current reality, and lobbied with increasing fervor for a new agreement. By 1989, when the agreement finally collapsed, Costa Rica was selling more than 40 percent of its crop to markets outside the ICA at prices half or less of the ICA price. When cash could not be had, Costa Rica settled for barter, exchanging coffee for Czechoslovakian buses and Bulgarian power stations.[5]

Since the price received by Costa Rican producers (and, indirectly, by processors) was an average of the ICA and non-ICA prices, processors, exporters, the government and many producers became convinced that they would do no worse in a free market and they might even do better. Furthermore, demand for quality coffee was expanding exponentially, while consumption of ordinary brands languished. Costa Rican processors and many in the industry became convinced that their low costs, high efficiency, and quality coffee would prevail in a free-market struggle against the giants of the coffee world. "Costa Rica Blockades Brazil" read one headline describing Costa Rica's struggle for a better deal in the International Coffee Organization.[6]

But as some of those interviewed now ruefully admit, the fate of the world coffee trade is decided far beyond the borders of Costa Rica no matter how efficient its coffee industry. The world and the world coffee trade had changed dramatically since 1962. Conservative cold warriors had replaced liberals in Washington, and commodity schemes in general, especially those that offered low-cost coffee to the then-USSR and other Communist bloc non-ICA members, were viewed with suspicion.[7] Furthermore, the American roasting oligopoly was now faced with stagnant or declining demand, intense competition from purveyors of caffeine in soft drinks, and eroding profit margins. The only dynamic sector of the market, gourmet coffees, was pioneered by upstart entrepreneurs who had somehow introduced competitive capitalism into an industry that had for years successfully suppressed it.[8] To make matters worse, the American and other major roasters could not get the high-quality coffees they needed to compete in the new market. They were restricted to the low-grade Brazilian coffees under the old quota scheme. One thing remained constant—Brazil. The Brazilians continued insisting on their historic quota even though their production had declined markedly.[9]

As a result, an unlikely coalition emerged between a group of high-quality coffee producers (called "other milds" in the trade) led by Costa Rica, and consuming nations, led by the United States. The coalition demanded readjusted quotas to reflect changing demand for higher-quality coffee and an end to preferential non-ICA sales. The opposition, led by the traditional production leaders Brazil and Colombia, resisted. The June 1989 meeting of the International Coffee Organization ended in a deadlock.[10] On July 3 quotas were suspended. Coffee prices promptly collapsed, falling from approximately $140 per hundredweight in June to as low as $70, before recovering to the low $80s where they remained at the time of the interviews.[11] In real terms prices this low had not been seen since the Great Depression. The situation for less efficient processors and for many small producers was desperate. Surveying the economic damage to the nation's leading industry, *La Nación* expressed editorially the hope that the government "would reflect a little more before adopting such a decision in the future."[12] Although thanks to a frost in Brazil coffee prices have rebounded to close to historic highs at this writing, at the time of the interviews the processors were faced with an economic disaster brought about by their commitment to free-market principles.

The processing elite, however, was shaken but unmoved by these economic reversals and remained true to its neo-liberal free-market principles and its faith in Costa Rican coffee. They also continued to back the Costa Rican government position of larger quotas or a free market. Nevertheless, many seemed stunned by the results of the policy they had enthusiastically supported and continued to back. "Costa Rica wants a larger quota," said one, "and we allied with the United States and the consuming countries . . . but I think prices have fallen further than anyone would have anticipated at the time." "We couldn't go on under the old system where half the coffee was sold at very low prices," said another, "but I never thought it would stabilize at such low levels." "I believe in a free market, that in the end it will be best for us . . . but it's a buyers' market, and the buyers are taking advantage of it to get the lowest prices they can," was another typical view. It appears not to have occurred to the more enthusiastic free-market advocates that prices might actually fall as far as they did in a deregulated economy. This is not to say that markets were in any sense "free." The principal beneficiaries of the price drop were the oligopolistic roasters in the developed world, who failed to pass the lower prices on to consumers. The net effect of the collapse of the ICA was a substantial transfer of wealth from the underdeveloped to the developed world.

Despite the adverse economic situation, most of the processors were at least able to break even, and some were able to make money even at the low prices prevailing in 1990. But they candidly acknowledged that the situation for smaller, less efficient producers and for some processors was critical. "Any producer with yields less than 30 *quintales* per *manzana* is going to lose money," said one processor, noting that the national average was close to twenty. "Of course there are many large producers who average more than that. But the rest are going to lose money. They are going to lose a lot of money." "At these price levels a lot of producers are abandoning production . . . many of the small and medium producers lack the resources to care for their groves adequately and many of them may leave production," said a government adviser. Several processors, however, said that they were able to make money in production on their own farms. But for the small producers and inefficient processors the collapse of the accord was an economic disaster.

Almost all those interviewed viewed the future with optimism nonetheless, and most had the financial resources to view the price situation in the long term. Their belief in the competitive position of Costa Rican coffee in the world market remained unshaken. "Costa Rica has very good yields and will survive the shakeout," said one. "I think the solution will be a gradual decline in production and an eventual equilibrium between supply and demand over a period of four or five years and a stabilization of prices," said another processor. "Costa Rica is a very technically advanced producer and the quality is good, so we can sell all we can produce. So we expect the situation for Costa Rica to improve over the next 3 or 4 years," said the government adviser. "The techniques of cultivation are the most advanced in the world. And Costa Rica produces high-quality coffee which is in demand . . . we can continue to succeed even without the accord," was another typical view.

Processors were well aware of the exponential expansion of the gourmet coffee market in the United States, and viewed the future prospects for high-grade Costa Rican coffee as excellent. They also though that the changes in Eastern Europe, particularly the addition of 17 million confirmed coffee drinkers to the German market, would increase demand for high-quality coffee. One extremely efficient processor, turning a profit even after the collapse of the accord, was actively marketing his own brand with the name of his mill, much in the manner of chateau-bottled wine. Another efficient large-scale processor was also marketing a gourmet brand named after one of his mills, this time in conjunction with a major multinational European roaster. A third was a principal organizer of an International Coffee Week in Costa Rica. The program brought together representatives from gourmet coffee chains and quality coffee buyers from all over the world for a week-long seminar on the virtues of Costa Rican coffee.

It is likely that these efficient, knowledgeable, large-scale processors and producers will survive, as those interviewed suggested, the coming shakeout in the world coffee economy. And it may be, as the majority of processors confidently expect, that the situation will improve as many producers withdraw from the market and demand for gourmet coffee rapidly expands. Five years after the interviews the Brazilian frost had raised prices to bonanza levels, but whether this is a permanent change or a temporary aberration remains to be seen. In any case, the extent of the fall in prices was still a surprise to most of those interviewed, and it is clear that at least some of the processors will not have the resources to survive until the expected recovery. The situation for the small producer is even grimmer. The overall effect of Costa Rica's successful blockade of Brazil in the world coffee organization is likely to be a substantial increase in the degree of concentration in both production and processing. If this does occur, it will continue long-standing trends that had already produced a new class of agro-industrial mega-processors and rendered obsolete the aristocratic producer-processors that have dominated the industry since its inception.

Farewell to the Ruling Class? Transnational Capital and the Coffee Elite

The transformation in the Costa Rican coffee economy initiated by the Liberación program not only created difficulties with the international coffee cartel but also dramatically altered the internal structure of the processing industry itself. For the processors whose profits depended on the volume of coffee processed, the dramatic expansion of coffee production resulting from the Liberación reforms represented the potential for greatly increased revenues. But at the same time, the success of the Liberación cooperative program greatly decreased the share of the total crop controlled by the private sector, and the limits on processor margins enacted in Law 2762 limited their ability to take advantage of the increased demand for processing to increase their own margins. Still, even taking into account co-op production, the absolute amount of coffee controlled by private processors increased greatly and, even with limited margins, revenues to the private sector also increased. Despite its opposition to the statism of Figueres, the coffee processing elite was one of the chief beneficiaries of the Liberación coffee program.

But the benefits of the Liberación program for the coffee elite were unevenly distributed. For some they represented a remarkable opportunity, for others a threat. Those processors who could find the capital to expand their facilities or purchase additional mills to take advantage of the increased production greatly increased their revenues. Furthermore, plant expansion enabled successful processors to take advantage of economies of scale and technical advances to lower their costs and improve their margins. On the other hand, the expanded role of cooperatives, the limits on processor margins, and the expansion of existing private processing capacity greatly intensified competitive pressures on all processors, particularly those lacking the financial resources to expand. The Liberación coffee program converted what had been a low-volume, high-margin, local monopoly business into a high-volume, low-margin, intensely competitive enterprise.[13]

As a result, the processing elite itself began to differentiate into a powerful group of successful, high-volume, highly capitalized, large-scale processors, and an ever weaker group of marginal, small-scale processors often operating with obsolete equipment and volumes too small to generate economies of scale. The small-scale processors bore the brunt of the Liberación reforms. The restrictions on processor margins were less important to the low-margin, high-volume processors, while the restricted margins often deprived the smaller processors of the capital they needed to modernize their antiquated plants. The large processors' economies of scale offset, to some extent, the cooperatives' advantages in tax exemptions and preferential financing. But in the case of the small private processors, these concessions often conferred a decisive competitive advantage upon the co-ops. The large processor, well-known in the international trading community, could usually secure external financing. The small processor could not, and received little or no support from the national bank oriented toward small producers and co-ops.[14]

As might be expected, the result was an ever smaller number of processing plants of increasing size and an ever greater concentration of private processing capacity in a few successful firms. There were 221 private processing plants in Costa Rica in 1935—a number only slightly reduced from the 256 in 1890. By 1972 there were 114. By the 1986–87 harvest only 68 private mills remained. Forty of these were controlled by the 20 leading firms and 26 by the five leading firms. In 1962 there were only two processing plants with capacities greater than 25,000 *fanegas* (1 *fanega* = 400 liters).[15] By

1986–87 there were, including co-ops, 27 of this size or larger, and they processed three-quarters of the national crop. The number of plants processing fewer than 5,000 *fanegas* went from 82 to 4. Furthermore, by the 1980s a private processing firm with 25,000 *fanegas* was no longer part of the processing elite. The five leading firms, with production of between 100,000 and 300,000 *fanegas* each, controlled almost three quarters of the privately processed coffee. These multi-plant, large-scale, mega-processors, all of whom also controlled exporting houses, now dominate the industry.[16]

Competition even among the surviving giants for clients and coffee was intense, and the capital requirements strained even their resources. This pressure was exacerbated after 1982, when a Unidad administration required that coffee processors obtain external financing in dollars rather than rely on the national bank or other internal sources. This decision exposed processors to exchange rate instabilities, deepened their dependence on foreign sources of capital, and, of course, effectively eliminated smaller processors, unknown outside the country, from the capital markets. In 1986 the then third-ranked firm, Aguilar y Cía., declared bankruptcy. At the time of the interviews the company was reorganizing under bankruptcy protection and was seeking backing from foreign capital. In 1989 the firm that typically ranked either first or second in total coffee processed, La Meseta, declared bankruptcy after overextending itself in the competition for client coffee and new processing plants. Even for the industry's largest firms, survival was becoming increasingly difficult without the aid of foreign capital, and sometimes with it.[17]

Transnational capital has become increasingly important in the Costa Rican coffee industry, especially for the largest and most powerful firms. Although foreign capital had always been important in finance and export, for the first time major multinational corporations became directly involved in coffee processing itself. At the time of its bankruptcy, La Meseta was owned by the Swiss chocolate and coffee giant Jacobs Suchard, which itself was taken over in 1989 by Philip Morris. Aguilar, the third-ranking firm, was actively negotiating a partnership with a foreign multinational as a solution to its own bankruptcy. The fourth-ranking firm, Montealegre S.A., was in fact a partnership between the Costa Rican family and a German firm, Vokert. The fifth-ranked firm, El Emperador, was controlled by the English multinational food chain Rainer Ltd. although the Costa Rican manager was a member of the Rohrmoser family. Of the top six firms only Peters and ORCAFE, the latter owned by José Antonio Orlich Bolmarcich, remained completely independent of foreign capital in 1990. Peters, the leading firm in 1990, had a European marketing agreement with the Swiss multinational Nestlé. These leading firms, allied with foreign capital, controlled three quarters of the privately processed coffee in Costa Rica, and exported almost all of it through firms that they also controlled.

In 1990 these leading mega-processors, often allied with foreign capital, were the first and by far the most economically important of three main groups of private processors. A second group of medium-sized processors of between 30,000 and 100,000 *fanegas* was still, for the most part, controlled by traditional coffee families, although interviews revealed that three of the dozen or so firms in this category were in fact partnerships with multinational firms. These firms succeeded by occupying a particular ecological and economic niche or, as one of their executives said, by "running between the legs of the giants." Another processor in this group described himself as "a high quality rather than a volume producer," despite the fact that his plant typically processed 60,000 to 70,000 *fanegas*, an amount that twenty years ago would have ranked him among the two or three largest processors in Costa Rica. Other producers in this group combined coffee with sugar cane to take advantage of the seasonal labor demands of the two crops, and all of these were located outside the central plateau where competition in coffee was most intense. These firms were strong enough and sufficiently specialized to continue successfully running between the legs of the giants, although the collapse of the accord intensified competitive pressures on all of them.[18]

The third group comprised small, marginal firms under intense competitive pressure, which were considering leaving or had already left the industry. Since elite members to be interviewed were selected from the leading twenty firms (based on average production between 1950 and 1980), relatively few of these smaller processors were included. Some of these smaller processors were among the twenty leading firms, however, and some former owners of defunct firms or firms now controlled by others had in fact been interviewed, giving some indication of the situation of this group. For the most part these processors were or are under intense competitive pressure. Many simply process for their own farms and have given up competing for clients altogether. Some have sold or are thinking of selling their farms for residential development. If current trends continue, it is likely that few of these smaller firms will survive. Most will probably join the large numbers of private processors who have sold to co-ops or simply abandoned processing.

Often family transitions were the occasion for these smaller processors to leave an increasingly hostile environment. The father of one member of the old coffee aristocracy had run the farm himself until 1975, when he was eighty years old, without bringing in his three sons. Like many traditional processors, his firm processed the family production and had never bought much coffee from outsiders. In the 1980s, said one of the sons, when Tournon and Montealegre were expanding their operations, it proved more convenient to turn their coffee over to them: "we didn't have the volume to make economic sense, and there was a lot of competition for buying coffee, a lot of infighting between the mills. . . . We used to process ten thousand *fanegas* of our own coffee and purchase ten to fifteen thousand more. That's twenty, twenty-five thousand *fanegas,* which was a good sized mill in that time. But now Tournon and Montealegre are processing ninety or a hundred thousand *fanegas.*"

The Montealegre-Rohrmosers, he said, had urbanized their properties in what is now the Rohrmoser district of San José and had used the money to construct a new mill on the Río Virilla and buy a second mill in San Isidro. He himself had actually looked for a site along the same river for a new mill, but the price was too high and the deal fell through. His family sold off their machinery and the building now stands empty. And his family is no longer part of the processing elite, although they still grow coffee. "We could not keep up with the great mills of Tournon, Montealegre, Seevers, Peters" he said, mentioning two of the top five firms (Montealegre and Peters) and two more in the group of successful second-order firms (Seevers and Tournon). The former processor is now devoting his time to dairying, but losing money on his coffee farm as a result of the collapse of the ICA.

A member of one of Costa Rica's most famous political families, a close relative of Calderón Guardia and a descendent of the conquerors, sold his family processing plant to a foreign multinational after he approached retirement age. Like the processor who lost out to Tournon and Montealegre, his family had processed coffee from their own farms and from those of some of their relatives. His father had told him, he said, that it was too complicated to buy from other people since you had to advance money and could be caught in currency fluctuations, as had happened to him. Nor did his father believe in bank credit, which precluded any expansion. Competition increased dramatically, and they finally had to give up the few outside clients they did have. "There was competition from Atirro, Margot, Aquiares, two cooperatives," he said, mentioning two mills of successful second-order firms and a third (Margot) belonging to the industry leader, Peters. "There was a cooperative in La Suiza, and in La Aragón and Santa Teresita." By the time his father had died, in 1980, his traditional policies had precluded any mobility into the processing elite. The multinational firm expanded the plant to fifty thousand *fanegas* and is now among the second-order successful producers. But their Costa Rican manager is not a member of the coffee aristocracy—the only one of the twenty-two processors interviewed who was not.

The smallest processor among those currently active who were interviewed processed 10,000 to 15,000 *fanegas,* all from his own properties. The collapse of the ICA, he said, meant "we are in for some difficult times. There are always ups and downs in the coffee business, but the current crisis seems likely to last for several years." Since his farms were close to San José, he was thinking of changing his operation to real estate. "There is a considerable demand for land for residential development." Another processor had sold his large processing plant to a multinational firm and built a small plant to handle his own production. "There was intense competition from the co-ops," he said, "and I was retiring. So we decided to simplify things." There had been, he said, five co-ops competing directly with him, all benefiting from tax exemptions and preferential interest rates. Both men, members of traditional aristocratic families, had for different, although related, reasons ceased to be members of the coffee processing elite. Although it may be possible for some of these small firms to survive by processing their own coffee, they will in any case have lost the economic power that has traditionally accompanied coffee elite status in Costa Rica.

The transformation of the Costa Rican coffee economy has transformed its ruling class. The traditional aristocratic producer-processor is a vanishing species, maintaining his distinguished heritage while losing his economic base. The successful agro-industrial mega-processors are rapidly becoming the partners or even the hired managers of foreign transnationals. It is this group that dominates the private sector of what is still Costa Rica's leading industry, and voices the views of what is left of the coffee elite. Although the rise of the co-ops, the limits on processor margins, and the diversion of credit instituted by Liberación have put many processors under great pressure and eliminated many others, the successful leaders of the coffee processing industry regard these developments with equanimity. They, along with the co-ops, have in fact been the principal beneficiaries of the reforms. As one of the most perceptive observers of the coffee scene among those interviewed said, "You see two tendencies, one, the increasing importance of multinationals and, two, the growth of co-ops." He attributed both to the Liberación reforms, particularly the restricted processor margins.

Agro-Industry, Neo-Liberalism, and the Coffee Culture

Liberación Nacional accomplished a remarkable social transformation that required armed revolution elsewhere in the region to bring about—the liquidation of an important class fraction of the coffee elite. The elimination of the aristocratic producer-processors who had dominated the industry and the government since the nineteenth century severed any remaining connection that the Costa Rican coffee elite had to its agrarian fraction. The surviving mega-processors are a new breed of agro-industrialists, far removed from the traditional producer-processor. The liquidation of the aristocratic producer-processor was, in no small part, carried out by market forces aided by government policy, but assisted by the leading agro-industrial mega-processors themselves. It is not surprising that they should be among the most enthusiastic defenders of the Costa Rican way of life, including, but certainly not limited to, its newly transformed coffee economy. The harmonious, egalitarian mythical world of *la cultura cafetalera* seems far removed from the unregulated competition, mega-processing, and transnational capital of the emerging neo-liberal economic order in Costa Rica—a new world which the Liberación reforms created.

It remains to be seen how long an ideology that has its roots in the sociable relations of production of the early twentieth-century coffee economy of the central plateau can continue to coexist with agro-industry, transnational capital, and neo-liberalism. As the processor who contributed the phrase "la cultura cafetalera" to the interviews and to this book said in a defining statement of the white legend, "there has always been an egalitarian sense, a sense of community here, but we have lost a lot of that in the last twenty years. We became a lot more competitive." This competition has not as yet completely transformed elite ideology even as it has transformed the class structure of the elite itself. The elite remains true to *la cultura cafetalera* while at the same time arguing for competition and deregulation. The emerging agro-industrial elite of mega-processors has adopted the neo-liberal principles of free-market competition even at the cost of their short-run, and possibly long-run, profitability. How the new agro-industrial processing elite will reconcile the laissez faire principles of liberalism with the welfare state principles and state regulation of coffee is unclear. It is an emerging and central contradiction within the elite's and the nation's mythology of democratic egalitarianism and social peace.

9

Liberty and the Contra *in Nicaragua*

In 1979 some members of the Nicaraguan coffee elite and their allies in new agro-industries saw what they hoped might be an opportunity to realize their dreams of a Liberal revolution denied since 1893. The Sandinista party came to power in 1979 through a national unity alliance with progressive sectors of the Nicaraguan agro-export elite. Among the most active supporters of the revolution were members of the agro-industrial fraction of the elite, particularly in industrialized crops like cotton and sugar. Many of the agrarians, particularly the coffee planters, remained with Somoza and went down with him. Sandinista confiscation policy favored efficient agro-industrial producers and targeted the properties of Somoza and his allies and those with backward "feudal" labor relations, further enhancing the weight of the agro-industrial fraction in revolutionary Nicaragua. After the revolution, three quarters of agro-export production remained in private hands, not only in coffee but in cotton, cattle, and sugar.[1] The agro-industrial fraction of the elite had been essential to the success of the revolutionary coalition. It would also play a decisive role in the failure of the Sandinista experiment. The national unity alliance between the Sandinistas and the elite was based on the principles of a mixed economy, political pluralism, and non-alignment.[2] By the time the party lost power in 1990, the mixed economy was in chaos, political pluralism had led to electoral defeat, and the national unity alliance had dissolved into civil war polarized by Great Power rivalry. The national unity alliance that had made the revolution possible scarcely survived the first anniversary of that revolution.

The resignation of Violeta Chamorro and Alfonso Robelo from the revolutionary junta in April 1980 marked the beginning of the end of the alliance. For many coffee growers, however, the turning point was the death of Jorge Salazar, a prominent coffee grower and founder of the Coffee Growers' Association of Matagalpa, in a shoot-out with Sandinista police on November 17, 1980. Salazar had founded the Association in August, during the economic chaos following the revolution, in order to ensure the orderly marketing of the coffee crop. He rapidly recruited a following of several thousand coffee producers, many of them medium and small growers, in the key north central coffee region. Salazar went on to become a founder and first president of the Agricultural Producers Association of Nicaragua (UPANIC), an organization that brought together representatives of large producers of Nicaragua's principal commercial crops, and vice president of COSEP, in which UPANIC was a core member. UPANIC, before and after the death of Salazar, remained among the most intransigent of the Sandinistas' political opponents in COSEP, and the Coffee Growers' Association of Matagalpa was an enthusiastic supporter of the UPANIC position. Years after Jorge Salazar's death, officers of both UPANIC and the Matagalpa Association had his black-bordered picture on the wall of their offices. All regarded him as a martyr to Sandinista duplicity despite his apparent involvement in armed conspiracy against the government.[3]

By the second anniversary of the revolution, many of the most prominent coffee growers and other members of the agrarian elite associated with UPANIC and COSEP were in increasingly vigorous opposition to Sandinista rule. Anti-bourgeois rhetoric on the part of the Sandinistas and the arrest of the entire COSEP leadership in October 1981 for "destabilizing" the revolution further deepened bourgeois alienation. By 1982 interviews by Dennis Gilbert found "deep, often passionate disaffection" in all sectors of the bourgeoisie.[4] Nonetheless, a surprising number of coffee producers and other members of the agrarian elite remained in Nicaragua and continued trying to work in a system that many of them had initially supported but now distrusted.[5] As late as 1984, COSEP and other bourgeois representatives engaged in a prolonged negotiation with the Sandinistas over participation in national elections held that year before deciding, with United States encouragement, to boycott them. Even when bourgeois alienation was at its height, those members of the agrarian elite who remained in Nicaragua continued their economic relations with the revolutionary government and never entirely abandoned efforts at negotiation and accommodation. These efforts continued even after the Sandinistas' 1990 electoral defeat, and eventually led to the working relationship between the Sandinistas and President Chamorro.[6]

Cooperation between the Sandinistas and the agrarian elite waxed and waned during more than a decade of Sandinista rule. Rose Spaulding divides the post-revolutionary history of this unlikely alliance into three periods — the first two years of attempts at accommodation and cooperation, the period from 1982 to 1987 when relations reached rock bottom, and a third period, from 1988 to the Sandinista defeat in 1990, when serious but inconsistent efforts were made to revive the national unity alliance.[7] My interviews took place in July and August of 1986, when relations between the Sandinistas and the bourgeoisie were at their nadir and the contra war was at its height. By this time most members of the coffee elite had given up entirely on the Sandinistas and many were privately hoping for a contra victory or even a United States invasion.

Although in 1986 opposition to the Sandinistas was nearly universal among those interviewed, significant differences were evident in both the tone and content of this opposition. Those interviewed also differed in their expressed willingness to negotiate with the Sandinistas and in their general sympathy with the revolution and its goals. On the basis of these attitudes those interviewed can be placed in three categories: "politicals," "technicals," and "patriotic producers." The politicals were in general associated with the leadership of the Coffee Growers' Association of Matagalpa or UPANIC and its other affiliates, all actively opposed to Sandinista rule. They were more interested in politics than economics or technology, rejected any possibility of accommodation, and denounced the Sandinistas in the language of cold war anti-communism. The technicals were often just as opposed to Sandinista policy, frequently belonged to the same private associations, but were more interested in the technical and economic aspects of production than in politics, were considerably more willing to compromise, and were less given to cold war rhetoric. They eschewed the outspoken opposition and high political profile of the Association leadership.

"Patriotic producer" was a term used by the Sandinistas to refer to private farmers believed to be loyal to the revolution, particularly those associated with the Sandinista-dominated National Association of Farmers and Ranchers (UNAG). Initially the Sandinistas had founded UNAG to compete with the private UPANIC associations dominated by the agrarian bourgeoisie, but by 1986 the organization was making active efforts to recruit large producers as members. Although the overwhelming majority of large producers remained loyal to the private sector associations, a small number actually joined the Sandinista farmers' organization. Interviews revealed that some of these producers were scarcely more enthusiastic about the revolution or the Sandinistas than those affiliated with the private associations, but their willingness to risk public identification with the Sandinistas set them apart from other growers. "Patriotic producer" will be used here to refer to all associates of UNAG, whatever their views, and to those members of other associations who were generally sympathetic to the Sandinistas even if they opposed specific government policies. But patriotic producers themselves, as well as other growers, acknowledged that they were a small and unrepresentative minority of large producers.

All three groups agreed in general on specific failings of the Sandinistas and the reasons for the breakdown of the national unity alliance, even though they differed markedly on relations with the Sandinistas and other issues. The alliance had been based on a commitment by both the Sandinistas and the bourgeoisie to three basic principles: a mixed economy, political pluralism, and non-alignment. Both sides professed allegiance to these principles throughout the Sandinista period. It is clear, however, that the Sandinistas and the bourgeois had different understandings of these principles and the policies they implied.[8] Moreover, it is unclear to what extent the principles were generally accepted within the party, even among the dominant national unity fraction that first proposed them, and government policy shifted continually during a decade of Sandinista rule.[9] By 1986 most members of the bourgeois were convinced that the Sandinistas had abandoned all three principles, if they had ever supported them in the first place. "The Sandinistas promised political pluralism, a mixed economy and non-alignment, and have done none of them," was a typical view. Nevertheless, the principles provide a useful framework for examining both government policy and elite alienation during the Sandinista period.

The Mixed Economy and the State as the Center of Accumulation

Although a mixed economy usually implies a mixture of state and private enterprise operating in a free-market economy, it appears that the Sandinistas had a different interpretation; initially, the policies pursued "came down on the side of a fairly orthodox principle of state centralization and the creation of a planned economy . . . [with] strong indirect controls over the remaining private sector."[10] In practice this meant that the state would be privileged as the "center of accumulation," and that government controls would effectively eliminate product, labor, capital, and producer- and most consumer-goods markets in the nominally private sector.[11] The Nicaraguan economy bore no relation to the "mixed economies" of Western Europe, even though the Sandinistas maintained warm relations with Western European social democratic parties. Despite orthodox economic adjustment policies introduced in 1986 and, with a vengeance, in 1988–89, state control remained the economic model until the Sandinista electoral defeat in 1990.[12]

While the Sandinistas reorganized the economy, they vastly increased expenditures for basic human needs, including massive food subsidies, and initiated an expensive state-led development program. The result, as Forest Colburn noted, was a "classic pattern" in the immediate post-revolutionary period in small Third World countries—disorganization of production accompanied by massive increases in consumption and investment, creating an acute fiscal and foreign exchange crisis.[13] In Nicaragua agro-export production declined by almost fifty percent while consumption and investment exploded, especially in response to the demands of the contra war.[14] The resulting chronic fiscal and balance-of-payments deficits were made up with monetary emissions and foreign borrowing that in turn led to hyperinflation, massive foreign debt, and a parasitic speculative sector.[15] By 1989 inflation had reduced workers' real wages to 10 percent of their 1979 levels, GNP per capita declined by 60 percent, and hyperinflation and price distortions had created what one sympathetic government-sponsored report called an "economy of chaos."[16]

Sandinista agricultural policies followed what might be called, after Robert Bates, the failed African model—taxes on export agriculture combined with the substitution of project-specific subsidies and state development projects for market price incentives.[17] In the Sandinista case the tax was imposed by the massive gap between internal and external prices for export commodities; market incentives were largely eliminated by state controls; and production was encouraged by subsidies on credit and imported inputs. Most of the agrarian development budget was spent on state agro-industrial projects, whose long run viability was debatable and benefits to private producers negligible.[18] Despite an intense internal debate with "peasantist" proponents of small producers and market incentives, most of whom were associated with the Agrarian Research Institute (CIERA), the state-centered agro-industrial model prevailed at the Ministry of Agriculture until late in the Sandinista period.[19]

The state-centered model also influenced Sandinista agrarian policy. After a wave of confiscations of properties of the Somozas and their close allies immediately after the revolution, agrarian reform was deemphasized and direct action by the landless to seize land was discouraged by persuasion or, when necessary, direct state action. The confiscated Somoza properties were converted into state farms and cooperatives; relatively little land was distributed to the landless. An agrarian reform law was not announced until the second anniversary of the revolution, and even then it was extremely conservative by Latin American standards. The law affected only estates larger than 350 hectares in Pacific Nicaragua and 700 hectares in the interior, effectively leaving out the entire private estate sector in export agriculture. These provisions strongly implied continued support for large-scale farming, state or private. Even larger farms could only be confiscated if they were abandoned or rented in "precapitalist" sharecropping arrangements. By the beginning of 1984 only 5 percent of the arable land had been distributed to less than 20,000 families.[20] Although the pace of reform quickened in the next two years in response to Sandinista fears of an eroding peasant political base, most of the affected land was accounted for by an extensive titling program for peasant squatters in the interior, displaced by expanding coastal agro-export production.[21]

In 1985 landless peasants encouraged by Sandinista agricultural organizations invaded both state and private farms in Masaya and precipitated a confrontation between the influential Bolaños clan, leaders of the agro-export "middle" bourgeoisie, and the government. The confiscation of the Bolaños properties, after the Masaya region had been declared a special agrarian reform zone and exempted from the restrictions of the 1981 law, was another turning point in the deteriorating relations between the government and the agrarian bourgeoisie.[22] In January 1986 a new law extended the agrarian reform to "underused" and rented, as well as abandoned, land and greatly accelerated the pace of confiscation. Under this law much confiscated land and some state farm land was finally redistributed to peasant small holders or cooperatives. The year 1986 was the peak year for confiscations, with over 400, and the low point in bourgeois-Sandinista relations. By 1988, however, concerns about declining production and the failed national unity alliance led Agrarian Reform Minister Wheelock to declare the reform over. Only three properties were confiscated in that year.[23] The damage to bourgeois confidence in stable property relations, however, had already been done.

The Sandinista state-centered model of agro-industrial development directly attacked the political, proprietary, and economic base of private accumulation in the agro-export sectors, despite continual public affirmations of commitment to the mixed economy. The result was a marked decline in the incentives for private capital accumulation, a subsequent decline in investment and production, an increasingly acrimonious debate over economic policy, and a near total collapse of business confidence. By 1986, when the interviews were conducted and, by almost all indicators, bourgeois-Sandinista relations had reached their nadir, the large growers interviewed required surprisingly little prompting to provide a detailed critique of the Sandinista policy. Although the tone varied, there was surprisingly little disagreement among "politicals," "technicals," and "patriotic producers" on the specific problems of Sandinista agrarian policy. Although the opinions of the agrarian bourgeoisie are, by definition, unrepresentative of Nicaraguan opinion generally, they do reveal the economic behavior, experience, and attitudes of a class fraction that was of decisive importance for the economic and political survival of the Sandinistas.

Producers against the State: Free Markets and Free Men

If a single theme animated the agro-industrial bourgeoisie's political and economic opposition to the Sandinistas as expressed in the interviews, it would be the idea of freedom. An officer of the Association of Coffee Growers of Matagalpa, member of one of Nicaragua's most socially prominent families and leading candidate for high posts in the agriculture ministry under both the Sandinista and Chamorro regimes, when asked what he would tell the Sandinistas if he were their adviser, replied: "Liberty (*libertad*), in one word liberty—economic freedom, political freedom. That we be allowed to buy and sell freely without government control and restrictions." If "progress" was the dominant theme of the El Salvadoran elite and "democracy" of the Costa Rican, then "libertad" (which may be translated as either "liberty" or "freedom") was the dominant theme of the Nicaraguan elite's opposition to the Sandinistas.

Paradoxically, exactly the same theme underlay the growers' opposition to Somoza and their initial *support* for the Sandinistas. Under the dictatorship the problem was Somoza-centered, not state-centered, accumulation. The Somozas tended to treat the state as their personal possession and they and a charmed circle of political associates divided the spoils of institutionalized corruption and business favoritism.[24] The growers deeply resented the corruption, intrusiveness, and backwardness of the Somocista state. As one of them said, "He [Somoza] ran the country as if it were his private farm . . . he treated the assets of the state as his personal possession." Or as another described it, "a few allies of Somoza doing all the business—getting all the land, having all the political power." "He wanted to control everything, and a lot of people resented it," observed another. The growers' principle of economic freedom was continually violated under Somoza.

Although Somoza offended the growers' principles, he did not adversely affect the direct economic interests of most of them. On the contrary, he succeeded in providing a business climate that enabled large agro-exporters to thrive. The growers said the economic situation in the prerevolutionary period had been excellent. None reported any difficulties in purchasing agricultural supplies they needed or selling their crop at world market prices in the generally free markets prevailing in the Somoza period. Although most resented Somoza's corruption and favoritism, only one had experienced interference in his own business. The objection to Somoza's economic policies was "global, not specific" as one prominent cotton grower said. "The cotton growers opposed Somoza as citizens, not as cotton growers." Those seeking explanations for the growers' support for revolution in short-run economic self-interest will be disappointed.[25] Most growers regarded the business climate under Somoza, as one of them told the author, as "fantastic."

Sandinista policies of state-centered accumulation, on the other hand, represented a threat to both the growers' principles and their economic survival. As a thoughtful political neutral who was one of Nicaragua's two or three most productive growers said ruefully, "You know, it's paradoxical. We had complete [economic] freedom in the midst of a dictatorship. And now we have no freedom at all." Another prominent grower, who publicly followed a three-generation tradition of political neutrality while privately expressing outspoken opposition to the Sandinistas, said: "We are not running a private business any more. Our role is purely symbolic. They [the government] come in and tell you what to do." Sandinista Minister of Agriculture and Agrarian Reform Jaime Wheelock's vision of "producers without power" and "administrators" in a state-led economy was widely understood and widely resented by the growers. As they saw it, the same ideological commitment to fair and free competition that had led them to enter a coalition with the Sandinistas against Somoza now led to growing distrust of the Sandinistas and the breakdown of that coalition.

Few growers had any doubts that the Sandinista economic model was state-centered accumulation with only a temporary or transitional role for private producers. And almost all of those interviewed, including politically moderate technicals and even some Sandinista sympathizers, believed that the eventual goal was a Soviet-style command economy. Officers of UNAG, but not most large-producer UNAG members, said they believed the mixed economy was a reality. For most of those interviewed the mixed economy was "a myth," sustained largely for the benefit of opinion abroad. As one member of the Matagalpa Association said, "They are masters of propaganda. The U.S. doesn't understand this. Everything they do is for external consumption." "They tell that to foreigners," said a prominent cotton grower of the mixed economy, "but everything is directed." Even a technically oriented, politically moderate coffee producer, when asked about the Sandinistas' commitment to a mixed economy, replied "lies, they're all lies. Everything they say is a lie."

Politically oriented growers believed that the state-centered agro-industrial model was simply a local manifestation of the international Communist conspiracy being imposed on Nicaragua from without. "They are Marxist-Leninists and their plan is to convert this into another Cuba," said one coffee grower who was active in the Matagalpa Association. "That's what they did in Cuba," said another aristocratic coffee grower of the agrarian reform: "first they took the big farms, then they took the medium ones. It's part of their plan. First Nicaragua, then Salvador, then the United States." Another coffee grower interrupted the interviewer's questions on agrarian policy to tell him that he really should be studying "Operation Kremlin. The plan of the Kremlin for expansion through Cuba and Nicaragua." He then argued, with apparent seriousness, that Daniel Ortega, in the service of Operation Kremlin, intended to expand the revolution to Salvador, Guatemala, and then to Mexico ("a powder keg"). "And then you will have refugees with red kerchiefs running across your border," starting "an uprising in Texas."

Such true believers would, of course, be predisposed to see a Soviet-style command economy in almost any conceivable Sandinista future. But technically oriented moderates and Sandinista sympathizers said the same thing in less colorful language. One prominent grower, who had been close to many Sandinista leaders during the revolution and had resigned from the board of the directors of the Matagalpa Association because he disagreed with their hard-line political positions, nonetheless concluded: "They [the Sandinistas] are not the same as they were. I think it was Richard Nixon who said that the Communists say one thing when they are trying to gain power, but do something different when they gain it." Another grower, interviewed at the suggestion of a MIDRINA (Ministry of Agriculture and Agrarian Reform) official, who regarded him as a model producer, said, "there will be no private farmers, that's the line. I have a good friend in the Front [the FSLN] and he tells me." Another moderate and technically proficient producer said he had shelved plans to expand "because of the Communist system, this move to Socialism—whatever you want to call it."

None of those interviewed argued that a Soviet-style system had yet arrived, and many were aware of the internal debates within the Sandinista Directorate itself over the pace and nature of socialist reform. But they regarded the debates as tactical only and the future direction set once and for all, no matter what the present policies implied. "Look," said one grower in English, "you come here and you don't see Soviet-style collective farms. You don't see an East German-style security system and you think it isn't communism. But even the Communists know that state farms can't work . . . It's just a new version of the Communist system." A moderate cotton grower, who said he would stay in Nicaragua and continue producing if the government moderated its position, nonetheless referred to what he called "this Communist system." He had heard Arturo Cruz say, on a Voice of America broadcast, that there are both radicals and moderates in the National Directorate, but he himself thought that the government was "more radical every day." "It's just a dispute about the pace of change," said another cotton grower of the opposition of the official Nicaraguan Communist Party to Sandinista policy. "The Communist Party wants an immediate change, but it's not convenient for them [the Sandinistas] now."

With the exception, once again, of a very small number of UNAG officers and allies, none of the producers saw any future for themselves, other large producers or, many said, even for small and medium producers in the Sandinista model of state-centered accumulation. Almost all expected to be confiscated in the long run, and many expected the end to come sooner. One coffee grower, when asked if he thought there would be a future for private growers in five years, replied, "no, not in one year. The pressure is increasing all the time." Another replied that the future of the large growers was "uncertain in the long run, possibly the short run." "I think this is my last year of planting cotton," said one moderate, technically oriented grower. Another cotton grower gave an estimate of two years before large producers disappeared. He had recently been part of a delegation that had visited Guatemala to explore possibilities of cotton production there. "When the war [that is, the contra war] is over, we are all going to be gone," said a dissident UNAG member.

As might be expected of producers with such profound pessimism concerning their own immediate future, substantive questions on specific Sandinista agricultural policy were frequently met with skepticism and impatience. When asked what the Sandinistas could do to improve the economic situation of large producers, one coffee grower close to the Matagalpa Association replied derisively, "Get out of the country!" Another noted that economic questions were beside the point—the real questions were political—and a third interrupted the interviewer to tell him that economic questions were a waste of time. Although such comments were common, they were not universal, and even among such profound skeptics it was usually possible to pursue specific economic issues. In fact a detailed economic critique does emerge from the interviews, even though the producers' fundamental belief in the ultimate triumph of a Soviet command economy made the discussion academic for many of those interviewed.

Confiscations and Insecurity

Growers complained bitterly and almost universally about the Sandinistas' policy of confiscations, and it is clear that this, more than any other single factor, was responsible for their profound pessimism concerning their own future and the government's ultimate intentions. Confiscations, occurring almost daily at their peak in 1986, when the interviews were conducted, were conclusive evidence for most producers that they were expendable and that a command economy was the goal. "It's like a sword swaying over our heads all the time," said the secretary of the Matagalpa Association, speaking of the confiscation policy. "One day the bell tolls for my neighbor, the next day for me," said another, "there isn't any future for private producers in Nicaragua. We are just subsisting." "There is no private economy," said a third, "when you can take everything away." Still another producer consulted each issue of the official register to see who else among his friends and colleagues had been confiscated. For most of the growers an end to confiscations was a prerequisite for any successful economic policy, while their continuation was fatal to the national unity alliance.

None of the growers expressed any disagreement with the confiscations of the properties of the Somoza family and their allies immediately after the revolution, but most viewed more recent confiscations as arbitrary, illegal, and, often, politically motivated. When he was asked about the reasons for the confiscation of a neighbor's estate, one grower replied, "there aren't any reasons. They wanted the land and they took it." "Your deeds are worth nothing," said another, "just pieces of paper." "They can say at any time that you are subject to confiscation. If you speak out politically they will confiscate your estate," said a cotton grower. Nicolás Bolaños, one of the growers interviewed, contended that the confiscation of the Bolaños brothers' cotton enterprise, SAIMSA, was "revenge against Enrique [Nicolás's brother and the head of COSEP] because he spoke out against the government." In fact many spokespersons for the bourgeoisie were among those confiscated, lending support to these assertions.[26]

The confiscation of the Bolaños properties was viewed as a critical turning point by a number of producers, because it demonstrated to them that even efficient producers were not safe. As might be expected, this was a particularly sore point with the most efficient producers. Noting that his neighbor and himself were the two most efficient producers in their Department, one producer insisted that "efficiency is not a protection against confiscation. They confiscate efficient producers. It is a question of political support." His neighbor's wife said she thought that the government kept her husband in business because he was a "model producer." "He has the highest yields in the entire country," she said but then, referring to Nicolás Bolaños as an example of an efficient producer, added, "they took his lands and his brother Enrique's too." She and her husband supported both the confiscation of the Somoza properties and the confiscation of idle land, but "why were they confiscating efficient farms?" "They always find some pretext," said one of Nicaragua's most efficient cotton producers, pointing to the confiscation of efficient producers and mentioning Bolaños by name. "For example, I allow my workers to cultivate subsistence plots. So they could accuse me of having *precaristas, colonos* ["precapitalist" land tenure arrangements, illegal under the 1981 agrarian reform law], and not using my land efficiently."

One of the more thoughtful growers saw a vicious circle at work in confiscations. "There are a good many growers, those at the [Matagalpa] Association, who take a completely negative attitude. They're afraid they will be confiscated so they don't invest and their production declines and they abandon acreage and then their farms get taken over. Or they spend all their time in Miami, which leads to the same results. It is a vicious cycle." Another grower had lost his land in a peasant land invasion because it was considered unused pasture even though the land was not used because the herd had been stolen during the revolution and its aftermath. He too saw a vicious cycle. "You can't use the land because you don't have cattle, and if you're not using the land, you lose it." Even the regional representative of UNAG in Matagalpa, herself from a prominent coffee family, acknowledged the problem but claimed that UNAG had had some success in reversing unfair confiscations. And, as she pointed out, "you can't just go off to Miami and expect an administrator to run a coffee estate." On the other hand, another grower claimed that a friend had his estate confiscated while he was in Miami for medical treatment.

Given the prevailing insecurity, investment beyond what was necessary to maintain production was irrational, and with one or two exceptions growers simply shelved expansion and indefinitely postponed replantings. "There is no point in investing in coffee if it's going to be taken away," was one typical view of a Matagalpa Association activist. "They [the Sandinistas] are more interested in politics than in economics. So they continue the confiscations for political reasons even though they know it will affect production," said a technically oriented and highly productive grower. "The government has created this uncertainty, this mistrust," said a nominal UNAG member, but vehement Sandinista critic, of the confiscation policy, "and no one is investing or expanding." The threat of confiscation served both to maintain minimal levels of production in the short run in order to forestall confiscation based on abandonment or "decapitalization," and to discourage investment that would make possible increases or forestall declines in production in the long run.

The confiscation policy affected, directly or indirectly, almost all of those interviewed. Many of them had lost some or, in two cases, all of their lands to confiscations, many had experienced land invasions or other forms of political pressure against their lands, almost all knew close friends who had lost their lands, and with one or two exceptions (both members of UNAG) all expected to lose their lands eventually. Many had shelved expansion plans in anticipation of eventual confiscation and maintained minimal production levels to avoid immediate confiscation. By the time of the interviews in 1986, the mixed economy with a place for the large private producer had become a political fiction for most of those interviewed. The government's policy of continual piecemeal confiscation had destroyed its economic credibility and squandered its political support among these large producers. It had also significantly reduced the production potential of the private agro-export sector. According to those interviewed, other Sandinista private-sector economic policies simply exacerbated this effect.

The Nominal Market Economy

Although both the Sandinistas and their bourgeois opponents thought that state-centered accumulation would eventually prevail, most agro-export production during the Sandinista period remained under private ownership. Strong indirect government controls, however, eliminated most market forces in this nominally private sector. Foreign trade in agro-export commodities was a state monopoly, and export products were sold to government trading boards at fixed prices. Credit was made available at negative real interest rates, and little consideration was given to the credit-worthiness of the recipients. The acute foreign exchange crisis made it difficult if not impossible to obtain imported agricultural inputs such as tractors and fertilizer even at exorbitant black market prices, and both foreign exchange and inputs were allocated by government agencies and producer organizations. Rates of pay for each agricultural task were set by the government and fell increasingly behind inflation, seriously eroding rural living standards and undermining the rural labor market. Seriously depressed real estate prices froze most land sales, other than distress sales, and confiscations undermined the market that did exist. As a result, no effective markets existed in land, labor, capital, producer goods, or export crops. The results of these indirect controls were price distortions, production disincentives, declining production, and mounting bourgeois alienation.

Product Prices, Profits, and Incentives. Growers complained bitterly about administered prices for export crops, particularly coffee, which, they argued, were too low to provide an investable surplus. Prices were paid in local currency at levels which in real terms were a small percentage of the hard currency prices prevailing in international markets. In the 1985–86 crop year, for example, the world price for coffee was at a cyclical high of $180 dollars per hundred pounds (*quintal*). Growers had been paid 15,000 cordobas plus an "incentive" in dollars of $5 a hundredweight for export quality beans. By the beginning of July 1986, when the interviews began, 15,000 cordobas was worth only $12.50 at the official parallel market rate and even less at the black market rate. The government retained the foreign exchange difference between external and internal prices, in effect imposing a substantial export tax—in this example more than 90 percent. The more politically outspoken growers denounced such price levels as little better than theft, and even growers more sympathetic to the revolution acknowledged that at such prices it was difficult to make an operating profit let alone accumulate sufficient funds to reinvest in standing crops or equipment. In fact, the effective export tax levels realized through the internal-external price differential would have eliminated any incentive to produce if they had not been offset by price controls on other factors of production.

Although prices were set at levels which theoretically permitted an operating profit to be realized at the artificial market prices for land, labor, producer goods, and capital, little or no investable surplus was realized by any of the growers. In fact, little attention seems to have been given to the distinction between operating profits and profitability, that is, sufficient return on investment to encourage reinvestment in equipment or standing crops. As one cotton grower noted when asked if production were profitable, "Yes, in terms of this Communist system . . . the government calculates costs and allows a certain profit. So it is profitable in a limited sense." He went on to point out that his total profits, the local currency equivalent of $2,500, would hardly begin to pay for the replacement costs, which he estimated at $40,000, of one engine for a crop-dusting aircraft, let alone for replacement and upkeep on his twenty tractors and associated agricultural implements. He had, however, been able to obtain from the government imported Russian tractors at even more unrealistic prices and conceded that the government was actually subsidizing cotton producers. "The price structure is completely crazy," said a coffee grower, "you can't calculate costs."

The situation for coffee growers was even worse. Most said that they had barely been able to pay their operating expenses or make a minimal operating profit during the revolutionary period. Even a politically neutral grower who favored negotiation with the government complained that "they paid us ridiculous prices in cordobas and it was impossible to make any money. Producers would sell off cattle to earn enough money to keep their estates running because if they didn't they could be confiscated. There was no incentive to produce." The wife of one of the most efficient growers in Nicaragua said that she and her husband had been reduced to investing money from her mother's family to keep the estate running. A neighbor and another efficient producer said that he and his operation "were just maintaining themselves. We have chickens and that has helped us raise money and food. The chickens have been a big help." "The coffee grower has no choice," said another grower, because he "has a huge investment tied up in the trees and he can't leave them. . . . And the government has treated him the worst of all." "They really abused us," concluded another leading coffee producer.

With minimal or non-existent operating profits and no investable surplus there was little or no reinvestment. One producer noted that "nobody has planted any new coffee trees since the revolution," and interviews with other growers generally confirmed his observation. "We are replacing trees, but no, we are not expanding—just trying to maintain ourselves," was a typical view. "You need a surplus to invest," said another grower, "but at these prices you aren't getting any . . . I keep going with bank credit—all the money I am investing comes from the bank. Without it I wouldn't be investing at all." Most growers said they limited themselves to routine maintenance, just enough to keep the groves producing, but not enough to insure the long run health of the groves. One UNAG officer suggested that "the government thought that you really did not need to take care of coffee trees—that they just kept producing."

Price distortions actually created incentives for disinvestment in coffee because more money could be made in other crops sold in the internal market at uncontrolled prices. "People would shift to pasture land, which was less expensive and less difficult to maintain," said a national officer of UNAG, "so if a farmer had an old coffee grove he would clear it out and replace it with pasture." "Other producers are growing soft maize and selling it in ears—much more profitable than coffee since the government considers it a luxury food and is not controlling the price," said her father, another prominent but politically neutral coffee grower. A loyal member of UNAG said he was considering planting additional coffee, but he reserved his real enthusiasm for expanding milk production, which he could sell profitably on the internal market. One grower made more money from discarded coffee beans sold on the uncontrolled domestic market than on export-quality beans sold to the government. Even for growers most sympathetic to the revolution, government pricing policy created no incentives for investment. For many others it was simply another example of the irrationalities of a "communist" system.

Producer Goods: Shortages and Political Allocation. The acute foreign exchange crisis and efforts to resolve it through administrative allocation of imports and foreign exchange effectively eliminated the market in agricultural inputs, created scarcities of critical items, drove up black-market prices, and required further government efforts to supply these items. Almost all growers complained of shortages of critical items like chain saws (for pruning coffee trees) and agro-chemicals (essential in cotton cultivation). One of Nicaragua's leading producers had an employee assigned full time to searching for spare parts. The wife of another grower said she and her husband "went nuts" trying to find spare parts and inputs. A shrewd UNAG member used almost every question in the interview as an opportunity to lobby for a new truck to haul his coffee harvest in the faint hope that the interviewer might have some influence. Another UNAG member had waited more than two years for a truck and was unable to transport his current crop, let alone expand production.

A prominent coffee grower who had been Nicaragua's largest egg producer had been forced to give up his chickens since he could not obtain imported fertilized eggs, incubation equipment, or veterinary supplies in sufficient quantities to permit industrial production. Even chicken wire was unobtainable. Fumes from a nearby volcano had eaten through the cages, leaving the chickens to run wild over the estate. A cotton grower said that he and some colleagues had tried to find a chemical that had to be applied to the crop between the 25th and 40th day of growth. The chemical was unavailable in the major cotton region of León, but they finally located some in the port of San Juan del Sur 100 miles to the south. They sent a representative in a truck who succeeded in obtaining the chemical, but the shipment never reached León. The truck broke down and there were no replacement parts. The cotton grower who told this story devoted a substantial part of his living room to storing spare parts which, he said, he didn't need now but might in the future. "You have to . . . buy the parts before you need them," he concluded.

When inputs were available they could usually only be obtained through the Sandinista farmers' organization, UNAG. This was, as one UNAG officer conceded, a substantial incentive to join the organization. "They can take advantage of the Swedish aid program, zinc for horses, milling machines for grain, spare parts sold through UNAG. You can't get these things through the Association." An Association officer agreed, "If you are a member of UNAG you get everything, credit, inputs, fertilizers. But we [Association members] have to buy it on the black market at 200 times the official price." Another grower contended that there were plenty of tractors in the country but they were passed out on the basis of politics not economics, "they go to the state farms and the cooperatives, not to us." Many private growers nonetheless refused to join UNAG as a matter of principle; "It's a government organization, . . . you have to submit to the line of the Front (FSLN) and I am not going to do it." But even many UNAG members reported that they were unable to get critical inputs.

Labor Markets. Growers reported that labor was in short supply, although many attributed it to the demands of the contra war rather than the absence of a rural labor market. But they also argued that many workers had found more remunerative ways to make a living under prevailing economic conditions, and that agricultural wages were inadequate to attract labor or to support workers. When asked to describe their greatest problem, a number of growers cited labor scarcity as a result of call-ups for military service. "The shortage of field hands," said one grower asked to name his principal problem, "as a result of the militia and military service which, in turn, are a result of the war." One technically proficient grower who was expecting a bumper crop nonetheless anticipated a substantial loss because there was insufficient labor to collect a premature fall of coffee berries. He attributed the scarcity to the war. Another grower complained of both the shortage and poor quality of labor. "All the workers have become vagabonds and live by robbing people . . . They can make more money stealing things than they can by working." A third producer contended that it was "more profitable to steal maize from a farm and sell it on the black market . . . than work." He argued that the black market was an even bigger problem than the military service in accounting for the labor shortage. "A good many rural people have moved to the city to take advantage of low food prices and government support," said a UNAG member, "and others have moved to escape the war so there are many fewer peasant producers around to supply labor."

Most growers compared rural living standards and wage levels unfavorably with the pre-revolutionary period, although they admitted that they could not afford to pay more given internal coffee prices even if the government would permit them to pay more, which it would not. "And who are the real exploiters of the poor?" asked one politically oriented producer. "They [the government] only allow my workers four ounces of rice a day. I want to give them more so who is exploiting the workers?" Another grower claimed that his workers had actually come to him and asked why he didn't pay them as much as he did in 1979. "At what we pay them they can't even buy clothes. And if I paid them any more, which I can't afford to do anyway, then I am a bad administrator." Another grower cheerfully admitted that he had been unable to give his workers a negotiated wage increase because the government had disallowed it.

Credit Markets. One factor of production not in short supply, however, was credit. Many growers said that they kept producing largely because of the easy availability of credit and the fear of confiscation. "Basically it's the credit," said one coffee grower when asked why he continued producing. "As long as they're willing to advance it you can keep producing." "All the money I am investing comes from the bank. Without it I wouldn't be investing at all," said another coffee grower. "They [the Sandinistas] are extremely liberal with credit and it is easy to get," said another grower, "there is no real problem." When asked if credit was difficult for him to obtain a leading cotton grower conceded that "really it isn't. There is an adequate supply of credit." None of the private growers interviewed complained of any difficulty obtaining credit.

The easy availability of credit alone was not sufficient to permit increasing or to maintain constant production. Those interviewed did not hesitate to attribute the substantial decline in production from pre-revolutionary levels (more than 50 percent by the time of the interviews)[27] to Sandinista policy. Indeed, some of the most outspoken politicals denied that the Sandinistas were interested in producing anything at all. "They're interested in politics not economics," said an officer of the Matagalpa Association, "they are not interested in producing anything. All they are interested in is in expanding their power. They just look around for more aid." "The economy is a basket case," said another outspoken political, "the only thing they're interested in is expansion. The only export of this country is revolution. That's the business they're in. They export revolution and the Russians send them wheat, oil, arms. That's the way the economy really runs." Even a sympathetic "patriotic producer" conceded that "they [the Sandinistas] weren't very concerned about coffee."

More technically oriented producers blamed the decline in production on fear of confiscations, shortages, price disincentives, unprofitability, and the general uncertainties of Sandinista economics. Small producers, said one technically oriented producer, "were beginning to advance technologically before the revolution, but now the farms are deteriorating or have been abandoned for lack of financial incentives." He thought it would be years before the damage could be reversed even under a favorable government policy. "If you don't maintain them [the coffee groves] they deteriorate, and the result was a great decline to about 500,000 *quintales* of coffee exported last year," said the grower who had argued that the government had little interest in proper maintenance. The two most efficient producers among those interviewed both said their yields were down considerably from 1979 as a result of labor and input shortages and investment disincentives. "It gets worse each year," said another technically oriented producer, who blamed the decline on economic mismanagement, particularly on state farms. "They say it's the war, but it's really management failure."

By the time of the interviews almost all of the growers, with the exception of one or two "patriotic producers," had given up on Sandinista agricultural policy and viewed any effort to change it as a waste of time. When asked whether he saw any possibility for flexibility on the part of the government, one technically oriented grower replied, "no, none. They are taking their orders, following orders from outside" [the Soviet Union]. "If you try to explain to them about prices they just say . . . you are part of the exploiting bourgeoisie," said an officer of the Matagalpa Association. When asked about a change in policy, a technically oriented producer said, "They are not going to change their line . . . the only solution is a total change, a total change in government." Although several of the patriotic producers and political neutrals said there actually had been a change in government policy for the better in the last year, with more financial incentives and more interest in production, by 1986 Sandinista economic policy had lost whatever credibility it once had with most growers.

The Sandinista policy of indirect government controls over the nominally private economy clearly contributed to bourgeois alienation and, if grower reports are to be believed, it was also a decisive influence on the decline in coffee production. The attempt to stimulate production through subsidized credit and inputs largely failed to accomplish its objectives, because these policies were more than offset by the adverse producer price policy and the shortages of labor and inputs. Price distortions not only created few incentives for investment; they actually stimulated disinvestment and the long-run deterioration of the groves because of minimal maintenance. While insisting on keeping a substantial private sector in export agriculture, the Sandinistas simultaneously created conditions which discouraged private accumulation and production.

Government policies of state-centered accumulation, piecemeal confiscations, and indirect market controls led to nearly unanimous rejection of the Sandinistas by the producer elite. The state-centered model of accumulation neglected the country's leading export, which did not lend itself to centralized agro-industrial production and was, for the most part, controlled by private producers large and small. The model also convinced many coffee producers that they had little future in a Sandinista Nicaragua. The policy of piecemeal confiscations generated immense hostility, discouraged investment, and reinforced the coffee producers' pessimistic view of their future. The indirect controls over the nominal private economy failed to increase production and instead stimulated economic disinvestment and decline, while deepening frustration. State-centered accumulation and the absence of markets in the "mixed economy" led to both economic and political failure.

The "mixed economy" became an area of conflict rather than consensus between the Sandinistas and the agrarian bourgeoisie. Indeed, it is likely that Sandinista economic policy alone would have driven the large producers into political opposition. But economic disagreements were exacerbated by conflicts over the theory and practice of democratic pluralism and by deteriorating political relations between the large producers and the government. The promise of democratic pluralism, like the promise of a mixed economy, became a major source of bourgeois discontent and a source of division rather than solidarity between the former partners in the revolutionary coalition.

Democratic Pluralism and Participatory Democracy

It was clear from the outset that the bourgeoisie and the Sandinistas had dramatically different views of democracy. For the bourgeoisie, democracy meant representative democracy with contested elections and oppositional rights. Their experience of powerlessness and isolation under the Somoza tyranny had made them, like the Costa Ricans but unlike the Salvadorans, firm believers in democracy even before the revolutionary decade of the 1980s. They opposed the Somozas not only because of their corruption and unfair competition but because they denied democratic rights. When asked why, if economic conditions were so good, did he oppose Somoza, one grower replied, "Because it was a dictatorship, the same family controlling everything for fifty years." Others said much the same thing. "We wanted a democratic system. And we wanted equality," said one. Another grower described with aristocratic disdain one of the electoral frauds in which he had been forced to participate during the years of the dictatorship.

The Sandinistas' commitment to political pluralism and democracy had therefore been an important reason for bourgeois support for the revolution, even if few growers had any illusions about the Sandinistas' own political views. "It was always clear that they [the Sandinistas] were Marxist-Leninists. I supported the revolution but we hoped that other groups might gain power and we might have real democracy," said one grower. "We hoped and believed what they said. We knew their position but . . . hoped there would be a democratic system," said another grower. "We believed the charter of Punta Arenas [July 12, 1979] when they [the Sandinistas] supported democracy," said a third. Commitment to Western-style democracy was therefore a major factor in bourgeois opposition to Somoza and initial support for the Sandinistas. It would also be a major factor in the collapse of that support.

The views of the Sandinistas on democracy, like their views on the economy, evolved over their years in power, so it is difficult to specify a single Sandinista model. At least initially, the Sandinistas gave greater weight to participatory than representative political forms and to popular hegemony rather than opposition political rights. In practice this meant an emphasis on "popular" organizations like the Association of Rural Workers (ATC), the National Union of Farmers and Ranchers (UNAG), and the Committee for the Defense of Sandinismo (CDS) and other organizations dominated by Sandinista militants. A Leninist party vanguard was to exercise leadership within these organizations and within the party itself. Nonetheless, the party accepted national elections in 1984 and 1990 and any doubts about the fairness of the latter were dispelled by the party's electoral defeat. As Dennis Gilbert notes, however, the party never clarified the relationship between its concept of popular democracy and Western-style representative democracy as expressed, for example, in the 1987 Constitution.[28]

The Sandinistas' initial support for popular and participatory forms of democracy led them to reject representative democracy as "democratism" and "liberal bourgeois ideology." In their view the "logic of the majority" was expressed by the party vanguard and the Sandinista-dominated "mass" organizations, not through the electoral process. In his 1980 speech announcing the indefinite postponement of national elections, Humberto Ortega rejected traditional elections as "a raffle among those who seek power," and argued that Sandinista democracy will "perfect revolutionary power . . . because the people hold power through their vanguard—the FSLN and its National Directorate." A party communiqué issued before Ortega's speech asserted that "bourgeois freedom has nothing to do with popular freedom which reflects the objective [that is, the class] interests of the people."[29] Since, as was noted above, "freedom of everything, economic freedom, political freedom," was the essence of the bourgeois position, this statement placed the government and the bourgeoisie on a collision course. In fact, as Ilja Luciak notes, the Sandinistas never resolved the contradiction between their support for the national unity alliance with the bourgeoisie and their commitment to hegemony by the popular classes, which most assuredly did not include the bourgeoisie.[30] The agrarian bourgeoisie had, conversely, become convinced that there was no possibility of either freedom or democracy in Sandinista Nicaragua, despite national elections and the continued debate among the Sandinistas themselves on the issue.

Sandinista Democracy: The View of the Agrarian Bourgeoisie

Those interviewed thought democracy, as they understood it, did not exist in Nicaragua. The more politically oriented argued that in politics, as well as in economics, the goal was a Soviet- or Cuban-style party dictatorship. "Elections are a fraud," said one politically oriented producer, "only one party was permitted to run an effective

campaign [in the 1984 elections] . . . You can't organize politically."
When asked to compare the political situation under the Sandinistas
with what it had been under Somoza, an officer of the National
Coffee Association said "elections are no different now. They are
predetermined. How can you have an election when there is no freedom to get involved before the election—we have all the worst
aspects of the Somoza system." An officer of the Matagalpa Association agreed and added that "things are much worse now," even
though he had been an active opponent of the Somozas' rule, which
he continued to denounced as a dictatorship.

A prominent cotton grower, who also shared the view that things
were worse politically under the Sandinistas than under Somoza,
argued that this was because of what he called the Sandinistas'
"Marxist-Leninist concept. They think of democracy in the style of
the East, not the West." "The problem is these Marxist-Leninist,
Communist, totalitarians, whatever you call them," said another
grower, adding, "the Sandinistas want to control everything, politics,
school, religion, production." When asked if there was any possibility of compromise, another politically oriented grower said, "no;
they are only interested in one thing—their Marxist-Leninist ideology. We're going to turn Nicaragua into another Cuba or Soviet
Union. You read in the paper about Kim Il Sung and the great
people's democracy." "It's their project, their system, totalitarian,
like Cuba or the Soviet Union. It's where they are getting their
orders," said a UNAG member whose views, despite his membership, were close to those of the Association.

All of these comments are by politically oriented growers, a number of whom are officers of private associations actively opposed to
Sandinista rule. Only UNAG officers defended representative democracy in Nicaragua, while technically rather than politically oriented growers expressed disappointment rather than rage that their
early hopes for democracy had not been realized. "We basically believed the Charter of Punta Arenas when they [the Sandinistas] supported democracy. The period of the revolution, the first government
of Violeta Chamorro and Alfonso Robelo, but after that they changed
and we found out it was all lies," said one coffee grower. "We hoped
that we could believe what they said," said another technically oriented producer of the Sandinistas; "we knew their politics, but be-

lieved they supported *los doce* . . . we hoped we would have a democratic system." Although most of the technicals were disappointed in the Sandinistas' political philosophy, they, unlike the politicals, were at least open to a more moderate policy. When asked if he would stay in Nicaragua and continue producing if the Sandinistas moderated their policies, one cotton producer readily agreed. But as the interviewer was leaving he called after him, "See you in Miami." Many of the technicals appeared receptive to Sandinista efforts at representative democracy, but, as this parting comment indicates, in 1986 they had little hope that such efforts were serious.

Democratic Rights and Civil Liberties

The Sandinistas had made respect for human rights one of the fundamental principles of the revolution and there were no mass executions or arbitrary vengeance against members of the old regime. Independent human rights groups reported that there were relatively few violations of human rights in Sandinista Nicaragua, and those that did occur were usually punished.[31] Nevertheless, under a state of emergency declared in 1982, most democratic rights were suspended, prior censorship was imposed on the press, and the activities of bourgeois political parties were restricted. The arrest of the entire leadership of COSEP in October 1981 for writing an open letter critical of the revolution signaled the limits of bourgeois political opposition even before the emergency decrees were in effect. But the 1984 election campaign was characterized by frank and often brutal criticism of the government by opposition parties, and the election itself was generally regarded as fair by international observers.[32] Even at the nadir of Sandinista-bourgeois relations in 1986, members of the bourgeoisie were willing, as their comments indicate, to attack the government in no uncertain terms in private conversation, although most said they would have been reluctant to do so in public. Not even the most outspoken politicals contended that a Soviet-style police state existed in Nicaragua, although a number argued that there would be one in the future.

Nevertheless, many of those interviewed felt that their political rights and liberties were in jeopardy in Sandinista Nicaragua. Politically prominent growers feared confiscation of their estates for their political views. Nicolás Bolaños, one of the most outspoken politicals, clearly felt that his estate had been confiscated because of his brother Enrique's criticism of the government as president of COSEP. The president of UPANIC, Ramiro Gurdian, also argued vehemently that his banana plantation had been confiscated because he had supported the United States suspension of Nicaragua's sugar quota. And the estate of another of those interviewed, an officer of the Matagalpa Association, was confiscated in 1988, after he resigned from a government-sponsored coffee advisory council. (Another of Bolaños's properties was confiscated at the same time for the same reason.) Political confiscations were a personal concern only for the politically active. Most growers thought they risked confiscation whether or not they spoke out politically simply because they were large growers. Nevertheless, confiscations directed against private-sector leaders increased the perceived risks of political action.

Most of those interviewed reported being under immense pressure from Sandinista police, militants, and mass organizations. "There is tremendous pressure on us all the time," said one UNAG member, "from the government, the ATC, the Front. They have threatened me personally . . . they point a gun at me—the ATC—pressure and more pressure." "They are increasing pressure on the private growers," said one efficient, technically oriented grower. "For example, two security men came to investigate me. They are trying to intimidate you, to pressure you." "The pressures are increasing," said the wife of another efficient grower. She reported that her husband "was investigated for applying for a visa to go to Costa Rica," and she feared for his safety. Visits by security forces were one of a number of forms of pressure on growers; others included arrest, violence, land invasions, and mob action or the threat of the same.

Only one of those interviewed reported that he himself had been arrested, but a number of others reported investigations or intimidation by security forces. The one grower who had been arrested turned out to be one of the revolution's most loyal supporters among those interviewed. He had gone to a party in another country, and a contra fund raiser had been present at the gathering. "It did look suspicious," he conceded. "So they arrested me, stripped me naked, completely naked and interrogated me. There was no physical violence, but there was considerable psychological abuse—you lost all track of time, of day or night. They didn't tell how long you would be held or what they would do with you." An UPANIC officer reported that he had been stripped and held naked in a room at the National Airport after returning from a business trip to Costa Rica. "A friend of mine was arrested and held for two weeks and then expelled from the country," said another grower who had not been threatened himself. "They don't break your jaw or tear off your lips. They put you in a chair, in a closed room—hot—and question you for hours." None of those interviewed reported anything other than detention and prolonged, psychologically abusive interrogation by the police.

Three of those interviewed reported death threats or actual killings, either during the revolution itself or in circumstances which did not suggest official complicity. "They [the Sandinistas] kill people," said a coffee grower; "they killed my father during the revolution." He went on to say that he believed that his father had been killed for being a Somocista. The wife of another grower believed that a relative, age thirty, was murdered by a Sandinista police chief, and said this was the fate she feared for her husband. A politically neutral grower said that he had been threatened by an army officer who said he would shoot him if the grower wouldn't lend him his truck. The officer was, he claimed, responsible for several killings after the revolution. "This is a guy who thinks nothing of killing." Although these reports could not be verified, they do not seem to indicate systematic police action but rather the possibilities for violence in a situation of revolution and civil war. But they do underscore the fear and pressure in which most growers worked in the Sandinista period.

Pressures from mass organizations and Sandinista militants and crowds added to their feeling of insecurity. The wife of the grower who had been investigated for applying for a visa to Costa Rica reported that on two recent occasions mobs had tried to burn their house down by dumping cans of gasoline in doorways and igniting them. She said she felt it was a systematic campaign to drive them out and confiscate their lands. Another grower claimed that the FSLN was encouraging workers on his estate to denounce him for the same reason. A politically neutral grower had recently experienced a land invasion by what he described as "the ATC and some people from the Front," although the invasion ended when a MIDINRA official persuaded the invaders to withdraw. One of a number of other growers who had experienced similar invasions acknowledged that it had taken place immediately after the revolution, but still "the threats continue. Threats of invasions of lands, threats of confiscations." Some growers reported being threatened by crowds of armed workers and one had actually been placed on trial by his own workers as a member of the "exploiting bourgeoisie," but these incidents seemed to have happened during and immediately after the revolution. Still the threat of crowd action seemed to trouble most growers. "There is no land invasion that is not organized and directed," said another grower, who had not experienced an invasion but expected one at any time.

Among those interviewed only some, but not all, UNAG members seem to have been exempt from such pressures. When asked if he had any problems with land invasions a UNAG member replied, "No, nothing like that . . . I haven't had any problems. I obey the laws. If you do, you don't have any problems." Another UNAG member not only said he had no problems with land invasions or other pressures but reported that the Sandinista youth organization and the FSLN had helped him recruit volunteer harvest labor. Another grower and UNAG officer pointed out that they were free to criticize the government, but admitted that the same criticisms coming from the Association could create problems. "The difference is the Association is making the criticisms basically to undermine the government, to support the counter-revolution. If the government thinks you are supporting the contra then you would have problems." But even technically oriented growers who were not active in the association reported pressures from the police and mass organizations. Although only active UNAG members seem to have achieved any immunity to political pressures, a technically oriented association member argued that "most of the large producers who join, join because they are frightened."

There is no denying that many if not most of those interviewed seemed frightened, although this did not prevent many of them from attacking both the government's economic policies and its civil rights record in private. But many insisted that they not be quoted by name, and almost all said they believed they could not make the same criticisms in public without risking arrest. One UNAG member, who was having dinner with a government official when the interview began, gave an entirely fraudulent set of pro-government answers as long as the official was present. As soon as the official left, he attacked the government and voiced enthusiastic support for a United States invasion. In another interview I asked how we could be talking critically of the government when the grower claimed there were no political rights in Nicaragua. He replied, "sure, but that's because we're speaking privately. If I were to go out on the street and say what we are saying here, I would be arrested." Even a political neutral sympathetic to the government acknowledged that "if you go out in the street and demand higher prices—no, that isn't possible," but argued that it was possible to negotiate in private. "You can't say one word of criticism of the government," said one of the most outspoken politicals, "you will be arrested, thrown in jail. Look what happened to Jorge Salazar."

Despite the government's commitment to human rights and, after 1984, to electoral democracy, the agrarian bourgeoisie in 1986 felt itself to be a threatened and persecuted minority. The limits on political rights imposed in the state of emergency contributed to this feeling, as did the elite's vulnerability to pressures from mass organizations and the security forces. By 1986 the contra war was at its height, and government security forces suspected, not without reason as the interviews indicate, that many large producers sympathized with the contra. Under these circumstances it is not surprising that a leading producer would be investigated or even arrested as a potential counter-revolutionary. Still, the pressures from mass organizations and the feelings of vulnerability stemmed in the final analysis from the elite's anomalous position in a revolutionary society governed by "the logic of the majority." The unresolved contradiction in Sandinista policy between the national unity alliance and popular hegemony contributed to the political alienation of the bourgeoisie. Even though they were not faced with a police state, the bourgeois found themselves without governmental representation or guaranteed security of their persons or property. Their official position in Sandinista society was well described by Sandinista Vice President Sergio Ramírez—"survivors of the shipwreck."

Governmental Access and Personal Relations

Despite the absence of electoral democracy and civil liberties during the Somoza period, the elite nevertheless had some access to the regime. But after the government reorganizations of 1979 and 1980, the bourgeoisie ceased to have its own representatives in influential positions and experienced increasing difficulties in influencing policy. This was not so much because the Sandinistas were unwilling to meet with prominent coffee and cotton growers; many growers in fact reported such meetings. But the meetings were often contentious and counterproductive, leading to more, not less, bourgeois alienation. As one Association member explained, "Look, in the early days of the revolution there were important cotton and coffee growers who were members of the agricultural ministry. They were technically competent, efficient producers. But they have all left, replaced by people who are incompetent. You can't negotiate with people who don't have any knowledge of production." Or as an officer of the Matagalpa Association put it, "Yes, we get together and have meetings. And we tell them what we want. But they do nothing. It is just propaganda."

Particularly at the beginning of the Sandinista period, the anti-bourgeois rhetoric of the Sandinistas further alienated the growers. "For a long time the government abused the coffee growers," said one government sympathizer. "We would go and try to say something to the ministry and they would not believe us. . . . We were the bourgeois exploiters." Another sympathetic grower agreed. "At the beginning, after the war [the revolution] we were seen as the enemy." And an official of the Matagalpa Association described his own frustration with meetings with government officials. "If you try to explain to them about prices, they just say 'you know why you think that—it's because you are part of the exploiting bourgeoisie'." "They call us the hated bourgeois, the exploiters of the workers," said an outspoken political activist in the Matagalpa Association. Although both of the two more sympathetic growers saw a major change in attitude in government ministries in the year preceding the interviews, the earlier attitudes had alienated many growers.

Meetings with government officials and government access generally seemed to confirm bourgeois suspicions of Sandinista intentions and further intensify the conflict. Given the wide gulf in economic policy, this outcome should not be surprising. As long as government policy emphasized state-centered agro-industrial development, there was little point in arguing for policies in favor of the private sector. At one meeting, at a time when coffee prices were low, one grower reported that Minister of Agriculture and Agrarian Reform Jaime Wheelock had said that "they might just let the entire coffee economy go." In another meeting with Wheelock, cotton growers who had come to request a review of confiscations were told, according to one of the growers present, that "if we review them, we may have to confiscate more." "He said that to a group of cotton growers," the grower said with incredulity. "I was right in the room and heard it with my own ears." Although by 1986 Wheelock was promising an end to confiscations and some growers reported a more favorable attitude in the ministry, much of the damage had already been done.

The available evidence and weight of scholarly opinion seem clearly to indicate that Sandinista economic policy was weighted against the private sector, and that conflict between the bourgeoisie and the Sandinistas was inevitable. Indeed, conflict was assured by the anomaly of a class of large producers in what was in effect, until the late 1980s, a command economy. The evidence on democratic pluralism is more mixed. It is clear that early Sandinista emphasis on participatory democracy, popular hegemony, and rule by the vanguard did not give much weight to bourgeois notions of electoral process or civil liberties. But most observers think that the 1984 elections were reasonably fair, and yet bourgeois representatives, supported by the private sector agrarian organizations, refused to participate. It may be that the despair concerning their economic future, evident in the interviews, made them unwilling to entertain any compromise with the Sandinistas; moreover, by 1984 the contra, backed by the United States, offered a non-democratic alternative route to power. United States pressure was certainly a major factor in the decision of the bourgeoisie not to contest the elections.[33] And the contra war itself placed immense pressures on the Sandinistas to increase surveillance and curtail civil liberties—behavior which, as the interviews indicate, further alienated the agrarian bourgeoisie.

Sandinista policy deserves a major share of the blame for both the political and the economic collapse of the mixed economy. The blame for the failure of the second principle of the revolutionary coalition, political pluralism, is more widely shared.

Non-Alignment and the Contra War

The third major principle of the national unity alliance, non-alignment, was a casualty of the contra war. Initially, the United States had been the revolution's principal aid donor, and much foreign aid also came from sympathetic Western European and Third World governments rather than from the Soviet bloc.[34] Although relations with the United States deteriorated, the revolutionary government continued to maintain its relations with Western European social democratic parties. In 1988, a report by the Swedish government on the state of the economy was largely responsible for moving the Sandinistas to embrace an orthodox economic stabilization program.[35]

The 1980 election of Ronald Reagan on a platform which strongly implied efforts to overthrow the FSLN, a renewal of cold war rhetoric in the United States, and the beginning of American support for the contras quickly ended whatever possibilities there might have been for continued U.S.-Nicaragua ties. Anti-imperialism, sympathy for Third World revolutionary movements, and a strategic alliance with the Soviet Union and Cuba had always been at the core of the Sandinista program. These commitments and the Sandinistas' deteriorating relations with the bourgeoisie made relations with the United States problematic under the best of circumstances. But the Reagan administration's insistence on viewing Nicaragua in terms of a cold war confrontation with the Soviet Union and its mounting support for the contra foreclosed normal relations, and made the Sandinistas increasingly dependent on Soviet military aid.[36]

By the time of the interviews in 1986, the politicals among those interviewed saw their relations with the Sandinista government in terms of the same cold war rhetoric used by the Reagan administration, and began to identify their interests with those of that administration. Support for the contra was universal among those classified as politicals and became widespread even among technically oriented producers and some nominally patriotic producers. Only a few UNAG members and one or perhaps two technically oriented producers expressed any reservations about the contras. Contra supporters among the politicals were surpassingly outspoken about their views, and even cautious technicals let it clearly be known where their sympathies lay. By 1986 the national unity alliance with the bourgeoisie had ended with most members of the agrarian bourgeoisie giving tacit, although probably not active, support to an armed movement dedicated to the overthrow of the Sandinista government. Differences among those interviewed on this issue were largely questions of political rhetoric.

For the politicals, the contra war and the Sandinistas' relations with the United States were defined in the polarized language of the cold war. The war was seen as a proxy battle between the United States and the Soviet Union, with the Sandinistas as mere agents of the latter. "Aren't the Sandinistas being paid by the Soviet Union," said one private association officer. "Where do the helicopters come from?" "There are thousands of Cuban soldiers in Nicaragua, 5,000 to 8,000," claimed another producer associated with the Matagalpa Association. "Under the Carter administration they had Panamanians," said a colleague of his at the Association, "but as soon as they got what they wanted from Carter, they expelled the Panamanians and brought in Cubans. It is just like Angola where the Cubans are killing Africans." "The Kremlin has exactly one line, and it's always the same, expansion, and that's what they are doing here," said another outspoken political. "They love the Soviet Union," said a leading cotton planter, "non-alignment is just another way of opposing the United States."

The Reagan administration was seen by the politicals as their loyal ally in the struggle against Soviet expansion; accordingly, Democrats in general and Congressional Democrats in particular were viewed with suspicion. Several producers asked about my party affiliation and seemed clearly disappointed with the answer (registered Democrat). One grower complained about "those Democratic Senators who filibuster . . . against contra aid." At least two growers volunteered that they were outraged when Daniel Ortega had traveled to the United States and "insulted" Ronald Reagan. Domestic opponents of Reagan administration policy were denounced as "communists" by one particularly vituperative anti-communist political. A number of growers were also suspicious of "internationalists" who, as one of them put it, "are just here to take a vacation in the tropics and see the revolution."

Despite the risks associated with support for the contra in Sandinista Nicaragua, several of the politicals not only did so but also backed U.S. military intervention. Some appeared to view the interview as an opportunity to lobby for military intervention. "Everyone would be down on the beach waving American flags," said a Matagalpa Association officer when asked about the possibility of such intervention. At least two growers tried to argue that failure to intervene would cause the United States itself to face invasion and Communist insurgency across the Rio Grande. Another political ridiculed intellectuals in the United States who drew false comparisons with Vietnam and Korea, where Communists had had Chinese backing. "But where is the China in Central America," he said. "You just send a fleet to either coast and they can't send ships or supplies." "When the Senate voted the $100 million [aid for the contra], 90% of the population were secretly happy," said a dissident UNAG member who also backed direct U.S. intervention.

Although such outspoken opinions were the defining characteristic of the group here called "politicals," even cautious technically oriented growers obliquely signaled their support for the U.S.-backed contra effort or, possibly, for invasion. When asked how Sandinista policy could be changed, one efficient technically oriented moderate replied, "Only through total change. And this will not come from within. There will have to be help, pressure from the outside." The wife of another efficient producer, after describing the various failings of the Sandinista system, made a gesture of prayer and said "There is only one God," in an appeal for divine (if not United States) intervention to end Sandinista rule. "They say there is no evil that lasts more than five years," she said, quoting a popular saying. "I think we definitely need a change," said an aristocratic Conservative opponent of Somoza in the context of discussing the contra war. "Why do they have a war? Because they have created an economic disaster and turned a lot of poor farmers against them." Another technically oriented producer introduced me to a friend by calling me a "cub of Reagan," making a politically daring play on the Sandinista slogan "cubs of Sandino" used for members of the Sandinista Popular Army (EPS).

Clear opposition to the contra and United States intervention was expressed by only a few UNAG members, one Association member, and the one political and organizational neutral among those interviewed. For members of the agrarian elite such opposition could be costly. The husband of one UNAG officer had been tortured to death by contra raiders on the family's coffee estate. The father of a UNAG member had been shot in a payroll robbery carried out by an army officer who, he believed, was defecting to the contra. Another member had narrowly escaped a contra ambush the day before the interview. Still another UNAG member worried about mines on the road to his coffee estate. The political neutral had lost several hundred head of cattle to a contra raid. "There is a lot of pressure, pressure from both sides," said the Association member sympathetic to the government. "There is pressure from the government. But also pressure from the contra to take up their position." All UNAG members but one faced direct threats from the contra; the one who did not was in fact an outspoken contra supporter.

Among the three types, the politicals had clearly taken a position of open disloyalty to the government. The technicals, while supporting the contras and possibly U.S. military intervention, seemed most concerned about effecting a real change in policy and might have supported the government under other circumstances. The small minority of patriotic producers had paid a great personal price for their loyalty to the government and disloyalty to their class. The government sympathizer among the Matagalpa Association members, who had resigned from the Association board because he disagreed with their political intransigence, said that "maybe 50 percent" of the Association members think politically and follow the Association line. "The rest think the way I do—it's better to stick to production." "They are interested in opposing the government," said a UNAG official of the Matagalpa Association. "Basically they simply want to find things to complain about. They think everything is bad." UNAG members were, of course, a negligible proportion of large coffee producers.

The extreme anti-communist and anti-Sandinista sentiment among the private Association officials and their followers, combined

with their enthusiastic support for the violent overthrow of the Sandinista government, would seem to make any renewal of the national
unity alliance difficult if not impossible. Indeed, COSEP and
UPANIC have in general opposed the de facto coalition between the
Chamorro government and the Sandinista-dominated armed forces
that emerged after the Sandinistas' electoral defeat. The loyalty of
the technically oriented producers, however, while lost at the time
of the interviews, might have been maintained or even regained with
different economic policies and an unequivocal support for parliamentary democracy from the outset. There is little doubt, however,
that the polarization introduced by the unremitting hostility of the
Reagan administration to any form of Sandinismo encouraged the
more intransigent anti-communist faction, and that the contra war
strained political tolerance on both sides and undermined the electoral democracy that it was supposed to establish. The extreme pressure that both supporters and opponents suffered, evident in the
interviews, is a dramatic indication of the practical political effect
of the contra war. In the end, collapse of the national unity alliance
depended in part on events outside Nicaragua's borders and outside
Sandinista control.

Conclusions

The agro-industrial fraction of the Nicaraguan elite joined the Sandinista revolution in pursuit of the vision of "liberty" that many of
their families had been seeking since the time of Zelaya. They were
to be disappointed once again under the Sandinistas. To the elite
"liberty" or "freedom" (*libertad*) meant "political freedom, economic
freedom, the freedom to buy and sell without government interference." At the core of this ideology is entrepreneurial freedom—the
ability to carry out the basic functions of capitalist accumulation
without governmental encumbrances. The vision also included the
development of a modern capitalist state that would efficiently dis-
charge its economic and administrative functions and facilitate industrial development through agro-exports. From the elite point of
view the Somocista state provided the economic freedom they
sought, but failed miserably at creating an efficient capitalist state
that would promote development. The Sandinistas deprived the elite

of this economic freedom and threatened the property and managerial discretion on which this freedom rested. Despite their explicit developmentalist objectives, the Sandinistas also failed to deliver an efficient, technically competent administration of the agro-export economy.

The agro-industrial vision of political freedom conflicted with Sandinista notions of participatory rather than representative democracy. For the agro-industrialists, political liberty meant not only freedom from government intrusion in the conduct of their businesses but freedom from restrictions on elite political activity and elite access to the state. During the revolutionary decade the Sandinistas provided considerable, but not unrestricted, freedom of political action for the elite, but elite access to and control over the state were limited by the dominance of the Sandinista party and popular organizations. Nevertheless the elite rejected opportunities, such as the 1984 election, when they could have gained more political access and almost from the beginning, as the example of Jorge Salazar demonstrates, were willing to use force to defeat the Sandinistas. At the root of the agro-industrial dissatisfaction with Sandinista politics were two incompatible visions of the economic order—state-centered accumulation and proprietary agro-export development. It is unlikely that any amount of political freedom would have resolved this contradiction.

The agro-industrial elite was much more concerned with "liberty" than "democracy." Much interview time was spent in discussions of the need for basic political rights for the bourgeoisie. Comparatively little attention was given to bringing what the Sandinistas called the popular classes into the political process, and even less to the question of what changes such incorporation would make in the distribution of wealth and power in Nicaragua. Nor was there much concern for the political rights of the Sandinistas themselves, as the nearly universal bourgeois support for the contra indicate. Many of those interviewed had risked their fortunes and in some cases their lives in a fight for the kind of freedom they sought under both Somoza and the Sandinistas. They were nonetheless willing, with varying degrees of enthusiasm, to support an anti-democratic organization officered by former members of Somoza's praetorian guard in order to regain their economic rights, whatever the cost in deprivation of political liberty to their opponents. This was not simply a return to the authoritarian agrarian past. The progressive agro-industrial sector of the elite was willing to use anti-democratic methods because its interests were threatened.

The agro-industrial elite's vision of "liberty" had helped bring down the old authoritarian agrarian order in Nicaragua and ensure the success of the Sandinista revolution. Yet the agro-industrialists had been unwilling and unable to accomplish this task by themselves. The armed leftist revolutionaries of the Sandinista Front had destroyed the old order and forced the elite to choose between the authoritarian past and an uncertain future. Ironically, the principal outcome of the Sandinista revolution has been the establishment of the electoral democracy sought by the agro-industrialists, not the socialist revolution sought by the Sandinistas. In the end, thanks to the failures of Sandinista economic policy and intervention by the United States, the agro-industrialists emerged as the principal victors of the socialist revolution they had backed. State-centered accumulation has been dismantled and neo-liberal private enterprise reestablished as the dominant mode of economic organization in Nicaragua.

The full incorporation of the left and the "popular classes" remains an unresolved problem in both the agro-industrialists' vision of "liberty" and post-Sandinista Nicaraguan political organization. The agro-industrial notion of "liberty" did not as a matter of course include the popular classes, represented, whether they liked it or not, by the Sandinistas. The interviewees stated many times that the solution to Nicaragua's problems was to get rid of the Sandinistas. Few seem troubled by the fact that the people who supported the party (over 40 percent of the vote in the 1990 elections) might be left without representation. What the agro-industrialists wanted was a limited "bourgeois" democracy in which liberty, property, and the market reigned supreme, and the bourgeoisie and their supporters acquired influence in the administration of a rational and efficient state. What was to be done with the overwhelmingly poor majority of the population was not included in the agro-industrial elite's limited version of bourgeois democracy.

The agro-industrialists proved to be an ambivalent and contradictory class in Nicaragua. They were a progressive force, particularly when contrasted to the authoritarian-agrarian order represented by the Somozas. They helped to make a significant breakthrough for democracy in Nicaragua. They were, however, ambivalent at best about the full incorporation of the Sandinistas' "popular classes" into the polity, and their commitment to democracy was variable, contingent on the absence of significant threats to their property or position. During the Sandinista era they were perfectly willing to back anti-democratic solutions when that position was threatened by a militant popular party. If the agro-industrialists are again threatened by an upsurge from below, democracy may prove to be an unstable and transient political form. The agro-industrialists may then be tempted, as they were in the Sandinista period, to seek authoritarian solutions. These solutions will not, however, be those of the old authoritarian agrarian order. That order is gone for good. In this sense the Nicaraguan revolution and the radical Sandinistas and liberal agro-industrialists who led it expanded the possibilities for human freedom. At this writing a permanent expansion of human freedom in Nicaragua remains largely in the realm of a possible but far from certain future.

IV

*Social Transformation and
Elite Narrative, 1979–1992*

10

Democracy and Revolution

The stories of "liberty" and "progress" told by the Salvadoran and Nicaraguan elites had their origins in nineteenth-century Liberal ideology and early twentieth-century class position. The Costa Rican story of "democracy" had its origin in the early twentieth-century society of small-holding coffee producers and aristocratic processors, but it was modified and institutionalized by the victors of 1948. The authoritarian ideologies that emerged from the 1930s crisis, particularly in El Salvador and Nicaragua, added to these stories a paranoid anti-communism that banished the counter-narratives of the left from public discourse and even private consciousness. Even in Costa Rica, where the counter-narratives survived in the policies of Liberación, anti-communism became an article of national faith. By the end of the decade of the 1980s elite ideologies had begun to undergo a significant shift to democratic neo-liberalism, which reflected the emergence of the agro-industrial fraction of the coffee elite as the dominant force in all three societies. This transition was still far from complete at the time the interviews were conducted.

The ideological transformation was accompanied by a profound political transformation. Between 1979 and 1992 El Salvador and Nicaragua moved from the oligarchic-dictatorial alliance that had dominated their politics since the 1930s to neo-liberal economic policies and uncertain representative democracy through authoritarian reaction and revolutionary socialism, respectively. Costa Rica, after a dangerous passage, moved from its traditional social democracy to a still uncertain future defined by neo-liberalism. These changes were accomplished by a radically new route to democracy—through socialist revolution from below. This revolution in turn was a consequence of the sea change in class structure: the rise of the agro-industrial elite and a vastly expanded semi-proletariat, caused by the postwar transformation of the agro-export economy. Ironically, then, the principal result of the socialist revolutions of the 1980s was the triumph of the agro-industrial elite and their vision of neo-liberalism and representative democracy. The defeat of the left in the 1980s, like their defeat in the 1930s, insured that their vision of an alternative to the elite vision of progress, liberty and now, finally, democracy would be purged once again from public discourse. This defeat was engineered by the United States, but it also revealed the weaknesses in the policies of the left, most evident in the economic failings of the Sandinista regime in Nicaragua.

As was noted at the outset, the different starting points of these three Central American societies in authoritarianism, revolutionary socialism, and social democracy, respectively, as well as their common destinations in democratic neo-liberalism, provide a way of testing what is still the most influential single account of the transformation of modern political structures—Barrington Moore's theory of the social origins of dictatorship and democracy. The Central American evidence suggests, however, a route to democracy very different from the one described by Moore or by most analysts of democratic transitions. This transition was one of ideas as well as political structures. The revolutionary voices of both the 1930s and the 1980s were banished to what Fredric Jameson calls the political unconscious in both the old order and the new.[1] How this came about is in part a question of the structural transformation emphasized by Moore and in part the ideological repressions emphasized by Jameson.

Central America and the Barrington Moore Thesis

In *The Social Origins of Dictatorship and Democracy* Moore argues that democracy is a product of a "bourgeois revolution" against a backward landed aristocracy ("no bourgeoisie, no democracy"), that authoritarian "fascist" regimes result from a coalition between a dominant landed aristocracy and a weak bourgeoisie, and that socialist revolution occurs when a mass revolt of cohesive peasant villages overwhelms landed and bourgeois classes weakened by a powerful agrarian bureaucracy.[2] This thesis has had a wide impact on the social sciences and has influenced numerous case studies of particular countries and regions.[3] It has been so widely employed in both classic and contemporary work on Central America that the contrast between the authoritarian North (Guatemala and El Salvador) and the democratic South (Costa Rica) has been interpreted almost entirely in Moore's terms as a result of stronger landed aristocracies in the North.[4] A recent encyclopedic review of the development of democracy in Europe, Latin America, and the Caribbean by Rueschemeyer, Stephens, and Stephens finds support for Moore's general argument while dissenting from some of its specifics.[5] The cases of El Salvador, Costa Rica, and Nicaragua confirm some of the most fundamental assertions of the model. But they also deviate from it in significant respects.

The fundamental problem, as the great Central American sociologist Edelberto Torres-Rivas points out, is that the clear division between a landed aristocracy and an industrial bourgeoisie implied by Moore's thesis is lacking in Central America and indeed in most of Latin America.[6] As a consequence of the dependent, peripheral role of these societies in the world economy, capitalism develops first in the countryside, not the city, and is based on agro-exports, not manufacturing. In the case of Central America in particular the agro-export elite was simultaneously *agrarian,* in that it produced coffee on large landed estates, and *agro-industrial* in that it drew much of its profit from processing coffee in factory-like installations. Diversification into other agro-exports, finance, or urban industry simply deepened this division because these activities were still tied to the agrarian sector. The agrarian and agro-industrial fractions of the elite are linked not only by kinship but by function, finance, ownership, and politics. The division between the agrarian and the agro-industrial fractions of the elite is fundamental to understanding what happened in Central America in the eighties and assessing the strengths and weaknesses of Moore's argument.

Moore, like many other theorists, both Marxist and non-Marxist, traces the development of democracy to a "bourgeois revolution" in which a rising industrial bourgeoisie and its political allies defeat the entrenched political power of the landed aristocracy.[7] The defeat of the Southern slave-holding aristocracy by the industrialists of the North in the U.S. Civil War is one of Moore's paradigmatic cases. The failure of bourgeois revolution can open the way to conservative authoritarianism (what Moore calls "fascism") through the continued dominance of the landlords, as in Moore's implicit comparative case of Germany. Given the close ties between the agrarian and agro-industrial fractions of the elite the prospects for a democratic resolution in the case of Central America are not promising. The inability of the agro-industrial fraction to separate itself from, much less defeat, the agrarian fraction, as well as the heavy weight of agriculture in the economic base of the elite as a whole, suggest that conservative authoritarianism would be the expected outcome. To this extent the Central American past provides convincing, if depressing, confirmation of Moore's thesis.

The dependence of the landed elite on what Moore calls "labor repressive agriculture" is the key element linking the landed elite with authoritarian anti-democratic politics. The use of extra-economic coercion in slavery, serfdom, or other forms of forced labor requires a powerful authoritarian state and precludes extension of citizenship or other legal rights to the working population. In their test of Moore's thesis Rueschemeyer, Stephens, and Stephens found that this key element of his theory "bore the test of repeated examinations across the countries studied."[8] They suggest, however, that landlords dependent on a large supply of cheap labor, whether recruited directly by force or not, are the key anti-democratic force, since considerable coercion may be necessary to maintain land concentration and suppress labor organization. As I have argued elsewhere, the combination of a landed class and an agricultural wage labor force is explosive. It can lead to revolutionary movements that can be repressed only by massive applications of force.[9] Perhaps the clearest case of this problem in Central America is in El Salvador, where the *matanza* of 1932 was necessary to continue depriving "free" wage laborers of their rights to political and union organization. The irreducible need for cheap or unfree hand labor in Central

American coffee production has tied landed elites to authoritarianism, and the bonds between the agrarian and agro-industrial fractions of the elite have committed the latter to the politics of the former.

Breaking the Alliance: Democracy through Socialist Revolution

El Salvador is the clearest case of the strength of the alliance and the extraordinary measures necessary to break it. The view that a division exists between what Italo López Vallecillos has termed the "agro-financial" and "agro-industrial-financial" fractions of the Salvadoran elite has become what Enrique Baloyra calls "the consensus of scholarly opinion on elite politics in El Salvador."[10] As López Vallecillos describes the division, the agro-industrial fraction "opposes any attempt to transform the rigid framework of land concentration and low salaries in its devotion to the plantation economy that is the basis of its income and profits." The agro-industrial fraction, in contrast, "tries to introduce changes in the economic system . . . and opts for less authoritarian political forms within the framework of liberal democracy, representative, but restricted and controlled."[11] Oscillation between these two elite strategies has long characterized Salvadoran politics; the temporary dominance of the more liberal faction in the 1920s led to the brief democratic opening under Araujo. In times of crisis, however, as in the 1930s and early 1980s, the positions of the two fractions converge on the retrograde policies of the authoritarian "agro-financial" fraction and the violent reimposition of an authoritarian political order. Democratic openings and mass murder have marked the extremes of this oscillation, which underwent more moderate swings in 1944, 1948, 1962, and 1972.

For democracy to develop in El Salvador, the agro-industrial fraction would have to sever its ties to the agrarian fraction and then break its power. In the past it had done neither. Paradoxically, it was precisely the capitalist rationalization of agro-export production that made the imposition of authoritarian controls after 1932 necessary and gave the agrarian sector such weight in Salvadoran elite politics. The technological revolution in coffee production carried out by the Salvadoran elite created substantial agrarian profits that then provided the capital for the financial and other sectors of the economy. Capitalist development therefore strengthened the position of the agrarian fraction rather than weakening it. The "magic square of oligarchic dominance" in El Salvador included production as well as processing, export, and finance. The development of the most fully proletarianized labor force in Central America was the other principal consequence of the capitalist rationalization of coffee production in El Salvador. The collision between a proletarianized labor force and a capitalist class tightly tied to the agrarian order was the root cause of the insurrection and massacre of 1932. The capitalist transformation of agricultural labor, not its absence as Moore suggested, led to the authoritarian solution.

The interdependence of the various fractions of the Salvadoran elite impeded the clear separation and inter-elite conflict assumed in the Moore model of democracy. In one way this outcome confirms Moore, since it is precisely the elite's ties to the agrarian order that inhibit democracy. The triumph of the agro-industrial fraction over the agrarian fraction, that is of the elite over itself, as assumed in the Moore model, is, however, a logical as well as a historical impossibility. Not only can there be no way into democracy as long as the agro-industrialists remain tied to the agrarians; there is no way that the agro-industrialists themselves can undo the knot. To provide an opening for democracy some way must be found to fracture an alliance held together by sinews of property and blood. Since this impetus cannot, under the circumstances of dependent agro-export development, ever come from the bourgeoisie, this class cannot, as in Moore's model, be the vanguard of democracy. In this sense the Moore model does not work in Central America.

In both El Salvador and Nicaragua cutting the knot between the agrarian and agro-industrial fractions of the coffee elite required the intervention of socialist revolutionaries. It is one of the consummate ironies of Central American radicalism that the model proposed by the Third International theorists of the 1930s, in which the Party vanguard would substitute for the absent bourgeoisie and bring about a bourgeois democratic revolution, is exactly what did happen, in disparate ways, in both Nicaragua and El Salvador. The revolution, of course, did not "grow over" into a permanent socialist revolution in either country, and at the end of the revolutionary decade the left had accomplished only a "bourgeois democratic revolution" and perhaps a partial one at that. Nonetheless the key blow that fractured the agrarian agro-industrial alliance of the coffee elite was provided by the armies of the left. Without them it is unlikely that a road would have been opened to parliamentary democracy. This may be in the end the greatest achievement of the revolutions of the 1980s. The cost in blood and destruction was great, but, as Tommie Sue Montgomery points out, the cost of preserving the old alliance might have been even greater.[12]

The fracture in the coffee elite is clearest in El Salvador, where the two fractions ended up in open warfare by the end of the 1980s. The triumph of the Cristiani faction after 1989 over the hard-line agrarians is what made possible the Chapultepec Treaty, the end of the war, and the transition to democracy. Cristiani, with his ties to ABECAFE and FUSADES, was clearly the representative of the agro-industrialists, just as the Cafetalera under de Sola was a redoubt of the rear-guard action being fought by the agrarians and their formidable allies in the military. There is little doubt that the war and particularly the offensive of 1989 made a tremendous difference in the minds of the elite. At the beginning of the decade ABECAFE had been willing to advocate a return to the solution of Martínez in 1932 and ARENA was still under the control of the murderer of Archbishop Romero. By 1990 almost no one in the dominant agro-industrial fraction of ARENA thought that the war could be won and that mass murder was still a viable political strategy. Certainly no one believed that a business revival was possible until the war ended. This was more than a question of economics, although it certainly was that. The elite's century-old dream of progress and economic development would be deferred forever without a settlement of the war. The settlement required a split between the agrarian and agro-industrial fractions of the elite and an accommodation between the latter and the left.

The big losers in the Cristiani victory and subsequent peace settlement were the agrarians. As the interviews with the losing faction of the Cafetalera make clear, the agrarians were well aware of this. Under Cristiani and the agro-industrialists the processors got back their mills and export trade and financial control over growers, who now had no way of protecting themselves against "market" (that is, processor) prices. The agrarian reform did not affect the most profitable operations of the processors, nor those of the urban industrialists and merchants. If the peace accords are fully carried out, perhaps as much as a quarter of Salvador's agricultural land (although almost none of the prime coffee land) will be affected, severely weakening the landed fraction.[13] The homicidal commanders who had repressed labor (and whose dismissal was called for in the accord) would not be needed if the labor force was to be given citizenship rights and the low-wage rural economy abandoned. The neo-liberal future of export-based industrialization and manufacturing for a renewed Central American common market certainly was not going to depend on a nation of forced laborers. Finally, access to an extended NAFTA or even continued access to the North American market was incompatible with the murder of priests. Significant aspects of the old order were discarded in the peace settlement and the FUSADES economic plan. Yet the most important institution of the old regime remained largely intact—the army. The old agrarian order is gone. But the nature of the new neo-liberal order is still to be defined.

Processors against Democracy: The Absent "Bourgeois Revolution" in Costa Rica

In Costa Rica the agrarian fraction of the elite was weakest because there were many more small and medium producers and the elite was dominated by the processors. As Lowell Gudmundson has pointed out, the Costa Rican case would seem to lend considerable support to Moore's theory. "A commercially-based processor group constitutes what amounts to a primarily non-landed elite, a working 'bourgeois' for all practical purposes, and the development of petty bourgeois groups [that is, the small and medium coffee growers], both allies and adversaries in political and economic terms, leads eventually to competitive electoral regimes."[14] This application of Moore's model has become the accepted explanation of Costa Rican democratic exceptionalism.[15] There is, as Gudmundson also points out, one glaring inadequacy in this account.[16] The triumphant bourgeoisie did not back a "bourgeois revolution" to bring about democracy and the extension of the franchise. They backed a counter-revolution against the regime that maintained its power through the extension of an effective franchise to the working classes. It was Figueres and his armed social democrats who opened the way for democracy by excluding the coffee elite from power and resolving the protracted political crisis resulting from the elite's unwillingness to accept the democratically imposed reforms of Calderón.[17]

The elite did not, however, back counter-revolution because they were a landed class dependent on "labor repressive" agriculture, nor because a sharp division between landowners and agricultural wage laborers required force to maintain it. Labor relations on Costa Rican estates never approached the militarization of Salvadoran rural society. In the 1930s the processors faced only the most moderate and gentlemanly of protests from the small producers who dominated rural villages. Class relations did approach the harmonious ideal of processing elite ideology even if they were not based on their mythical image of rural egalitarianism. The axis of class cleavage lay between a "working bourgeois" of "commercially-based processors," and a "petty bourgeois" of small and medium coffee growers. The Costa Rican processing elite was an agrarian bourgeoisie more like *(mutatis mutandum)* Moore's English commercial farmers than his Prussian Junkers. In Moore's model there is no requirement that the bourgeoisie be urban. An agrarian bourgeoisie can carry the struggle for democracy, as in the English case. In Costa Rica in the forties the agrarian bourgeoisie of the coffee elite did not do this. The absence of a labor repressive landed class in Costa Rica made the development of democracy possible. This development did not, however, depend on the leadership of the agrarian bourgeoisie.

The behavior of the Costa Rican agrarian bourgeoisie in the 1940s confirms the general finding of Rueschemeyer, Stephens, and Stephens that the bourgeoisie has seldom been the class pushing for the full democratic extension of the franchise. It also calls into question the entire concept of "bourgeois democratic revolution" as it has been used in both Marxist and non-Marxist social science. Rueschemeyer and the Stephenses found that the bourgeoisie could be a progressive force in winning the civil rights necessary for the defense of markets and property, but middle and working classes were usually responsible for the extension of full democratic political rights. The bourgeoisie could be an ally in this process, but just as often it was not, particularly if hard pressed by a challenge from the left. This is precisely what happened in Costa Rica. Faced by a democratic challenge from the Communists and Calderón, the agrarian bourgeois went into increasingly strident and ultimately violent opposition to that challenge. They had been comfortable with the elite-dominated "bourgeois democracy" of Don Cleto and Don Ricardo. They were intransigent in the face of the real political incorporation of the working class.

The concept of bourgeois revolution is in need of substantial revision, as the work of Rueschemeyer and the Stephenses as well as a critical reconsideration of the paradigmatic (negative) case of Germany indicate.[18] The history of the agrarian bourgeoisie in Costa Rica in the twentieth century supports the notion that a bourgeoisie, agrarian or industrial, holds a concept of democracy essentially limited to the civil, legal, political, and intellectual rights that make the development of scientifically based market capitalism possible. What the bourgeois wants, not surprisingly, is a limited "bourgeois" democracy guaranteeing market-based capitalism. When the extension of democracy threatens to restrict market-based capitalism and weaken their own position, the bourgeois can become vehement opponents of democracy. Still, their opposition to democracy is not a matter of their own survival, as it is for the labor-repressive agrarians. This most fundamental assertion of Moore's has been amply confirmed by later research, including that reported here. But the idea that inclusive electoral democracy results from a "bourgeois revolution" led by the bourgeoisie itself is no longer tenable.

The breakthrough to effective electoral democracy in Costa Rica was led, as it was in El Salvador, by armed leftist revolutionaries in another example of the route to democracy through revolution from below. Although the tactical alliance between Figueres and the coffee elite in the civil war makes it appear that this was a rightist revolt, in fact, as the coffee elite was to find out to its sorrow, this was not the case. Figueres and the Communists and Calderón did not differ significantly on the social and labor reforms of Calderón. Structurally, Figueres carried out the armed revolution that Calderón and the Communists could not or would not make for themselves. Figueres's plans to revolutionize the economy by diverting the economic surplus generated by coffee into an ambitious state-led development program went far beyond Calderón's program. Figueres, however, was not representing labor or the working classes generally but acted on behalf of a nascent agro-industrial bourgeoisie in the making. The principal consequence of Figueres's developmentalism was the strengthening of the agro-industrial fraction of the Costa Rican elite, including the coffee elite. This fraction had been only weakly developed in Costa Rica because of the relative economic weakness of the coffee elite. The Costa Rican elite lacked the control over production of the Salvadorans, lost control over bananas to Minor Keith and the Americans, and lacked a market for domestic manufacture because of poverty and land concentration in the countryside.

Figueres's revolution and Liberación policies created the agro-industrial elite and made possible a breakthrough for democracy that the bourgeoisie itself was incapable of making. Liberación policies in coffee created a new agro-industrial group of mega-processors, some of the most important of whom, like the Peterses and the Bolmarciches, were tied politically to Figueres. It also caused the eclipse and virtual liquidation of the old *cafetaleros*, who depended on small-scale processing and control of their own landed estates. Liberación policies also created new agro-industrial fortunes in rice, sugar, bananas, and cattle and, eventually, in export platform manufacturing, tourism, and the "agriculture of change" (that is, nontraditional export crops). The triumph of the agro-industrial fraction that had caused open warfare in El Salvador had been accomplished by more gradual and peaceful but no less ruthless economic means. The old cafetaleros are gone forever in Costa Rica, replaced by the agro-industrial mega-processors, their allies in other sectors of the economy, and foreign capital. Oscar Arias Sánchez, like Alfredo Cristiani, is at the core of the new agro-industrial order in Central America. Through his peace plan Arias and his allies among his counterparts in El Salvador and Nicaragua succeeded in cementing the victory of the agro-industrial fraction of the elite throughout the region.

In Costa Rica the triumph of the agro-industrialists and their ideology of neo-liberal democracy brings with it a peculiar set of contradictions. The agro-industrial elite created by the statist developmentalism policies of Figueres is now more or less committed to a neo-liberal program opposed to these very policies. The confusion of the Costa Rican processors over the collapse of the International Coffee Agreement is representative of this contradiction. In 1990 they faced bankruptcy as a result of the neo-liberal policies which, in alliance with the United States, they had backed. Similarly, they were more than a little ambivalent about the nationalized banking system that had done so much to strengthen the agro-industrial class in Costa Rica. Finally, although the elite's commitment to the social reforms of Calderón as a guarantor of social harmony and peace remained undiminished in 1990, it remains to be seen if an agro-export-based welfare state is compatible with neo-liberal structural adjustment programs and the other costs of allegiance to the U.S.-backed neo-liberal order in Central America. Since the welfare state was, as the coffee processors said, one of the things that kept Costa Rica out of the Central American cauldron, its demise could only be viewed with concern. Finally, neo-liberalism strikes at the sense of community at the heart of "la cultura cafetalera." What will replace it remains to be seen.

Nicaragua: Bourgeois Revolutionaries in a Socialist Revolution

In both El Salvador and Costa Rica the agro-industrial fraction of the coffee elite, incongruously allied with armed leftist revolutionaries, provided the impetus for the development of democracy and neo-liberalism. In Nicaragua, however, the United States intervention and its institutional legacy in the form of the Somoza regime prevented the development of a strong agro-industrial fraction in coffee. The Nicaraguan coffee elite did not achieve a rationalization of either processing or production and remained the most under-developed and technologically backward in the region. Although a technological transformation of the industry had begun in the 1960s, it was not far enough advanced at the time of the revolution to have created a strong agro-industrial fraction. Although some coffee growers backed the revolution, the anti-Somoza opposition was led by the new agro-industrial elite generated by the new post-World War II export crops, above all cotton. Cotton production as it developed in Nicaragua was a capital-intensive industry using tractors, crop-dusting aircraft, petrochemicals, and, eventually, mechanical harvesters; it also generated an associated industry in cottonseed oil manufacture. Leaders of the "middle bourgeois" opposition to Somoza, such as Robelo, Lacayo, and Bolaños, were part of the agro-industrial cotton elite.

The expansion of sugar after the Cuban revolution also broadened the economic base of the aristocratic conservative families tied to the San Antonio sugar mill, including most notably Pedro Joaquín Chamorro. The Chamorro-Lacayo alliance not only expressed the continued importance of kinship in Nicaraguan political life but also underscored the dominance of the postwar agro-industrial producers of cotton and sugar over the backward agrarians in coffee. Many large coffee growers, including the largest, Anastasio Somoza, retained the semi-feudal labor relations and backward technology of an agrarian rather than an industrial elite. Many of them remained allied to the authoritarian Somoza regime and went down with him. Others, among them some of Nicaragua's most efficient and technically advanced growers, allied with the revolution and the middle bourgeoisie led by Robelo and the Bolaños brothers. The affinity of a landed elite for authoritarian solutions, postulated by Moore, is as true in Nicaragua as it was in El Salvador and Costa Rica.

Nevertheless, the break between the authoritarian Somoza regime and the agro-industrialists was not made by the agro-industrialists themselves. Once again an outside force of armed leftist revolutionaries was necessary to bring about the final rupture between the two fractions of the elite. The presence of armed leftist guerrillas and mass uprisings in the cities heightened the Somocista repression and disrupted economic activities. As was clear from the interviews, the repression extended to many of the elite and their families, including most notably Pedro Joaquín Chamorro. In the end the presence of the FSLN-led urban uprisings forced the agro-industrial fraction to choose between an uncertain revolutionary future and continued allegiance to the authoritarian patterns of the past. Many chose to back the revolution, and by so doing brought down the Somoza regime. Without the pressure of the insurrection they may never have made this sharp break with the past. It is significant, however, that they preferred even socialist revolution to continued dominance by the Somozas.

As the interviews make clear, what the bourgeois wanted was, as one of their leaders put it, "liberty, in one word liberty . . . economic freedom, political freedom, . . . that we be allowed to buy and sell freely without government interference." Or as Carlos Vilas observed, they wanted "a modern capitalist state that would efficiently perform its political economic functions."[19] As the growers' bitter complaints about the tyranny, corruption, and backwardness of the Somoza state indicated, these objectives were not satisfied in the old regime. Despite having what they described as complete economic freedom under the Somozas, the agro-industrial elite still wanted a liberal bourgeois revolution to establish the political framework that would enable them to develop the full potential of agro-industrial capitalism. They had been trying to carry out this postponed bourgeois revolution since 1893. In 1979 the most advanced agro-industrialists thought they saw another opportunity and seized it. That they proved to be mistaken, at least in the short run, did not change their fundamental objectives, which they pursued with renewed vigor under the Sandinistas.

These objectives were more directly concerned with liberty than democracy in its most inclusive sense. Although all of those interviewed said they wanted democracy and objected to both the Somozas and the Sandinistas for denying it, their statements and actions indicate that they did not necessarily have in mind the full political incorporation of the lower classes and their parties. As was the case in both El Salvador and Costa Rica, what the agro-industrialists of Nicaragua wanted was a bourgeois revolution in the limited sense—restrictions on state interference in the economy and representation for propertied interests in the state. Their refusal to grant legitimacy to the Sandinistas, their withdrawal from electoral politics in 1984, and their support for the contra indicate that their tolerance for incorporating the lower classes into politics was limited at best. Throwing the Sandinistas out of the country by force of arms, as some of the more vociferous politicals wanted, was not a democratic solution. Nicaragua provides still another confirmation of the fundamentally ambivalent attitude of the agrarian bourgeoisie to democracy.

The principal division among those interviewed, however, was precisely over this issue. The anti-communist, anti-Sandinista politicals wanted the Sandinistas expunged from Nicaragua by whatever means necessary. The more cautious technicals were convinced that some fundamental change was necessary, perhaps to be accomplished by outside intervention, but they were much more willing to work with the Sandinistas in a fully democratic regime that would include representation for both the lower and upper classes. These divisions continued after the Sandinista defeat. The politicized producer organizations and COSEP took the lead in opposition to the Chamorro-Sandinista alliance, while most of the technically oriented producers did not object to the alliance. Although the complex sequences of revolutionary politics make prediction of political views from economic position difficult, in general, as the distinction between politicals and technicals itself suggests, it was the agro-industrial fraction of those interviewed who were most willing to compromise with the Sandinistas. The two most technically sophisticated coffee producers in Nicaragua were in favor of compromise, as were most of the agro-industrial cotton growers (although not the Bolaños brothers).

Despite the differences between Nicaragua, Costa Rica and El Salvador, their transitions to democracy share some fundamental characteristics. In all three cases, just as Barrington Moore argued, a sharp break with labor-repressive agriculture and the agrarian past is necessary for the development of democratic institutions. This condition is not, however, sufficient. The agrarian and agro-industrial fractions of the Central American elite are interdependent, and the latter has been unable to separate itself from the former without the armed intervention of the left. Furthermore, even when an agrarian bourgeoisie has been able to separate itself from the landed fraction, democracy is not necessarily the result. The agro-industrial bourgeoisie is satisfied with guarantees of property and markets and the political rights necessary to make these things possible. The extension of the franchise in representative democracy requires the intervention of other groups; in these three countries, of the armed left. The Central American cases then lend support to Moore's assertion regarding landlords, but not the bourgeoisie. The breakthrough for democracy is not caused by the latter. The cases of El

Salvador, Costa Rica, and Nicaragua also suggest that a new model may be necessary to account for the contemporary wave of democratic transitions.

Revolution from Below and the Transition to Democracy

As James Dunkerly has pointed out, the transition to democracy takes on a very different form in Central America than in the Southern Cone of Latin America (Argentina, Uruguay, Chile) and other semi-peripheral regions that have become the model for theorizing about the current wave of "transitions to democracy."[20] In the Southern Cone model of "democracy by default," the exhaustion of state-centered import-substitution industrialization, compounded by the debt crisis of the 1980s, led to a loss of foreign and domestic business support and subsequent voluntary withdrawal of the military from rule after it had disarticulated the left through political repression.[21] In Central America, state-centered import-substitution industrialization was not the dominant pattern except in an attenuated form in Costa Rica, and Costa Rica's democracy dates to 1948, long before the current wave of transitions. The praetorian military dictatorships of Central America have little in common with the "bureaucratic authoritarianism" of the military regimes of the Southern Cone, and the Central American militaries, to put it mildly, did not leave voluntarily. Nor was the Central American left disarticulated, at least not until it tried to assume a democratic role. The Central American crisis began with mass protests in the late 1970s, five years before the debt crisis began to destabilize military regimes elsewhere.

Nor was the process of democratic transition in Central America similar to the historical development of democracy in Europe and North America. Rueschemeyer, Stephens, and Stephens conclude their review of the development of democracy in Europe and the Western Hemisphere by explaining that capitalism and democracy are related because "capitalist development weakens the landed upper class and strengthens the working class as well as other subordinate classes."[22] In Central America, however, capitalist agro-export development strengthened the landed class through its alliance with the agro-industrialists and inhibited the development of urban industrial working and middle classes. These classes, so important to the extension of democracy in the West and in the transition to democracy in the Southern Cone and elsewhere in Latin America, are simply not present in Central America.[23]

Yet there are important parallels with transitions elsewhere, even if the central class actors are different in Central America. The long postwar expansion of capitalism created new classes and new class dynamics that could no longer be contained in an imperial order built on narrowly based authoritarian regimes backed by United States military assistance, in an alliance held together by the ideological glue of fanatical anti-communism. Both the structural and ideological bases of this system have now fallen apart. The emerging crisis of world capitalism after 1973, which eventually led to the debt crisis in the Southern Cone in the 1980s, was already making itself felt in Central America and elsewhere, in sharply rising prices for petroleum and petrochemical imports and increasing pressures on real wages.[24] The slowing of the world economy after 1973 helped to set off the Central American crisis, but its root causes were the success of the postwar agro-export-based expansion and the failure of authoritarian governments to deal with the social welfare needs of the expanding semi-proletariat and informal sector that this expansion created.

As Gay Seidman has demonstrated in a comparative study of Brazil and South Africa, parallel processes were at work in more developed societies. The success of import-substitution industrialization strategies in semi-peripheral authoritarian regimes such as Brazil and South Africa in the post–World War II era created new social movements that could not be contained within these regimes.[25] The creation of a vastly expanded industrial working class on the one hand, and a vast impoverished urban informal sector on the other, both consequences of successful industrialization without redistribution, created the conditions for what she calls "social movement unionism." The close connections between the workplace and the squatter settlements where most workers lived aided movement organizing. The closed politics of authoritarian regimes in turn radicalized the union movement. Critical for the success of social movement unionism was a split between the industrial elite and the state as the world economy entered its downturn after 1973. Given a choice between strengthening the authoritarian state apparatus sufficiently to repress the workers' movements and making an accommodation with them, the new industrial bourgeoisie abandoned its allies in the military, opening the way for democratic regimes in both South Africa and Brazil.

Although the classes are different, the process, in broad outline, is remarkably similar in Central America. Here the most important social actors are the urban informal sector and the rural semi-proletariat instead of the working class. The organizers are Marxist guerrillas rather than social movement labor unionists, and an agro-industrial class fraction substitutes for the industrial bourgeoisie. Nevertheless, just as in Brazil and South Africa, popular mobilization splits the more progressive sector of the bourgeoisie off from its authoritarian allies, opening the way for democracy. In Central America only armed revolutionaries could break the two fractions of the elite apart and separate the more progressive agro-industrialists from their allies in the military and the landed oligarchy. In the absence of a working class, revolutionary mass mobilization was the one way to incorporate the masses into a political process, since they could not be organized into unions or social democratic parties. The driving force in both kinds of transitions is the successful postwar capitalist expansion, followed by the downturn after 1973. The underlying economic trends also account for the remarkable simultaneity of the transitions in places as diverse as Southern Africa, the Southern Cone, and Central America.

The Central American experience, however, stands out as a distinct form of the transition to democracy—through socialist revolution from below. The entirely unexpected and, from the point of view of the left, unintended consequence of the failed socialist revolutions in Central America in the 1980s (and the successful social democratic revolution in Costa Rica in 1948) was the triumph of electoral democracy and neo-liberalism. Despite the disparate histories of the three countries, some elements of the revolutionary road to democracy are common to all three. First, an armed revolution by the left splits the agro-industrial and agrarian fractions (or in the case of Costa Rica creates an agro-industrial fraction). Intervention, or the threat of intervention, by the United States blocks or undermines a victory by the left. Nevertheless, the authoritarian structures of the old regime are dismantled or weakened under the threat of revolutionary armed force. The power of the landed elite is then reduced either through agrarian reform as in El Salvador and Nicaragua or through economic attrition as in Costa Rica. Finally, in response to pressure from the debt crisis and the IMF and the United States, the left's agenda is contained and a new neo-liberal economic model is constructed centered on exports and transnational capital. The agro-industrial fraction of the elite emerges triumphant in this process, with the defanged left in a decidedly secondary although legitimate political role.

What caused this revolutionary transition? The root cause was the post-war success of world capitalism that transformed the class structure of the Central American export economies. In 1930 the patterns of class relations in El Salvador, Costa Rica and Nicaragua were dissimilar, creating very different prospects for dictatorship, democracy, and revolution in each. By 1980 all the systems under the impact of the agro-export bonanza were converging, at varying rates, on a single pattern of class division between a capital intensive agro-industrial elite and a semi-proletariat of displaced and largely unemployed former workers and farmers. These new classes could not be contained in the archaic political structures of the old dictatorial-oligarchic alliance. The armed left led the legions of the semi-proletariat and informal sector into battle against the authoritarian order. The agro-industrial elite was the ultimate beneficiary of the route to democracy through socialist revolution. The presence of a large semi-proletariat remains an unresolved contradiction of the new agro-industrial order.

As the history of the crises of both the 1930s and the 1980s indicates, the route by which class relations translate into politics and ideology is complex and filled with unexpected twists and turns. Yet the convergence of class relations in all three countries is the fundamental reason for the similarity in political outcome, just as the divergence in class relations at the beginning of the 1930s is the reason for the dramatic differences in the three political systems when the 1980s began. The social origins of democracy and dictatorship in Costa Rica and El Salvador at the start of the 1980s were the historical outcome of the way class relations were polarized in the coffee order in each country at the beginning of the century. The presence of a revolutionary socialist regime in Nicaragua in 1979 was the historic consequence of the U.S. military intervention that frustrated the Liberal revolution of the coffee elite. In 1992 the dominance of the agro-industrial elite in all three countries was the key to the success of the Arias plan and the convergence on neo-liberalism and democracy.

The triumph of the agro-industrial elite and democracy depended on the destruction of the agrarian-authoritarian order inherited from the 1930s. The destruction went farthest in Costa Rica, where au-thoritarian structures were in any case weakly developed thanks to the dominance of the "coffee pact" in political life. The abolition of the army in 1948 eliminated the possibility of an authoritarian so-lution, at least in the short run. Nevertheless the 1980s crisis caused a dramatic militarization of Costa Rica and threatened to reopen this possibility. In Nicaragua too, the revolution destroyed the armed structure of the state by liquidating the National Guard. Although the concept of a Sandinista Party army has been eliminated, the new national army, based on the Sandinista army and commanded by Ortega ally (and Granada aristocrat) Joaquín Cuadra, is highly un-likely to return to the past. In El Salvador the transition is much less complete since much of the old military structure remains de-spite the purge of the most abusive commanders and the reorgani-zation or elimination of the other security forces. The army still enjoys much of its old immunity from legal prosecution, and the judicial system is still weak and vulnerable to threats.[26] There are a great many people in El Salvador and Nicaragua with both the ex-perience and the inclination to use armed force in political crises.

Acceptance of the new democratic order is most advanced in Costa Rica, where democracy was central to national and elite ideology. In Nicaragua and El Salvador important fractions of the elite remain unreconciled to the incorporation of the left into the electoral polit-ical system: not only the hard line agrarians but some members of the agro-industrial elite itself. In El Salvador the sincerity of elite commitment to democracy varied considerably even within the agro-industrial fraction. A minority appeared genuinely committed to democracy as a matter of principled belief. Others clearly regarded a democratic opening as a tactical move compelled by wartime pres-sures. Most were somewhere in between. In 1990, as was noted earlier, most of the elite seemed to be indifferent as to whether the left ended up in the National Assembly or in their graves. In Nicaragua the "politicals" among those interviewed wanted the Sandinistas out of the country, and if COSEP's current policies continue to reflect their thinking, some still do. Except in Costa Rica, elite acceptance of democracy is not deeply rooted in either institutions or ideology and liable to be reversed under pressure.

Analysis of the behavior of the agro-industrial bourgeoisie in Central America confirms the results of other researchers indicating, contrary to Moore's theory, that bourgeois support for full extension of the franchise is conditional and dependent on the conjuncture of political forces. Under pressure the agro-industrial elite could well return to authoritarian structures. Such pressures are very likely as neo-liberal policies strip state protection from the poor and expose the population to the full force of market mechanisms. In the short run, and possibly the long run as well, neo-liberal policies have only increased the size and misery of the semi-proletariat and informal sector that were a key element in the revolts in the first place.[27] Containing disorder from this sector is an increasing problem not only in Central America but elsewhere in the hemisphere. Greater involvement of the military in urban policing functions in El Salvador and elsewhere is one indication of this problem, as is the instability of nominally democratic systems like Peru or Venezuela.[28]

Although the Central American experience does not confirm Moore's assertions in regard to the bourgeoisie, it does tend to support his most fundamental assertion—that a "revolutionary break with the past" is necessary for the development of democracy.[29] Of all the Latin American countries currently involved in transitions to democracy only Costa Rica, El Salvador, Nicaragua, and possibly Mexico have made such a revolutionary break with the past. Elsewhere democracy has been the result of what Terry Karl calls "transitions from above," in which elites negotiate or dictate the terms of the transition and the economic and military institutions of the old regime remain intact.[30] Under such circumstances the vicious Latin American cycle of democratic opening and popular mobilization followed by violent and authoritarian elite reaction may resume, and the current wave of "transitions" may prove to be transitory.

The strategic problem of democratic transitions, according to Adam Przeworski, is "how to get to democracy, without either being starved by those who control productive resources or killed by those who have arms."[31] The example of Latin America's oldest (and possibly only) stable democracy, Costa Rica, is instructive.[32] The revolutionaries of 1948, structural allies if strategic opponents of the left, succeeded in eliminating the military threat by eliminating the military and constructed a welfare state that provided some minimal protection from physical want for much of the population. In Nicaragua too the old military is gone, but the dismantling of the Sandinistas' rudimentary welfare state has put malnutrition, if not starvation, back on the national agenda. In El Salvador the military remains but was forced to accept a purge of its leadership, the loss of its policing functions, and the integration of ex-guerrilla combatants into the security structure—changes that, taken together, have no real parallel in other contemporary South American democratic transitions. Those with productive resources, however, are no more inclined to share them than they were before 1979.

In some respects, then, the conditions for the consolidation of democratic rule (and the continuation of consolidated democracy in Costa Rica) are actually better in Central America than they are in many democratic "transitions from above," in Latin America and elsewhere, where there was no revolutionary break with the past and the institutions of the old regime remain intact. Indeed, it remains to be seen whether democratic transitions from above, without Moore's "revolutionary break with the past," can *ever* lead to stable, consolidated democracy.[33] Recent developments in Peru, Colombia, Venezuela, and Mexico, where instability, political violence, or military disloyalty followed negotiated transitions, indicate that the issue is far from decided.[34] Instability has also characterized Central American transitions, particularly in Nicaragua, but the institutions of the old order are gone for good.

The most fundamental obstacles to democracy in Central America and in Latin America more generally remain—the profound inequalities of wealth and power that are the region's inheritance from its tragic past. The recent neo-liberal economic reforms have only served to increase this inequality. Reducing these inequalities was always the central message of the Central American left, in the 1930s as well as in the 1980s. The triumph of neo-liberalism and democratic ideology after 1992 has once again eclipsed the issue of inequality but hardly eliminated it as a reality of Central American life. Once again the example of Costa Rica is instructive. Only in Costa Rica has the reduction of inequality through welfare state measures, issues championed by the left, become an accepted part of elite ideology, public policy, and national consensus. Only Costa Rica can reasonably lay claim to the designation of consolidated democracy, certainly in the region and very possibly in all of Latin America. The deep and increasing inequalities in El Salvador and Nicaragua continue to threaten the breakdown of democracy, even the renewal of civil war, despite the changes of the revolutionary decade.

The road to democracy through socialist revolution from below has profoundly changed the political and economic institutions of Central America. It has also brought about a substantial change in the realm of ideas, a process frozen in time in the interviews conducted at the moment of transition in all three countries. Particularly in El Salvador and Nicaragua, the shift from one way of organizing political and social life to another was accompanied by considerable ideological strain and discomfort clearly evident in the interviews. They revealed not only the contradictions, structural and ideological, of the old order collapsing around the elite but the contradictions that the new order shared with the old. In the 1980s the ideological ghosts of the 1930s rebels returned to haunt the hearts and minds of the principal beneficiaries of the oligarchic-dictatorial regimes founded on their corpses. They continue to haunt the new neo-liberal order, protestations of the end of the left or even the end of history notwithstanding.

11

From Liberalism to Neo-Liberalism

The rise of the agro-industrial elite and the political transition to democracy through revolution from below were accompanied by a profound ideological transformation. Traditional nineteenth-century Central American liberalism, modified by the Depression crisis to include authoritarian anti-communism, was replaced by the new orthodoxy of neo-liberalism and democracy. The alternative visions of the left were once again in eclipse, just as they had been after the Depression. Neo-liberalism emerged as the hegemonic ideology of the triumphant agro-industrial elite. Yet a close analysis of the conversations of the elite reveals that in the realm of consciousness, and even more the unconscious, the issues raised by the left in the 1930s and 1980s are very much alive. Neo-liberalism, like liberalism before it, neglected significant aspects of Central American reality. The growing semi-proletariat that had been the cause of the revolutions in the first place was outside the precepts of the new philosophy, except as a group soon to vanish through capitalist development. Yet it is now the fastest growing class throughout the region. Neo-liberalism, like liberalism, brought with it its own contradictions.

Understanding these ideological transformations and contradictions requires a different, although related, set of concepts than those useful for understanding the political and economic transformation of Central America. Three concepts in particular clarified the transformation in the realm of ideas as expressed in the stories the elite told in the interviews: (1) ideology and ideological mystification as outlined originally by Marx; (2) narrative, a concept developed originally in critical literary studies but increasingly adopted by social scientists; and (3) the idea of the "political unconscious" as developed by Fredric Jameson and explicated by William Dowling.[1] The three concepts are actually closely related both in theory and in practice, and provide a way of tying the ideological transformation to the structural transformation of Central American political economy discussed in the previous chapter. They also provide a disciplined way of penetrating beneath the surface of the stories told in the interviews to detect the unconscious contradictions present in the minds of the elite as well as in the deep structure of their societies. Together they help to understand both what is said in the interviews, and, more importantly, what must be left unsaid.

Ideology, Narrative, and the Political Unconscious

The concept of ideology is used in two related but distinctly different ways in the social sciences.[2] First, it can simply mean a set of ideas or ways of thinking held by a group about the social organization of a society, without necessarily making any judgment about the truth or falsehood of those views. In this sense of the term any group, whether dominant or subordinate, can have an ideology, and the accuracy of the ideology as a reflection of the social structure is an empirical question subject to research. In its second meaning, which can be traced to Marx himself, ideology is an inherently distorted or mystified view of the social structure. Only distorted or mystified views of social reality count as ideology, and ideology is always produced by a process of mystification. A polemical version of this view finds ideology only in the views of one's political opponents and, as Mannheim noted, can lead to dogmatism and unscientific thinking. This was not, however, the position taken by Marx himself, nor is his position inherently unscientific.

As Jorge Larrain has pointed out, Marx in his early writings, particularly *The German Ideology*, described the precise process by which ideological ideas were generated.[3] Marx's model does not deny the possibility that the view held by the ruling class or any other class for that matter can accurately represent social reality, but asserts that such views do not constitute ideology. Ideology is that set of beliefs that is a product of a particular social process of inversion, first in the realm of reality, and second in the realm of ideas. The production of ideology is an attempt to resolve in the realm of ideas contradictions that are unresolvable in the realm of social reality. Ideologies are therefore always an expression of fundamental and unresolvable contradictions, unresolvable, that is, short of a revolutionary dissolution of those contradictions. Religious ideas that God created humankind, for example, are an ideological inversion of the creation of gods by humans, and thus mystify inverted relations of subordination in which the primary producers are seen as dependent on the will of the surplus extractors, rather than the reality of the exploiters' complete dependence on the labor of the producers.

Ideologies are, then, always inverted reflections of what Marx saw as the "innermost secret, the hidden foundation of the entire social construction . . . the direct relation of the owners of the conditions of production to the direct producers."[4] It is not simply a matter of "false consciousness." Not all false ideas constitute ideology. Ideology is the product of a particular social and intellectual process that creates a double inversion, first in the realm of production, second in the realm of ideas. In Marx's early work it is the unbearable reality of exploitation that requires resolution in ideology. In his later work he sought the causes of this process of inversion in the workings of capitalism itself. The commodity form inverted the real relations of capitalists and workers by converting the unfreedom of the workers' subordination to capital to the freedom of the labor market. The sphere of exchange is "a very Eden of the innate rights of man. There alone, rule Freedom, Equality, Property and Bentham,"[5] and exchange relations conceal the unfreedom and inequality of capitalist property relations. In both the early and the late Marx, ideology inverts and conceals fundamental contradictions. In the early Marx the inversion is a result of the unbearable misery of the human experience under capitalism; in the later Marx it is a product of the workings of the capitalist system itself.

Marx's theory of ideology as mystification finds a parallel in the concept of "narrative," which is, in Hayden White's words, "not a neutral medium for the representation of events" but "the very stuff of a mythical view of reality."[6] Narratives, whether in literature or in real life, are stories that have a beginning, middle, and an end, a cast of characters, a set of events, and a sequence of action leading to a resolution of the problem with which the narrative began.[7] Most important for the analysis of ideology, narratives have an organizing principle which gives meaning, coherence, and moral purpose to the story, and which, according to White, is what distinguishes narrative from a simple chronological listing of events.[8] The organizing principle governs not only the unfolding of the story but also the selection of events and the evaluations of characters and their actions. Ideological mystification enters in the moral and evaluative selection and construction of sequences of events into a narrative or "story." As John Thompson observes, "stories are told which justify the exercise of power by those who possess it—situating them within tales that recount the past and anticipate the future."[9] The dominant narratives of a society are the narratives of its ruling class.

The concept of narrative was first developed in literary studies, where it has produced an immense philosophical and critical literature. It has been more recently applied to the social sciences.[10] There are significant differences between fictional narratives and the stories of everyday life. Most notably, the narrators are telling the story about themselves and their social group, and the story involves real events and real people. Such narratives, as Charlotte Linde observes, involve "moral comments about the way things are, the way things ought to be, and the kind of person the speaker is."[11] When the speaker is telling a story about a social group of which he or she is a member, the story may be called, according to George Steinmetz, a "social narrative." Steinmetz also observes that such stories may be told by more than one individual, producing a collective portrait of a group or "collective narrative".[12] It is such collective social narratives, told by members of the coffee elite about themselves, that are the central focus of this analysis.

It is also useful to distinguish between stories told about social groups by historians and others with specialized training, and those told by lay persons. Steinmetz calls lay social narratives "ethno-histories," to distinguish them from the formal accounts of trained historians (which may themselves have narrative properties).[13] Sometimes the latter are termed "expert narratives." Although the interviews focused on recent events, members of the coffee elites, singly and collectively, presented "ethno-histories" of their respective nations, sometimes beginning with the colonial period but more commonly with the rise of coffee in the nineteenth century, as a frame for the conversation. Ethno-histories and other collective social narratives, like all narratives, have an organizing evaluative principle that gives them meaning; it constitutes the basis for the group's "mythical view of reality," the narrative expression of its core ideological mystifications. It is what conceals the real contradictions of the group's social position. This notion of the evaluative or organizing principle is the narrative concept most useful in the study of ideology, because it converts real events into an ideologically mystified story.

It soon became evident in the research reported here that the Central American coffee elites had stories they wanted to tell the interviewer whether he wanted to hear them or not. In one way or another these stories were told whatever the specific questions asked. They were often told with considerable feeling and urgency and sometimes took on an almost confessional quality. They seemed to be told as much for the narrator's benefit as the interviewer's. The "fundamental contradictions" concealed by the ideological mystifications of narrative were being revealed with terrifying immediacy during the Central American civil wars. Elite narrative justifications of their own existence were being contradicted by daily experiences outside their doors. An extraordinary task of narrative construction and reconstruction was required to preserve the smooth surface of the ideological order. Often the task proved too demanding and the narrative (and the interview) threatened to break down into an unpleasant argument or worse. In retrospect, these breaks in the fabric of the narrative proved to be extremely revealing of the psychic and social contradictions the elite was struggling to contain. They were clues to the content of what Fredric Jameson has called the "political unconscious."[14]

Jameson's political unconscious is not a direct application of Freud's theory of the unconscious but is based on an analogy with Freud's account of psychological life. Here the contradictions that require repression and denial are not psychosexual impulses but the contradictions of history itself, and they are hidden not in neurotic symptoms but in narratives, which may be viewed as a kind of symptom of the underlying contradiction. For Jameson, a committed Marxist, these contradictions are the same as those of Marx—the relation of the primary producer to the extractors of surplus. The goal of critical analysis is to bring to the surface the repressed and buried reality of these fundamental contradictions of history. As William Dowling observes, "What Jameson gives us in short is an idea of History, intolerable to the collective mind, a mind that denies underlying conditions of exploitation and oppression much as the individual consciousness denies or shorts out the dark and primal instinctuality of the unconscious."[15] Narrative in Jameson's theory tells us the specific ways in which history is denied or repressed. It is a symptom of the work of political repression.[16]

Jameson's theory brings together Marx's idea of ideological mystification, the concept of narrative, and the original idea of the "political unconscious" into a single theory of the historical determinants of ideology. Jameson himself applied the idea to the analysis of literary texts, above all the novel. There is no reason in principle that it could not also be applied to collective social narratives like those produced by the Central American coffee elites. The problem then becomes not simply to claim that some hidden contradiction "explains" the narrative but to discover the specific ways in which the narrative denies or represses history.[17] Personal narratives like those that emerged in conversations with the coffee elites provide some clues to these specific processes not available to the analyst of literary texts. These are real people attempting to justify themselves to themselves as well as to the interviewer, and the emotional and interpersonal tensions created in that effort are plainly visible. Fundamentally, however, the process of interpretation requires a contrast between the evaluative principle involved in elite members' construction of their "ethno-histories" and the "underlying conditions of exploitation and oppression." The question of what the elite leaves out is as important therefore as what it puts in. Most important of all is the organizing principle that guides the selection.

El Salvador: Progress and Silence

Few better illustrations could be found of Walter Benjamin's dictum—"there has never been a document of culture which was not at the same time a document of barbarism"—than the history of El

Salvador. A determined effort, both official and unofficial, was made to repress the most profound contradiction of El Salvador's history by obliterating the evidence of the insurrection and massacre of 1932. All societies and their ruling elites construct historical fabrications, but few go to the length of removing all newspapers referring to an event from public libraries. This positively Orwellian construction of an official narrative of Salvadoran history was so successful that analysts refer to a "political culture of silence"—one that so thoroughly expunged all traces of the counter-narratives of the 1930s that the left virtually had to begin from scratch in the 1970s.[18] Before the 1970s successive military regimes were remarkably successful in fostering an official legend which, as Thomas Anderson described it, had "blood thirsty mobs butchering thousands of middle-class citizens, and of a heroic army that barely managed to turn back the barbarian wave."[19] It is in this context that the army's official slogan, "as long as the army lives, the country lives," evokes deep historical memories.

In the 1980s the ideological as well as the political order of the ancien regime began to crack under the strain of renewed revolution. Nevertheless, for some members of the elite interviewed in 1990, the old ideological order was still unproblematic. I was dumbfounded to discover that members of the hard-line agrarian fraction could discuss the mass murder of their political opponents in a matter-of-fact way that betrayed no embarrassment or emotional tension or apparently any knowledge of how such conduct was viewed in the rest of the world. The view of the hard-line agrarian fraction was a historical survival of the coffee elite's view, propounded in *El Café de El Salvador* in 1932, that the "serene severity" of the government had been necessary to counteract the "disorientation" in the minds of simple peasants. The official story of the old regime reversed the role of perpetrator and victim so that the massacres were not the murder of unarmed civilians at all but an act of self defense. The repression and isolation of El Salvador during the long night of military rule made it possible for elites to believe what most outsiders see as a bizarre historical reversal. In the 1980s some members of the hard-line agrarian fraction continued to believe the story. For other agrarians and for most of the agro-industrial fraction both the story and the structures it defended had begun to unravel.

The strain of this ideological change was evident in interviews, particularly with members of the agro-industrial fraction least comfortable with the ideology and policies of the old regime. It soon became evident that there were three areas of the interview that created the most tension and had to be approached with caution, if at all, by the interviewer. The first and by far the most sensitive issue was human rights *(derechos humanos)*. Even the use of the term itself was frequently met with suspicion, and it was almost inevitably dismissed as enemy propaganda or turned back on the interviewer ("What about the human rights of our soldiers?"). The FMLN was a second area of tension. It proved impossible to use the word "rebel" *(rebelde)* in the interviews without being corrected. The approved discourse was "subversive" *(subversivo)* or "terrorist" *(terrorista)*. Mention of the "structural reforms" demanded by the rebels (and to some extent by the revolutionary junta) also created tension. To raise the issue risked being bracketed with the Christian Democrats, or worse, the FMLN "subversives." There were other areas in the interviews, such as INCAFE coffee policies, about which the elite openly expressed outrage, but the issues of human rights, popular rebellion, and structural reform evoked a qualitatively different response. These touched on the contents of the political unconscious that were not part of acceptable discourse in politics or in interviews. Raising these issues interrupted the stories that the elite wished to tell about itself.

In El Salvador the evaluative organizing principle of the story, as we have seen, was the elite as the vanguard of progress through coffee-led agro-export development that would raise the standard of living of all Salvadorans, including particularly the "poorest of the poor" (as they are now called in government rhetoric). The agro-industrial elite's story of progress began with the arrival of the European immigrants who revolutionized coffee growing and raised tiny El Salvador to be a world leader in coffee. In the elite's view the rest of the economy, including urban industry, depended on agro-exports, as did government tax revenues, social services, consumer goods, and rural living standards. This part of the story was often defended with convincing arguments grounded in the political economy and economic history of El Salvador. This progress, which had brought El Salvador to the verge of industrial take-off, was interrupted by the corrupt statism of the Christian Democrats, who threatened to destroy the coffee economy and all of the nation's hopes for industrial progress. Fortunately, the Cristiani administration would return the coffee economy to the economic vanguard who had built it in the first place, allowing them to resume the march of progress.

The actual events and actors in Salvadoran history were arranged to fit the story of "progress," and evaluated positively or negatively according to whether they inhibited or advanced elite-directed agro-export development. Actors and events that did not "fit" were left out. The Christian Democrats, not the FMLN, are seen as the principal villains in this particular morality tale, a bit of casting which is also consistent with ARENA rhetoric in campaign rallies. Remarkably, the FMLN and the civil war are excluded from the narrative of Salvadoran history. They were foreign terrorists or subversives, not really Salvadoran at all. The army is also strangely absent, as are the poor as an active political force. Areas excluded from the narrative by its organizing principle of progress are, as might be expected, the areas of greatest tension in the interviews. Human rights violations, a popular insurrection, and the revolution's demand for changes in the structure of society do not fit into the narrative of progress or the concept of an elite acting for the good of society. Their very existence contradicts the elite vision of itself as the bearers of progress and development for *all* Salvadorans. Yet the organizing principle itself points to the specific historical contradictions that this principle is designed to contain.

What are these contradictions? The interviews point to two principal ones. First, the explosive issue of human rights brings up the agro-industrial elite's uncomfortable ties to the authoritarian agrarian order. Second, recognition of the FMLN as the representative of a legitimate popular rebellion and a serious discussion of the need for "structural reform" would call into question the structure of accumulation, the "underlying conditions of exploitation and oppression," on which the agro-export economy is built. To open a discussion of human rights would immediately open the "acts of barbarism" in 1932 and again in 1981–82 that were committed to maintain the agro-export order. To discuss the rebels or structural reform would raise the counter-narrative of the long-dead rebels of 1932 and the very lively rebels not far from the armed guards at the office door. It is they who raise most forcefully the economic contradictions at the heart of the agro-export order and threaten to carry out the real resolution of contradictions that find only mystified resolution in the elite narrative of progress. As long as the elite remains committed to both authoritarianism and the agro-export model these contradictions can only be resolved by the narrative denial of their existence. The hard-line agrarians repressed both contradictions. For the agro-industrial fraction the first contradiction had begun to be a subject for resolution in the real rather than the narrative world.

At the moment of the interviews the agro-industrial elite was beginning to try to resolve the contradiction of their support for the authoritarian order through negotiations with the FMLN. The November offensive had convinced many of them that the war was unwinnable. They were, therefore, in the process of cutting their ties to the military and the old order that, as the interviews indicate, they had never been enthusiastic about in the first place. Their new position was nonetheless fraught with contradictions, and to some extent it still is. The assassination of the Jesuits at the precise moment that the leader of the agro-industrial fraction, Alfredo Cristiani, was holding discussions with Ignacio Ellacuria and Segundo Montes underscored their contradictory position. It was, however, something the elite wanted to talk about, by way of distancing themselves from the event and the authoritarian order that it represented. To members of a party founded by the murderer of an archbishop this involved the painful work of making the political unconscious a subject of conscious political negotiation. It was clear in the interviews that the political leaders among the agro-industrial fraction had decided to sacrifice some of the worst commanders as the price of peace. This was eventually done, but the army as an institution remains. The move to democracy broke the authoritarian narrative as well as political order, but it only partly resolved the underlying contradiction.

Popular rebellion and structural reforms, however, raise even more fundamental issues for the elite narrative of progress. As any reasonably objective study of agro-export development in El Salvador will show, development of the agro-export economy has been accompanied by the dispossession and immiseration of much of the population.[20] Indeed, that is what caused the rebellions of both 1932 and 1979–1992. After one hundred and fifty years of trying, the agro-export economy has not created the comfortable working and middle classes of the developed world; instead, it has left many people no better off and possibly worse off than before. In El Salvador the story of coffee has been, for most of the population, not the "Gift of God" but the devil's curse. This of course is the story told by the rebels of 1932 and the 1980s. It cannot be admitted into the elite narrative without calling the elite's own existence into question. The elite firmly believes that a new democratic agro-industrial order organized along neo-liberal lines will permit it to dispense with the authoritarian past and resume the march of progress. Whether they are right is an empirical question, but early indications are not encouraging. If the agro-industrialists are wrong, then neo-liberalism will be what it appears to be—the latest version of a story told to put the issues of the rebels of 1932 and 1979–1992 back into the political unconscious.

Nicaragua: Liberty and the Contra

As was the case in El Salvador, the ruling historical narrative of Nicaragua was written by the victors of the conflict of the 1930s, and the legitimacy of the regime depended on denying its original complicity in murder. *El verdadero Sandino* (The True Sandino), which is to say an inversion of the true Sandino, written by Anastasio Somoza from documents purloined from his murdered followers, paints Sandino as a barbaric murderer and a thief motivated by lunacy, mysticism, and (like the rebels of El Salvador) the international Communist conspiracy. Anti-communism provided a convenient ideological justification for the Somoza dictatorship, even if it never became the article of religious faith it did in El Salvador. Somoza's justification for his primary act of barbarism is remarkably similar to that of the Salvadoran military: both claimed to have acted to save the nation from hordes of crazed Communist murderers from the lower orders. Somoza's myth never gained the currency of the Salvadoran story. His regime always seemed based on cynical political manipulation rather than ideology, especially to the many members of the elite excluded from the charmed circle of dynastic power. Sandino, however, was successfully banished from national discourse, along with the national humiliation by the United States that he fought against. In this respect the Somozas' ideological reconstruction succeeded.

The narrative of the agro-industrial fraction of the elite had been constructed in opposition to the Somozas, and later against the Sandinistas. If the organizing principle in the Salvadoran interviews was "progress," the organizing principle in the Nicaraguan interviews was "liberty": "freedom to buy and sell freely, political freedom, economic freedom." The elite narrative placed its members at the center of the struggle for liberty under Somoza and under the Sandinistas; both regimes emerge as villains in this drama. The contras and the contra war were largely absent from this narrative. As in El Salvador, neither the propertyless poor nor changes in the distribution of wealth and power appear in the narrative, although the failures of Sandinista state-centered accumulation strategies are a central element. Here the areas of tension in the interviews were precisely those areas excluded from the organizing principle of "liberty." The tension pointed to the same two fundamental contradictions as in El Salvador—the elite's relationship to authoritarian solutions, in this case the contra, and its dependence on the unequal authority structures of the agro-export economy, represented once again by the revolutionary party.

Perhaps the clearest example of the first of these two contradictions is the way the elite talked about the deaths of Jorge Salazar and Noel Rivera. Salazar was a martyr of the Coffee Growers Association of Matagalpa, its followers, and its allies in COSEP. His black-bordered picture was on the walls of their offices, a visible reminder, in their stories, of Sandinista betrayal of the elite struggle for political freedom. The inscription under his picture asserted

> We will not go to Miami;
> We will not give in.
> And if we go to the mountains,
> It will be to produce foreign exchange
> For the nation.

Yet despite the inspirational verse, Jorge Salazar had been killed plotting to go to the mountains to join the beginnings of the contra rebellion, not to plant coffee for export. No one interviewed mentioned this fact, although Salazar was mentioned frequently, always portrayed as a victim of Sandinista perfidy. Noel Rivera was mentioned by no one except his wife, Gladys Bolt, and his father-in-law, even though in the small world of Matagalpa coffee planters, and indeed in the country as a whole, this notorious murder was well known. Since he had been murdered by the contras, the deed did not fit the bourgeois narrative of a struggle for liberty from oppression. The contras, as the American president frequently stated, were "freedom fighters," not murderers.

Despite their professed commitment to liberty, the elite were backing an armed anti-democratic movement led by members of the former Nicaraguan National Guard and funded by the United States.[21] The politicals' enthusiastic embrace of the contra and of U.S. intervention underscored their previous support for the political structure of the protectorate and the Somoza regime based on the Nicaraguan National Guard. A virulent anti-communism was the ideological glue that held these contradictory images of "liberty" and National Guard repression together. This topic proved to be the most explosive issue in the interviews. The more outspoken politicals rejected any frame for the narrative which did not regard the Sandinistas as agents of an international Communist conspiracy. The premise of the interview itself, focused on questions of Sandinista agrarian policy, was rejected by many of the politicals. The real story, as one of them instructed, was the story of the efforts of the Soviet Union and Cuba to take over the hemisphere. Since the Sandinistas were "communists," they need not be extended political or human rights. Contra terror, unmentioned in the interviews, could be justified against "communists." In reality the contras' abysmal record of human rights violations exceeded by an order of magnitude anything done by the Sandinistas.[22]

The other emotional issue, as in El Salvador, was the question of the legitimacy of the revolutionary party in Nicaraguan society and government. The sensitivity of this issue was revealed in the very first interview, when the only reply to a question asking what the Sandinistas could do to improve the situation in coffee was, "Get out of the country." The perceived illegitimacy of the Sandinistas was clearly related to the issue of contra violence against "communists," since most of the politicals and even some of the technicals saw the Sandinistas as irredeemably tied to the Soviet Union or a Soviet-style regime. It also spoke to another issue: the Sandinistas' efforts to change the distribution of wealth and power in Nicaragua. As in El Salvador, the tensions surrounding the revolutionary party touched on a contradiction deeper even than the elite's ties to the authoritarian order now past—the underlying inequalities of the agro-export economy itself, of which they were the vanguard. The two fundamental structural contradictions of the agro-industrial fraction of the elite, their relationship to the authoritarian agrarian order and their relationship to the lower classes in the agro-export system, were the most explosive issues in Nicaragua as they had been in El Salvador. Contra tactics indicated the price some members of the elite were willing to pay to restore that system.

The Nicaraguans interviewed were divided over these ideas. The Communist conspiracy and the need for a United State invasion were the principal defining elements of the group called "politicals." The "technicals" were much more willing to consider working with the Sandinistas, much less given to anti-communist diatribes, much more ambivalent about the contra, and much more realistic in their perception of the Sandinistas. There was less tension in these interviews because there was less need to try to banish elements of reality into the political unconscious. The technicals would, and presumably have, come to terms with the Sandinistas as a force in Nicaraguan society, although they reject their policy of state-centered accumulation, which, in any case, seems to have ended up in the dustbin of history. As in El Salvador, a significant fraction of the elite had moved to cut its ties with the authoritarian order. Under the Sandinistas some did fall back toward the authoritarian solutions of the American protectorate and the Nicaraguan National Guard. Many, however, remained willing to give up on the old order entirely, a position that made the Sandinista-Chamorro coalition possible. This resolution, achieved in the realm of reality, made anti-communist rhetorical excesses unnecessary for the technical agro-industrial fraction. They, like the agro-industrialists of El Salvador, were moving toward the neo-liberal democratic model. The politicals remained tied to the authoritarian structures of the past.

The Salvadoran elite organized its story around progress, the Nicaraguans around liberty. Both initially supported authoritarian states to maintain order. Together they expressed the principles of the nineteenth century Liberals, "Peace [meaning order], Liberty, and Progress." The choice of each nation's elite to emphasize one part of the Liberal heritage (while sharing an ambivalence about "order") is significant. The principal contradiction in El Salvador had always been the glaring economic inequalities created in the name of progress for all by the success of the coffee agro-export economy. The central contradiction in Nicaragua, whose coffee economy never made much progress, had been the loss of political liberty caused by the United States intervention and the Somozas, and the rejection of Sandino and later the Sandinistas whose stated aim was to restore it. Each elite chose to emphasize elements of the Liberal agenda which not only reflected important historical realities of its nation, but also hid the principal contradiction on which its wealth was based. The Salvadoran elite narrative of progress hid the agrarian inequalities that were the central theme of the counter-narratives of the left. The Nicaraguan elite narrative of liberty justified the suppression of the counter-narrative of national liberation of Sandino and the Sandinistas. Elite narrative histories are created out of national historical contradictions that were not of the elite's own choosing. The narratives themselves, however, reconstruct that history in accord with a narrative principle that removes these specific historical contradictions to the realm of the political unconscious.

Costa Rica: Anti-Communism and the Myth of Rural Democracy

If "progress" was the organizing principle of the Salvadoran stories, and "liberty" of the Nicaraguan, then "democracy" was clearly the theme of the Costa Rican elite. The white legend of rural egalitarianism and democracy based on coffee was not only the organizing principle of elite interviews but a central element in the Costa Rican "national ideology" shared by coffee producers large and small and by much of the rest of the society. It is in many ways a much more effective myth than the organizing principles of either the Salvadoran or the Costa Rican stories. It was unchallenged in either discourse or politics in the 1980s and was related in the interviews with little of the tension and desperation that accompanied the Salvadoran and

Nicaraguan stories. The Costa Rican elite was happy and proud to explain its national ideology to a foreign visitor and confident that the social welfare reforms added to the original model by Calderón (and initially resisted by the elite) had insulated them from the conflagration raging elsewhere. Such was the strength and acceptance of the story of rural egalitarianism and democracy that the only sign of the tensions that revealed its narrative and ideological character was the particular intensity with which the story was habitually told.

The only area in which any interruption in the smooth flow of the narrative occurred was around the issue of communism. In the context of the peace and harmony advocated by all members of the elite, it was disconcerting to hear an otherwise progressive and peaceful processor say that "the only good Communist is a dead Communist." Almost all those interviewed reaffirmed anti-communism as the article of national faith that it in fact is. Some of the older people still remembered "comunismo criollo," but most considered communism to be a foreign and thoroughly un-Costa Rican implant that threatened the peace, tranquility, and democracy of the white legend. Although anti-communism had its origins in the 1930s, in the fears of small farmers of proletarianization and other changes associated with capitalism (which they blamed on Communists), it became a tenet of national faith during the conflicts of the civil war period. As John Patrick Bell observed, communism was *the* issue during the hostilities.[23] Communism became the negation of the Costa Rican national ideology and anti-communism, therefore, the negation of the negation and an essential element in that ideology. As in El Salvador and Nicaragua, the reigning national myth, in this case of peace, harmony, and democracy, was founded on an act of barbarism—the violent overthrow of Calderón, the deaths of 2,000 Costa Ricans, most of them government supporters, and the purge of Communists from Costa Rican life.

The myth of rural democracy had its origins in the sociable relations of production between small-holding coffee producers and the processing elite but, as Lowell Gudmundson has perceptively argued, was institutionalized as the national ideology by what he calls the "petty bourgeois" reformism of Figueres and Liberación.[24] An ideology that had its origins in elite paternalism became the ruling narrative of the progressive agro-industrial class-in-the-making that has come to dominate Costa Rica since 1948. It expresses the coalition between small coffee growers and progressive capitalists that (along with state employees) formed the core of the Liberación coalition after 1948. Even in 1948 it was a poor guide to Costa Rican class relations, since it left out the proletariat of the banana zones, the urban working class and the unemployed, the peons of Guanacaste, and the entire labor force of coffee pickers on which the economic system as well as the myth rested. Today it is an even less realistic portrait of Costa Rican class structure, even in the coffee economy that gave it birth. Liberación coffee policy has created a new class of capitalist small farmers allied with the new agro-industrial mega-processors, while at the same time it has impoverished and proletarianized many of the traditional peasant coffee farmers. The changes initiated by Liberación have accentuated the contradiction between processors and pickers that always was at the heart of the coffee order but was obscured by the prominence of peasant production in Costa Rica.

The groups left out of the myth of rural democracy in 1948, now joined by the urban informal sector, the growing semi-proletariat in coffee, and the workers in the new *maquila* industry, were and are the groups that the Communist counter-narrative always championed. The violent political suppression of the Communists erased these groups from both the elite and national narratives of democracy—an omission necessary to maintain both the political and ideological hegemony of the social democratic but capitalist reformers of 1948. As it happened in both El Salvador and Nicaragua, the revolutionary party and its narrative were relegated to the political unconscious. The repression has been much more successful in Costa Rica in part because the new Liberación agro-industrialists adopted the programs, but not the class analysis, of their opponents. Liberación (and the coffee elite) believe in *solidarismo,* not labor unions, particularly those led by Communists, and they have been very successful in keeping unions out of the private (although not the public) sector. They have also succeeded in keeping the growing number of groups that are exceptions to the myth of rural democracy out of the Costa Rican national ideology. Both anti-communism and the myth of rural democracy were enshrined as part of the national ideology by the victors of 1948.

Paradoxically, the success of Liberación in transforming the Costa Rican economy and creating a new agro-industrial elite, as well as a new class of capitalist small farmers, has only deepened the contradiction that the myth of rural democracy was constructed to conceal. The transformation of coffee has created an expanded rural semi-proletariat, and the expansion of capitalist ranching and the agriculture of change has driven people into the cities and increased the size of the semi-proletariat. Costa Rica's relatively generous welfare and housing policies have prevented these changes from undermining stability the way they did in Nicaragua and El Salvador, but these social policies are now threatened by the same neo-liberal policies the agro-industrial elite has adopted, in Costa Rica as elsewhere, as the new model for capitalist accumulation. In contrast to Nicaragua and El Salvador, in Costa Rica in 1990 no one in the coffee elite talked of authoritarian solutions to the country's problems. The inequalities of wealth and power and the immiseration of much of the population that is the other fundamental contradiction of the agro-export order, in either its traditional Liberal or neo-liberal variant, remain in Costa Rica as much as they do in El Salvador and Nicaragua.

Does Narrative Matter? Mystification and Class Relations

The narrative themes of progress, democracy, and liberty in El Salvador, Costa Rica, and Nicaragua, respectively, as well as the common theme of anti-communism, served to structure the elite's view of itself, its society, and its view of the crisis of the revolutionary decade. They determined what was said and what was not said in the interviews. But do the narratives themselves matter? Is there anything that the narratives and their ideological distortions add to our understanding of the transformation of Central American society that is not equally well or better rendered by close attention to the underlying transformations in class relations and politics? From the perspective of narrative theory the question itself runs the risk of posing a false choice between elite narrative and one of the flawed meta-narratives of the social sciences. The political economy of the transformation of class relations itself could be viewed as simply one version of such a meta-narrative rather than as an expression of the intractable realities of material life.[25] It has been the contention of this work, however, that in Central American history narrative matters, and it matters in particular because it is closely tied, both as cause and consequence, to the material realities of human experience in the agro-export economy. To resolve the tensions between narrative and political economy by subsuming either one into the other ignores one of the central dilemmas of contemporary social science — the relationship between the two.

The narratives of the Central American coffee elites are rooted in their class position and historical experience. The successful rationalization of the Salvadoran coffee industry is the historical basis of the Salvadoran elite's belief in progress, just as the sociable relations of production in Costa Rica are the basis for elite narrative themes of democracy and social harmony. The Nicaraguans' commitment to liberty reflects the dreams of the coffee elite from the Zelaya period through the Sandinistas, frustrated in historical fact as well as in ideology. Communists really did exist in Central America even if they were not so foreign or ferocious as they have become in elite memory. All the same, these views are ideological in the original sense intended by Marx. They mystify and deny unbearable social contradiction. There is no room in the Salvadoran story for the "black legend" of economic exploitation of agricultural labor; nor in the Costa Rican for people left out of the idealized rural democracy of the coffee districts of the central plateau; nor in the Nicaraguan for the poor denied a political voice by a limited notion of liberty. The narrative themes reflected material class relations at the same time they denied them.

It is also not the case that these narrative themes made little difference compared to the sea changes of underlying political economy and class relations. When I began my field work in Nicaragua, for example, I, like many others, was convinced that an economic crisis and Somoza's greed had affected producers' profits and thereby alienated them from the regime. I found to my surprise that coffee and cotton producers uniformly described their economic situation in the 1970s as excellent, and almost none reported any incidents of direct interference in their own businesses. I persisted in my questioning along this line until one grower in exasperation said, "The cotton growers opposed Somoza as *citizens*, not as cotton growers." He was right. The growers' commitment to *libertad,* the dominant theme in their narrative and the basic demand of Liberals since 1893, is a much better predictor of their behavior in the revolutionary decade and after than their material interest. They allied with Marxist-Leninist rebels against a system which, as Somoza himself sagely observed, "had enabled them to build up their fortunes." After the assassination of Chamorro, their sentiment was well expressed by the elite member who would rather live under communism than under Somoza. As Dennis Gilbert notes, if at the beginning of the Sandinistas' decade in power the agro-industrialists had not been committed to ideas of liberty and democracy because of their experience under the Somozas, they might well have ended up as fascist by its end.[26] They *were* so committed, however, and for the most part, despite their flirtation with the contra, remained so, greatly improving the chances for Nicaraguan democracy in the post-Sandinista period.

In Costa Rica too political economy provides an indispensable, but partial, view of events. Oscar Arias's behavior in the crisis of the 1980s was widely supported by the elite, as my interviews with his business partners and other members of the elite indicated. What economic interest caused him and other members of his class to jeopardize trade relations and economic aid in the midst of a debt crisis by embarking on a collision course with the United States through the Arias peace plan? Political economy provides a partial answer at best. The supreme importance of social peace and harmony in elite narrative and Costa Rican national ideology explains much more of Arias's behavior and its support by much of the elite and a majority of the electorate. Arias deserved his peace prize. He believed in peace, leading agro-industrialist though he was. Even in El Salvador, where political economy imposed the cruelest choices, the ideas of the elite made a difference. To my considerable surprise, what the elite told me in interviews in 1987 and 1990, opinions that represented a shift toward democratic themes not present in the traditional Salvadoran elite narrative of progress, proved an accurate prediction of what they would do in 1992 at the bargaining table.

Perhaps this is to say little more than what Max Weber said long ago—that " 'world images' that have been created by 'ideas' have, like switchmen, determined the tracks along which action has been pushed by the dynamic of interest."[27] But Weber also denied vigorously that he intended "to substitute for a one-sided materialistic an equally one-sided spiritualistic interpretation of culture and history."[28] Avoiding such one-sidedness is the peculiar power of Jameson's theory. It makes narrative ideological representations its central focus, without losing sight of their grounding in material human experience. It is precisely the narrative ordering of events by the elite that embodies the ideological distortion of history which relegates the barbarism of the Central American past to the political unconscious. No amount of narrative reconstruction can, however, erase history and raise the dead of 1932 from their mass graves or restore the Jesuits to life. The real history of Central America was written by the lives, and with tragic frequency the violent deaths, of real human beings. It is lived human experience, not narrative, that defines history. Only the contrast between this history and narrative reveals the ideological distortions of the latter.

In Central America it is the contrast between the lived experience of the majority of the population and the stories told about these experiences by the coffee elite that reveal the denials and distortions of those stories. Without the weight of past historical scholarship on Central American political economy it would be impossible to make this contrast and evaluate the elite narrative, not just the stories but what is left out of them. The omissions, as Jameson's theory would suggest, are the contradictions of the agro-export order. This is as true of the newly emerging narratives of neo-liberalism as it was of the traditional Liberal order of nineteenth-century Central America, out of which the elite narratives reported here were constructed. Ultimately, then, both ideologies are tied to the contradictions of underlying class relations and can be transformed only when those relations are transformed. This is what happened during the revolutionary decade that led Central America from authoritarianism and liberalism to democracy and neo-liberalism.

Revolution, Democracy, and Neo-Liberalism

In the 1980s Central America found a new route to the transition to democracy—through socialist revolution from below. Just as Barrington Moore had argued, breaking the power of the lords of the land was necessary for the triumph of democracy. Contrary to Moore, however, the agro-industrial bourgeoisie could not carry out this task itself. They and the landlords were two fractions of the same elite. The actions of the armed left were necessary to fracture the alliance and break the power of the landlords. Even then the agro-industrial bourgeoisie proved ambivalent about the full incorporation of the lower classes. It was the armed left that fought for the full extension of the democratic franchise. Although the socialist revolutionaries destroyed the old order and opened the way for democracy, the ironic outcome of their efforts was the triumph of the agro-industrial bourgeoisie and neo-liberalism. Nevertheless the revolutionaries succeeded in removing one of the two principal contradictions that the Central American agro-export order had inherited from the 1930s — the ties between the agro-industrialists and the authoritarian agrarians. The defeat of the left insured that the other fundamental contradiction — between the elite and the semi-proletariat created by the expansion of the agro-export economy — remained.

The essence of Jameson's theory of the political unconscious, like Marx's theory of ideological mystification, is that resolutions in the narrative order depend on resolutions of real contradictions in the social order. The fracture of the agro-industrial-agrarian alliance removed that particular contradiction and, therefore, the need for its ideological mystification. Anti-communism had been the most important ideological element concealing the brutality of the agrarian authoritarian order. As in the United States during the McCarthy era, the anti-communism of the Central American coffee elites had nothing to do with a putative international Communist conspiracy. Instead it was an ideological inversion of what the elite had done to their "communists" in 1932, 1934, and 1948 and was trying to do, once again, at the beginning of the 1980s. Anti-communism made it possible for the elite to both justify and deny the crimes of the old order. The transition to democracy through revolution destroyed that order, thereby eliminating the need for its mystifications in anti-communist ideology. Conveniently, the Communist menace itself disappeared at almost precisely the same moment. Fortunately, since communism no longer existed, it was no longer necessary to invent it.

The failure of the socialist revolution, however, left the second contradiction, between the agro-export elite and the poor, unresolved. This contradiction was the deeper of the two, since the authoritarian order had come into being in the first place to suppress its expression in the revolutionary movements of the 1930s. Elite narratives of progress, liberty, and democracy concealed this contradiction in ways that inverted the actual historical experience of each society. In El Salvador "progress" for the coffee elite meant immiseration for the proletarianized rural population; in Costa Rica the myth of a rural "democracy" of small property owners concealed the propertyless majority created by agro-industry; in Nicaragua "liberty" hid those whose liberty had been denied to create the wealth of the agro-industrialists. The organizing principle of each story contains the denial of the same contradiction—the dependence of all three elites on an unskilled labor force of coffee pickers and the progressive displacement of much of the rural population into the informal and semi-proletarian sectors by agro-export agriculture. This contradiction was the cause of the revolutions of both the 1930s and the 1980s. It was also the principal theme of the left, now rhetorically consigned to oblivion by the triumphant agro-industrial elite.

Neo-liberalism is the dominant ideology of the agro-industrial elite. The old liberalism of authoritarian state intervention has been replaced by the new liberalism of democratic deregulation. Anti-communism, rendered superfluous by the destruction of the authoritarian order it sustained, has been replaced by the end of communism. The narrative currents of "progress," "liberty," and "democracy" flowed together into the neo-liberal orthodoxy of economic progress through democracy and free markets. So far, however, neo-liberal economic strategy has had no more success in stimulating real economic progress in Central America than it is having in the former Soviet Union. The wealthy elite still faces a poverty-stricken population, many now outside the labor market altogether. To the degree that neo-liberal policies are taken seriously and the remaining state industries and state protections for the poor are eliminated, the contradiction can only deepen. If present economic trends in Central America continue, the neo-liberal vision will reveal itself to be simply the latest effort to construct a narrative that, like Central Amer-

ican Liberalism and anti-communism before it, banishes oppositional ideologies to the political unconscious and conceals the fact
that in Central America (and elsewhere) the unrestricted workings
of capitalism are, once again, creating unprecedented wealth for the
few at the expense of the general impoverishment of the many.

Appendix A

Marriages and Descendents of Children
of James Hill and Dolores Bernal Nájera

Children
Grandchildren Great Grandchildren Great Great Grandchildren

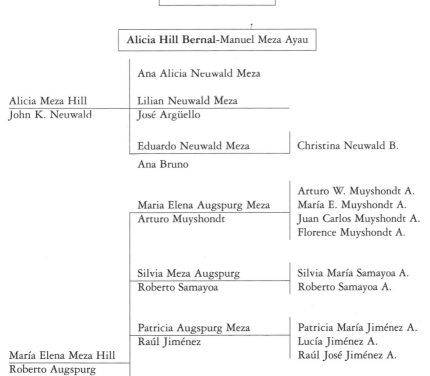

Roberto Hill Bernal		
No descendents		

Alicia Hill Bernal-Manuel Meza Ayau

	Ana Alicia Neuwald Meza	
Alicia Meza Hill	Lilian Neuwald Meza	
John K. Neuwald	José Argüello	
	Eduardo Neuwald Meza	Christina Neuwald B.
	Ana Bruno	
	Maria Elena Augspurg Meza	Arturo W. Muyshondt A.
	Arturo Muyshondt	María E. Muyshondt A.
		Juan Carlos Muyshondt A.
		Florence Muyshondt A.
	Silvia Meza Augspurg	Silvia María Samayoa A.
	Roberto Samayoa	Roberto Samayoa A.
	Patricia Augspurg Meza	Patricia María Jiménez A.
	Raúl Jiménez	Lucía Jiménez A.
María Elena Meza Hill		Raúl José Jiménez A.
Roberto Augspurg		

Marcia Alicia Augspurg Meza Jaime Escalón	Carolina Escalón A. Jaime Roberto Escalón A. Gerardo Escalón A.	
Eleonora Augspurg Meza Gabriel Llort	Marcos Llort A. Eleonora Llort A. Diego Llort A. Cristina Llort A.	

Roberto Manuel Augspurg M.

Ricardo Augspurg Meza

María Eugenia Palomo Meza Ricardo Sugrera	Ricardo Andrés Sugrera P. Arturo Sugrera P. Marco Sugrera P.
Jaime Roberto Palomo Meza Debbie Linka	Jaime Roberto Palomo L. Cristina Palomo L. Francesca Palomo L.

Loly Meza Hill
Roberto Palomo

Lolita Palomo Meza Jorge Girón	Gabriela Girón P.
Lorena Palomo Meza Roberto Celasco	Gerardo Celasco P. Sergio Celasco P.
Carmen Elena Palomo Meza David Mohlman	Katherine Mohlman P.

Patricia Meza Tinoco Federico Bustamante	Carolina Bustamante M. Javier Bustamante M.
Irma Alicia Meza Tinoco Guillermo Rivera	Francesca Rivera M. Adriana Rivera M.

Arturo Meza Hill
Anabel Tinoco G.

Anabel Meza Tinoco
Guillermo Kruseman

Claudi Elena Meza Tinoco

Manuel Antonia Meza Tinoco

María Hill Bernal-Francisco Llach

Eduardo Llach Hill
Nancy Cady

Eduardo Llach Cady   Lydia Llach S.
Elizabeth Schwartz

Deborah Llach Cady   Alvaro Valdés Ll.
Alvaro Valdés   Roberto Arturo Valdés Ll.

María Eugenia Llach Cady
James Shipman
Cecilia Llach Cady
Miguel Llach Cady

Roberto Llach Hill
Leonor Guirola

Roberto Llach Guirola
Alexa Llach Guirola
Marcos Llach Guirola
Diego Llach Guirola

Jaime Hill Bernal-Berta Argüello Escalón

Jaime Hill Argüello
Roxana Tinoco G.

Cynthia Guirola

Alexandra Hill Tinoco
Roxana Hill Tinoco
Jaime Hill Tinoco
Eduardo Hill Tinoco
Julia Adriana Hill Guirola

Florence Hill Argüello
Roberto Mathies
   Regalado

Florence María Mathies Hill
Roberto Mathies Hill

Ana Carolina Mathies Hill   Carolina María Alvarez M.
Luis R. Alvarez
Claudia Mathies Hill
Ernesto Mathies Hill

Harold Hill Argüello | Alberto Hill Dutriz
Johanna Dutriz | Johanna Hill Dutriz
| Juan Marcos Hill Dutriz

Ricardo Hill Argüello | Patricia Hill Call.
María Eugenia Call. | Alexa María Call.

Eduardo Hill Bernal

No descendents

Federico Hill Bernal-Emma Valiente Rivas

	Ana Mercedes Avila Hill	Ana Haydeé Méndez A.
	Marcos Méndez	
		Francisco José Mendieta A.
	María Fermina Avila Hill	Rodrigo Alfonso Mendieta A.
Haydeé Hill Valiente	Francisco Mendieta	Diego Mendieta A.
Francisco Avila Meardi		
	María Dolores Avila Hill	Héctor Federico Chacón A.
	Héctor Federico Chacón	Ricardo Francisco Chacón A.
	José Federico Avila Hill	

	Roberto Manuel Hill Llanos	
	Ana Julia Hill Llanos	
	Edgar Puente	
Robert Hill Valiente		
Ana Julia Llanos	María Raquel Hill Llanos	Andrés Roberto Puente H.
	Alvaro Puente	Juan Marco Puente H.
	Bertha Haydeé Hill Llanos	

	Dolores Haydeé Hill S.	
	Federico Santiago Hill S.	Federico Alejandro Hill V.
	Ana Ruth Valdés	

| Frederico Hill Valiente
Regina Esther
  Schonenberg | Regina Eugenia Hill S.
Rafael Trigueros Hecht | Ana Regina Trigueros H.
Alejandra Eugenia Trigueros H.
Juan Rafael Trigueros H.
Camelia Teresa Trigueros H. |
| | María Teresa Hill S.
Federico Batlle Castillo | Johanna Michelle Batlle H.
Dallana Elizabeth Batlle H.
Virginia Regina Batlle H. |

María Eugenia Hill Valiente

Ana Dolores Hill Bernal-Mario Tierello

| Ana Dolores Hill Bernal
Mario Tierello | Mario Ernesto Tierello Hill
María Eugenia Duke | Juan Antonio Tierello D. |

Manuel Hill Bernal

No descendents

Julia Hill Bernal-Terence O'Sullivan

| Ellen O'Sullivan Hill
Ernesto Regalado
  Dueñas (+) | Ernesto Regalado O'Sullivan
Arturo Regalado O'Sullivan |
| Philip Danby | |

Source: Familia Hill B., *James Hill* (San Salvador: Privately published for the Hill B. Family by Editorial Delgado, 1988).

Appendix B

Selection of the Interview Population

The plan of the study called for interviews with members of leading coffee dynasties who were managing the family's principal coffee firm; when this was not possible, other family members were substituted. Most of those interviewed were active executives or estate owners. In order to represent the dominant elite fractions, the original plan of the study called for interviewing members of dynastic families controlling the 20 leading processing firms in Costa Rica, the 20 leading private producers in Nicaragua, and the 15 leading processors and the 15 leading producers in El Salvador. Only in Costa Rica, where excellent record keeping by the Office of Coffee and the absence of acute class polarization in the society made both identification of and access to members of the elite relatively straightforward, could this plan be followed completely.

In El Salvador, then at the height of the civil war, interviews could only be obtained by personal introductions by other elite members known and trusted by the interviewee. Members of the elite in high governmental and cultural positions were helpful in arranging such interviews, so the population frame was redefined to include individuals in leadership positions in the principal coffee organizations. In Nicaragua personal introductions were also often indispensable, and the absence of good records made identification of leading producers difficult. The same strategy of contacts through official organizations was pursued in Nicaragua. Despite these difficulties, comparison of the economic positions of the people interviewed with statistical information on the coffee elite as a whole and with the characteristics of the sectors represented by each organization made it possible to determine which components of the elite were in fact represented in the interviews.

Interviews usually took place in the executive's office, either in town or at the mill or farm, and averaged one hour and fifty minutes each. With the exception of public figures who did not request anonymity, such as President Cristiani, all of those interviewed were promised anonymity. In most cases, particularly in El Salvador and Nicaragua, the interviews could not have been conducted without such a guarantee. Most interviews were conducted in Spanish, but the interviewer responded in English or Spanish depending on the preferences of the interviewee. Recording was out of the question under wartime conditions in El Salvador and Nicaragua, and to insure comparability interviews were not recorded in Costa Rica either. The author was able to take notes, however, and interviews were transcribed, in English, from these notes immediately after the interview. Every effort was made to capture the exact words of those interviewed, but something has no doubt been lost in translation or in memory. Quotations in the text are from these transcriptions. The exact procedures in the selection of those to be interviewed are briefly described below for each country.

El Salvador

All those interviewed were contacted through personal introductions from individuals well known to them. Efforts were made to contact coffee elite members who were either (a) officers or recent past officers of the principal coffee organizations, including both ABECAFE and ASCAFE, or (b) executives or proprietors of leading processors and exporters ranked by coffee volume. Some of those interviewed, of course, fell in both categories. I had a number of additional interviews and informal conversations with persons in government and private life knowledgeable about the industry, some of whom were also from elite families but not officers of associations or executives of leading firms. They are therefore not included in the analysis of interview data except for background information. Statements by members of the coffee elite in the Salvadoran press were reviewed in INCAFE's "Recortes de Periódicos" collection for the period 1979– 1989. The collection attempts to include all articles on coffee in all leading San Salvador daily newspapers. Four of the interviews were conducted in July 1987 and the remainder in February, March, and April 1990. Five ABECAFE members (three of them associated with one firm) and one leader of the dissenting faction of ASCAFE declined to be interviewed. Two more ABECAFE members whose offices were contacted were out of the country at the time of the interviews.

Costa Rica

The list of leading firms was derived from a list developed by Gertrude Peters Solórzano for her exhaustive study of the recent history of large Costa Rican processors ("Formación y desarrollo del grupo cafetalero en la communidad empresarial costarricense: historia de las empresas cafetaleras en Costa Rica, 1950–1982," (Escuela de Historia, Universidad Nacional, Heredia, Costa Rica, 1984), and her "Historia reciente de las grandes empresas cafetaleras 1950–1980," pp. 241–263 in *Historia, problemas y perspectivas agrarias en Costa Rica,* special number of *Revista de Historia* (Heredia, Costa Rica: Universidad Nacional, 1985). Peters included all processing plants that, on average, processed more than 20,000 *quintales* (1 *quintal* = 100 lbs.) of coffee annually in the period 1950–1980 ("Historia reciente," p. 245). There was a total of 34 plants on Peters's list, but some were controlled by the same family groups. The population for the present study was defined by determining the ownership of each plant through the registry maintained at the Institute of Coffee and combining plants controlled by a single firm into a single processing enterprise. This procedure yielded a total of 22 owners of the 34 processing plants. In two cases owners of two or more processing plants had the same surname (the Montealegres with three firms and the Bolmarciches with two). Under the assumption (which proved to be erroneous) that all these firms were operated as a unit by the respective families, the firm with the largest production in each family group was selected for the study population. The result was a list of twenty firms representing the twenty largest processors in the period 1950–1980.

In each case efforts were made to interview the current president of the firm; in two cases the president was unavailable so the vice president was interviewed instead (both of these officers were involved in day-to-day management). In almost all cases the president was also the principal shareholder or partner in the firm. Interviews revealed that the firms controlled by members of the Montealegre and Bolmarcich families were in fact independent and even competitive units. One additional firm controlled by a Montealegre was therefore included in the population. Two firms had been sold to multinational firms since Peters's study, and each case both the present and former owners were interviewed. One firm had gone out of the processing business, and another was reorganizing under bankruptcy protection. In both cases the immediate past president was interviewed. The executive of one firm (one of the two largest, unfortunately) failed to respond to repeated requests for an interview, and a second executive was out of Costa Rica at the time of the interviews. The president of the exporters' association, who had worked for a number of processing firms, was also interviewed. The total number interviewed was therefore 22 individuals representing 18 of the twenty leading firms in the period 1950–1980. Except for changes in ownership in two cases, the one bankruptcy, and the one departure from the industry, all of these firms were still the leading private processing firms in 1990. All of the top ten firms and most of the top twenty in 1990 were included in a list derived from the twenty leading firms of the 1950–1980 period. All of the interviews took place between May and August 1990.

Use of Peters's list made it possible to take advantage of the extensive historical and documentary research she had already conducted on the firms included in the interview population. (She had also interviewed some executives herself but did not focus on their social and political views.) The author is deeply grateful for the gracious and generous assistance of Gertrude Peters Solórzano, who provided much useful background information and also kindly made available unpublished manuscripts and primary data from her study. Her researches provide the framework for the present study. Unless otherwise noted, however, all the interview material reported here was my own.

Nicaragua

The list of producers was constructed by first interviewing officers and former officers of the major national and regional producers' organizations in coffee and cotton who were themselves large producers (six producers). Both private and generally anti-governmental producers' organizations and the formally independent but generally pro-government National Union of Farmers and Ranchers (UNAG) were included. These officers as well as staff members of the organizations were then asked to recommend others with whom the author could speak (nine producers). This network was supplemented by names selected randomly from a list of registered cotton growers and from a list of large private coffee producers prepared by the National Development Bank (and kindly provided by David Dye). Finally, two producers, who were also officers of a regional private growers' association, were contacted through the recommendation of the Ministry of Agricultural Development and Agrarian Reform (MI-DINRA), bringing the total number of officers and former officers to eight and the total number interviewed to 23. Five of the growers (including two officers) belonged to UNAG, one was a member of both UNAG and a private growers' association, one refused to join any organization, and all of the others were affiliated with private producers' associations. Officers and members of both UNAG and private producers' associations indicated that almost all large growers were affiliated with private associations and only a handful with UNAG. Only large growers were interviewed. A large grower was defined as a coffee grower who was producing or had produced in the recent past 1,500 *quintales* a year, or a cotton grower with 300 *manzanas* (1 *manzana* = .69 ha.) or more registered in the 1983–84 crop year. One cotton grower was included even though he planted only 150 *manzanas* because he was a national representative of UNAG. All of the interviews were conducted in July and August of 1986.

Notes

Introduction

1. Although the revolutionary challenge in Guatemala was defeated in 1982, the civil war there continues as it has for more than thirty years.

2. James Dunkerly in *The Pacification of Central America* (London: Verso, 1994), p. 3, gives an estimate, which he calls conservative, of 160,000 dead. John Booth and Thomas Walker in *Understanding Central America* (Boulder: Westview, 1989), p. 2, estimate 200,000 dead. Both give the same figure of two million refugees.

3. Enrique G. Dubón, "La concentración de la actividad económica en la agroindustria del café," Documento de Trabajo, *Boletín de Ciencias Económicas y Sociales*, no. 8 (San Salvador: Universidad Centroamericana José Simeón Cañas, August 24, 1982), app. 2 (no pagination).

4. Oscar Arias Sánchez is the son of Juan R. Arias Trejos, through whom he traces his ancestry to Vázquez de Coronado, and Lilliam Sánchez Cortés, the daughter of Julio Sánchez Lépiz. See Samuel Z. Stone, *The Heritage of the Conquistadors: Ruling Classes in Central America from Conquest to the Sandinistas* (Lincoln, Nebraska: University of Nebraska Press, 1990), p. 168; and Ana Virginia Arguedas Chaverri and Marta Ramírez, "Contribución al análisis de empresas: el caso de Julio Sánchez Lépiz (1862–1934)" (Tesis de Licenciatura, Universidad Nacional, Heredia, Costa Rica, 1985), p. 422.

5. Author's interview with a leading coffee processor, San José, Costa Rica, July 19, 1990.

6. Carlos M. Vilas, "Family Affairs: Class, Lineage and Politics in Contemporary Nicaragua," *Journal of Latin American Studies* 24 (May 1992):309–341.

7. Ibid.

8. Barrington Moore, Jr., *Social Origins of Dictatorship and Democracy: Lord and Peasant in the Making of the Modern World* (Boston: Beacon, 1966).

9. Gudmundson's observation is in "Central American Agrarian History and the Barrington Moore Thesis," unpublished paper, University of Oklahoma, n.d. p. 1. The starting point for any comparative analysis of the coffee elite in Central

America is Ciro Flamarion Santana Cardoso's essay, "Historia económica del café en Centroamérica (siglo XIX): estudio comparativo," *Estudios Sociales Centroamericanos* (enero-abril 1975):9–55. Themes developed in this work are also elaborated in Cardoso and Héctor Pérez Brignoli's *Centro América y la economía occidental (1520–1930)* (San José: Editorial de la Universidad de Costa Rica, 1977). The comparative works of Central American sociologist Edelberto Torres-Rivas include "Síntesis histórica del proceso político," in *Centroamérica hoy,* ed. Edelberto Torres-Rivas, et al. (Mexico, D.F.: Siglo Veintiuno, 1975), pp. 9–118; *Crisis del poder en Centroamérica* (San José: Editorial Universitaria Centroamericana, 1981); (with Jan L. Flora) "Sociology of Developing Societies: Historical Bases of Insurgency in Central America," in *Central America: Sociology of Developing Societies,* ed. Jan L. Flora and Edelberto Torres-Rivas (New York: Monthly Review, 1989), pp. 32–55. More recently North American sociologist Robert G. Williams has built on this tradition in his *States and Social Evolution: Coffee and the Rise of National Governments in Central America* (Chapel Hill: University of North Carolina Press, 1994). Anthony Winson implicitly applies the Moore model to the case of Costa Rica in his *Coffee and Democracy in Modern Costa Rica* (New York: St. Martin's Press, 1989). Enrique Baloyra applies it explicitly to Central America as a whole with particular emphasis on El Salvador and Nicaragua in "Reactionary Despotism in Central America," *Journal of Latin American Studies* 15 (Nov. 1983):295–319. John Weeks, "An Interpretation of the Central American Crisis," *Latin American Research Review* 21, no. 3 (1986):31–53 makes a parallel argument drawing heavily on Baloyra. Deborah Yashar also uses Moore's framework in her comparative study of Guatemala and Costa Rica, "Demanding Democracy: Reform and Reaction in Costa Rica and Guatemala" (Ph.D. diss., University of California, Berkeley, 1992). Gudmundson explicitly and correctly includes me in the list of authors influenced by Moore. He cites my earlier works, *Agrarian Revolution* (New York: Free Press, 1975) and "Social Theory and Peasant Revolution in Vietnam and Guatemala," *Theory and Society* 12 (Nov. 1983):699–737.

1. Revolution and the Coffee Elite

1. Ciro Flamarion Santana Cardoso, "Historia económica del café en Centroamérica (siglo XIX): estudio comparativo," *Estudios Sociales Centroamericanos* 4 (enero-abril 1975):15.

2. Samuel Stone, *La dinastía de los conquistadores,* 3rd ed. (San José: Editorial Universitaria Centroamericana, 1982), p. 191.

3. Carolyn Hall, *El café y el desarrollo histórico-geográfico de Costa Rica*, 3rd ed. (San José: Editorial Costa Rica, 1982), p. 53.

4. Rafael Menjívar, *Acumulación y desarrollo del capitalismo en El Salvador* (San

José: Editorial Universitaria Centroamericana, 1980), p. 130; Dubón, "Agroindustria del café," Anexo II.

5. Michael J. Schroeder, " 'To Defend Our Nation's Honor': Toward a Social and Cultural History of the Sandino Rebellion in Nicaragua, 1927–1934" (Ph.D. diss., University of Michigan, 1993), pp. 108–109.

6. Hall, *El café*, p. 45; Stone, *Dinastía*, p. 100–102; Ciska Raventos, "La burguesía cafetalera," *Trabajo* 2 (1987):8.

7. Eugenio Herrera Balhary, *Los alemanes y el estado cafetalero* (San José: Editorial Universidad Estatal a Distancia, 1988), pp. 165–166, 155–158, and author's interview with a leading coffee processor, San José, July 19, 1990.

8. Hall, *El café*, p. 53; Arguedas Chaverri and Ramírez, "Julio Sánchez Lépiz," pp. 367, 422; Oficina del Café, *Registro de Beneficiadores*, circular no. 577, 19 Dec. 1975, p. 4, and circular no. 244, 22 Dec. 1989, p. 9.

9. According to Mayra Achio and Ana C. Escalante in *Azúcar y política en Costa Rica* (San José: Editorial Costa Rica, 1985), p. 130, the major sugar mill, Taboga, is controlled by Rodrigo Arias Sánchez, Oscar's brother, as well as several other leading Liberacionistas. Raúl López lists the Sánchez Cortés as one of the leading families in the cattle industry ("Sobre la fracción ganadera de las clases dominantes," *Trabajo* 2 (1987):17.

10. On El Salvador see Eduardo Colindres, "La tenencia de la tierra en El Salvador," *Estudios Centroamericanos* 31, nos. 335/336 (Sept.-Oct. 1976):471 for a list of the leading coffee producers and exporters in 1970–71. All are descendents of immigrants or distinguished republican or colonial families. In Nicaragua no such definitive listing is available, but studies by Rosario Sanabria ("The Rise of Coffee Production in Nicaragua: Social Composition of Plantation Owners as of 1910," Ann Arbor: Department of Sociology, University of Michigan, May 1988) and Michael Schroeder for Matagalpa-Jinotega ca. 1930 ("Our Nation's Honor," pp. 108–109) indicate that the elite is overwhelmingly of either aristocratic or foreign origins. In my own interviews in Nicaragua in 1986 only one of the 17 leading coffee growers I contacted was from indisputably plebeian origins.

11. Colindres, "Tenencia de la tierra," pp. 471–472, 469.

12. James Dunkerly, *The Long War: Dictatorship and Revolution in El Salvador* (London: Verso, 1983), p. 53. Robert T. Aubey, "Entrepreneurial Formation in El Salvador," *Explorations in Entrepreneurial History*, 2nd ser., 6 (1968–69):273.

13. Dunkerly, *Long War*, pp. 54, 127; Paul Heath Hoefel, "The Eclipse of the Oligarchs," *New York Times Magazine*, 6 September 1981, p. 23.

14. Details on the career of Herbert de Sola are from R. Macarezi, *Don Herbert de Sola (ensayo biográfico)* (El Salvador: Tipografía Ungo, 1966). Dunkerly, *Long War*, p. 141 refers to the de Solas as part of the aperturista sector of the landed bourgeoisie. Orlando de Sola's views are discussed at length in Chapter 6. The one member of the de Sola family who consented to be interviewed for this study was among the most progressive of those interviewed in any family group.

15. Details on the life of James Hill are from *James Hill* (San Salvador: privately published by Editorial Delgado in 1988 for the Hill-Bernal family). Coffee processing ranks are from the appendix to Dubón, "Agroindustria del café." The family's economic interests are listed in Aubey, "Entrepreneurial Formation," p. 276, and in Eduardo Colindres, *Fundamentos económicos de la burguesía Salvadoreña* (San Salvador: Universidad Centroamericana, José Simeón Cañas Editores, 1977), pp. 201, 219, 248–249.

16. Author's interviews, Matagalpa, Nicaragua, August 3, and August 17, 1986. Information on John (Juan) Bolt's estate in 1930 is from Schroeder, "Our Nation's Honor," p. 109, who incorrectly lists him as a German planter.

17. The 1910 estate size is from Sanabria (based on 1910 census), "Rise of Coffee Production," p. 47; 1930 from Schroeder, ibid.

18. Author's interview, Matagalpa, August 12, 1986.

19. Ibid. For accounts of the Christmas party raid see John Booth, *The End and the Beginning: The Nicaraguan Revolution,* 2nd ed. (Boulder: Westview Press, 1985), p. 142 and George Black, *Triumph of the People: The Sandinista Revolution in Nicaragua* (London: Zed, 1981), pp. 86–87.

20. Author's interviews, Matagalpa, Nicaragua, August 3 and 17, 1986. Reed Brody, *Contra Terror in Nicaragua: Report of a Fact Finding Mission, September 1984– January 1985* (Boston: South End Press, 1985), p. 178.

21. In one notorious case members of the elite were kidnapped by a ring of army officers closely linked to elite member and death-squad organizer, Héctor Antonio Regalado. See Tommie Sue Montgomery, *Revolution in El Salvador: From Civil Strife to Civil Peace,* 2nd ed. (Boulder: Westview, 1992), p. 205. Two of Orlando de Sola's associates were machine-gunned to death in attacks for which the FMLN denied responsibility. The murders were probably related to internal struggles within ARENA and the coffee elite (see Chapter 6).

22. See Chapter 9.

23. Luis Sebastián, "El camino económico hacia la democracia," *Estudios Centroamericanos* 35, nos. 372/373 (oct.-nov. 1979):950; Colindres, "Tenencia de la tierra," p. 471.

24. Aubey, "Entrepreneurial Formation," and Colindres, *Fundamentos económicos,* pp. 101–104.

25. Data on processing ranks for 1980–81 are from Dubón, "Agroindustria del café"; for 1970–71 from Colindres, "Tenencia de la tierra," p. 471.

26. Lopéz, "Fracción ganadera," p. 17. Author's interview, San José, July 18, 1990.

27. See app. 2, pp. 165–193, of Francisco Esquivel's *El desarrollo del capital en la industria de Costa Rica, 1950–1970* (Heredia, Costa Rica: Editorial de la Universidad Nacional, 1985).

28. Stone, *Dinastía de los conquistadores.*

29. Stone, *Heritage of the Conquistadors,* pp. 111–112.

30. Author's interviews, San José, July 18, July 19, 1990.

31. José María is the son of Figueres *père's* first wife, Henrietta Boggs, a North American. Dynastic expectations are, however, well established in Costa Rican politics. When José María's stepmother (also a North American) Karen Cristina Figueres was reading the first scriptural passage at funeral services for Don Pepe in June 1990 and her voice broke slightly, her stepson stepped forward to finish the reading. According to the *Tico Times* several voices in the crowd whispered, "There's the next president." They were right (*Tico Times,* 15 June 1990 p. 15).

32. Vilas, "Family Affairs," p. 334.

33. Ibid. On business groups see Jaime Wheelock, *Imperialismo y dictadura: crisis de una formación social* (Mexico, D.F.: Siglo Veintiuno, 1975), pp. 199–201 and Harry W. Strachen, "The Role of Business Groups in Economic Development: The Case of Nicaragua" (DBA diss., Harvard University, 1972). According to Strachen, p. 151, the BANIC and BANAMERICA groups controlled 70% of the total assets of the private financial sector.

34. Strachen ("Business Groups," p. 100) argues that in Nicaragua the business group is a solution to "underdeveloped financial systems" and is crucial in investment and credit transactions, minimizing risk. The core of both of Strachen's financial groups is a network of aristocratic families.

35. Miles Wortman, writing on Central America, notes, "How did the notable eighteenth-century families survive through all the bloodshed and political turmoil of the epoch, the constant civil wars, forced exiles, and expropriations of land and wealth . . .The answer is: the family, the cousin, the brother-in-law or the son, in sum, the network too entrenched to be removed by political turmoil, too powerful socially to be discounted, and sufficiently flexible to bend with political change, to guard the cousins' holdings or to save the brother in-law from execution," pp. 77–78 in Diana Balmori, Stuart F. Voss, and Miles Wortman, *Notable Family Networks in Latin America* (Chicago: University of Chicago Press, 1984).

36. As Enrique Baloyra notes in the case of coffee domination of commercial finance in El Salvador, "There was nothing inherently conspiratorial about all this. The product of credit extended for commercial operations was simply the product of concentrated and overlapping ownership and the network of relations resulting from it." *El Salvador in Transition* (Chapel Hill: University of North Carolina Press, 1982), p. 29.

37. José María and Mariano Montealegre, for example, were both educated in London and became what are believed to be Costa Rica's first physician and engineer respectively (Stone, *Dinastía,* pp. 261–262). Herbert de Sola's son Orlando was educated at the Menlo School in San Francisco and spent a year at Oxford before completing his education as a physician in Paris. In El Salvador he became Vice Rector of the National University, Dean of the Medical School, Minister of

Health, and a founder of the hospital La Merced. His brother Ernesto was awarded the first Bachelors degree in Architecture from M.I.T. ever received by a Salvadoran, became one of the country's first trained architects, and was responsible for the design of more than 350 structures in El Salvador (Macarezi, *Don Herbert de Sola,* pp. 94–96). Oscar Arias attended Boston University and did graduate work at the University of Essex and the London School of Economics, receiving a doctorate and becoming Professor of Political Science at the University of Costa Rica. His doctoral dissertation, published as *Quién gobierna en Costa Rica* (San José: Editorial Universitaria Centroamericana, 1984), concludes that the proposition that Costa Rican political life has democratized after the 1948 revolution is false (p. 241).

38. Dennis Gilbert, "The Oligarchy and the Old Regime in Peru" (Ph.D. diss., Cornell University, 1977), p. 251, notes that the Prados, one of the Peruvian oligarchy's leading families, were "at their economic and political zenith" between 1948 and the early 1960s.

39. Maurice Zeitlin and Richard Earl Ratcliff, *Landlords and Capitalists, The Dominant Class of Chile* (Princeton: Princeton University Press, 1988), pp. 252–257.

40. Balmori, et al., *Notable Family Networks,* p. 230.

41. Knut Walter, *The Regime of Anastasio Somoza 1936–1956* (Chapel Hill: University of North Carolina Press, 1993), p. 53.

42. Torres-Rivas, "Síntesis histórica," p. 115.

43. Walter, *Anastasio Somoza,* pp. 54–55.

44. On military organization and relationship with the elite see William Stanley, "Inter-Elite Conflict and State Terrorism in El Salvador" (paper presented to the 16th International Congress of the Latin American Studies Association, Crystal City, Va., 4–6 April, 1991). As Enrique Baloyra observes, "the military institution emerged as the dominant political actor, filling the power vacuum created by the crisis of the oligarchy that began in 1932," *El Salvador in Transition* (Chapel Hill: University of North Carolina Press, 1982), p. 18.

45. For accounts of the transformation of the Central American agro-export economy in the postwar era see Robert Williams, *Export Agriculture and the Crisis in Central America* (Chapel Hill, University of North Carolina Press, 1986); Victor Bulmer-Thomas, *The Political Economy of Central America Since 1920* (Cambridge: Cambridge University Press, 1987); Charles D. Brockett, *Land, Power and Poverty: Agrarian Transformation and Political Conflict in Central America* (Boston: Unwin Hyman, 1988), esp. chap.3, pp. 41–65, "The Postwar Transformation of Central American Agriculture"; and James Dunkerly, *Power in the Isthmus* (London: Verso, 1988), chap. 5, pp. 169–219, "Uneven Development, 1950–1980." Between the late forties and the late seventies Central American cattle production more than doubled, sugar production tripled, but cotton production increased more than

tenfold. Coffee yields and production nearly doubled (Dunkerly, pp. 189, 187). All of these sources provide roughly the same portrait of the transformation of the political economy of agro-exports based on detailed analysis of economic data.

46. Dunkerly, *Power in the Isthmus,* pp. 194–195, 211; Brockett, *Land and Power,* pp. 54–55. Williams, *Export Agriculture,* pp. 163–165.

47. For El Salvador William L. Durham provides a convincing demonstration of the displacement as the combined effect of agro-export expansion and population growth in his *Scarcity and Survival in Central America: Ecological Origins of the Soccer War* (Stanford: Stanford University Press, 1978). For the region see Dunkerly, *Power in the Isthmus,* pp. 179–201; Brockett, *Land and Power,* pp. 68–76; Williams, *Export Agriculture;* and Bulmer-Thomas, *Political Economy,* pp. 201–207.

48. Dunkerly, *Power in the Isthmus,* p. 210, notes that "both increased dependence on seasonal wages in the rural economy and the limited size of the manufacturing working class have reduced the social distinctiveness of underemployment and marginalized petty trading, generalizing the experience of partial or temporary wage labour to such an extent that it has become far more common over the last thirty years than that of 'pure' worker or peasant."

49. On the role of the rural semi-proletariat in Nicaragua see my "Cotton and Revolution in Nicaragua," in *State versus Markets in the World-System,* ed. Peter Evans, Dietrich Rueschemeyer, and Evelyn Huber Stephens (Beverly Hills, Ca.: Sage, 1985), pp. 91–116, and Orlando Nuñez Soto, *El Somocismo y el modelo capitalista agro-exportador* (Managua: Departamento de Ciencias Sociales de la Universidad Autónoma de Nicaragua, n.d.). Carlos Vilas in *The Sandinista Revolution: National Liberation and Social Transformation in Central America* (New York: Monthly Review, 1986) shows that the social base of the urban insurrection was among informal sector workers and students. Jenny Pearce's field research in Chalatenango and Rafael Cabarrús's in Aguilares have demonstrated conclusively that it was the rural semi-proletariat that provided the mass base of the FMLN. Similar conclusions are reached by Timothy Wickham-Crowley from statistical data. See Jenny Pearce, *Promised Land: Peasant Rebellion in Chalatenango, El Salvador* (London: Latin American Bureau, 1986); Carlos Rafael Cabarrús, *Génesis de una revolución: Análisis del surgimiento y desarrollo de la organización campesina en El Salvador* (Mexico, D.F.: Centro de Investigaciones y Estudios Superiores en Antropología Social, 1983); Timothy Wickham-Crowley, *Guerrillas and Revolution in Latin America: A Comparative Study of Insurgents and Regimes Since 1956* (Princeton: Princeton University Press, 1992), pp. 243–244.

50. The Monimbó uprising began on February 21, 1978, after Somoza's National Guard attempted to break up a crowd leaving a funeral mass for Pedro Joaquín Chamorro, assassinated on January 10. On February 26 Sandinista President Daniel Ortega's brother Camilo was killed leading Monimbó residents in battle with the National Guard. Subtiava exploded on March 3.

51. See note 49 above.

52. Vilas, *Sandinista Revolution,* pp. 101–122.

53. Williams, *Export Agriculture,* pp. 129–134.

54. Dunkerly, *Power in the Isthmus,* pp. 363–364.

55. Pearce, *Promised Land,* p. 151.

56. Ibid.

57. Phillip Berryman, *The Religious Roots of Rebellion: Christians in Central American Revolutions* (Maryknoll, New York: Orbis Books, 1984), pp. 7–24; Booth, *The End and The Beginning,* pp. 124–125.

58. Penny Lernoux, *Cry of the People: The Struggle for Human Rights in Latin America—The Catholic Church in Conflict with U.S. Policy* (New York: Penguin, 1982), p. 465.

59. Dennis Gilbert, *Sandinistas* (Oxford: Basil Blackwell, 1988), p. 20.

60. Ibid., pp. 22–23.

61. Baloyra, *El Salvador in Transition,* p. 101.

62. "Jimmy Carter did what the communists couldn't do—he brought socialism to El Salvador. He destroyed our free enterprise system," said a member of the Salvadoran oligarchy quoted in Robert Armstrong and Janet Shenk, *Face of Revolution* (Boston: South End Press, 1982), p. 159. A conversation between the author and another (very drunk) upper-class Salvadoran got off to a shaky start when the latter volunteered, "I want to kill Jimmy Carter." Sara Miles and Bob Ostertag report in "D'Aubuisson's New ARENA," *NACLA Report on the Americas* 23 (July 1989):21, that ARENA campaign rallies were "among the most visibly anti-Yankee events in Latin America." Anger at the United States was almost equalled by outrage at the Christian Democrats. For further variations on this theme see Chapter 6.

63. William Stanley, "State Terrorism."

64. On D'Aubuisson and the founding of ARENA see Montgomery, *Revolution in El Salvador,* pp. 132–134, 157; Yolanda Baires Martínez, "Orígenes y formación del Partido ARENA," unpublished paper (San José, n.d); and Chris Norton, "The Hard Right: ARENA Comes to Power," in *A Decade of War: El Salvador Confronts the Future,* ed. Amjali Sundaram and George Gelber (New York: Monthly Review, 1991), pp. 196–215.

65. Montgomery, *Revolution in El Salvador,* p. 157; Baires, "Partido ARENA," p. 12.

66. Dunkerly, *Long War,* p. 185; Montgomery, *Revolution in El Salvador,* p. 260.

67. See Miles and Ostertag, "D'Aubuisson's New ARENA."

68. See Fundación Salvadoreña para el Desarrollo Económico y Social, *Memoria de labores 1988* (San Salvador: Fundación Salvadoreña para el Desarrollo Económico y Social, 1989?), "Miembros de la Fundación," pp. 46–49.

69. On the role of the bourgeoisie in the revolution see Booth, *End and the*

Beginning, pp. 97–103; Gilbert, *Sandinistas,* chap. 5, pp. 105–127, "The Bourgeoisie and the Revolution," and my "Revolution and the Agrarian Bourgeoisie in Nicaragua," in *Revolution in the World System,* ed. Terry Boswell (New York: Greenwood, 1989), pp. 99–128.

70. "One does not," explained a Nicaraguan banker to Dennis Gilbert some years later, "kill people of a certain social condition." Gilbert, *Sandinistas,* p. 108.

71. Author's interview, Managua, Nicaragua, August 5, 1986.

72. The other members were lawyer Ernesto Castillo, priests Fernando Cardenal and Miguel D'Escoto, intellectuals Carlos Tünnermann and Sergio Ramírez, and professionals Ricardo Coronel, Casimiro Sotelo, and Carlos Gutiérrez. George Black, *Triumph of the People,* p. 104.

73. Shirley Christian, *Nicaragua: Revolution in the Family* (New York: Vintage, 1986), p. 78. This is a valuable source on the upper-class family involvement in the revolution despite an anti-Sandinista bias so pronounced that at one point the author quotes approvingly a source comparing a Sandinista crowd to a Nazi Nuremberg rally (p. 198).

74. Gilbert, *Sandinistas,* p. 107. Nevertheless important members of the BANIC and BANAMERICA bloc, including most notably Pedro Joaquín Chamorro himself, were active in the opposition. Alfonso Robelo's GRACSA was tied to BANIC. Felipe Mántica and Emilio Baltodano of los Doce were both founders of BANAMERICA. So was Enrique Dreyfus, President of COSIP. See Wheelock, *Imperialismo y dictadura,* p. 158.

75. GRACSA continued expanding into related industries in the Sandinista period and remains once again, under Lacayo's leadership, a key economic actor in Nicaragua. See Rose Spaulding, "Capitalists and Revolution: State-Private Sector Relations in Revolutionary Nicaragua (1979–1990)" (paper presented at the 16th International Congress of the Latin American Studies Association, Crystal City, Va., April 4–6, 1991), p. 25.

76. Information on the Bolaños-Geyers and SAIMSA was kindly supplied by Nicolás Bolaños-Geyer in an interview with the author, Managua, July 7, 1986.

77. My calculations indicate that 64 of the 109 patronymic family groups with more than 200 *manzanas* (1 mz. = .69 ha.) in cotton in Nicaragua in 1977 were still producing in 1983–1984, although only 6 (including the Bolaños) with 1,000 *manzanas* or more were still producing. In the north central coffee region only 21 of the 51 growers producing 1,500 *quintales* (1 *quintal* = 100 lbs.) in 1977 were still producing in 1983–84. See my "Revolution and the Agrarian Bourgeoisie," p. 115.

78. Ibid. and Spaulding, "Capitalists and Revolution," p. 4.

79. On the origins of the alliance see Black, *Triumph of the People,* pp. 104–106, for a view sympathetic to the FSLN; Christian, *Revolution in the Family,* pp. 43–45, for a view sympathetic to the bourgeoisie; and Donald C. Hodges, *Intellectual*

Foundations of the Nicaraguan Revolution (Austin: University of Texas Press, 1986) for an analysis of the ideological underpinnings of the alliance. For the reconstitution of the alliance after the Sandinista electoral defeat, see Vilas, "Family Affairs," Spaulding, "Capitalists and Revolution," and Mark Everingham, "From Insurrection to *Concertación* in Nicaragua: Alliances, Businessmen and Elite Consensus" (paper presented at the 17th Congress of the Latin American Studies Association, Los Angeles, Sept. 24–27, 1992).

80. For a detailed analysis of the consolidation of Sandinista rule and the exclusion of the bourgeoisie see Stephen M. Gorman, "Power and Consolidation in the Nicaraguan Revolution," *Journal of Latin American Studies* 13 (May 1981):133–149. See also Anthony Winson, "Nicaragua's Private Sector and the Sandinista Revolution," *Studies in Political Economy* 17 (Summer 1985):71–106; Gilbert, *Sandinistas,* 108–111; and Christian, *Revolution in the Family,* pp. 171–186.

81. Of the confiscated cotton estates, 49% were returned to their former owners, as were 35% of the coffee estates. Many confiscated estates were, however, turned over to farm workers or demobilized soldiers from the Sandinista and contra armies. Rose Spaulding, "From Revolution to Neo-Liberalism: Private Sector Ambivalence in Post-Revolutionary Nicaragua (1990–1992)" (paper presented at the 17th International Congress of the Latin American Studies Association, Los Angeles, Sept. 24–27, 1992).

82. Ibid., p. 29.

83. Excellent summaries of events in Costa Rica in this period are provided by Dunkerly, *Power in the Isthmus,* chap. 11, pp. 589–655, "Costa Rica: Stability at a Price"; and Dario Moreno, *The Struggle for Peace in Central America* (Gainesville: University Press of Florida, 1994), pp. 83–90. For a Costa Rican view see the issue of *Aportes 5,* "Una nueva historia se escribe en el sur" (julio-agosto 1985). The issue editorial begins (p. 3), "A national sentiment exists that the nation is threatened." One banana workers' union official told the author in September 1985 that "after 1979 some people in the movement thought that Costa Rica was in a prerevolutionary situation and that the revolution was a few days or weeks away. They wanted to create a *foco* for revolutionary action in the banana zone." The debate over revolution versus reform split the banana workers' union.

84. Dunkerly, *Power in the Isthmus,* pp. 644–645, and Moreno, *Struggle for Peace,* p. 83. For a colorful although nonetheless useful portrait of the campaign, see Seth Rolbein, *Nobel Costa Rica* (New York: St. Martin's Press, 1989), pp. 163–187.

85. Author's interview, San José, Costa Rica, July 19, 1990.

86. Moreno, *Struggle for Peace,* pp. 82, 86.

87. Ibid., p. 90, Dunkerly, *Power in the Isthmus,* p. 645.

88. See Ralph Lee Woodward, *Central America: A Nation Divided* (New York: Oxford University Press, 1985) for the definitive account of the impact of liberalism on Central America as a whole. On the influence of liberalism and positivism

on the Costa Rican coffee elite, particularly the so-called Generation of 1888 or the Olympians, see Stone, *Dinastía de los conquistadores*. Liberal ideology and its impact in El Salvador are described in Rafael Guidos Véjar, *El acenso del militarismo en El Salvador* (San Salvador: Universidad Centroamericana Editores, 1980); Rafael Menjívar, *Acumulación y desarrollo del capitalismo en El Salvador* (San José: Editorial Universitaria Centroamericana, 1980); and David Browning, *El Salvador: Landscape and Society* (Oxford: Clarendon Press, 1971). On the Liberal revolution of José Santos Zelaya in Nicaragua see Benjamin Teplitz, "The Political and Economic Foundations of Modernization in Nicaragua: The Administration of José Santos Zelaya" (Ph.D. diss., Howard University, 1973); Charles S. Stansifer, "José Santos Zelaya: A *New Look* at Nicaragua's '*Liberal*' Dictator," *Revista Interamericana* 7 (Hato Rey, Puerto Rico) (Fall 1977):468–85; and Alberto Lanuza, Juan Luis Vázquez, Amaru Barahona, and Amalia Chamorro, *Economía y sociedad en la construcción del estado en Nicaragua* (San José: Instituto Centroamericano de Administración Publica, 1983).

89. Edelberto Torres-Rivas, *Interpretación del desarrollo social en Centroamérica* (San José: Editorial Universitaria Centroamericana, 1972), p. 85.

90. Woodward, *Central America,* p. 175.

91. The classic statement of the association is in Seymour Martin Lipset's 1959 paper, "Some Social Requisites of Democracy: Economic Development and Political Legitimacy," *American Political Science Review* 53 (March 1959):69–105. For a comprehensive review and empirical test of the idea see Dietrich Rueschemeyer, Evelyn Huber Stephens, and John D. Stephens, *Capitalist Development and Democracy* (Chicago: University of Chicago Press, 1992). They conclude (p. 272) that "the level of democratic development cannot be simply read off from the level of capitalist development."

92. C. Wright Mills, *The Sociological Imagination* (New York: Grove Press, 1961), p. 6. For Mills this intersection defined the scope of the sociological imagination.

93. I have been particularly influenced by a series of articles in a special section of the Fall 1991 and Winter 1992 issues of *Social Science History,* particularly George Steinmetz's "Reflections on the Role of Social Narratives in Working-Class Formation: Narrative Theory in the Social Sciences," pp. 489–516. As William Sewell (Fall 1991, p. 487) notes in his introduction, "narrative" has been used to cover a variety of concepts including what could equally well be called ideology. As it is used here, it will refer to what Steinmetz calls "social narratives," the stories that social actors tell about themselves. Both terms, "ideology" and "narrative," refer to the same interview transcripts so the choice of one or the other is a matter of theoretical interpretation. Both concepts have associated, although distinct, bodies of theoretical literature that are useful in making sense of the interview materials. These issues are discussed in more detail in the concluding chapter.

94. The collections called "Recortes de Periódicos" were maintained in the libraries of the Instituto Nacional del Café in San Salvador (reorganized under the Consejo Salvadoreño del Café during the period of the research) and Oficina del Café in San José. In both cases the office collects all articles in major national newspapers dealing with coffee.

95. On neo-liberal policies in Central America see James Dunkerly, *The Pacification of Central America: Political Change in the Isthmus 1987–1993* (London: Verso 1994), pp. 12–18. On Latin America more generally see John Walton and Jonathan Shefner, "Latin America: Popular Protest and the State," in *Free Markets and Food Riots: The Politics of Global Adjustment,* ed. John Walton and David Seddon (Oxford: Blackwell, 1994), pp. 97–134.

96. On the adoption of the neo-liberal program by Chamorro see Spaulding, "From Revolution to Neo-Liberalism." The implementation of neo-liberal policies actually began in the waning days of the Sandinista regime (see Richard Stahler Sholk, "Stabilization, Destabilization and the Popular Classes in Nicaragua, 1979–1989," *Latin American Research Review* 25, no. 3 [1990]:55–88) but were greatly extended by Chamorro. On Cristiani's policies see Dunkerly, *Pacification,* pp. 16–17; Miles and Ostertag, "D'Aubuisson's New ARENA"; and Chapter 6 below. On Costa Rica see Karen Hansen-Kuhn, "Sapping the Economy: Structural Adjustment Policies in Costa Rica," *The Ecologist* 23 (Sept./Oct. 1993):179–184.

97. I am indebted to Rose Spaulding ("From Revolution to Neo-Liberalism," p. 4) for this observation. Spaulding also notes, however, that the economic policies of the United States and the International Monetary Fund exerted "an influence over economic policy in the region that has not been seen since the Alliance for Progress era." As Walton and Shefner note in "Latin America: Popular Protest and the State," p. 101, structural adjustment policies were applied by the IMF with "striking uniformity across debtor nations" and required as a condition for continued lending "currency devaluation, increased interest rates, reduced imports, greater freedom to foreign capital, elimination of tariff protections, privatization of state-owned firms, and, above all, reduced public expenditures in the form of cuts in state subsidies for food, transportation, petroleum products, education and health services."

2. Class and Class Relations

1. Edelberto Torres-Rivas, "Síntesis histórica del proceso político," in *Centroamérica hoy,* ed. Edelberto Torres-Rivas, Gert Rosenthal, Eduardo Lizano, Rafael Menjívar, and Sergio Ramírez (Mexico, D.F.: Siglo Veintiuno, 1975), pp. 27–29.

2. Transport, roasting, soluble coffee manufacture, distribution, and retail sales were always controlled by agents of the importing nations. See Bart S. Fisher, *The International Coffee Agreement: A Study in Coffee Diplomacy* (New York: Praeger,

1972), pp. 50–51; Vernon D. Wickizer, *The World Coffee Economy with Special Reference to Control Schemes* (Stanford, Calif.: Food Research Institute, 1943), pp. 55–56; Michael Sivetz and Herbert E. Foote, *Coffee Processing Technology,* vol. 2 (Westport, Conn.: Avi Publishing, 1963), p 279.

3. Michael J. Biechler, "The Coffee Industry of Guatemala: A Geographic Analysis" (Ph.D. diss., Michigan State University, 1970), p. 109; J. C. Cambranes, "Café sangriente," *Polémica* 3 (1982):18–31; C. R. Montenegro, "La explotación cafetalera en Guatemala 1930–1940" (Tesis de Licenciatura, Universidad de San Carlos, 1976), p. 144; Guillermo Nañez Falcón, "Erwin Paul Dieseldorf, German Entrepreneur in the Alta Verapaz of Guatemala 1865–1900" (Ph.D. diss., Tulane University, 1970), p. 81; Dirección General de Estadística, *Censo Cafetalero 1950* (Guatemala: Dirección General de Estadística, 1953), p. 5; (1971), pp. 245, 248.

4. On El Salvador see David Browning, *El Salvador: Landscape and Society* (Oxford: Oxford University Press, 1971), p. 179; Eduardo Colindres, "La tenencia de la tierra en El Salvador," *Estudios Centroamericanos* 31, nos. 335/336 (1976): 470–471; L. Sebastián, "El camino económico hacia la democracia," *Estudios Centroamericanos* 31, nos. 372/373 (1979):950–951. On differences between El Salvador and Guatemala see Ciro F. S. Cardoso, "Historia económica del café en Centroamérica (siglo XIX)," *Estudios Sociales Centroamericanos* 4 (enero-abril 1975):9–55; and Torres-Rivas, "Síntesis histórica."

5. Carolyn Hall, *El café y el desarrollo histórico-geográfico de Costa Rica,* 3rd ed. (San José, Editorial Costa Rica, 1982); Mitchell Seligson, *Agrarian Capitalism and the Transformation of Peasant Society: Coffee in Costa Rica.* Special Studies Series no. 69, Council on International Studies (Buffalo: State University of New York, 1975), and *Peasants of Costa Rica and the Development of Agrarian Capitalism* (Madison: University of Wisconsin Press, 1980); Cardoso, "Historia económica," and "The Formation of the Coffee Estate in Nineteenth Century Costa Rica," in *Land and Labour in Latin America,* ed. K. Duncan and I. Rutledge (Cambridge: Cambridge University Press, 1977), pp. 162–202; Anthony Winson, *Coffee and Democracy in Modern Costa Rica* (New York: St. Martin's Press, 1989), pp. 21–23. See also John Patrick Bell, *Crisis in Costa Rica* (Austin: University of Texas Press. 1971), p. 6; Torres-Rivas, "Síntesis histórica," p. 70.

6. Eduardo Baumeister, "Notas para la discusión de la cuestión agraria en Nicaragua" (paper presented at the Third Congress of Nicaraguan Social Sciences, Managua, October 1982). In the debate over Nicaragua Wheelock argued that the coffee elite remained backward, facilitating imperial control over Nicaragua. Baumeister thought that the middle strata in coffee could support Sandinista agrarian policies if they were not so exclusively focused on agro-industrial production. Wheelock represented the other pole of this debate in Sandinista Nicaragua.

7. The system used here is based on those developed by Ricardo Falla for research in the Department of Jinotega, Nicaragua, described by A. Gariazzo, E. Incer, D. Dye, and R. Soley in "Estrategia de reproducción económico-social de los pequeños productores cafetaleros: casos de Matagalpa y Carazo," unpublished (Managua: Instituto de Investigaciones Económicas y Sociales, 1983), p. 28; and by the Centro de Investigaciones y Estudios de la Reforma Agraria, *Las Clases Sociales en el Agro* (Managua: Centro de Investigaciones y Estudios de la Reforma Agraria, n.d.), for Nicaragua as a whole. For a more detailed discussion of the development of this index see my article "Coffee and Politics in Central America," in *Crises in the Caribbean Basin,* ed. Richard Tardanico (Newbury Park, Ca.: Sage, 1987), pp. 153–157.

8. The Nicaraguan data actually conceal substantial regional variation. For a more detailed discussion of this issue see my "Coffee and Politics in Central America," pp. 159–162.

9. For descriptions of the Guatemalan forced labor system see James W. Bingham, "Guatemalan Agriculture During the Administration of President Manuel Estrada Cabrera, 1898–1920" (MA diss., Tulane University, 1974); Cambranes, "Café sangriente"; Julia Garlant, "Developmental Aspects of Barrios' Agrarian Program, Guatemala, 1871–1885" (MA diss., Tulane University, 1968); Kenneth J. Grieb, *Guatemalan Caudillo: The Regime of Jorge Ubico, Guatemala 1931– 1944* (Athens, Ohio: University of Ohio Press, 1979); David J. McCreery, "Debt Servitude in Rural Guatemala: 1876–1936," *Hispanic American Historical Review* 64, no.4 (1983):735–759; Nañez, "Erwin Paul Dieseldorf."

10. The contracting system is described in Nañez, ibid., pp. 317–348; Joseph J. Pansini, "El Pilar, a Plantation Microcosm of Guatemalan Ethnicity" (Ph.D. diss., University of Rochester, 1977), pp. 9–21; and Lester J. Schmid, "The Role of Migratory Labor in the Economic Development of Guatemala" (Ph.D. diss., University of Wisconsin, 1967), pp. 181–204.

11. Wheelock, *Imperialismo y dictadura,* p. 92; H. Trujillo, "La formación del estado en El Salvador," *Estudios Sociales Centroamericanos* 10, no. 28 (1980):128.

12. Bingham, *Cabrera,* p. 105.

13. The reliability of the Nicaraguan density data is questionable, as it appears to be census practice to assume rather than count 1,000 trees per *manzana.*

14. United Nations Food and Agriculture Organization, *Production Yearbook,* vols. 14 and 34 (Rome: United Nations Food and Agriculture Organization, 1960, 1981).

15. Juan Pablo Duque, *Informe del jefe del departamento técnico sobre su viaje de estudio a algunos países cafeteros de la América Central,* Federación Nacional de Cafeteros de Colombia (Managua: Asociación Agrícola de Nicaragua, 1938).

16. For cross-national surveys see Helen L. Hearst, "The Coffee Industry of Central America" (MA diss., University of Chicago, 1929); Jamaica Coffee In-

dustry Board, *Report* (Kingston: Jamaica Coffee Industry Board, 1959). For individual countries see Mauricio Domínguez, "The Development of the Technological and Scientific Coffee Industry in Guatemala, 1830–1930" (Ph.D. diss., Tulane University, 1970); Nañez, "Erwin Paul Dieseldorf"; A. Gariazzo, E. Incer, D. Dye, and R. Soley, "El subsistema del café en Nicaragua" (paper presented at the Second Seminar on Central America and the Caribbean, Managua, February 9–12, 1983), and "Estrategia de reproducción"; Carolyn Hall, *Formación de una hacienda cafetalera: 1889–1911* (San José: Editorial Universidad de Costa Rica, 1978), and "El café"; Paul C. Morrison and Thomas L. Norris, "Coffee Production and Processing on a Large Costa Rican *Finca,"* *Papers of the Michigan Academy of Science, Arts, and Letters* 39 (1954):309–322; Larry K. Laird, "Technology versus Tradition: The Modernization of Nicaraguan Agriculture" (Ph.D. diss., University of Kansas, 1974); David Radell, *Coffee and Transportation in Nicaragua: Field Work Report* (Berkeley: Department of Geography, University of California, 1964).

17. Duque, *Informe,* p. 45; Hearst, "Coffee Industry," p. 120; Harold Playter, *Nicaragua: A Commercial and Economic Survey* (Washington, D.C.: U.S. Government Printing Office, 1927), p. 26; Radell, "Coffee and Transportation," p. 48.

18. Laird, "Modernization," p. 92; Radell, "Coffee and Transportation," pp. 25, 51.

19. Radell, ibid., p. 16.

20. Domínguez, "Coffee Industry in Guatemala," pp. 134, 138.

21. Duque, *Informe,* p. 5; Costa Rica Instituto de Defensa del Café de Costa Rica, "El Instituto levanta el censo cafetalero del país: resúmen general de la república," *Revista del Instituto de Defensa del Café de Costa Rica* 3, no. 14 (1935):59.

22. Domínguez, "Coffee Industry," p. 167.

23. Sivetz and Foote, *Coffee Processing,* p. 54; Wellman, *Coffee,* p. 370.

24. For technical descriptions of the process see Sivetz and Foote, ibid., pp. 55–57; Wellman, ibid., pp. 370–374; Wickizer, *World Coffee Economy,* pp. 41–45.

25. Laird, "Technology versus Tradition," p. 92; Radell, *Coffee and Transportation,* pp. 51–52; Instituto Centroamericano de Administracíon de Empresas, *Finca "Santo Domingo"* (Managua: Instituto Centroamericano de Administración de Empresas, 1981), pp. 6–11; Morrison and Norris, "Costa Rican *Finca,"* pp. 318–322.

26. Enrique Baloyra, *El Salvador in Transition* (Chapel Hill: University of North Carolina Press, 1982), p. 25; Domínguez, "Coffee Industry," p. 264; Hall, *El café,* p. 87; Radell, *Coffee and Transportation,* p. 25.

27. Fawzi Habib, "The Course and Problems of an Export Economy: The Case of El Salvador" (Ph.D. diss., Duke University, 1958), p. 138; Hall, *El café,* p. 45; Daniel Slutzky and Esther Alonso, *Quién es quién en la caficultura nacional* (San Salvador: Universidad de El Salvador, 1971), p. 21–22; Wheelock, *Imperialismo y dictadura,* pp. 144–145.

28. Colindres, "La tenencia de la tierra," p. 471; Nañez, "Erwin Paul Dieseldorf," pp. 385–410; Stone, *Dinastía,* pp. 347–351.

29. Duque, *Informe,* p. 40, 47–48; Hearst, "Coffee Industry," pp. 42–44; Seligson, *Peasants of Costa Rica,* p. 34.

30. Duque, ibid., pp. 45–46; Radell, "Coffee and Transportation," pp. 27, 54.

31. Biechler, "Coffee Industry," p. 18; Duque, *Informe,* p. 50; Nañez, "Erwin Paul Dieseldorf," pp. 251–253, 284.

32. Biechler, ibid., pp. 171–172.

33. Duque, *Informe,* p. 51; Hall, *El café,* pp. 50–51; Hearst, *Coffee Industry,* pp. 139–140.

34. Domínguez, "Coffee Industry," pp. 264–265.

35. Duque, *Informe,* p. 51.

36. Laird, "Modernization," p. 92; Radell, "Coffee and Transportation," pp. 24–26, 51.

37. Wellman, *Coffee, Botany,* Plate 27.

38. Wheelock, *Imperialismo y dictadura.*

39. On land values see Cardoso, *Coffee Estate,* p. 175; Stone, *Dinastía,* p. 96. On wage levels see Duque, *Informe,* p. 58; Hearst, "Coffee Industry," p. 125.

40. Morrison and Norris, "Costa Rican *finca*," Hall, *Hacienda cafetalera.*

41. Hall, *El café,* pp. 153, 159; Seligson, "Agrarian Capitalism," p. 28.

42. Sebastián, "El camino," pp. 950–951.

43. Asociación Cafetalera de El Salvador, *Primer censo nacional del café* (San Salvador: Asociación Cafetalera de El Salvador, 1940), pp. 183–199. The census lists the names of the owners of all processing plants in the country as well as the holders of all export licenses listed by export brand name. Although the number of export brands is only an approximate measure of export activity, the listing of owners by name makes the 1940 census a particularly valuable source on the overlap in processing and export in El Salvador.

44. Compare the lists in Table 8 with the listing of the Salvadoran oligarchy presented in Robert T. Aubey, "Entrepreneurial Formation in El Salvador," *Explorations in Entrepreneurial History* 6 (1968–1969):268–285; or in Eduardo Colindres, *Fundamentos económicos de la burguesía salvadoreña* (San Salvador: Universidad Centroamericana, 1977).

45. Edelberto Torres-Rivas, "State Making and Revolution in Central America," lecture given at the Center for Research on Social Organization, University of Michigan, November 19, 1982.

46. República de Nicaragua, *Censo cafetalero* (Managua: República de Nicaragua, 1910).

47. Richard Millet, *Guardians of the Dynasty* (Maryknoll, N.Y.: Orbis, 1977), p. 51.

48. The Guatemalan revolution of 1944–1948 was based on urban middle-

class mobilization and action by disaffected military officers; it was not a peasant revolt. Peasant mobilization accompanied the revolution, especially during the Arbenz regime (1950–1954), but this was only possible because of state backing. When Arbenz was overthrown in 1954, peasants were savagely repressed and the *status quo ante* restored.

49. Robert G. Williams, *Export Agriculture and the Crisis in Central America* (Chapel Hill: University of North Carolina Press, 1986), p. 14.

50. James Dunkerly, *Power in the Isthmus* (London: Verso, 1990), p. 191.

51. According to Dunkerly, ibid., p. 192, in Nicaragua, where the difference is most pronounced, cotton requires 74 worker days per year per *manzana,* while coffee requires 160.

3. Farabundo Martí and the Failure of Revolutionary Socialism

1. Thomas Anderson, *Matanza: El Salvador's Communist Revolt of 1932* (Lincoln: University of Nebraska Press, 1981), p. 159.

2. Anastasio Somoza García, *El verdadero Sandino o el Calvario de las Segovias* (Managua: Tipografía Robelo, 1936).

3. The definitive account of the insurrection and the subsequent massacre is Anderson's *Matanza,* which draws on contemporary accounts of anti-communist journalists Joaquín Méndez, *Los sucesos comunistas en El Salvador* (San Salvador: Imprenta Funes & Ungo, 1932) and Jorge Schlesinger, *Revolución comunista* (Guatemala: Editorial Unión Tipográfica, 1946), as well as first-person interviews and other primary materials. The testimonial of Communist leader Miguel Mármol many years after the event, as transcribed by Salvadoran poet and revolutionary Roque Dalton in *Miguel Mármol,* trans. by Kathleen Ross and Richard Schaff (Willimantic, Ct.: Curbstone Press, 1987), is an invaluable account from the Communist side. The researches of the late Salvadoran sociologist Segundo Montes, conducted in the central area of the revolt in Sonsonate in the 1970s and presented in *El compadrazgo: Una estructura de poder en El Salvador* (San Salvador: Universidad Centroamericana José Simeón Cañas, 1987) are also invaluable. The revolt has generated a considerable interpretative and analytical literature, including Rafael Guidos Véjar, *El ascenso del militarismo en El Salvador* (San Salvador: Universidad Centroamericana José Simeón Cañas, 1988); Douglas Kincaid, "Peasants into Rebels: Community and Class in Rural El Salvador," *Comparative Studies in Society and History* 29 (July 1987):466–494; Alejandro Marroquín, "Estudio sobre la crisis de los años treinta en El Salvador," *Anuario de Estudios Centroamericanos* 3 (1977):115–160; Héctor Pérez Brignoli, "Indios, comunistas y campesinos: La rebelión de 1932 en El Salvador," *Cuaderno Agrario* 5 (San José: Escuela de Historia, Universidad Nacional de Costa Rica, 1991); and Leon Zamsoc, "Class Conflict in an Export Economy: The Social Roots of the Salvadoran Insurrection of 1932," in

Sociology of Developing Societies: Central America, ed. Jan L. Flora and Edelberto Torres Rivas (New York: Monthly Review Press, 1989), pp. 56–75. Valuable descriptions and analysis of the revolt can also be found in the general works on El Salvador of Alastair White, *El Salvador* (New York: Praeger, 1973) and Everett Wilson, "The Crisis of National Integration in El Salvador, 1919–1935" (Ph.D diss., Stanford University, 1970). Rodolfo Cerdas Cruz, *La hoz y el machete: La Internacional Comunista, America Latina y la revolución en Centroamérica* (San José: Editorial Universidad Estatal a Distancia, 1986), provides an analysis of the effects of the Communist International on the insurrection.

4. Anderson, *Matanza,* pp. 123–124, 131–132; Montes, *El compadrazgo,* p. 191; Dalton, *Miguel Mármol,* p. 308. Montes, ibid., pp. 188–191 provides a thorough review of various authors' casualty estimates, most of which are derived directly or indirectly from estimates by military officers. Anderson, ibid., pp. 134–135, reviews many of the same sources plus his own interviews with military officers involved in the repression, and concludes that 10,000 would be a reasonable figure given the physical problems of disposing of so many people in such a short time with the forces available. Montes, on the other hand, bases his estimates on direct reports of executions and the physical mass of bodies reported by survivors, and reaches the much higher number of 25,000. Although he reports an extreme reluctance on the part of survivors to talk about the revolt even forty years after the event, his estimates are the only ones based on primary researches in the area of the revolt.

5. Roque Dalton, "We All," reprinted in *El Salvador at War: A Collage Epic,* ed. Marc Zimmerman (Minneapolis: MEP Publications, 1988), p. 65.

6. Dalton, *Miguel Mármol,* pp. 304, 317; Anderson, *Motanza,* p. 205.

7. Méndez, *Los sucesos comunistas,* preface.

8. Quoted in Lisa North, *Bitter Grounds: Roots of Revolt in El Salvador* (Westport, Conn.: Lawrence Hill, 1985), p. 40.

9. Quoted in Pérez Brignoli, "Indios," p. 1.

10. Quoted in ibid., p. 23.

11. Quoted in Wilson, *Crisis,* p. 136.

12. The alienation of communal and public lands is described in detail in David Browning, *El Salvador: Landscape and Society* (Oxford: Clarendon Press, 1971), and in Rafael Menjívar, *Acumulación originaria y desarrollo del capitalismo en El Salvador* (San José: Editorial Universitaria Centroamericana, 1980).

13. Menjívar, *Acumulación,* p. 148.

14. Browning, *El Salvador,* p. 204.

15. Guidos Véjar, *El ascenso,* p. 102.

16. Pérez Brignoli, "Indios," p. 25.

17. Browning, *El Salvador,* pp. 170–171.

18. Menjívar, *Acumulación,* p. 149.

19. Guidos Véjar, *El ascenso,* p. 102.

20. Marroquín, *Estudio,* p. 123.

21. Anderson, *Matanza,* p. 54

22. Guidos Véjar, *El ascenso,* p. 102.

23. White, *El Salvador,* p. 99.

24. Dalton, *Miguel Mármol,* p. 307.

25. Anderson, *Matanza,* p. 30.

26. Dalton, *Miguel Mármol,* p. 287.

27. White, *El Salvador,* p. 94.

28. Anderson, *Matanza,* p. 27.

29. Ibid., pp. 40, 53, 74, 75.

30. Dalton, *Miguel Mármol,* p. 230.

31. Anderson, *Matanza,* p. 27.

32. Miguel Mármol notes that "neither in the Party nor in the Young Communist League was there at that time a cellular organization." Dalton, *Miguel Mármol,* p. 151.

33. Guidos Véjar, *El ascenso,* p. 115.

34. For accounts of the Pío Bosque and Araujo administrations see Anderson, *Matanza,* pp. 40–48, Guidos Véjar, *El ascenso,* pp. 114–118; Marroquín, "Estudio," and White, *El Salvador,* pp. 95–99.

35. Marroquín, "Estudio," p. 145.

36. Alberto Masferrer, *El minimum vital* (Guatemala City: Tipografía Nacional de Guatemala, 1950), p. 189.

37. Marroquín, "Estudio," pp. 144–145.

38. Ibid., pp. 146–147.

39. Anderson, *Matanza,* p. 44–46.

40. Marroquín, "Estudio," p. 148.

41. Anderson, *Matanza,* p. 52.

42. White, *El Salvador,* p. 99.

43. Guidos Véjar, *El ascenso,* p. 118.

44. Anderson, *Matanza,* p. 51.

45. Ibid., pp. 52–53.

46. Dalton, *Miguel Mármol,* pp. 224–225.

47. Marroquín, "Estudio," p. 149.

48. Anderson, *Matanza,* p. 54.

49. Araujo continued to believe until the end of his days that Martínez was responsible for the coup. Anderson, *Matanza,* p. 62, concludes that "Martínez was not aware of the details of any one plot, but was fully aware that something was in the wind, and was ready to profit by whatever occurred." White, *El Salvador,* p. 112, note 39, who, like Anderson, interviewed officers involved in the coup, also concludes that Martínez and other high ranking officers had no prior knowledge of the coup.

50. Manuel Caballero in *Latin America and the Comintern 1919–1943* (Cambridge: Cambridge University Press, 1986), p. 52, notes that "the Comintern had practically nothing to do with it [the insurrection]. As far as is known, it seems to have been a spontaneous initiative of the Salvadoran Communists." Miguel Mármol told Roque Dalton, "I'd like to pause here and use it to say once and for all that we didn't receive 'orders' nor 'watchwords' from the Communist International to 'make' the insurrection . . . the decision, the preliminary analysis and the form in which the actions were embarked upon were exclusively ours" (Dalton, *Miguel Mármol,* p. 291). Anderson in *Matanza,* p. 84, concludes: "Martí and his immediate aides . . . appear to have acted largely on their own with a minimum of direction and aid from the international communist movement. . . . Russia served chiefly as an inspiration to the revolutionaries."

51. Dalton, *Miguel Mármol,* pp. 290–291.

52. According to Manuel Caballero (*Comintern,* p. 44), the International did not consider the Salvadoran Communist Party to be one of the "real" sections of the International in Latin America but one of the "minor" parties. "Minor" refers not to the party's strength but its importance in the Comintern.

53. Cerdas Cruz, *La hoz,* pp. 274, 276.

54. Ibid., p. 273.

55. Dalton, *Miguel Mármol,* pp. 171, 195.

56. Caballero, *Comintern,* p. 55.

57. Anderson, *Matanza,* p. 24; Cerdas Cruz, *La hoz,* p. 273.

58. Dalton, *Miguel Mármol,* p. 80.

59. Anderson, *Matanza,* p. 22.

60. Dalton, *Miguel Mármol,* pp. 140, 197.

61. Caballero, *Comintern,* p. 9.

62. Milorad M. Drachkovitch and Branko Lazich, "The Communist International," in *The Revolutionary Internationals, 1864–1893,* ed. Milorad M. Drachkovitch (Stanford: Stanford University Press, 1966), pp. 159–202, and Kermit E. McKenzie, *Comintern and World Revolution 1928–1943* (New York: Columbia University Press, 1964), provide useful overviews of International thinking and strategy. Caballero's *Latin America and the Comintern* and Cerdas Cruz's *La hoz y el machete* provide excellent overviews of the Comintern in Latin and Central America respectively.

63. V. I. Lenin, *Left Wing Communism: An Infantile Disorder* (New York: International Publishers, 1934), pp. 17 and 82.

64. V. I. Lenin, *Proletarian Revolution and Renegade Kautsky* (New York: International Publishers, 1934), pp. 28, 12, and 11.

65. Jorge Arias Gómez, *Farabundo Martí* (San José: Editorial Universitaria Centroamericana, 1972), p. 73.

66. Marroquín, "Estudio," p. 147.

67. Dalton, *Miguel Mármol,* p. 290.

68. Anderson, *Matanza,* p. 81.

69. Dalton, *Miguel Mármol,* p. 229.

70. Ibid., p. 218.

71. Arias Gómez, *Martí,* pp. 13, 19.

72. Dalton, *Miguel Mármol,* p. 224.

73. Arias Gómez, *Martí,* p. 53. On the eve of his execution, however, Martí praised Sandino as one of the "few patriots in the world" (ibid., p. 154).

74. For descriptions of the International's Third World strategy see Cerdas Cruz, *La hoz;* Caballero, *Comintern,* pp. 65–106; and McKenzie, *World Revolution.*

75. Cerdas Cruz, *La hoz,* p. 303.

76. "Manifiesto del Comité Central del Partido Communista a las clases trajabadoras de la República: obreros, campesinos y soldados," reprinted in Roque Dalton, *Miguel Mármol: El Salvador 1930–32* (San Salvador: Editorial Universitaria, n.d.), p. 80.

77. Dalton, *Miguel Mármol,* p. 301; Anderson, *Matanza,* p. 117.

78. Dalton, *Miguel Mármol,* p. 152.

79. Cerdas Cruz, *La hoz,* pp. 298–305.

80. Anderson, *Matanza,* pp. 91, 93–96.

81. Dalton, *Miguel Mármol,* p. 290.

82. Anderson, *Matanza,* p. 158.

83. Ibid, pp. 15–21; Montes, *El compadrazgo,* pp. 177–200; Dalton, *Miguel Mármol,* p. 307.

84. Anderson, *Matanza,* p. 20.

85. See in particular Kincaid, "Peasants"; Montes, *El compadrazgo,* pp. 177–200; Pérez Brignoli, "Indios"; Zamsoc, "Class Conflict."

86. Montes, *El compadrazgo,* p. 191.

87. Méndez, *Los sucesos,* p. 105.

88. Asociación Cafetalera de El Salvador, "Contestación a la encuesta de la Asociación para el Estudio de Reformas Sociales," *El Café de El Salvador* 2 (July 1932):34–47. A critical analysis of the document is presented by Ovidio González, "Algunos elementos ideológicos de la clase dominante en el '32," Universidad Centroamericana José Simeón Cañas, *Boletín de Ciencias Económicas y Sociales* 6 (nov.-dic. 1984):384–397.

89. Asociación Cafetalera, "Contestación," p. 35.

90. Ibid., p. 42.

91. Ibid., p. 43.

92. Ibid., p. 41.

93. Ibid., p. 45.

94. Ibid., p. 37.

95. Ibid., p. 41.

4. Manuel Mora and the Rise of Euro-Communism

1. Careful historical studies of the firm of Tournon by Gertrude Peters ("La formación territorial de las grandes fincas de café en la Meseta Central: estudio de la firma Tournon; 1877–1955," *Revista de Historia* 9–10 (1980):81–167), and the processing operations of Julio Sánchez Lépiz by Ana Virginia Arguedas Chaverri and Marta Ramírez, "Contribución al análisis de empresas: el caso de Julio Sánchez Lépiz (1862–1934)" (Tesis de Licenciatura, Universidad Nacional, Heredia, Costa Rica, 1990), indicate that, in the early twentieth century, these firms were dependent in large part on coffee purchased from small and medium producers. Carolyn Stone notes in *El café y el desarrollo histórico-geográfico de Costa Rica*, 3rd ed. (San José: Editorial Costa Rica, 1982), p. 53, that "the strength of the coffee elite did not, nevertheless, rest on the possession of immense estates but rather in the control that they exercised over the processing and commercialization of the product," and further, that in Costa Rica's principal coffee region, the central plateau, "the registry of property of 1867 and following years, just as the Coffee Census of 1935, show clearly that the central plateau developed as a region where coffee farms of small and medium size, owned, for the most part, by peasants predominated."

2. Anthony Winson, *Coffee and Democracy in Modern Costa Rica* (New York: St. Martin's Press, 1989), p. 37; Víctor Acuña, "Clases sociales y conflicto social en la economía cafetalera costarricense: 'Productores contra beneficiadores' 1932–1936," *Revista de Historia*, número especial, *Problemas y perspectivas agrarias en Costa Rica* (Heredia, Costa Rica: 1985):189–190.

3. Rodolfo Cerdas Cruz, *La hoz y el machete: La Internacional Comunista, America Latina y la revolución en Centroamerica* (San José: Editorial Universidad Estatal a Distancia, 1986), p. 348; Acuña, "Clases sociales," p. 196.

4. The movement has been extensively studied by Víctor Hugo Acuña Ortega and his students. See Acuña, "La ideología de los pequeños y medianos productores cafetaleros costarricenses (1900–1961)," and Alfonso González Ortega, "El discurso oficial de los pequeños y medianos cafetaleros (1920–1940, 1950–1961)," both in *Revista de Historia* 16 (julio-diciembre 1987):137–191, and Acuña, "Clases sociales."

5. Acuña, "Clases sociales," pp. 190, 195.

6. Acuña, "La ideología," p. 152.

7. Ibid., pp. 141–144. The quotation from Manuel Marín Quirós appears on page 142. Changes in small-holder movement ideology concerning the processors after the 1940s are described in González Ortega, "El discurso," p. 176.

8. Acuña, "Clases sociales," pp. 188, 191–192.

9. Gloria Rodríguez, "The Coffee Order in Costa Rica, 1870–1889: Formation and Consolidation of a Structure of Domination" (Ph.D. diss., University of Sussex,

1983), pp. 77–78. See also José Luis Vega, *La formación del estado nacional en Costa Rica* (San José: Instituto Centroamericano de Administración Pública, 1981), pp. 283–311. On the generation of 1888 and the extension of the franchise see Samuel Stone, *La dinastía de los conquistadores* (San José: Editorial Universitaria Centroamericana, 1982), pp. 125–127; 222–224.

10. Acuña, "La ideología," p. 145.

11. John Patrick Bell, *Crisis in Costa Rica* (Austin: University of Texas Press, 1971), pp. 46–47.

12. Selections from *Trabajo* quoted in Cerdas Cruz, *La hoz,* p. 327. Mora's comments are quoted in Robert Salom, *La crisis de la izquierda en Costa Rica* (San José: Editorial Porvenir, 1987), p. 27. Party policy on social democrats and reformism as well as its view of the Soviet Union are described in Alejandro Gómez, *Rómulo Betancourt y el Partido Comunista de Costa Rica* (Caracas, Venezuela: Universidad Central de Venezuela, 1985), pp. 146 and 153–159.

13. Salon in *La crisis de la izquierda,* p. 29, dates the change to 1937 or thereabouts, but more moderate policies date from the Party's founding.

14. The "minimal program" is reproduced in Ana María Botey and Rodolfo Cisneros, *La crisis de 1929 y la fundación del partido comunista de Costa Rica* (San José: Editorial Costa Rica, 1984), pp. 119–122.

15. Cerdas Cruz, *La hoz,* p. 348.

16. For the development of the United Fruit Company activities in Central America see Frank Ellis, *Las transnacionales del banano en Centroamérica* (San José: Editorial Universitaria Centroamericana, 1983), pp. 30–74.

17. Conditions in the zone are described in Víctor Hugo Acuña, *La huelga bananera de 1934* (San José: Centro Nacional de Acción Pastoral y Centro de Estudios para la Acción Social, 1984), pp. 19–23, and Mitchell Seligson, *Peasants of Costa Rica* (Madison: University of Wisconsin Press, 1980), p. 67.

18. According to Cerdas Cruz (*La hoz,* p. 318) a group of Communists organized in Limón in 1929 and later joined with a group of law students in San José to form the Asociación de Resistencia Obrera, a precursor of the Communist Party of Costa Rica.

19. Acuña, *La huelga bananera,* p. 15.

20. Ibid., p. 17.

21. Marielos Aguilar, *Carlos Luis Falla: su época y sus luchas* (San José: Editorial Porvenir, 1983), pp. 76–96, discusses Falla's role in the strike and his writings on the banana zone.

22. Seligson, *Peasants,* pp. 70–71.

23. Aguilar, *Carlos Luis Falla,* p. 61.

24. Acuña, *La huelga bananera,* p. 29–31, 37.

25. Ibid.

26. The same debate broke out once again in the 1980s in the aftermath of the

Nicaraguan revolution (author's interviews with banana union representatives in San José and Río Frío, August 1985).

27. Quoted in Gómez, *Rómulo Betancourt,* p. 121. The article originally appeared in the September 30, 1934, issue of *Trabajo.*

28. Bell, *Crisis in Costa Rica,* pp. 46–48.

29. Quoted in Cerdas Cruz, *La hoz,* p. 349, note 14.

30. Ibid., p. 348.

31. Ibid., pp. 348, 350.

32. Ibid., p. 352.

33. Bell, *Crisis in Costa Rica,* p. 47.

34. Ibid., p. 13.

35. Cerdas Cruz, *La hoz,* pp. 346, 376.

36. For an account of Volio and his movement see Marina Volio, *Jorge Volio y el partido reformista* (San José: Editorial Costa Rica, 1972). See also Jorge Mario Salazar, *Política y reforma en Costa Rica 1914–1958* (San José: Editorial Porvenir, 1981), on the reformism of both Volio and González Flores.

37. Stone, *La dinastía,* pp. 292–292; Botey and Cisneros, *La crisis de 1929,* p. 64.

38. Botey and Cisneros, ibid., pp. 129–130.

39. Carlos Luis Falla, who was himself a shoemaker, wrote eloquently of the desperate situation of this trade in his short story "El taller" in *Tres cuentos* (San José: Editorial Costa Rica, 1975). Mora was the son of a cabinet maker.

40. Cerdas Cruz, *La hoz,* p, 317; Botey and Cisneros, *La crisis de 1929,* p. 116.

41. Botey and Cisneros, ibid., p. 130.

42. Bell, *Crisis,* p. 11.

43. The 1933 events are described in Aguilar, *Carlos Luis Falla,* pp. 60–61.

44. Manuel Rojas Bolaños, *Lucha social y guerra civil en Costa Rica 1940–1948* (San José: Editorial Porvenir, 1989), p. 85.

45. Jorge Mario Salazar Mora, *Calderón Guardia* (San José: Editorial Universidad Estatal a Distancia, 1980), pp. 21, 25.

46. Mark Rosenberg, "Social Reform in Costa Rica: Social Security and the Presidency of Rafael Angel Calderón," *Hispanic American Historical Review* 61 (1981):282.

47. Ibid., p. 279.

48. Salazar, *Calderón Guardia,* pp. 22–23.

49. Oscar Aguilar Bulgarelli, *Costa Rica y sus hechos políticos de 1948* (San José: Editorial Costa Rica, 1983), p. 31.

50. Ibid., pp. 44, 68, 73; Bolaños, *Lucha social,* pp. 51–52.

51. Rosenberg in "Social Reform in Costa Rica" argues persuasively that the social security act was a top-down initiative of Calderón and his closest advisers.

52. Aguilar, *Hechos políticos,* pp. 38–39.

53. Ibid., pp. 50–52.

54. Mora related this version of the events in interviews with Oscar Aguilar Bulgarelli (*Hechos políticos,* Anexo 1, pp. 489–491) and Samuel Stone (*Dinastía,* p. 301, note 2) among others.

55. Quoted in Aguilar, *Hechos políticos,* p. 511.

56. Bell, *Crisis,* p. 52.

57. The text of the letters exchanged by Mora and Sanabria are reproduced in Aguilar, *Hechos políticos,* pp. 59–64.

58. Ulate had actually been included in the initial slate of the Alliance of Workers, Peasants and Intellectuals, an electoral alliance formed for the 1930 election by many individuals later active in the Communist Party (Botey and Cisneros, *La crisis de 1929,* p. 66). His denunciation of the social guarantees was contained in an editorial in his newspaper *Diario de Costa Rica* in May 1942 (Rojas Bolaños, *Lucha social,* pp. 74–75) which nonetheless expresses grudging admiration for the Communists. Ulate had defended the participation of the Communists in Costa Rican life in their early years before becoming an outspoken anti-communist in the civil war period (Bell, *Crisis in Costa Rica,* pp. 52–53).

59. The so-called San Pablo Affair, from the name of the sunken vessel, is described in detail in Charles D. Ameringer, *Don Pepe* (Albuquerque: University of New Mexico Press, 1978), pp. 17–21. Ameringer (p. 24) notes that Figueres "had a temper and did not shrink from the use of violence." Figueres's view of Calderón as a dictator or potential dictator led him to seek an alliance with other Central Americans in an effort to overthrow dictatorship throughout the region. Figueres thus implicitly equated Calderón with the notorious tyrannies of Anastasio Somoza in Nicaragua, Jorge Ubico in Guatemala, and Tiburcio Carías Andino in Honduras (Ameringer, ibid., pp. 24–25).

60. In the 1946 elections, for example, the Calderón-Communist alliance carried San José and won overwhelmingly in the banana zone province of Limón, Guanacaste, with its pattern of large estates and impoverished campesinos, and the port province of Puntarenas. The opposition carried the coffee districts of the Meseta Central. Rosenberg notes that after his election Calderón surrounded himself with aristocratic Catholic reformers including the venerable Jorge Volio (Rosenberg, "Social Reform in Costa Rica," p. 283).

61. Rojas Bolaños, *Lucha social,* p. 93. Anthony Winson, *Coffee and Democracy in Modern Costa Rica* (New York: St. Martin's Press, 1989), p. 51. The more conservative elements of the oligarchy had backed León Cortés and his Democratic Party, but after his death in 1946 they had nowhere else to go other than Ulate. Stone (*Dinastía,* p. 309) refers to Ulate's National Union party as the party of the *cafetaleros.*

62. Samuel Stone (ibid., p. 309) notes that over half of the members of the Centro were descendents of noble families of the colonial period and 20% were

descendents of the conquistador Juan Vázquez de Coronado. Nevertheless, as Rojas Bolaños (*Lucha social*, p. 94) notes, the political orientation as well as the social origins of many of the members were middle class.

63. Jacobo Shifter, *La fase oculta de la guerra civil en Costa Rica* (San José: Editorial Universitaria Centroamericana, 1986), p. 70–71, argues that the Centro and Figueres were markedly anti-capitalist and favored a radical transformation of the economy through state action.

64. Calderón was running once again for the presidency after ceding the office to Calderonist Tomás Picado from 1944 to 1948.

65. Ulate won by 10,000 votes, but there is considerable evidence of irregularity in the voting, although it may never be known whether outright fraud was committed. The number of voters dropped from the 1944 election, despite the fact that interest in the election was at a fever pitch. The drop was greatest in areas such as Limón and Guanacaste, where the Communists and Calderón had been strong. Manuel Mora claimed that in a fair vote Calderón would have won by ten thousand votes (see the discussion and voting data in Shifter, *La fase oculta*, pp. 80–81). Mora's estimate is contained in his interview with Aguilar presented as anexo 6, p. 547 of *Hechos políticos*.

66. Winson, *Coffee and Democracy*, p. 62; Ameringer, *Don Pepe*, p. 70.

67. Ameringer, *Don Pepe*, pp. 86–87.

68. Ibid., p. 91.

69. Ibid., p. 88.

70. Ibid., p. 90.

71. Ibid., p. 105.

72. On the coffee program of Liberación, see Winson, *Coffee and Democracy*, pp. 99–110. Ameringer reviews the various autonomous entities in subsequent Liberación administrations in *Don Pepe*. See especially pages 98, 142, 251–252, 279.

73. Shifter, *La fase oculta*, pp. 112–115.

74. Bell, *Crisis in Costa Rica*, p. 160.

5. Augusto César Sandino and the Failure of Revolutionary Nationalism

1. Neill Macaulay, *The Sandino Affair*, 2nd ed. (Durham: Duke University Press, 1985), p. 225, reports that in the spring and summer of 1932 "there was fierce fighting in almost every department in Nicaragua."

2. The date of the official founding of the Communist Party is given by Knut Walter, *The Regime of Anastasio Somoza 1936–1956* (Chapel Hill: University of North Carolina Press, 1995), p. 105; Macaulay, *Sandino Affair*, p. 225, reports that clandestine Communists were active in the Atlantic Coast region in 1931–32.

3. For general histories of the complex events of this period see Ralph Lee Woodward, *Central America: A Nation Divided,* 2nd. ed. (New York: Oxford, 1985), pp. 194–202 and Karl Berman, *Under the Big Stick: Nicaragua and the United States since 1848* (Boston: South End Press, 1986).

4. For summaries of the voluminous literature on the Walker episode see Woodward, *Central America,* pp.136–146 and Berman, *Big Stick,* pp. 51–72.

5. On the differences between the political economy of León and Granada and the origins of their political rivalry, see David Richard Radell, "An Historical Geography of Western Nicaragua: The Spheres of Influence of León, Granada and Managua, 1519–1965" (Ph.D. diss., University of California, Berkeley, 1969); Alberto Lanuza, Juan Luis Vázquez, Amaru Barahona, and Amalia Chamorro, *Economía y sociedad en la construcción del estado en Nicaragua* (San José: Instituto Centroamericano de Administración Pública, 1983), particularly pt. 1, chap. 2, "Análisis de la estructura de la producción," by Lanuza, and pt. 2, chap. 1, "Las condiciones políticas de la formación del estado oligárquico," by Vázquez.

6. Benjamin Teplitz in "The Political and Economic Foundations of Modernization in Nicaragua: The Administration of José Santos Zelaya" (Ph.D. diss., Howard University, 1973), pp. 182–187, provides a detailed account of Conservative efforts to encourage coffee production. Teplitz's unpublished dissertation is still the best study available on Zelaya.

7. For accounts of the rise of the Liberal coffee elite see Lanuza, et al., *Construcción del estado en Nicaragua,* pp. 75–84 and 153–157; Jaime Wheelock Román, *Imperialismo y dictadura* (Managua, Nicaragua: Editorial Nueva Nicaragua, 1985); Jaime Biderman, "The Development of Capitalism in Nicaragua: A Political Economic History," *Latin American Perspectives* 10 (Winter 1983):7–32; and Michael Merlet, "El siglo diecinueve en Nicaragua: auge y derrota de la vía campesina (1821–1934)" (paper presented at the symposium "Las sociedades agrarias centroamericanas: siglos XIX y XX," Universidad Nacional, Heredia, Costa Rica, 1990). In 1867 Zelaya's father, José María Zelaya, was the sixth largest grower in Managua, then the center of Nicaraguan coffee production (Lanuza, et al., ibid., p. 79).

8. Teplitz, "Foundations of Modernization in Nicaragua," pp. 190–209; Lanuza, et al., ibid., pp. 158–162.

9. Teplitz, ibid., p. 228.

10. Ibid., p. 192.

11. Ibid., p. 231.

12. On the 1881 insurrection see Jaime Wheelock Román, *Raíces indígenas de la lucha anticolonialista en Nicaragua* (Managua: Editorial Nueva Nicaragua, 1981). Both the 1881 and 1895 revolts are described in Michael J. Schroeder, "To Defend Our Nation's Honor: Towards a Social and Cultural History of the Sandino Rebellion in Nicaragua, 1927–1934" (Ph.D. diss., University of Michigan, 1993), pp. 101–102.

13. Teplitz, "Foundations of Modernization in Nicaragua," p. 217.

14. Ibid., p. 221.

15. Ibid., p. 414, notes, "Under the Zelayists, national interests were equated exclusively with upper class interests."

16. On infrastructure development see Charles S. Stansifer, "José Santos Zelaya: A *New Look* at Nicaragua's '*Liberal*' Dictator," *Revista Interamericana* (Hato Rey, Puerto Rico) 7 (Fall 1977):478. Loan arrangements are described in Charles Edward Frazier, "The Dawn of Nationalism and Its Consequences for Nicaragua" (Ph.D. diss., University of Texas, 1958), p. 96.

17. As Berman, *Big Stick,* p. 149, notes, a persistent myth, encouraged apparently by Zelaya himself, was that his overthrow was a result of his nationalist objections to a canal treaty (see, for example, Gregorio Selser, *Sandino* (New York: Monthly Review, 1981), p. 26; Stansifer, "José Santos Zelaya," p. 483; Woodward, *Central America,* p. 195). There is no evidence in support of this contention; in fact Zelaya's foreign minister signed a protocol agreeing to the main provisions of a draft canal treaty in December 1901 (Berman, ibid.). The decision to build the canal in Panama had nothing to do with objections by the Nicaraguans (see David McCullough, *The Path Between the Seas: The Creation of the Panama Canal 1879–1904* (New York: Simon and Schuster, 1977), p. 327).

18. Stansifer, "José Santos Zelaya," pp. 473, 475–476.

19. Ibid., pp. 480–482. See also Berman, *Big Stick,* pp. 137–140, Woodward, *Central America,* pp. 191–194.

20. Teplitz, "Foundations of Modernization," p. 242.

21. Craig L. Dozier, *Nicaragua's Mosquito Shore: The Years of British and American Presence* (Birmingham: University of Alabama Press, 1985), p. 159.

22. Dozier's *Mosquito Shore* is the most detailed scholarly study of the Mosquitia.

23. On Bluefields as leader in banana exports, see Dozier, *Mosquito Shore,* p. 143; on La Luz and Los Angeles Company, Berman, *Big Stick,* p. 143; on the Emery firm, Dozier, ibid., p. 142. The estimate of American control of investment is by Ambassador Lewis Baker as quoted in John Findling, "The United States and Zelaya: A Study in the Diplomacy of Expediency" (Ph.D. diss., University of Texas, 1971), p. 14.

24. R. L. Morrow, "A Conflict between the Commercial Interests of the U.S. and Its Foreign Policy," *Hispanic American Historical Review* 10 (Feb. 1930):13, quoted in Dozier, *Mosquito Shore,* p. 157.

25. As Findling, "United States and Zelaya," p. 227, notes, "throughout Zelaya's sixteen year reign the United States pursued a diplomacy marked by expediency and a concern for an isthmian canal."

26. After examining in the U.S. National Archives detailed accounts of controversies involving American citizens, Stansifer ("Jose Santos Zelaya," p. 478) concludes that in fact most concessions were granted for reasons of economic development and cancelled for cause, not nationalism.

27. On the Emery claim see Berman, *Big Stick,* pp. 143–144.

28. The text of the Knox Note is presented in United States Department of State, *Foreign Relations of the United States* (Washington, D.C.: Government Printing Office, 1909), p. 452.

29. I am indebted to Walter LaFeber for bringing the Root speech to my attention in his *Inevitable Revolutions: The United States in Central America* (New York: Norton, 1983), p. 36. Quotations in the text are from the transcript of the speech as presented in *Foreign Relations*, p. 1457.

30. In an address at the University of California, Berkeley, on March 23, 1911. As McCullough (*Path between the Seas,* p. 384) points out, a more accurate description might have been, as Roosevelt said later in private, that the canal was handed to him "on a silver platter." As in Nicaragua in 1909, a local rebellion became the occasion for the dispatch of U.S. warships.

31. Roosevelt annunciated the doctrine in a speech on the Dominican Republic, but the same principle would be applied throughout the region (LaFeber, *Inevitable Revolutions,* p. 37).

32. Findling, "United States and Zelaya," p. 9.

33. Ibid., p. 168.

34. Quoted in Harold Denny, *Dollars for Bullets: The Story of American Rule in Nicaragua* (Westport, Conn.: Greenwood Press, [1929] 1980), p. 3.

35. As Woodward, *Central America,* p. 191, notes, "Fiscal intervention in Santa Domingo began in 1904, and it escalated to military occupation in 1916. A similar fate befell Haiti in 1915."

36. See Stansifer, "José Santos Zelaya," on the image and the reality; Berman, *Big Stick,* p. 143, on yellow journalism. Quotes from the Knox Note are from *Foreign Relations* (1909), p. 452.

37. Berman, *Big Stick,* p. 150.

38. See, for example, Selser, *Sandino,* p. 27.

39. See note 17 above.

40. On the origins of the United States military intervention see Richard Millet, *Guardians of the Dynasty* (Maryknoll, N.Y.: Orbis Books, 1979), pp. 15–36. Good general histories of the intervention are also presented in Berman, *Big Stick,* pp. 151–181, and Woodward, *Central America,* pp. 196–201.

41. Colorful and often polemical contemporary accounts of the United States financial protectorate are presented in Rafael Nogales Méndez, *The Looting of Nicaragua* (New York: M. McBride, 1928); Denny, *Dollars for Bullets;* J. A. H. Hopkins and Melinda Alexander, *Machine Gun Diplomacy* (New York: Lewis Copeland Company, 1928); and James T. Wall, *Manifest Destiny Denied, America's First Intervention in Nicaragua* (Washington, D.C.: University Press of America, [1933] 1981). Berman's *Big Stick,* pp. 151–181, remains the most useful scholarly account.

42. According to Nogales, *Looting of Nicaragua,* p. 21, the coffee economy was managed as follows: "The New York concerns in control of the Bank of Nicaragua controlled also the coffee market by means of an institution which they owned and which was called the Companía Mercantil de Ultramar. Their system was very simple. The bank would advance money to the coffee growers at the rate of ten to eighteen per cent a year, with the understanding that their crops would have to be sold to the Companía Mercantil de Ultramar for a price lower than the market price."

43. The Board of Directors of the Bank was brought back to Nicaragua from New York in 1938 by Somoza García (Walter, *Regime of Anastasio Somoza,* p. 75).

44. David R. Radell, "Coffee and Transportation in Nicaragua" (Department of Geography, University of California, Berkeley, 1964), p. 54. In the early part of the century desperate coffee planters conceived of a bizarre plan to compensate for the lack of rail or road connections from the north central coffee region and the coast. A crude path was cleared between Matagalpa and León and a tracked steam engine was purchased to run on it. "El Tren de Matagalpa," as this notorious innovation was called, made only six trips, each accompanied by a mule train to carry water for the boilers, before damage from the rough track halted operations.

45. Wheelock, *Imperialismo y dictadura,* p. 166.

46. Henry L. Stimson, *American Policy in Nicaragua* (New York: Charles Scribner's Sons, 1928), p. 88.

47. On the Tipitapa agreement and its role in the formation of the Nicaraguan National Guard see Millet, *Guardians of the Dynasty,* pp. 54–56.

48. Macaulay, *Sandino Affair,* p. 48.

49. Robert Edgar Conrad (trans. and ed.), in his Introduction to *Sandino: The Testimony of a Nicaraguan Patriot, 1921–1934* (Princeton: Princeton University Press, 1990), p. 17.

50. Donald C. Hodges, *Intellectual Foundations of the Nicaraguan Revolution* (Austin: University of Texas Press, 1986), p. 136. "We consider the war we are undertaking to be a continuation of his [Zeledón's] own," said Sandino himself (as quoted in Hodges, ibid.).

51. Ibid., pp. 107–152, provides an excellent overview of Sandino's construction of Nicaraguan history as revealed in observations scattered throughout his writing. Sandino's theory of the canal is described on p. 116.

52. Schroeder, "Our Nation's Honor," pp. 63–64.

53. As Hodges, *Intellectual Foundations,* p. 136, notes, "Opposition to the treaty is the thread tying together his participation in the constitutionalist war, his defense of Nicaraguan sovereignty against the American intervention, and his final escalation of military action with virtually no help from abroad."

54. Most scholarly commentators see anti-Yankee nationalism as the core of Sandino's beliefs (see Macaulay, *Sandino Affair;* Selser, *Sandino;* Schroeder, "Our

Nation's Honor"; Karl Berman in his Introduction to *Sandino without Frontiers* (Hampton, Va.: Compita Publishing, 1988); and Richard Grossman, "Patria y Libertad: Sandino and the Development of Peasant Nationalism in Northern Nicaragua" (paper delivered at the 17th International Congress of the Latin American Studies Association, Los Angeles, September 24–27, 1992). Later Sandinista interpreters have emphasized his anti-imperialism and have tried to find in him a "proletarian guerrilla" and precursor of later "national liberation" struggles including their own. (See Carlos Fonseca Amador, *Sandino: guerrillero proletario* (Managua(?): Secretaría Nacional de Propaganda y Educación Política del FSLN, 1980(?)); Víctor Tirado López, *Sandino y la doctrina de liberación nacional* (Managua: Editorial Vanguardia, 1989); Humberto Ortega Saavedra, *Cincuenta años de lucha Sandinista* (Managua: Ministerio de Interior, n.d.); Sergio Ramírez, "The Relevance of Sandino's Thought," pp. 123–132 in Berman's *Sandino without Frontiers*). It may be fairly said, as does Dennis Gilbert in *Sandinistas* (New York: Basil Blackwell, 1988), that the Sandinistas "read Sandino through Marx." Hodges, *Intellectual Foundations,* has emphasized Sandino's mystical and spiritual side and tried to find anarchist and Marxist influences in his thought. There is in fact considerable evidence of the former, but most students of Sandino, and most other readers of his work, including the present author, find the latter assertion unconvincing (for example Conrad, *Sandino: Testimony of a Nicaraguan Patriot,* p. 17, note 39, and Schroeder, "Our Nation's Honor," p. 59, both explicitly reject Hodges' contention of anarchist or Marxist influence). Hodges never backs up with any direct evidence his contention (*Sandino's Communism,* p. 3) that Conrad is incorrect in asserting that Hodges has nowhere demonstrated that Sandino ever read Mexican anarchist Flores Magnon. In fact Flores Magnon is never mentioned by Sandino in any of his published writings or interviews.) Paradoxically, Anastasio Somoza in his *El verdadero Sandino o el Calvario de las Segovias* (Managua: Tipografía Robelo, 1936) also gives great weight to Sandino's mysticism and his alleged communism. Except for Schroeder and Grossman, who had access to interviews with survivors of Sandino's army conducted after the Sandinista revolution, all of these interpretations rely for the most part on the same sources, particularly Sandino's own writings, mostly letters and manifestos (many of which are collected in Conrad, *Sandino: Testimony of a Nicaraguan Patriot*); books by contemporary journalists Carlton Beals, *Banana Gold* (Philadelphia: Lippincott, 1932); José Román, *Maldito país* (Managua: Editorial Unión, 1983); and Ramón Belausteguigoitia, *Con Sandino en Nicaragua* (Managua: Editorial Nueva Nicaragua, 1981); which are by far the most revealing sources on Sandino's personality, motivations, and ideas; and a book by contemporary sympathizer Gustavo Alemán Bolaños, *Sandino: El libertador, la epopeya, la paz, el invasor, la muerte* (Mexico: Ediciones del Caribe [1932], 1980), as well as the many captured documents in Somoza's book. Schroeder and also Macaulay make extensive use of the archives of the United States Marine and National

Guard operations against Sandino. The differences among the interpreters are more a reflection of their own differing political and intellectual perspectives than differences in the primary source material. My own attempt to adjudicate among the competing interpretations is based on a reading of these secondary sources plus an examination of Sandino's published writings (they are not extensive) and the contemporary journalistic accounts. All quotations from Sandino in the text, unless otherwise noted, are from the Conrad collection. The best overall account is probably still Macaulay's *The Sandino Affair.*

55. Schroeder, "Our Nation's Honor," p. v.

56. Ramírez, "Relevance of Sandino's Thought," p. 123.

57. As he explained to journalist José Román, *Maldito país,* p. 70.

58. Hodges, *Intellectual Foundations,* p. 113.

59. Schroeder, "Our Nation's Honor," p. 63; Hodges, *Intellectual Foundations,* p. 112.

60. Schroeder, ibid. Sandino's first manifesto of July 1, 1927 is reproduced in Conrad, *Testimony,* pp. 74–77.

61. Quoted in Berman, *Sandino without Frontiers,* p. 2.

62. Sandino told José Ramón that he had explained to the workers at San Albino that he was a socialist, not a Communist (*Maldito país,* p. 57). He referred to the coming "proletarian explosion" in his famous "Light and Truth" manifesto of February 15, 1931 (Conrad, *Testimony,* p. 362) and expressed his faith in the workers and peasants in his "Message to the Urban and Rural Workers of Nicaragua and of All Latin America" of February 26, 1930 (Conrad, ibid., p. 311). Even Fonseca concedes that Sandino's demands were limited to "calling for the withdrawal of the interventionist forces and respect for national sovereignty" (Carlos Fonseca, "Viva Sandino," in Berman, ed., *Sandino without Frontiers,* p. 113).

63. Reading about Simón Bolívar reportedly moved Sandino to tears (Macaulay, *Sandino Affair,* p. 53).

64. As quoted in Arias Gómez, *Farabundo Martí,* p. 154.

65. Macaulay, *Sandino Affair,* p. 158.

66. "Conversations with Ramón Belausteguigoitia, February 1933," in Conrad, *Testimony,* p. 455.

67. Schroeder, "Our Nation's Honor," pp. 142, 146, 265, 272: Macaulay, *Sandino Affair,* pp. 54, 73, 88.

68. Sandino's analysis of the San Albino mine is presented in his second manifesto of July 14, 1927 (Conrad, *Testimony,* pp. 79–81).

69. "Conversations with Ramón Belausteguigoitia, February 1933," in Conrad, *Testimony,* pp. 455–56; Schroeder, "Our Nation's Honor," p. 514.

70. As quoted in Macaulay, *Sandino Affair,* p. 211.

71. As quoted in ibid., p. 226.

72. Schroeder, "Our Nation's Honor," p. 236.

73. Ibid., p. 515.

74. Grossman, "Patria y Libertad," p. 4.

75. Schroeder, "Our Nation's Honor," p. 225.

76. The picture is reproduced, for example, in an unnumbered appendix to Ortega's *Cincuenta años de lucha Sandinista.* The photo's authenticity was vouched for by Pennington himself, although he denied beheading the soldier personally (Macaulay, *Sandino Affair,* p. 229).

77. Schroeder, "Our Nation's Honor," p. 380.

78. Schroeder, ibid., p. 434. For a summary of Marine depredations see Macaulay, *Sandino Affair,* pp. 228–229, and in greater detail, Schroeder, ibid, pp. 440–485.

79. Quoted in Macaulay, *Sandino Affair,* p. 234.

80. On the conclusion of the war and Sandino's assassination see Macaulay, *Sandino Affair,* pp. 236–254.

81. Schroeder, "Our Nation's Honor," pp. 7, 12, reports that the Guard went on an eight-day killing rampage in which, as in El Salvador, prisoners were executed in groups of 50.

82. Somoza, *El verdadero Sandino,* pp. 563–564.

83. Selser, *Sandino,* p. 201.

84. In a letter to Gustavo Alemán Bolaños, March 16, 1933 (Conrad, *Testimony,* p. 468).

85. Sandino hoped to unite the Nicaraguan Labor Party with dissident Liberals, but conversations with representatives of the former ended inconclusively (Macaulay, *Sandino Affair,* p. 146).

86. Macaulay notes that in 1931–32 "economic distress in the banana country was exploited by both Communists and Sandinistas" (ibid., p. 225).

87. Schroeder notes that "the El Jícaro mining region [i.e., near San Albino] and the zone of intensive coffee expansion east of San Rafael del Norte and Jinotega" were the regions that Marine intelligence reports indicate were the areas of greatest Sandinista support. Comparison of the "Map of Reported Marine 'Contacts' with Sandino's Insurgents 1927–1932" (Map 8.10, p. 328) with maps of intensive coffee cultivation (Map 3.4, p. 107) and gold mining (Map 4.1, p. 131) in Schroeder's dissertation indicate an almost perfect overlap between the "Contacts" and gold or dispersed intensive coffee cultivation. The area of most concentrated intensive coffee cultivation around the town of Matagalpa has few contacts, but this area was heavily garrisoned by Marines who could rely on the support of the many local coffee growers in the area. The economic origins of the insurrection seem clear even if economic issues played little role in the movement's ideology.

88. "Conversation with José Ramón on the Coco River, March 1933," in Conrad, *Testimony,* pp. 500–501.

89. Despite the widespread myth of a mestizo Nicaragua, a substantial indig-

enous population existed in northern Nicaragua well into the Sandino period. As has already been noted, there were two Indian rebellions in the region in the last two decades of the nineteenth century (Jeffrey L. Gould, "Vana Ilusion! The Highlands Indians and the Myth of Nicaragua Mestizo, 1880–1935," *Hispanic American Historical Review* 73 (August 1993):393–429).

90. It is not surprising, therefore, that many northern Nicaraguan Indians joined the Conservative revolt against Zelaya (Gould, ibid., p. 409).

91. Anthony D. Smith, *The Ethnic Origins of Nations* (Oxford: Blackwell, 1986), p. 24.

92. The most detailed exposition of this school and its influence on Sandino is Hodges, *Sandino's Communism.*

93. Román, *Maldito país,* p. 183.

94. "The army . . . is enveloped in a spiritual power so grand that it represents the most potent ideal army that America has had since the times of the liberator," claimed Belaustiguigoitia (quoted in Schroeder, "Our Nation's Honor," p. 224).

95. Reproduced in Conrad, "Testimony," pp. 361–362.

96. In Hodges's *Sandino's Communism,* and Somoza's *El verdadero Sandino.*

97. Marvin Harris, *Cows, Pigs, Wars and Witches: The Riddles of Culture* (New York: Vintage, 1975), pp. 239–240.

98. On his last evening of life he was discussing plans with Liberal President Juan B. Sacasa to establish a public company to exploit the gold deposits of the Río Coco. Sacasa's wife was to be the major shareholder (Macaulay, *Sandino Affair,* p. 254). As has been noted, Sacasa did nothing about the murder of Sandino or his followers. Not one of the leading upper-class families of Nicaragua supported Sandino's crusade (Schroeder, "Our Nation's Honor," p. 502).

99. Jaime Wheelock's *Raíces indígenas* and especially his influential *Imperialismo y dictadura* are examples of such analysis. See also Orlando Nuñez Soto, *El somocismo y el modelo capitalista agroexportador* (Managua: Departamento de Ciencias Sociales de la UNAN, n.d.), and Ricardo Morales, *La dominación imperialista en Nicaragua* (Managua: Secretaría Nacional de Propaganda y Educación Política del FSLN, 1980), as well as the extensive writings of FSLN founder Carlos Fonseca.

6. Agro-Industrialists versus Agrarians in El Salvador

1. Antonio Pérez Bennett, Armando Molina Mena, Edwin Napoleón Lozo, and Ernesto Mauricio Magaña, "Investigación sobre la crisis del café en el año 1974: beneficiadores" (San Salvador: Facultad de Ciencias Económicas, Universidad Centroamericana José Simeón Cañas, 1975), p. 24.

2. See, for example, "Junta de gobierno de la Asociación Cafetalera de El Salvador" in *El Café de El Salvador* 3 (January 1933), facing p. 1.

3. Carmen Candray de Aquino, et al., "El Salvador, 1929–1932" (San Salvador:

Departamento de Ciencias Políticas y Sociología, Universidad Centroamericana José Simeón Cañas, 1977), pp. 44–45, 52; and Pérez Bennett, et al., "Investigación sobre la crisis del café," pp. 29–31.

4. Compare the listings of the Cafetalera boards for the 1970s presented in Eduardo Colindres, *Fundamentos económicos de la burguesía salvadoreña* (San Salvador: Universidad Centroamericana Editores, 1977), pp. 151–152, with the list of leading processors in Enrique G. Dubón, "La concentración de la actividad económica en la agroindustria del café," Documento de Trabajo, *Boletín de Ciencias Económicas y Sociales,* no. 8, app. 2 (San Salvador: Universidad Centroamericana José Simeón Cañas, August 24, 1982). The leading processors include such famous names as de Sola, Daglio, Liebes, Llach, Battle, Prieto, Salaverría, Cristiani, Menéndez, Homberger, and Hill. None of these names appear on the Cafetalera board listings.

5. See the previous note and *Memoria de labores 1988,* "Miembros de la Fundación," pp. 46–49 (San Salvador: Fundación Salvadoreña para el Desarrollo Económico y Social, n.d. [1989?]).

6. Rank order in terms of coffee processing taken from Dubón, "Concentración de la actividad económica," app. 2, "Beneficiadores privados y volúmen de café y procesado (1980–81)."

7. See for example ABECAFE's paid announcements in *El Diario de Hoy:* 6 Feb. 1984, p. 45; 9 Feb. 1984, p. 25; 13 Feb. 1984, p. 59; 16 Feb. 1984, p. 35; 3 Mar. 1984, p. 33; 5 Mar. 1984, p. 45; and 19 Mar. 1984, p. 69.

8. "La caficultura, regalo de Dios," in-house document, Asociación Salvadoreña de Beneficiadores y Exportadores del Café, San Salvador, n.d. [1989]. In the personal collection of Miguel Angel Salaverría.

9. Cecilia Elizabeth Saade de Saade and Evelyn Rivas de Rosal, "La concentración en la producción de café y las modificaciones inducidas por el proceso de reforma agraria: período 1971–1982" (Tesis de Licenciatura, Universidad Centroamericana José Simeón Cañas, 1983), p. 116.

10. The date of Barrios's death, 29 August, is celebrated as the Día Nacional de Caficultura in recognition of his role in initiating Salvadoran commercial production. See for example, "En Día de la Caficultura destacan valor del café," *El Diario de Hoy,* 30 Aug. 1986, p. 5; and "El Capitán General Gerardo Barrios impulsa la siembra de café," *El Diario de Hoy,* 29 Aug. 1988, p. 15.

11. Ralph Lee Woodward, Jr., *Central America, A Nation Divided,* 2d ed. (Oxford: Oxford University Press, 1985), p. 163.

12. "El problema del INCAFE," *Estudios Centroamericanos* 42, no. 461 (1987):242–45.

13. *El comercio exterior del café y la economía nacional* (San Salvador: Asociación Salvadoreña de Beneficiadores y Exportadores de Café, n.d.), p. 48.

14. "Ley sobre INCAFE parecida a la legislación nicaragüense," *El Diario de Hoy,* 4 Jan. 1979, p. 3.

15. Roberto López, "La nacionalización del comercio exterior en El Salvador: mitos y realidades en torno al café," Latin American and Caribbean Center Occasional Papers no. 16 (Miami: Latin American and Caribbean Center, Florida International University, 1986), p. 31.

16. The statement was actually made by General Adolfo Blandón, Chairman of the Joint Chiefs of Staff of the Salvadoran Armed Forces, in a meeting held on 21 Aug. 1986 with representatives of the Cafetalera and other private-sector organizations. See "Pdte. Duarte tiene que rectificar, dice Blandón," *El Diario de Hoy,* 22 Aug. 1986, p. 3.

17. See "Asamblea aprueba ley del Consejo Salvadoreño del Café," *El Diario de Hoy,* 19 Oct. 1989, p. 2; "Crean Consejo del Café y se reforma el INCAFE," *La Prensa Gráfica,* 20 Oct. 1989, p. 3; "Asamblea aprobó la venta libre de café al exterior," *Diario Latino,* 20 Oct. 1989, p. 6; and "8 representantes en Consejo del Café," *El Mundo,* 20 Oct. 1989, p. 32. Both ABECAFE and the Cafetalera were represented on the board of the council, along with representatives of the marketing and agrarian reform cooperatives.

18. ABECAFE paid announcement, *Diario Latino,* 24 Nov. 1977, p. 19, quoted in James Dunkerly, *The Long War: Dictatorship and Revolution in El Salvador* (London: Junction, 1982), p. 113.

19. Italo López Vallecillos, "Fuerzas sociales y cambio social en El Salvador," *Estudios Centroamericanos* 34, nos. 369–370 (julio–agosto 1979):558.

20. This acceptance is limited, at best. The processing plant workers' union, SICAFE (Sindicato de la Industria del Café), continues to denounce human rights violations against its officers and members during labor disputes. For examples, see SICAFE's paid announcements in *El Mundo:* 29 Jan. 1986, p. 19; and 13 May 1989, p. 26.

21. The victorious faction consisted of de Sola, President Francisco García Rossi (who died in 1987), René Domínguez Hernández, Doña María Teresa de Padaoni, Gerardo Escalón Gómez, Andrés Rodríguez Celis, Carlos Raúl Calvo, Jorge Amando Alabí, and Julio Funes Hartman. The defeated faction, led by Cafetalera President Arturo Simeón Magaña, elected a separate president and board and briefly claimed legitimate control of the association before ceding to the de Sola faction, which had elected its own president and board. See "División entre gremio cafetalera del país," *El Diario de Hoy,* 30 May 1984, p. 2; and "Violenta sesión de los cafetaleros ayer," *Diario Latino,* 30 May 1984, p. 20.

22. De Sola's columns appeared regularly in *El Diario de Hoy.* Examples include "INCAFE defiende lo indefendible," 26 Oct. 1985, p. 4; "Como lograr la paz," 25 July 1986, p. 6; and "El Salvador ante la OIC," 15 June 1989, p. 6. For representative statements by García Rossi, see "Piden al gobierno parar destrucción caficultura," *El Diario de Hoy,* 15 July 1986, p. 3; and "Desarrollo de los pueblos descansa en libre empresa," *El Diario de Hoy,* 9 Aug. 1986, p. 7. García Rossi was

killed in an automobile accident in the United States on 17 June 1987. For representative columns by Calvo, see "Entierro socialista para El Salvador!" *Diario Latino,* 11 Apr. 1986, p. 6; "El comunitarismo es totalitario," *El Diario de Hoy,* 15 Aug. 1986, p. 20; and "Las reformas estructurales y la guerra," *El Diario de Hoy,* 23 Sept. 1986, p. 21. Paid announcements referred to the Duarte and IN-CAFE policies as "irrational and suicidal" and obedient to "a Marxist-Leninist ideology imposed from abroad" that had brought the country to "a blood bath, exodus, unemployment, and the destruction of the economy." See *El Diario de Hoy,* 21 Sept. 1987, p. 45; 18 Apr. 1986, p. 22; and 24 Feb. 1987, p. 41.

23. For accounts of the election campaigns, see "División entre gremio," *Diario de Hoy,* 30 May 1984, p. 2; "Violenta sesión," *Diario Latino,* 30 May 1984, p. 20; "Táctica de la D.C.: dividir al gremio," *El Diario de Hoy,* 30 May 1986, p. 3; and "Triunfa en la cafetalera planilla del Dr. García Rossi frente a la de la 'oposición' " *El Mundo,* 29 May 1986, p. 2. See also "Alertan por intentos de dividir gremio cafetalero," *El Diario de Hoy,* 27 May 1988, p. 3; and "Denuncia pública: Juntas Departamentales de Ahuachapán, Cabañas, Cuscutlán, Morazán, San Miguel, Sonsonate y Usulután," *El Diario de Hoy,* 26 May 1988, p. 43; "Cafetaleros superan situación y eligen nueva junta directiva," *El Mundo,* 26 June 1989, p. 7; "Elección fraudulenta denuncian cafetaleros," *El Diario de Hoy,* 22 June 1989, p. 3; "La Asociación Cafetalera de El Salvador aclara," *El Diario de Hoy,* 7 July 1989, p. 35; and "¿Por qué hay dos directivas en Asociación Cafetalera?" *El Diario de Hoy,* 28 Feb. 1990, p. 7. Five of the nine members of the victorious slate in 1989 had been members of slates defeated by the de Sola faction in earlier elections, and four were from the defeated 1984 board. For charges and counterchaiges, see "Alertan por intentos de dividir gremio cafetalero," *El Diario de Hoy,* 27 May 1988, p. 3; and "Cafetalera sólo es un cascarón, dice presidente," *El Diario de Hoy,* 27 May 1989, p. 2.

24. See "Cafetaleros santanecos apoyan directiva central," *El Diario de Hoy,* 12 June 1984, p. 31.

25. Paul Heath Hoeffel, "The Eclipse of the Oligarchs," *The New York Times Magazine,* 6 Sept. 1981, p. 28.

26. "Muere Ex-Presidente Napoleón Duarte," *El Diario de Hoy,* 24 Feb. 1990, p. 1.

27. "La verdad sobre el troglodismo," *El Diario de Hoy,* 17 June 1987, p. 6.

28. "He's a Rightist (No Doubt about It)," *The New York Times,* 11 Aug. 1989, p. A4.

29. "La verdad sobre el troglodismo," *El Diario de Hoy,* 17 June 1987, p. 6.

30. "Resúmen semanal," *Proceso* 10, no. 390 (28 June 1989):9. See also note 25.

31. Edgar Chacón, president of the Instituto de Relaciones Internacionales, was assassinated by unknown assailants on 30 June 1989. His colleague Gabriel Payés was killed under similar circumstances on 19 July of the same year. See "Crónica

del mes," *Estudios Centroamericanos* 44, nos. 493–494 (nov.–dic. 1989):1139. The attacks on de Sola's house were reported in an interview with a close associate.

32. "Resúmen semanal," *Proceso* 11, no. 474 (22 May 1991):6.

33. The list of delinquent borrowers also included the governor of Ahuachapán and former Cafetalera President Arturo Simeón Magaña, who had led the faction defeated by de Sola and García Rossi in 1984, as well as a number of other members of important coffee families. See "Dan lista de deudores al Banco Hipotecario," *Diario Latino,* 1 Nov. 1989, p. 6.

34. See "Nudo de paradojas en el caso del Banco Hipotecario," *El Mundo,* 3 Nov. 1989, p. 29.

35. Segundo Montes, "El problema de los derechos humanos en El Salvador," *Estudios Centroamericanos* 44, nos. 493–494 (nov.-dic. 1989):1095–1108.

7. Democracy and Anti-Communism in Costa Rica

1. Víctor Hugo Acuña Ortega, "La ideología de los pequeños y medianos productores cafetaleros costarricenses (1900–1961)," *Revista de Historia* 16 (Universidad Nacional, Heredia, Costa Rica) (julio-diciembre 1987):152.

2. Lowell Gudmundson, *Costa Rica Before Coffee* (Baton Rouge, La.: Louisiana State University Press, 1986), p. 1.

3. Theodore Creedman, *Historical Dictionary of Costa Rica* (Metuchen, N.J.: Scarecrow Press, 1977), p. x.

4. Gudmundson, *Costa Rica,* p. 1.

5. Ibid., pp. 151–153; Ciro Flamarion Santana Cardoso, "Historia económica del café en Centroamérica (siglo XIX): estudio comparativo," *Estudios Sociales Centroamericanos* (enero-abril 1975):9–55. Jeffery M. Paige, "Coffee and Politics in Central America," in *Crises in the Caribbean Basin,* ed. Richard Tardanico (Newbury Park, Ca.: Sage, 1987), pp. 141–190.

6. Gudmunson, *Costa Rica,* p. 161; Acuña, "La ideología," p. 152; Alfonso González Ortega, "El discurso oficial de los pequeños y medianos cafetaleros (1920–1940, 1950–1961)," *Revista de Historia* 16 (Universidad Nacional, Heredia, Costa Rica) (julio-diciembre 1987):161; Gloria Rodríguez, "The Coffee Order in Costa Rica, 1870–1889: Formation and Consolidation of a Structure of Domination" (Ph.D. diss., University of Sussex, 1983), p. 257.

7. Acuña, "La ideología"; González, "El discurso oficial"; Gudmundson, *Costa Rica,* p. 153.

8. On El Salvador see Eduardo Colindres, *Fundamentos económicos de la burguesía Salvadoreña* (San Salvador: Universidad Centroamericana Editores, 1977), and Robert T. Aubey, "Entrepreneurial Formation in El Salvador," *Explorations in Entrepreneurial History* 6, 2nd ser. (1968–69):268–285. Samuel Stone, in a study of industrial investments in Costa Rica from 1960 to 1970, notes "the almost total

absence of coffee producers" (*La dinastía,* p. 352). A similar absence is noticeable in the list of proprietors of major Costa Rican industrial enterprises presented in app. 2 (pp. 165–193) in Francisco Esquivel's *El desarrollo del capital en la industria de Costa Rica, 1950–1970* (Heredia, Costa Rica: Editorial de la Universidad Nacional, 1985).

9. For an analysis of the coffee elite's views in the earlier period see Anthony Winson, *Coffee and Democracy in Modern Costa Rica* (New York: St. Martin's Press, 1989), pp. 28–32. The following quotation from a leading coffee ideologue is, according to Winson (p. 31), typical of the period: "The growth of the rural population in the cities is the effect . . . of a badly understood policy of protection for non-agricultural industry. It is precisely industrialism which creates social problems in agricultural countries. . . . There is no room for transformation industries in countries where capital is so scarce and with a low acquisitive power. The social argument, that is, the employment opportunities offered in these industries for labour, is a sentimental one because, firstly, these workers are badly paid and secondly, they would be better off in the countryside."

10. See Esquivel, *El desarrollo del capital,* app. 2, pp. 165–193.

11. *La Prensa Libre,* 23 July 1983; *La Nación,* 5 March 1986, p. 25A.

12. Víctor H. Acuña, "Classes sociales y conflicto social en la economía cafetalera costarricense: productores contra beneficiadores (1932–1936)," pp. 181–212 in *Historia, problemas, y perspectivas agrarias en Costa Rica,* special number of *Revista de Historia* (Heredia, Costa Rica: Universidad Nacional, 1985).

13. Ciska Raventós Vorst, "El café en Costa Rica: desarrollo capitalista y diferenciación social de los productores (1950–1980)" (Tesis de Maestría, Universidad de Costa Rica, 1983), pp. 29–32. See also Dagoberto Vargas Castillo, "Sabe usted como se fija el precio de su café," *Noticiero del Café* 16 (San José: Instituto del Café, diciembre 1986):2–3; "Cincuenta años de actividad cafetalera," *La Nación,* 24 July 1983, p. 26A, and "Nace la Oficina del Café," *La Nación,* 24 July 1983, p. 28A.

14. Mitchell Seligson, "Agrarian Capitalism and the Transformation of Peasant Society: Coffee in Costa Rica," Special Studies Series 69, Council on International Studies (Buffalo: State University of New York, 1975).

15. *La Nación,* 15 June 1985, p. 4A.

16. See note 1, Chapter 4.

17. Acuña, "Productores contra benficiadores," pp. 141–144.

18. González, "El discurso oficial," pp. 176–186.

19. Acuña, ibid., p. 144.

20. On the 1930s see Winson, *Coffee and Democracy,* pp. 28–32. On the nineteenth century see Rodríguez, "The Coffee Order," pp. 114–203.

21. See Gustavo Blanco and Orlando Navarro, *El solidarismo* (San José: Editorial Costa Rica, 1984) for a discussion of the history and development of the movement in Costa Rica.

8. Neo-Liberalism and Agro-Industry in Costa Rica

1. Anthony Winson, *Coffee and Democracy in Modern Costa Rica* (New York: St. Martin's Press, 1989), pp. 93–113; Víctor Manuel Pérez Solano, "Treinta y dos años de investigación sistemática y transferencia tecnológica del cultivo de café en Costa Rica, 1950–1982" (San José: Oficina del Café, 14 de febrero 1983), p. 28; Instituto del Café de Costa Rica, Departamento de Liquidaciones, "Cosecha 1989–1990: total de café declarado por los beneficios."

2. Frederick F. Claimonte and John H. Cavanagh, "TNCs and the Global Beverage Industry," *The CTC Reporter* 30 (Autumn 1990):28.

3. Bill Saporito, "Can Anyone Win the Coffee War?" *Fortune,* May 21, 1990, p. 100.

4. Bart S. Fisher, *The International Coffee Agreement: A Study in Coffee Diplomacy* (New York: Praeger, 1972), provides a political interpretation of the 1962 agreement. See also Richard L. Lucier, *The International Political Economy of Coffee* (New York: Praeger, 1988), and James Mwanda, John Nichols, and Malcolm Sargent, *Coffee: The International Commodity Agreements* (Hampshire, England: Gower, 1985), for discussions of the economic aspects of the accord.

5. See "País tendrá problemas en ventas del café," *La Prensa Libre,* 11 March 1989, p. 4; "Tensión en el mundo del café," *La República,* 2 April 1989, p. 4A; and "No nos hincamos ante los grandes," *La Nación,* 14 June 1989, p. 31A, for typical discussions of Costa Rica's problems with the ICA. "C.R. venderá café a los socialistas," *La República,* July 1988, p. 3, and "Bajo trueque venderá más café a Checoslovaquia," *La República,* 10 August 1989, p. 2, describe the barter arrangements with socialists states.

6. *La República,* 3 March 1987, p. 2. On Costa Rican perceptions of expansion in the market for quality coffees see "C. Rica trás mercado de cafés de calidad," *La República,* 17 August 1988, p. 13, and "Costa Rica promociona comercio de café fino," *La Nación,* 30 October 1988, p. 5A. Arturo Lizano, executive secretary of the National Chamber of Exporters, publicly argued, for example, that if Costa Rica could not achieve a new ICA treaty, "a free market is better" (*La Nación,* 8 April 1989, p. 5A). Minister of Foreign Trade Luis Diego Escalante, who represented Costa Rica in the 1989 ICO negotiations, expressed the same optimistic view of free markets (*La República,* 15 June 1989, p. 6A).

7. In contrast to the position of the Kennedy administration when the ICA was first negotiated in 1962, Bush administration officials displayed a notable lack of interest in the fate of Third World coffee producers. Agriculture secretary Clayton Yeutter, for example, announced that the United States would negotiate a new accord but only if "it serves the needs and desires of the consuming nations." He went on to contend that even Colombia, a major producer, would be "better off without an international agreement over a 20- or 30-year period," although he

conceded that "there may be short-run considerations here" (*Wall Street Journal,* Eastern Edition, 11 September 1989, p. C13).

8. "A Cold War Over Coffee," *New York Times,* 29 October, 1989, sec. 3, p. F1; "Boom in Fancy Coffee Pits Big Marketers, Little Firms," *Wall Street Journal,* Eastern Edition, 6 November 1989, p. B1; Saporito, "Coffee War," pp. 99–100.

9. Robert J. Samuelson, "The Coffee Cartel: Brewing Up Trouble," *Washington Post,* 26 July 1989, p. A25.

10. On Costa Rica's role in the negotiations, see "Costa Rica bloqueó Brasil en OIC," *La República,* March 3, 1987, p. 2, and "Aislar a Brasil busca C.R. en lucha cafetera," *La República* 15, June 1989, p. 6A.

11. On Costa Rica's reactions to the price drop see "Mercado libre rige precio del café," *La Nación,* 4 July 1989, p. 20A; "País presenta hoy plan de retención de café," *La Nación,* 17 January 1990, p. 34A.

12. *La Nación,* 8 November 1989, p. 14A.

13. See Winson, *Coffee and Democracy,* pp. 127–140; Nora C. Garita Bonilla and María del Rosario León Quesada, "Diferenciación al interior del bloque cafetalero" (Tesis de Licenciatura, Universidad de Costa Rica, 1977); Ciska Raventós Vorst, "El café en Costa Rica: desarrollo capitalista y diferenciación social de los productores (1950–1980)" (Tesis de Maestría, Universidad de Costa Rica, 1983), pp. 1–48, and Gertrude Peters Solórzano, "Historia reciente de las grandes empresas cafetaleras 1950–1980," en *Historia, problemas, y perspectivas agrarias en Costa Rica,* special number of *Revista de Historia* (Heredia, Costa Rica: Universidad Nacional, 1985), pp. 242–243, for discussions of the effect of Liberación policies on the processing sector. All agree that the Liberación reforms greatly benefited large scale processors at the expense of smaller and marginal processors. This conclusion is also supported by the interview data reported below. Samuel Stone (*La dinastía,* p. 147), on the other hand, concludes that the reforms have "destabilized the country's most productive sector," but his conclusions seem to describe the period before the recent dramatic expansion of production.

14. Winson, ibid., Garita Bonilla and León Quesada, ibid., Raventós, ibid., and Peters, ibid. See also Ciska Raventós Vorst, "La burguesía cafetalera," *Trabajo* 2 (1987):5–11.

15. One *fanega* of unprocessed coffee berries yields approximately 100 lbs. or one *quintal* of processed beans.

16. Data on processing plants from Paige, "Coffee and Politics," p. 176; Raventos, "La burguesía cafetalera," pp. 6–8, and computations by the author based on Instituto del Café, "Cosecha 1989–1990."

17. Information on bankruptcies obtained from interviews with a member of the Aguilar firm and with competitors of La Meseta.

18. This typology is based on interviews and calculations of firm total processing capacity from Instituto del Café, "Cosecha 1989–1990."

9. Liberty and the *Contra* in Nicaragua

1. George Irwin, "Nicaragua: Establishing the State as the Center of Accumulation," *Cambridge Journal of Economics* 7 (June 1983):128; David F. Ruccio, "The State and Planning in Nicaragua," in *The Political Economy of Revolutionary Nicaragua,* ed. Rose J. Spaulding (Boston: Allen & Unwin, 1987), pp. 64–65.

2. On the origins of the alliance see George Black, *Triumph of the People* (London: Zed, 1981), pp. 104–106; Shirley Christian, *Revolution in the Family* (New York: Vintage, 1986), pp. 43–45; Donald C. Hodges, *Intellectual Foundations of the Nicaraguan Revolution* (Austin: University of Texas Press, 1986), pp. 239–241.

3. The most detailed account of the Salazar affair is contained in Christian, *Revolution in the Family,* pp. 197–215. Christian, a conservative critic of the Sandinistas, nonetheless concludes that Salazar was deeply implicated in an attempted coup. The exact circumstances of Salazar's death, however, remain in dispute. Information on the Association of Coffee Growers of Matagalpa was provided by interviews with Association officials.

4. Dennis Gilbert, *Sandinistas* (Oxford: Basil Blackwell, 1988), p. 119.

5. Calculations by the author based on Nicaraguan government statistics indicate that by 1986 less than half of the prerevolutionary large producers were still in control of their estates, principally from the "middle" bourgeoisie. See my "Revolution and the Agrarian Bourgeoisie in Nicaragua," in *Revolution in the World-System,* ed. Terry Boswell (New York: Greenwood, 1989), pp. 113.

6. The process of accommodation, called "concertación" in Nicaragua, began in the last two years of Sandinista rule. See Mark Everingham, "From Insurrection to Concertación in Nicaragua: Alliances, Businessmen, and Elite Consensus" (paper presented at the 17th International Congress of the Latin American Studies Association, Los Angeles, September 24–27, 1992).

7. Rose Spaulding, "Capitalists and Revolution: State-Private Relations in Revolutionary Nicaragua (1979–1990)" (paper presented at the 16th International Congress of the Latin American Studies Association, Washington, D.C., April 4–6, 1991).

8. This was particularly true in regard to the mixed economy and political pluralism. See the discussion in Gilbert, *Sandinistas,* pp. 114–117 and Spaulding, "Capitalists and Revolution."

9. Gilbert, commenting on Sandinista agrarian policy, notes that "an astrologer might have as good a chance as anyone else of divining the long-term direction of Sandinista agrarian policy" (*Sandinistas,* p. 104). In his prologue to Alejandro Martínez Cuenca's memoirs (*Sandinista Economics in Practice* [Boston: South End Press, 1992], p. 1), Vice President Sergio Ramírez went so far as to deny that any Sandinista model existed as such.

10. Amalia Chamorro Z. and Richard A. Della Buono, "The Political Economy of the Sandinista Electoral Defeat," *Critical Sociology* 17 (Summer 1990):96.

11. Irwin, "The State as the Center of Accumulation"; Ruccio, "The State and Planning in Nicaragua"; David Kaimowitz, "Nicaragua's Experience with Agricultural Planning: From State Centered Accumulation to the Strategic Alliance with the Peasantry," *Journal of Developing Studies* 24 (July 1988):115–135; Michael Zalkin, "Food Policy and Class Transformation in Revolutionary Nicaragua, 1979–1986," *World Development* 15 (July 1987):961–984.

12. On the 1986 adjustment see Robert Pizarro, "The New Economic Policy: A Necessary Readjustment," pp. 217–232 in Spaulding, ed., *Political Economy.* On 1988–89 see Swedish International Development Authority, *Nicaragua: The Transition from Economic Chaos toward Sustainable Growth* (Stockholm, 1989).

13. Forrest D. Colburn, *Post-Revolutionary Nicaragua: State, Class and Dilemmas of Agrarian Policy* (Berkeley: University of California Press, 1986), p. 16.

14. Bill Gibson, "The Nicaraguan Economy in the Medium Run," *Journal of Interamerican Studies and World Affairs* 33 (Summer 1991):28–29.

15. Gibson, ibid.; Swedish International Development Authority, *Nicaragua: The Transition;* Richard Stahler Sholk, "Stabilization, Destabilization, and the Popular Classes in Nicaragua, 1979–1989," *Latin American Research Review* 25, no. 3 (1990):55–88.

16. Swedish International Development Authority, *Nicaragua: The Transition.*

17. Robert Bates, *Essays on the Political Economy of Rural Africa* (Berkeley: University of California, 1987), p. 107.

18. David Kaimowitz, "Nicaragua's Experience"; and Forrest P. Colburn, "Class, State and Revolution in Rural Nicaragua: The Case of los Cafetaleros," *The Journal of Developing Areas* 18 (July 1984):501–518; and Colburn, *Post-Revolutionary Nicaragua,* pp. 68–82. See also Joseph Collins, *What Difference Could a Revolution Make* (New York: Grove Press, 1986). The Tipitapa-Malacatoya sugar mill alone absorbed half of the agricultural ministry agro-industrial development budget (Collins, p. 189).

19. For representative statements by members of the CIERA group see Eduardo Baumeister and Oscar Neira Cuadra, "The Making of a Mixed Economy: Class Struggle and State Policy in the Nicaraguan Transition," in *Transition and Development: Problems of Third World Socialism,* ed. Richard R. Fagen, Carmen Diana Deere, and José Luis Coraggio (New York: Monthly Review, 1986); pp. 171–191. David Kaimowitz, "Nicaragua's Experience"; and Michael Zalkin, "Food Policy."

20. Gilbert, *Sandinistas,* p. 93.

21. On the agrarian reform see Ilja A. Luciak, "Popular Hegemony and National Unity: The Dialectics of Sandinista Agrarian Reform Policies, 1979–1986," *LASA Forum* 27 (Winter 1987):15–19, and "The Political Economy of Transition," unpublished, Department of Political Science, Virginia Polytechnic Institute and State University, n.d., and Spaulding, "Capitalists and Revolution," pp. 12–18.

22. Luciak, "Popular Hegemony," p. 17.

23. Spaulding, "Capitalists and Revolution," p. 34.

24. Edelberto Torres-Rivas described the Somozas' regime as "Sultanic," after Max Weber's categorization in which "the chief tends to treat his position of authority as a personal prerogative, almost as his private property." See Torres-Rivas, "Síntesis histórica del proceso político," in *Centroamérica hoy,* ed. Edelberto Torres-Rivas, et al. (Mexico, D.F.: Siglo Veintiuno, 1975), p. 75, and Max Weber, *The Theory of Social and Economic Organization,* ed. Talcott Parsons, trans. A. Henderson and Talcott Parsons (New York: Free Press, 1947).

25. This is the assumption of much writing on bourgeois opposition to Somoza. See, for examples, Orlando Núñez Soto, "El Somocismo y el modelo capitalista agroexportador" (Managua: Departamento de Ciencias Sociales de la Universidad Autónoma de Nicaragua, n.d.), pp. 112–177; Julio C. López, Orlando Núñez Soto, Carlos Fernando Chamorro Barrios, and Pascual Serres, *La caída del Somocismo y la lucha Sandinista en Nicaragua* (Ciudad Universitaria Rodrigo Facio: Editorial Universitaria Centroamericana, 1980), pp. 56–58; Adolfo Gilly, *La nueva Nicaragua* (Mexico, D.F.: Editorial Nueva Imágen, 1980), pp. 93–94; George Black, *Triumph of the People* (London: Zed Press, 1981), pp. 66–68; Henri Weber, *Nicaragua: The Sandinista Revolution* (London: New Left Books, 1981), p. 26; Robert G. Williams, *Export Agriculture and the Crisis in Central America* (Chapel Hill: University of North Carolina Press, 1986), pp. 161–163. This was in fact my working hypothesis when I arrived in Nicaragua (see my "Cotton and Revolution in Nicaragua," in *States versus Markets in the World-System,* ed. Peter Evans, Dietrich Rueschemeyer, and Evelyn Huber Stephens [Beverly Hills: Sage, 1985], pp. 91–114). Carlos Vilas in his *The Sandinista Revolution* (New York: Monthly Review Press, 1986), p. 91, is, however, a notable dissenter from the conventional view. The issue of short-run economic interest, as well as the general role of the agrarian bourgeoisie in the revolution, are discussed at greater length in my "Revolution and the Agrarian Bourgeoisie."

26. Ibid., p. 15.

27. The contrast with neighboring Costa Rica is particularly dramatic. While Nicaraguan production had by 1989 reached a low point of a little more than 50% of its 1978–79 average, Costa Rica had increased its production in the same period by more than 50% (United Nations Food and Agriculture Organization, *FAO Yearbook: Trade of the United Nations,* FAO Statistics Series no. 91, vol. 33, (1979), pp. 77–79 and vol. 44 (1990), pp. 88–90).

28. Gilbert, *Sandinistas,* p. 34. For an insightful discussion of the Sandinistas' view of democracy see Luciak, *Political Economy of Transition,* pp. 21–29.

29. Both the communiqué and Ortega's speech are quoted in Gilbert, *Sandinistas,* pp. 34 and 35 respectively.

30. Luciak, *Political Economy of Transition,* p. 27.

31. See Americas Watch Committee, *Human Rights in Nicaragua* (New York:

Americas Watch, 1984, 1985, 1986, 1987), and Amnesty International, *Nicaragua: The Human Rights Record* (London: Amnesty International, 1986).

32. "Report of the Latin American Studies Association Delegation to Observe the Nicaraguan General Election of November 4, 1984," *LASA Forum* 15 (Winter 1985).

33. On this point there seems little doubt. See Pastor, *Condemned to Repetition,* p. 249.

34. Barbara Stallings, "External Finance and the Transition to Socialism in Small Peripheral Societies," in Fagen et al., eds., *Transition and Development*, pp. 54–78.

35. Swedish International Development Authority, *Nicaragua: The Transition.*

36. For discussion of the impact of the Reagan administration on United States Nicaraguan relations, see Pastor, *Condemned to Repetition*, pp. 230–261, and Gilbert, *Sandinistas,* pp. 162–164.

10. Democracy and Revolution

1. Fredric Jameson, *The Political Unconscious: Narrative as a Socially Symbolic Act* (Ithaca: Cornell University Press, 1981).

2. Barrington Moore, Jr., *Social Origins of Dictatorship and Democracy* (Boston: Beacon, 1966). Quotation is on p. 414.

3. For reviews of this literature see Jonathan Wiener, "Review of Reviews," *History and Theory* 15 (1976):146–175; Dennis Smith, "Discovering Facts and Values: Barrington Moore," in *Vision and Method in Historical Sociology,* ed. Theda Skocpol (Cambridge: Cambridge University Press, 1984), pp. 313–355. For applications to specific cases see David Abraham, *The Collapse of the Weimar Republic: Political Economy and Crisis* (New York: Holmes and Meier, 1986); Dwight B. Billings, *Planters and the Making of the New South: Class, Politics, and Development in North Carolina, 1865–1900* (Chapel Hill: University of North Carolina Press, 1979); Jonathan Wiener, *Social Origins of the New South: Alabama 1860–1885* (Baton Rouge: Louisiana State University Press, 1978); Timothy Tilton, "The Social Origins of Liberal Democracy: The Swedish Case," *American Political Science Review* 68 (1974):561–581; Gail Stokes, "The Social Origins of Eastern European Politics," *Eastern European Politics and Society* 1 (Winter 1987):30–74; Guillermo O'Donnell, *Modernization and Bureaucratic Authoritarianism: Studies in South American Politics* (Berkeley: Institute of International Studies, 1973); Misagh Parsa, *Social Origins of the Iranian Revolution* (New Brunswick, N.J.: Rutgers University Press, 1989); John Stephens, "Democratic Transition and Breakdown in Western Europe," *American Journal of Sociology* 94 (March 1989):1019–1077.

4. See Introduction note 9.

5. Dietrich Rueschemeyer, Evelyn Huber Stephens, and John D. Stephens,

Capitalist Development and Democracy (Chicago: University of Chicago Press, 1992), p. 270.

6. Edelberto Torres-Rivas, "Síntesis histórica del proceso político," in *Centroamérica hoy,* ed. Edelberto Torres-Rivas, Gert Rosenthal, Eduardo Lizano, Rafael Menjívar, and Sergio Ramírez (Mexico, D.F.: Siglo Veintiuno, 1975), pp. 27–29. Similar observations on Latin America generally are made by Maurice Zeitlin and Richard Ratcliff in *Landlords and Capitalists: The Dominant Class of Chile* (Princeton: Princeton University Press, 1984), pp. 150–152.

7. For a discussion of the concept in the paradigmatic German case see Geoff Eley, "The Social Construction of Democracy in Germany, 1871–1933," in *The Social Construction of Democracy,* ed. Reid Andrews and Henick Chapan (New York: New York University Press, forthcoming). The key non-Marxist statement of this position is by Ralf Dahrendorf in *Society and Democracy in Germany* (Garden City, N.Y.: Doubleday, 1967). For a critical review see Rueschemeyer, Stephens, and Stephens, *Capitalism and Democracy,* pp. 57–63.

8. Rueschemeyer, Stephens, and Stephens, *Capitalism and Democracy,* p. 270.

9. Jeffery M. Paige, *Agrarian Revolution: Social Movements and Export Agriculture in the Underdeveloped World* (New York: Free Press, 1975).

10. See Italo López Vallecillos, "Fuerzas sociales y cambio social en El Salvador," *Estudios Centroamericanos* 34, nos. 369–370 (julio–agosto 1979):557–90; and Enrique Baloyra, *El Salvador in Transition* (Chapel Hill: University of North Carolina Press, 1982), p. 28. See also Rafael Guidos Véjar, "La crisis política en El Salvador, 1976–1979," *Estudios Centroamericanos* 34, nos. 369–370 (julio–agosto 1979):507–526; Guidos Véjar, *El ascenso del militarismo en El Salvador* (San Salvador: Universidad Centroamericana Editores, 1980), pp. 81–82; Rafael Menjívar, *Acumulación y desarrollo del capitalismo en El Salvador* (San José, Costa Rica: Editorial Universitaria Centroamericana, 1980), pp. 127–130; E. A. Wilson, "The Crisis of National Integration in El Salvador, 1919–1935" (Ph.D. diss., Stanford University, 1970), pp. 132–133; and James Dunkerly, *The Long War: Dictatorship and Revolution in El Salvador* (London: Junction, 1982), p. 54. For a dissenting view see Wim Pelupessy, "El sector agroexportador de El Salvador: La base económica de una oligarquía no fraccionada," *Boletín de Estudios Latinoamericanos y del Caribe* 43 (1987):53–71.

11. López Vallecillos, "Fuerzas sociales," p. 588.

12. Tommie Sue Montgomery, *Revolution in El Salvador: From Civil Strife to Civil Peace,* 2nd ed. (Boulder, Co.: Westview, 1992), p. 261.

13. Elisabeth Jean Wood, "Rural Social Relations, Democracy and Development in El Salvador: Agrarian Politics and the Negotiated Resolution of the Civil War," unpublished, Leverett, Mass. October 31, 1993, p. 54.

14. Gudmundson, "Moore Thesis," p. 10.

15. See, for example, Ciro F. S. Cardoso and Héctor Pérez Brignoli, *Centro*

América y la economía occidental (1520–1930) (San José: Editorial de la Universidad de Costa Rica, 1977), p. 318; Edelberto Torres-Rivas, *Repression and Resistance: The Struggle for Democracy in Central America* (Boulder, Co.: Westview, 1989), pp. 138–139; Robert Williams, *States and Social Evolution: Coffee and the Rise of National Governments in Central America* (Chapel Hill: University of North Carolina Press, 1994), pp. 230–231, and Deborah Yashar, "Demanding Democracy: Reform and Reaction in Costa Rica and Guatemala, 1870s-1950s" (Ph.D. diss., University of California, Berkeley, 1992), pp. 70–71. Anthony Winson in *Coffee and Democracy in Modern Costa Rica* (New York: St Martin's, 1989), p. 170–171 also stresses the absence of labor-repressive agriculture in Costa Rica but attributes the coffee elite's opposition to Calderón to the persistence of what he calls "landlord capitalism" rather than to the resistance of an emerging agro-industrial bourgeoisie to democracy.

16. Gudmundson, "Moore Thesis," p. 11.

17. The fact that the elite waged the civil war in the name of democratic elections does not affect this conclusion. The fairness of the elections was precisely the issue that precipitated the war. There is no conclusive evidence either way. The willingness of the elite in general and of Figueres in particular to use violence against the democratically elected Calderón and Picado regimes long preceded the election dispute.

18. Eley, "Democracy in Germany."

19. Carlos Vilas, *The Sandinista Revolution* (New York: Monthy Review Press, 1986), p. 132.

20. James Dunkerly, *The Pacification of Central America: Political Change in the Isthmus, 1987–1993* (London: Verso, 1993), p. 7. Susanne Jonas makes the same point in her analysis of Central American electoral transitions in the mid-1980s ("Elections and Transitions: The Guatemalan and Nicaraguan Cases," in *Elections and Democracy in Central America,* ed. John A. Booth and Mitchell A. Seligson (Chapel Hill: University of North Carolina, 1989), n. 1, p. 151). In the Introduction to the Latin American volume of their classic work, *Transitions from Authoritarian Rule* (Baltimore: Johns Hopkins, 1986), p. 10, which emphasizes the Southern Cone, Guillermo O'Donnell, Philippe Schmitter, and Laurence Whitehead explicitly exclude revolutionary transitions to democracy like those in Central America and even claim that such transitions are unlikely if not impossible. Revolution may occur in "patrimonial regimes" but does not lead to democracy.

21. The term "democracy by default" to describe the South American model was coined by Laurence Whitehead ("The Alternatives to 'Liberal Democracy': A Latin American Perspective," *Political Studies* 40 (special issue 1992:158). Whitehead restricts the term to South America, explicitly excluding Central America (ibid., p. 149). See Marcelo Cavarozzi, "Beyond Transitions to Democracy in Latin America," *Journal of Latin American Studies* 24 (Oct. 1992):667 for a detailed de-

scription of the model of democracy as a result of the collapse of the "state-centered complex." The starting points for Cavarozzi's analysis are Guillermo O'Donnell's notion of "bureaucratic authoritarianism" in the Southern Cone as an initial response to the exhaustion of import-substitution industrialization (in *Modernization and Bureaucratic Authoritarianism*), and the "transitions paradigm" developed by O'Donnell, Schmitter, and Whitehead (see note 20). See also Hector E. Schamis, "Reconceptualizing Latin American Authoritarianism in the 1970s," *Comparative Politics* (January 1991):201–220 for a parallel analysis of the breakdown of "bureaucratic authoritarianism" in the Southern Cone stressing changes in economic policy. Jeffrey Frieden in *Debt, Development and Democracy* (Princeton: Princeton University Press, 1991) also emphasizes the role of the debt crisis in the transition to democracy in Argentina, Brazil, Chile, Mexico, and Venezuela. Stephen Haggard and Robert R. Kaufman's review of important Asian as well as Latin American semi-peripheral democratic transitions in *The Political Economy of Democratic Transitions* (Princeton: Princeton University Press, 1995) finds that economic crisis in general (including, but not limited to, the debt crisis) undermines business support for military regimes and, when the military itself is divided, leads to military withdrawal and the installation of democratic regimes. Bruce Cumings has extended the Southern Cone model to the case of South Korea in his "The Abortive *Abertura:* South Korea in the Light of Latin American Experience," *New Left Review* 173 (1989):5–32.

22. Rueschemeyer, Stephens, and Stephens, *Capitalist Development and Democracy*, p. 271.

23. The role of the working class in democratic development has been emphasized not only by Rueschemeyer, Stephens, and Stephens, but also by Ruth Berins Collier and David Collier in their recent comparative study of Latin America, *Shaping the Political Arena: Critical Junctures, the Labor Movement, and Regime Dynamics in Latin America* (Princeton: Princeton University Press, 1991). See also J. Samuel Valenzuela, "Labor Movements in Transitions to Democracy," *Comparative Politics* 21 (July 1989):445–472, and Göran Therborn, "The Rule of Capital and the Rise of Democracy," *New Left Review* 103 (1977):3–41.

24. James Dunkerly, *Power in the Isthmus: A Political History of Modern Central America* (London: Verso, 1988), p. 211.

25. Gay W. Seidman, *Manufacturing Militance: Workers' Movements in Brazil and South Africa* (Berkeley: University of California Press, 1994).

26. For discussion of the security forces in the transition and the emerging judicial and human rights situation see Jack Spence and George Vickers, *A Negotiated Revolution: A Two-Year Progress Report on the Salvadoran Peace Accords* (Cambridge, Mass.: Hemisphere Initiatives, 1994), and Gary Bland, "Assessing the Transition to Democracy," in *Is There a Transition to Democracy in El Salvador?*, ed. Joseph S. Tulchin (Boulder, Co.: Lynne Rienner, 1992), pp. 163–206.

27. As James Dunkerly *(Pacification,* p. 17) notes, eighteen months after Violeta Chamorro's election 50% of the Nicaraguan labor force was un- or under-employed and 69% was unable to meet basic food needs. He observes that modest official levels of unemployment conceal deeper "marginalization and impoverishment . . . even in Costa Rica, where in 1990–1991 some 27,821 families were classified poor for the first time, an 18.4% increase." One indication of the general economic deterioration is the return of cholera to the region, a disease unseen in Central America since the 1850s.

28. See Douglas A. Kincaid and Eduardo Gamarra, "Disorderly Democracy: Redefining Public Security in Latin America" (paper presented at the Annual Conference of the Political Economy of the World System Section of the American Sociological Association, Miami, Florida, April 22, 1995).

29. Moore, *Social Origins,* pp. 426–431.

30. Terry Lynn Karl, "Dilemmas of Democratization in Latin America," *Comparative Politics* 23 (Oct. 1990):9. In Karl's typology the category of transitions to democracy through revolutions from below is an empty cell, although she allows that "developments in Nicaragua and Mexico may soon challenge this assumption."

31. Adam Przeworski, "The Games of Transition," in *Issues in Democratic Consolidation: The New South American Democracies in Comparative Perspective,* ed. Scott Mainwaring, Guillermo O'Donnell, and J. Samuel Valenzuela (Notre Dame: Notre Dame University Press, 1992), p. 105.

32. As J. Samuel Valenzuela (in Mainwaring, et al., *Democratic Consolidation,* pp. 93–94) notes, "consolidated democracies have been a rarity in Latin America. Costa Rica since the 1950s, Venezuela since the 1960s, Chile from the mid-1930s to 1973, Uruguay from the mid-1930s to the Bordaberry presidency, and perhaps Argentina in the mid 1920s." Venezuela has experienced two attempted coups in the last five years and the democratic regimes in Chile, Uruguay, and Argentina mentioned by Valenzuela were all ended by military coups, leaving Costa Rica as the only extant "consolidated" democracy.

33. Moore himself was skeptical concerning the future of Indian democracy precisely because India had made no such revolutionary break with the past *(Social Origins,* p. 431).

34. Peter Hakim and Abraham F. Lowenthal, surveying the Latin American scene in 1990, observed that "democracy in Latin America is far from robust. It is nowhere fully achieved, and it is most firmly established in those few countries where it was already deeply rooted a generation ago" ("Latin America's Fragile Democracies," in *The Global Resurgence of Democracy,* ed. Larry Diamond and Marc F. Plattner (Baltimore: Johns Hopkins University Press: 1993), p. 293). Their observation was made even before instability in Mexico and Venezuela became evident.

11. From Liberalism to Neo-Liberalism

1. The presentation of Marx's theory of ideology is based on Jorge Larrain's perceptive analysis in *Marxism and Ideology* (London: MacMillan, 1983); the application of narrative owes much to George Steinmetz's "Reflections on the Role of Social Narratives in Working-Class Formation: Narrative Theory in the Social Sciences," *Social Science History* 16, no. 3 (Fall 1992):489–516. Jameson's idea of the political unconscious is presented in *The Political Unconscious: Narrative as a Socially Symbolic Act* (Ithaca: Cornell University Press, 1981). William C. Dowling in *Jameson, Althusser, Marx: An Introduction to the Political Unconscious* (Ithaca: Cornell University Press, 1984) modestly claims to have written only an introduction to Jameson's provocative but difficult work. Actually, Dowling's book, in addition to admirably accomplishing this limited goal, also represents a theoretical work in its own right, developing and extending Jameson's theory in significant ways. It is Dowling's reading of Jameson that will be emphasized here.

2. Exactly the same distinction is made by Jorge Larrain in his selection on "Ideology" in *A Dictionary of Marxist Thought,* ed. Tom Bottomore (Cambridge, Mass.: Harvard University Press, 1983), pp. 218–222, and by Harry M. Johnson in *The International Encyclopedia of the Social Sciences,* ed. David Sills (New York: MacMillan, 1968), p. 76. See also John B. Thompson, *Studies in the Theory of Ideology* (Cambridge: Polity Press, 1984), p. 76.

3. Larrain, *Marxism and Ideology.*

4. Karl Marx, *Capital,* vol. III, trans. Ernest Unterman (Chicago: Charles H. Kerr, 1909), p. 919.

5. Karl Marx, *Capital,* vol. I, trans. Samuel Moore and Edward Aveling (Chicago: Charles H. Kerr, 1908), p. 195.

6. Hayden White, *The Content of the Form: Narrative Discourse and Historical Representation* (Baltimore: Johns Hopkins University Press, 1987), p. ix.

7. According to George Steinmetz, "Social Narratives," p. 497, adapting the concept for sociological use, narrative has "a beginning, a middle and an end, and the movement toward the end is accounted for by conflicts, causal explanations and the sequence of events." Seymour Chatman, in a basic text in literary theory, writes that a narrative contains "a chain of events (actions, happenings), plus what might be called the existents (characters, items of setting)." Chatman, *Story and Discourse: Narrative Structure in Fiction and Film* (Ithaca: Cornell University Press, 1978), p. 19.

8. White, *Content of the Form,* pp. 19–20.

9. Thompson, *Theory of Ideology,* p. 11.

10. For general overviews of the concept in literary studies see Chatman, *Story and Discourse;* Wallace Martin, *Recent Theories of Narrative* (Ithaca: Cornell University Press, 1986); and J. Hillis Miller, "Narrative," in *Critical Terms for Literary*

Study, ed. Frank Lentricchia and Thomas McLaughlin (Chicago: University of Chicago Press, 1990), pp. 66–79. On social science applications see the special section, "Narrative Analysis in the Social Sciences," *Social Science History* 16, nos. 3 and 4 (Fall 1991 and Winter 1992), particularly articles by Steinmetz, Somers, and Hart, and the general introduction by William Sewell, pp. 479–488; and the special issue "Narrative Analysis: An Interdisciplinary Dialogue," *Poetics* 15 (April 1986).

11. Charlotte Linde, "Private Stories in Public Discourse: Narrative Analysis in the Social Sciences," *Poetics* 15 (April 1986), p. 187.

12. Steinmetz, "Social Narratives," pp. 489–490.

13. Ibid., p. 503.

14. Jameson, *Political Unconscious;* Dowling, *Jameson, Althusser, Marx.*

15. Dowling, *Jameson, Althusser, Marx,* pp. 77–78.

16. A similar reading of Marx, based on an observation by Lacan, is presented in Slavoj Zizek's essay, "How Did Marx Invent the Symptom," in his *The Sublime Object of Ideology* (London: Verso, 1989), pp. 11–53.

17. Ibid., p. 115.

18. Mario Lungo Uclés, *El Salvador en los 80: Contrainsurgencia y revolución* (San José: Editorial Universitaria Centroamericana, 1990), p. 150.

19. Thomas Anderson, *Matanza,* 2nd ed. (East Haven, Conn.: Curbstone Press, 1992), p. 205.

20. The definitive works are those of David Browning, *El Salvador: Landscape and Society* (Oxford: Oxford University Press, 1971), and William L. Durham, *Scarcity and Survival in Central America: Ecological Origins of the Soccer War* (Stanford: Stanford University Press, 1978).

21. Forty-six of 48 positions in the FDN (Fuerza Democrática Nicaragüense; Nicaraguan Democratic Force or "contra") military structure were held by former guardsmen, including the position of top commander held by Enrique Bermúdez. Reed Brody, *Contra Terror in Nicaragua: Report of a Fact Finding Mission: September 1984-January 1985* (Boston: South End Press, 1985), p. 13.

22. See Americas Watch, *Human Rights in Nicaragua: Reagan Rhetoric and Reality* (New York: Americas Watch, 1985).

23. John Patrick Bell, *Crisis in Costa Rica* (Austin: University of Texas Press, 1971), p. 41.

24. Lowell Gudmundson, *Costa Rica Before Coffee: Society and Economy on the Eve of the Export Boom* (Baton Rouge: Louisiana State University Press, 1986), p. 161.

25. Margaret R. Somers ("Narrativity, Narrative Identity, and Social Action: Rethinking English Working-Class Formation," *Social Science History* 16 [Winter 1992]:605) argues that social science meta-narratives such as modernization, industrialization, or the transition from feudalism to capitalism may distort sociological analysis by pressing historical experience into a false totalizing principle,

much in the way that social narratives (Somers calls them "onotological narratives") distort historical events to fit their organizing principle. Somers's solution is not, however, to abandon efforts at sociological generalization but to adopt sociological concepts to history, not the other way around. Rejection of such "meta-narratives" is, as Pauline Roseneau notes, a fundamental principle of post-modern thought (*Post-Modernism in the Social Sciences: Insights, Inroads and Intrusions* [Princeton: Princeton University Press, 1991], pp. 84–85). Charlotte Linde, "Private Stories," p. 196 also notes that scientific discourse itself can be treated as narrative, although she adds that narrative analysis may be employed without such an assumption.

26. Dennis Gilbert, personal communication, January 9, 1996.

27. *From Max Weber,* eds. Hans Gerth and C. Wright Mills (London: Routledge, 1970), p. 280.

28. *The Protestant Ethic and the Spirit of Capitalism* (London: Allen and Unwin, 1974), p. 183.

Index